Imaginary Penalities

Edited by
Pat Carlen

WILLAN
PUBLISHING

Published by

Willan Publishing
Culmcott House
Mill Street, Uffculme
Cullompton, Devon
EX15 3AT, UK
Tel: +44(0)1884 840337
Fax: +44(0)1884 840251
E-mail: info@willanpublishing.co.uk
website: www.willanpublishing.co.uk

Published simultaneously in the USA and Canada by

Willan Publishing
c/o ISBS, 920 NE 58th Ave, Suite 300
Portland, Oregon 97213-3786, USA
Tel: +001(0)503 287 3093
Fax: +001(0)503 280 8832
E-mail: info@isbs.com
website: www.isbs.com

First published 2008

ISBN   978-1-84392-375-6 paperback
       978-1-84392-376-3 hardback

British Library Cataloguing-in-Publication Data

A catalogue record for this book is available from the British Library.

Project managed by Deer Park Productions, Tavistock, Devon
Typeset by GCS, Leighton Buzzard, Bedfordshire
Printed and bound by T.J. International Ltd, Padstow, Cornwall

Imaginary Penalities

Contents

Acknowledgements   *vii*

About the contributors   *ix*

Imagine   **xiii**
Pat Carlen

1 **Imaginary penalities and risk-crazed governance**
   Pat Carlen   1

2 **Imaginable insecurities: imagination, routinisation
   and the government of uncertainty post 9/11**
   Pat O'Malley and Philip D. Bougen   26

3 **The first casualty: evidence and governance in a
   war against crime**
   Tim Hope   45

4 **Inventing community safety**
   Adam Edwards and Gordon Hughes   64

5 **Telling sentencing stories**
   Jacqueline Tombs   84

6 **The 'seemingness' of the 'seamless management'
   of offenders**
   Anne Worrall   113

7   Pain and punishment: the real and the imaginary in
    penal institutions
    Joe Sim   135

8   Imaginary reform: changing the postcolonial prison
    Andrew M. Jefferson   157

9   The imaginary constitution of wage labourers
    Magnus Hörnqvist   172

10 Re-imagining gendered penalities: the myth of
    gender responsivity
    Kelly Hannah-Moffat   193

11 Risking desistance: respect and responsibility in
    custodial and post-release contexts
    Mark Halsey   218

12 'The best seven years I could'a done': the reconstruction
    of imprisonment as rehabilitation
    Megan Comfort   252

13 Re-imagining justice: principles of justice for divided
    societies in a globalised world
    Barbara Hudson   275

References   295
Index   329

Acknowledgements

I owe an immense debt of gratitude to all the contributors and to Brian Willan of Willan Publishing. Their intellectual liveliness and wise counsel made the editing of this book a very pleasurable experience.

About the contributors

Philip Bougen is on the faculty at the Anderson Schools of Management, University of New Mexico. His current research is in the areas of catastrophe risk, catastrophic disorganisation and security policy.

Pat Carlen is a sociologist. Publications include: *Magistrates' Justice*; *Women's Imprisonment*; *Jigsaw: A Political Criminology of Youth Homelessness*; and *Official Discourse* (with Frank Burton). Awarded the American Society of Criminology's Sellin-Glueck Prize (1997) for outstanding international contributions to Criminology, she is presently Editor-in-Chief of the *British Journal of Criminology*.

Megan Comfort is a sociologist at the Center for AIDS Prevention Studies at the University of California, San Francisco (UCSF) and a visiting fellow at the Mannheim Centre for Criminology at the London School of Economics and Political Science. Her book, *Doing Time Together: Love and Family in the Shadow of the Prison*, was published by the University of Chicago Press, 2008.

Adam Edwards is a lecturer in the Cardiff University School of Social Sciences. His principal research interests are in governance and the regulatory state, the politics of law and order and the sociology of criminological knowledge. Publications include *Crime Control and Community* (with Gordon Hughes) and *Transnational Organised Crime* (with Pete Gill).

Mark Halsey teaches in the School of Law at Flinders University. He is the author of *Deleuze and Environmental Damage* and his work on young people and incarceration has appeared in *Punishment and Society, Journal of Criminal Law and Criminology,* and *Probation Journal.*

Kelly Hannah-Moffat is Associate Professor of Criminology at the University of Toronto. Publications include: *Punishment in Disguise: Governance in the Canadian Women's Federal Prisons; An Ideal Prison* (edited with Margaret Shaw); and *Gendered Risk* (edited with Pat O'Malley).

Tim Hope is Professor of Criminology at Keele University. Of his many publications, most relevant to this book are: 'Pretend it doesn't work: the "anti-social" bias in the Maryland Scientific Methods Scale', *European Journal on Criminal Policy and Research,* 11: 275–96; 'Pretend it works: evidence and governance in the evaluation of the Reducing Burglary Initiative', *Criminal Justice,* 4 (3): 287–308.

Magnus Hörnqvist teaches in the Department of Criminology, Stockholm University. Publications include his doctoral thesis, *The Organised Nature of Power.* Other research projects include studies on the implementation of crime prevention (Allas vårt ansvar i praktiken) and anti-terror policies (Laglöst land) in Sweden.

Barbara Hudson is Professor in Law at The University of Central Lancashire. Publications include: *Justice through Punishment; Penal Policy and Social Justice; Racism and Criminology* (with Dee Cook); *Race, Crime and Justice; Understanding Justice;* and *Justice in the Risk Society: Challenging and Re-affirming Justice in Late Modernity.*

Gordon Hughes is Professor of Criminology at Cardiff University. Co-editor of many books, he has also published the following monographs: *Understanding Crime Prevention: Social Control, Risk and Late Modernity* and *The Politics of Crime and Community* (with Adam Edwards).

Andrew Jefferson is a psychologist working at the Rehabilitation and Research Centre for Torture Victims in Copenhagen and is co-founder of the Scandinavian Studies of Confinement research network. Publications include 'Prison Officer Training and Practice in Nigeria', *Punishment and Society,* 9 (3); 'Reforming Nigerian prisons: a 'deviant' state' *BJC* 45 (4); 'Therapeutic Discipline?', *Outlines: Critical Social Studies,* 1.

Pat O'Malley is University Professorial Research Fellow in Law at the University of Sydney. Recent publications include *Risk, Uncertainty and Government*; *Governing Risks*; and *Gendered Risks* (with Kelly Hannah-Moffatt). Current projects include the analysis of fire prevention and urban security networks (with Steven Hutchinson) and a monograph on *Monetary Justice and Control Societies*. In 2002 he was awarded the American Society of Criminology's Sellin-Glueck Prize for outstanding international contributions to Criminology.

Joe Sim is Professor of Criminology at Liverpool John Moores University. Publications include: *Medical Power in Prisons*; *British Prisons* (with Mike Fitzgerald); *Prisons under Protest* (with Phil Scraton and Paula Skidmore); and *The Carceral State* (forthcoming).

Jacqueline Tombs is Professor of Criminology and Criminal Justice at the Glasgow Caledonian University. Publications include: *Reducing the Prison Population: Penal Policy and Social Choices*; *A Unique Punishment: Sentencing and the Prison Population in Scotland*; *The British Crime Survey: Scotland* (with G. Chambers); and *Prosecution in the Public Interest* (with S. Moody).

Anne Worrall is Professor of Criminology at Keele University. Publications include: *Offending Women: Female Lawbreakers and the Criminal Justice System*; *Punishment in the Community: Managing Offenders, Making Choices* (with Claire Hoy); *Girls' Violence: Myths and Realities* (edited with Christine Alder); *Gender, Crime and Justice*; and *Analysing Women's Imprisonment* (both with Pat Carlen). She has also been a member of the Parole Board for England and Wales.

Imagine

Pat Carlen

An Emperor who cares too much about clothes hires two
swindlers who promise him the finest suit of clothes from the
most beautiful cloth. This cloth, they tell him, is invisible to
anyone [who is] either stupid or not fit for his position. The
Emperor is nervous about being able to see the cloth himself so
he sends his ministers to view it. They see nothing, yet praise
the cloth. When the swindlers report a suit of clothes has been
fashioned, the Emperor allows himself to be dressed in their
creation for a procession through town. During the course of the
procession, a small child cries out, 'But he has nothing on!' The
crowd realizes the child is telling the truth and begins laughing.
The Emperor, however, holds his head high and continues the
procession.[1] (From *The Emperor's New Clothes*, a fairy tale by
Hans Christian Andersen).

In *Interesting Times*, the historian Eric Hobsbawm argues that after the
attack on the World Trade Centre in New York in September 2001

a sudden gap appeared between the way the USA and the rest
of the world understood what had happened on that awful day.
The world merely saw a particularly dramatic terror attack with
a vast number of victims and a momentary public humiliation
of the USA. Otherwise the situation was no different from
what it had been since the Cold War ended, and certainly no
cause for alarm for the globe's only superpower. Washington
announced that September 11th had changed everything, and
in doing so, actually *did* change everything, by in effect declaring

itself the single-handed protector of a world order and definer of threats against it. Whoever failed to accept this was a potential or actual enemy.

(Hobsbawm 2002: 411)

A tantalising feature of human societies is that knowledge of their ever-changing conditions of existence is reflexively denied us. This self-denial of knowledge apparently bugged Adam and Eve in the Garden of Eden (rightly so, in my opinion) and has teased humankind ever since. Aristotle taught that we grasp new knowledge via metaphor and then lose it as it transmogrifies into myth. In different, but related, discourses, other and more recent writers have been concerned with the functions and features of ideological knowledge as partial truth (for example, Mannheim 1960/1936; Lukacs 1971/1923) or as a necessary pre-condition for the production of new knowledge (for example, Althusser 1971; Hirst 1976a and 1976b). Sociologists (pre-eminently Max Weber 1947) have been intrigued by the attempts of bureaucracies to routinise knowledge in order to control its product (see O'Malley and Bougen, Chapter 2), while other scholars, especially linguistic philosophers, have continued, in the tradition of Aristotle, to examine the poetic and linguistic structuring of discourses, especially rhetorical discourses.

One of the most important conceptual advances for the analysis of rule-usage – that is, analysis of the relationships between all the rules available for us to draw on in shaping and justifying action both before and after the event and those which we actually use when we want to get things done – is Noam Chomsky's (1971) seminal distinction between competence and performance. Competence refers to people's abstract knowledge of the rules – the rules in repertoire; and performance refers to their ability successfully to combine them to achieve a variety of public and private meanings – the rules in play (Carlen 1976. See Edwards and Hughes, Chapter 4 and Tombs, Chapter 5 on performatives).

The eponymous imaginary penalities analysed in this book are primarily concerned with structures of ideological penal policies and practices; with how variously fashioned political and populist rhetorics about the most effective ways to combat crime, risk and security-threat have ossifying tendencies to become closed and taken-for-granted realities of governance, inhibiting, corrupting and atrophying any suggestions and opportunities for more open-ended imaginative discourses on social cohesion and justice (such as, for instance, Hillyard et al. 2004).

The book itself has an unusual history. It began life as a research paper which tells the story of a new prison whose original goals had been much modified in the few months it had been opened, but whose staff and headquarters' administrators insisted that though the original goals were completely unachievable they themselves must, none the less, act 'as if' those original goals were still in place (see Carlen, Chapter 1). As a sociologist, I was intrigued by the questions raised by such a situation, but the lively and engaged response to the paper when delivered in several different venues was unexpected. People told me that the 'imaginary' syndrome I had outlined was a feature of organisations far removed from the prison – in hospitals, civil service, local government, universities and schools, to name but a few – while myriad examples of the undesirable effects of newly fashioned imaginary penalities on contemporary criminal justice and penal systems were recounted by justice practitioners and researchers alike.

Initial correspondence with criminologists in other jurisdictions indicated that imaginary penalities feature widely, but differently, in both global and local modes of crime and security governance. Further discussion suggested that, although they might well be characterised as having all the attributes usually ascribed to ideological knowledges in general, the specific genesis and modes of sustenance of today's imaginary penalities inhere in almost-hidden structures of cultural and penal governance; in micro-structures veinously facilitating the bureaucratic routinisation of knowledge (see O'Malley and Bougen, Chapter 2; Hope, Chapter 3) and the creation of acquiescence in official discourses on crime, lawbreaking and risk (see Carlen, Chapter 1; Tombs, Chapter 5; Hannah-Moffat, Chapter 10; Comfort, Chapter 12). It is, incidentally, because of the complexity of this web of imaginaries that many of the following chapters present very detailed descriptions. The silent build-up of social auditing and penal programming machinery (whatever its original purposes and concomitant other functions) now too often also operates to discipline and silently silence those whose views do not sit easily with attempts by governments and state bureaucracies to 'govern through crime' (Mathiesen 2004; Simon 2007). Imaginary penalities are not easily penetrated.

The concept of 'imaginary penalities', moreover, though theoretically suggestive to many people already puzzling over the totalising and tightening grip which official law and order discourses have recently had on public knowledge about crime and punishment, has served less as a conceptual framework and more as an orientational device for the authors of the empirically based studies presented here. None the less, one further theoretical distinction was required, if we were to avoid the implication that all official responses to crime and security threats must always and already be imaginary. Accordingly, once it had been decided to use the concept of imaginary penalities to inform analysis of some micro-structures of penal governance, it also became important to differentiate between 'imaginary penalities' (with their tendencies to silence or subvert challenges to official penal orthodoxies) and the irrepressible 'social imagination' which is forever open to debate about new conceptions of social relations and justice (see, for example, Hope, Chapter 3; Edwards and Hughes, Chapter 4; Sim, Chapter 7; Jefferson, Chapter 8; Comfort, Chapter 12; Hudson, Chapter 13).

Imaginary Penalities is about one set of contemporary epistemic contests: ideological and political battles over the manufacture and policy-harnessing of crime, risk and security knowledges. But, more specifically, its focus is upon the micro-politics of selected dimensions and sites of the many imaginary penalities presently dominating local, national and international responses to criminal threat. The overarching substantive argument linking the chapters is: *that because imaginary penalities are (amongst other things) obstructive of new knowledge about crime they should be opposed by more imaginative, open and pluralistic approaches to the governance of law and order.* The main theoretical focus is upon questions of ideology, knowledge and critique. The empirical thrust aims at contributing rich and analytic descriptions of how global trends and national policies are realised in imaginary form at local level and have deleterious effects not only on crime control, but also on the quality of justice nationally and internationally.

From imaginary penalities to imaginative quests for new understandings of crime, punishment and security

The term 'imaginary' has been employed most recently and productively by Charles Taylor in his book *Modern Social Imaginaries* (2004), where he defines 'imaginary' as

> the ways people imagine their social existence, how they fit together with others, how things go on between them and their fellows, the expectations that are normally met, and the deeper normative notions and images that underlie these expectations. (Taylor 2004: 23)

But although Taylor's treatise contains much of relevance to the themes of *Imaginary Penalities*, the perspective on imaginary that most influences the concept from which the present volume takes its title, owes more to the writings of Jacques Lacan (1977) and Louis Althusser (1971). It was first put together by Frank Burton and Pat Carlen in their book *Official Discourse* (1979); Lacan's psycho-analytic employment of 'imaginary' was adopted and adapted as a metaphor to denote an ideological consciousness which constantly strives for entry into the symbolic community upon which its existence depends – but only on its own terms. Oppositional or contradictory knowledge is excluded.

Althusser had already used the term 'imaginary' to describe a mode of knowing which he characterised as being 'unscientific' and 'non-theoretical' and that usage appealed to Burton and Carlen because it theorised ideology (the already known) as being a necessary precondition to knowledge rather than as being the opposite of some godlike truth. Lacan's original metaphoric usage, however, also remained attractive because of its processual features, its highlighting of the necessary tension between what, in this book, are called 'imagination' and 'imaginary': 'imagination' denoting a never-ending quest for new knowledge; and 'imaginary' the process and product of ideological structures attempting either to suppress or incorporate it. (See Carlen, Chapter 1 for a more detailed exposition and some illustrations of the concept of imaginary penalities.)

Six of the essays in this book investigate empirically one or more dimensions of the tensions between imaginative approaches to crime, punishment and security and the varied manifestations of contemporary imaginary penalities (Carlen, Chapter 1; Tombs, Chapter 5; Sim, Chapter 7; Jefferson, Chapter 8; Hannah-Moffat, Chapter 10; Halsey, Chapter 11). Three essays untangle a web of imaginaries in relation to seamless justice (Worrall, Chapter 6); prison labour (Hörnqvist, Chapter 9); and rehabilitation (Comfort, Chapter 12). Three more focus on the conceptual difficulties of distinguishing between 'imagination' and 'imaginary' (O'Malley and Bougen, Chapter 2; Hope, Chapter 3; Edwards and Hughes, Chapter 4). The book's final chapter (Hudson, Chapter 13) suggests some possibilities for re-imagining justice, a cosmopolitan justice based not on some imaginary unity of interests of already-divided nations but on a judicial discourse recognising, and attempting to accommodate, the competing values of strangers in a globalised world.

Dimensions of imaginary penalities

The bureaucratisation of imagination

Pat O'Malley and Philip Bougen in Chapter 2 remind us that imagination is an indispensable precondition for knowledge, especially of the previously unimaginable, such as large-scale terrorist attacks. Yet, they also demonstrate that even when governments actively seek imaginative solutions to otherwise unknowable problems, imaginative endeavours in relation to risk are constantly atrophied by bureaucratic routinisation in the name of actuarial security. And, as the imagination is routinised and becomes myth (often, though not necessarily, an imaginary ossification of the bizarre rather than the probable) the new knowledge that imagination was originally exhorted to seek is destroyed – and at the very moment of its birth. For, to quote Paul Hirst (1976b), 'ideology is always a form of the creation of recognition'.

The bureaucratisation of imagination is also discussed by Tombs (Chapter 5) in relation to sentencing; and Hannah-Moffat (Chapter 10) in relation to Risk, Need and Responsivity Programmes for women in Canada.

Imaginary truths

In Chapter 3, Tim Hope demonstrates how conjectural (imaginative) devices employed to aid statistical modelling can be selectively used to produce evidence in support of both official predictions and the success of government programmes of crime reduction. Selection between competing paradigms is, of course, a necessary precursor to scientific discovery. When, however, conjectural methods producing results seen to be of non-utility to the government of the day are opposed in secret, rather than in open debate, and results based on alternative conjectural methods are elevated to the status of truth (and, later, to the status of evidentiary truths as government predictions are reflexively fulfilled) the politically legitimated research results leave the realm of open conjecture (imagination) and enter the closed world of the imaginary.

Imaginary communities

Concern with the relationships between the already-known and the new is also the main theme of Chapter 4 where Adam Edwards and Gordon Hughes argue that, whatever their genesis, theorisations of community safety have to be taken seriously because they have political and regulatory effects. Yet, although imagination is one precondition for new practice, because of their other preconditions and contextual polyvalence, neither visions or representations of community, nor communities' actual practices, are ever reducible one to the other, or to their conditions of existence. Indeed, imaginary communities are invented as a consequence of the indulgence of an epistemic fallacy: the confusion of representation of community safety with its effective governing practices. To illustrate their point, Edwards and Hughes give an elegant exposition of the varied and sometimes contradictory effects that academic imaginings of 'community safety' have had on political discourses and local communities.

Apart from the general theoretical arguments being made here about the relationships between imagination and its imaginary constructs, the focus on imagined and imaginary communities also resonates with concerns expressed in other chapters about the ways in which imaginary penalities either implicitly or explicitly invoke a range of differing and contradictory 'communities' in support of their policies and practices (see Carlen, Chapter 1; Tombs, Chapter 5; Sim, Chapter 7; Jefferson, Chapter 8).

Exclusion of the other

The necessity for all discourses to choose between different paradigms and justificatory rules has already been discussed. What is important, in relation to the desired production of new knowledge for the better understanding of changing judicial, penal and security contexts, is that debate should be kept open to all kinds of arguments and expertise, including the expertise of those working in frontline judicial and penal contexts on a daily basis. One purpose of analysing imaginary penalities, therefore, is to assess which knowledges have been incorporated into judicial and penal discourses and which excluded.[2] This is the task undertaken by Jacqueline Tombs in Chapter 5 where she argues that as a result of sentencers being forced to adhere to the logic of actuarial risk assessments when passing sentence, the knowledge born of their experience as judges (that is, the discretion previously held to be a main plank of their discursive authority) is nowadays too often excluded from the sentencing process as the unaccountable Other which has to be suppressed in the service not of justice but of risk reduction. Furthermore, she suggests that the exclusion of judicial discretion from sentencing decisions may well account for the increasing numbers of minor offenders being gaoled in Scotland – even though judges fight back, when they can, by trying to pass sentences which are still imaginatively informed by their experience and remaining discretionary powers but which also appear to comply with the logic of pre-given risk assessments. However, although the attempts to limit judicial discretion have, by and large, been done under the rhetorics of accountability and consistency in sentencing, the probation service in England and Wales has been a much more direct casualty of the punitive populist turn in the governance of crime in the UK, as Anne Worrall demonstrates in Chapter 6.

Although English probation officers have attempted to make the official rhetoric of holistic justice a reality, they (and other non-custodial programme personnel) have increasingly come under attack in official reports on the management of offenders. As a result, they have attempted even stricter adherence to the imaginary penality which implies that 'all purposes of sentencing are compatible and achievable' (p. 131) and which, in so doing, also ejects all awkwardly non-populist understandings of the complexities of sentencing from officially approved penal discourse. One result, as Worrall argues in an authoritative critique of recent developments in the 'seamless' management of offenders in the UK, has been an increase in the numbers recalled to prison, as probation officers have attempted to avoid blame before any of the inevitable 'seams' show. This is not surprising. The imprisonment of offenders is, logically, the only safe option for workers in an essentially high risk profession which has always been the media's, and is now the government's, favourite scapegoat whenever offenders already serving non-custodial sentences commit further serious crimes.

Chapters 7–12 also include examination of what is excluded from the official discourses of imaginary penalities. Here, however, the main exclusion always relates to structural conditions, especially those relating to inequality, poverty or lack of rehabilitative resources outside the prison. As Magnus Hörnqvist insists in Chapter 9:

> the dominant focus is limited to individuals. Institutions and social structures never enter the analysis (van Berkel et al. 2002: 70). The response to social exclusion and unemployment is not seen to lie in structural change. More or less everything except the excluded individuals themselves is excluded from policy considerations. (p. 180)

Analysis of these very different imaginary penalities suggests that in systematically excluding more imaginative and politically embarrassing knowledges about crime and risk they also increase levels of penal pain and incarceration; and serve political ends far removed from the justifying rhetorics of reform, rehabilitation and human rights. It is primarily as a result of selective discursive exclusion of the Other of structural inequalities and power that imaginary penalities become peopled by imaginary prison officers and imaginary prisoners while inhabiting imaginary prisons and a proliferation of other imaginary penal contexts.

Imaginary prisons and imaginary prison officers

Joe Sim's Chapter 7 begins by identifying another excluded Other of recent British government discourse on crime. It includes

a range of crimes and social harms – domestic violence and murder, rape, deaths at work, deaths on the roads, racist and homophobic abuse, attacks and murders, income tax evasion, deaths in custody and state crime...(p. 136)

He then proceeds to detail a catalogue of exclusions which constitute modern imaginary prisoners and prisons before focusing on the making of modern prison staff in Britain. Here he presents a different imaginary to Carlen, Chapter 1.[3] For Sim's imaginary prison officers are described as

acting as if they *believe* they can and indeed *want* to deliver on the promised benefits of the prison if only more time, more resources, more managerial support and more public sympathy were forthcoming...(p. 146)

Inspiringly, however, and despite the grim picture he paints of British prisons, Sim ends the chapter with illustrations of his concluding argument that it is 'possible to imagine, develop and implement a penal politics that is not regressive and repressive'.

For a second example of an imaginary penality involving imaginary prison officers, Chapter 8 by Andrew Jefferson focuses on Nigeria. It highlights a concern about transnational imaginary attempts at penal reform which are increasingly occurring under the banner of human rights (see also Piacentini 2006). In Jefferson's analysis the excluded

Other of human rights training is identified as that which gave rise to the interventionary demand in the first place: the penal practices already embedded in local conditions and culture. His analysis, like that of Magnus Hörnqvist (Chapter 9), exposes the tendency of Western penal programmers to assume that the programme *is* the practice. At a time when human rights discourse has been used by the United States as an excuse for 'incursions into states' freedom of action and sovereignty' which many authoritarian third world leaders have then used as an excuse 'from making the economic and political reforms the West urges' (Hutton 2007: 223), Jefferson's chapter provides a timely warning: against parachuting Western penal values (here in the form of prison officers' training courses in prisoners' human rights) to non-Western countries without seriously taking into account the influence of pre-existing cultural and economic conditions (see also Arsovska and Verduyn 2008 and the discussion of cosmopolitanism in Hudson, Chapter 13).

Imaginary prisoners

The imaginary penalities analysed in the next four chapters all, to a greater or lesser extent, centre around complex constructions of imaginary prisoners. In Chapter 9 Magnus Hörnqvist provides a sophisticated exposition and analysis of previous and current theories about the relationship of imprisonment to labour markets, arguing that in today's prisons the aim is no longer to produce disciplined industrial workers but, rather, 'stress-managing service workers'. Hence the plethora of cognitive behavioural programmes which, though purporting to equip prisoners with wage-earning skills, are actually fashioned to make them come to terms with intermittent unskilled work and unemployment. On this analysis, imaginary prisoners (imaginary because they are officially defined as being unemployable unless given prison programming) are then turned by the same official discourses and programmes into imaginary wage labourers. But their chances of getting skilled work after cognitive behavioural training are no greater than they were before. (The partiality of the imaginary construction of prisoners in England is touched on by Joe Sim in Chapter 7; Hörnqvist's examples in Chapter 9 come from Sweden, but Chapters 10–12 illustrate that similarly partial constructions are to be found in Canada, Australia and the United States.)

Imaginary rehabilitation

The essays on imaginary rehabilitation by Kelly Hannah-Moffat (Chapter 10), Mark Halsey (Chapter 11) and Megan Comfort (Chapter 12) demonstrate how imaginary rehabilitation is constructed via the exclusion of those very same Other considerations which, in being central to prisoners' social identities, must also be central to any future desistance from lawbreaking. Thus, in Hannah-Moffat's analysis of the selective ways in which gender considerations have been incorporated into Risk, Need and Responsivity Programmes for women in Canada, structural and cultural factors such as the women's previous histories and ethnicity are either excluded from programme discourses for not being 'proven' risk factors or, alternatively, not even considered in relation to programmes which have already been pre-defined as gender-neutral. Similarly, in Mark Halsey's depiction of the lack of respect shown to young men in custodial and post-release contexts in Australia, the analytic focus is again on the discursive abstraction of prisoners from their social contexts. But here the absent Other of the discourse is constituted not only by lack of recognition of prisoners' biographies, but also by the lack of any concept of social interdependency. Hence, all talk about desistance from crime and recidivism reduction becomes imaginary. For, as Halsey argues, while young men in penal institutions continue to be shown so very little respect by their custodians *and* the emphasis of training programmes is upon individual responsibilities and endeavour, they are not being well prepared to imagine a law-abiding world characterised by mutually inclusive respect and reciprocity in social relationships. (See also Hudson, Chapter 13, on the importance of respect in social relations.)

Finally, in this trio of articles on rehabilitation and desistance, Megan Comfort examines how, in the absence of welfare provision outside prison, very poor prisoners and their families in the United States are able and willing to construct an imaginary rehabilitation. They abstract themselves from the pains and debilitations of imprisonment in order to escape for a while from 'the extraordinary degradation of life conditions for poor African Americans in the era of mass incarceration' (p. 252). And the United States is not alone in replacing welfare with imprisonment. What an irony it is that, in so many of the countries whose governments are currently preaching democracy and human rights to governments of other sovereign states, it is only in prison that the poorest citizens of these Western democracies can obtain the minimum living standards denied them on the outside.

But it could be different. And, like several of the other authors in this book, Comfort ends by suggesting that it *is* possible to conceive of ways of doing justice differently. 'Imagine...'

Imagine!

Which is what Barbara Hudson does in Chapter 13, where she sets out an imaginative and alternative way of re-conceiving justice. Unlike present conceptions of nation-state justice, cosmopolitan justice would not be based on an assumption of shared rationalities. Instead it would recognise and welcome difference and diversity. It would not set up imaginary criminals abstracted from their economic and cultural histories so that it might then more easily programme them to fit in with official rhetoric about the efficacy of current crime policies. Nor would it silence, via audit and stigmatisation, any justice workers holding views running counter to prevailing official discourses on crime and security. Instead, a cosmopolitan justice would attempt to 'find modes of accommodation and establish procedures of fair co-operation between groups and individuals who may have different and even conflicting interests and ideas of the good life' (p. 277). And lastly, one might add, in recognition of the inevitable attraction of bureaucratic routinisation to people who (as well as being imaginative!) have to choose between courses of action in order to get things done, a reflexively re-imagined justice would attempt avoidance of judicial closure by continuously reviewing and debating both its own and competing knowledges and modes of governance.

Choosing between alternatives and excluding some of them, together with the accompanying tendency to discursive closure, are unavoidable prerequisites of meaningful communication. All of us who discourse on crime and punishment are (wittingly or unwittingly) complicit in the making of imaginary penalities. But the effects of the imaginary can be limited; and the imaginary itself can be contested: first, by investigating what is excluded from its discourse; and then by analysis and exposure of the means by which the exclusion is effected. For the same knowledges that are incorporated into imaginary penalities are also those which, re-imagined differently, might one day give birth to new, more democratic and more socially enhancing responses to crime and security threats.

Notes

1 http://.en.ikipedia.org/wiki/Emperor's New Clothes
2 The discursive Other has to be recognised because it is implicated in the discourse's originating conditions but then it is excluded to enable and justify the discourse taking the form it does.
3 The object of knowledge is different: Carlen is attempting to explain how it was that everybody connected to the running of a prison could both explicitly deny the possibility of it achieving its objectives while at the same time explicitly claiming that they none the less had to act as if it could; Sim explains how some prison officers obstruct reforms while at the same time claiming that they support them.

Chapter I

Imaginary penalities and risk-crazed governance

Pat Carlen

Introduction

This essay develops the concept, identifies and analyses the phenomenon, and then discusses the challenge of, imaginary penalities.[1] The term imaginary penality is, in this chapter, used to denote penal policies and practices where agents charged with either the authorisation, development and/or implementation of a system of punishment address themselves to its principles and persist in manufacturing an elaborate system of costly institutional practices 'as if' all objectives are realisable. At the same time, however, they also recognise that, although their audited actions may be presented as evidence of the effectiveness of the project, when they act they must also address themselves to an other, oppositional but operational, penality with a material reality always and already subversive and, logically, destructive, of the objectives of the official penology. The term risk-crazed governance refers to a governmental mode which both cherishes and employs a pervasive social risk-consciousness as a tool of control, with the result that the demand for risk-protection becomes inelastic and far outstrips the capacity of governments to meet the demand (compare with Garland 1996).

The essay's main argument is that whereas previous eras saw the development of substantive and symbolic penalities which could be confronted and modified through internal empirical testing or external critique of their relevance as responses to lawbreaking, today, in risk-crazed states of governance, some elements of substantive penalities (for example, rehabilitation programmes) and some elements of symbolic penalities (for example, 'toughness' rhetoric) have combined in the imaginary penalities of an ever-encroaching and totalising criminal governance.[2]

The burden of the argument depends upon an analysis of the effect that the political strategy of punitive populism combined with that of the managerialist technique of social auditing has had on workers (especially professionals) in the criminal processing system. The research experience which initially provoked the analysis occurred in Australia; the empirical focus is primarily on the UK. It is hoped that this 'small canvas' and regional approach will complement some of the insights provided by recent 'large canvas' and global theorising which, useful though it has been in tracing out a palimpsest of social trends, has not, in my opinion, been quite so helpful in identifying local points of political intervention and discursive struggle.

Narrative

In October 2005 I did some research in an Australian prison, Optima.[3] It was a new institution designed to run re-integrative programmes for female offenders. The facilities were excellent and the staff were enthusiastic and non-punitive in style and philosophy.[4] But, from the beginning, I was struck by their insistence that the prison's well-publicised rehabilitative goals had no chance of realisation. In fact, what was most striking about Optima in October 2005, nine months after it had opened with a fanfare about its therapeutic ethos and re-integrative objectives, was that not one of the staff interviewed would say that the re-integrative objectives were being met, and none could see any possibility of them being met in the future. They gave four main reasons for their pessimism: that whereas the prison and programmes had been designed for sentenced prisoners, the rapidly increasing prison population at Optima was primarily made up of remand prisoners; that the majority of programmes had not been accredited (that is, given an official seal of approval for use in the prison); that all the staff and many of the prisoners knew that back-up programmes outside the prison were very few and far between, and in some geographical areas, non-existent; that many of the staff thought that, even if there had been any post-prison support programmes, such programmes would have been unlikely to appeal to prisoners who (variously) were going out to continuing drugs usage, no safe and secure accommodation and abusive men; or who simply assumed from their previous experience that, in the conditions to which they were returning, crime was most probably the best solution to their problems (compare with Halsey 2006b). Not surprisingly, therefore, because of the many barriers to achievement of the prison's objectives (barriers, incidentally, which lay quite beyond the control of the staff) and, also, because of the logical and practical difficulties of attempting to assess (for monitoring purposes) what contribution Optima had made to any post-prison lifestyle changes by its ex-inmates, staff revealed that they had informally modified the institution's foundational rehabilitative/re-integrative objectives, and had justified the modifications according to four main arguments:

- we cannot track how women perform after leaving prison; we can only ease their re-entry into the community;

- we cannot monitor how women perform after leaving prison; but we can monitor changes in the behaviour of the women while they are in prison;

- we cannot get information about the achievement of programme objectives (outputs), but we can monitor both how the programmes are run (inputs) and consumer [i.e. prisoner] satisfaction;

- we should move away from aiming for recidivism reduction and aim instead for intermediate goals, such as increasing the length of time a woman stays out of prison, or equipping her to be better able to live in the community without getting into criminal trouble.

All of which was very understandable in the impossible situation of the imaginary prisoners, imaginary programmes and imaginary community which the staff had had imposed on them from without. Yet, although the staff in interview were quite certain that operational modifications to Optima's objectives had been made and, moreover, argued vehemently that such modifications were justified, they were also adamant that they would not be making these amendments known to the judges and magistrates who would, therefore, continue to think that Optima's objectives were the re-integrative ones advertised by the Corrections Department at the opening of the prison. For, although prison personnel could only maintain their own realist position and respond to the imaginary penality in coherent fashion by replacing the prison's impossible-of-realisation formal objectives with more realisable objectives rooted in their professional knowledge of the factors (for example, safe housing and drugs abstinence) most likely to be strategic in shaping lawabiding post-prison careers, at the same time, that very process of institutional goal replacement destroyed the prime justification (re-integration) for many of the more minor offenders being in Optima at all, thereby also undermining the officially proclaimed rationale for the existence of the prison, its staff, and, indeed, by extension, much of the carceral system.

Comment

That's the story. 'And so what?' you may be thinking. It is well known that there is nothing new about the existence of an observable contradiction between policy objectives and policy achievements (as a prison officer said, 'that's life'); there is nothing new about a prison's rehabilitative goals being undermined by lack of social and medical provision for released prisoners (as another prison officer said, 'that's always happened'); and there is nothing new about organisational goal adaptation in the face of material obstacles to achievement of the original goals (as the prison governor commented, 'that's professional discretion operating as it's meant to operate'). None of that was new to me. What, however, did surprise me was the knowing and collusive response of the penal personnel. By 'knowing' and 'collusive' I mean that not only did the interviewees admit to the inappropriateness of the prison programmes, they also implied that 'everyone knew', and that nobody could/would do anything about it. As the rest of this chapter attempts to make clear, I was gradually to come to the conclusion that their knowingness was born of a partial knowledge of the 'imaginary' nature of the penalities within which their professional consciousness was being reconfigured. Meanwhile, however, this was a different type of criminology or penality to any I had come up against before. For whereas the exposé criminology of previous eras repeatedly demonstrates how penal practitioners routinely claim to be doing one thing when they are observably doing something entirely different, nowadays exposé criminology has become somewhat redundant as, instead of either embracing or denying external critique, contemporary penal practitioners themselves point out that they obviously cannot do what governments claim they should be doing (that is, successfully addressing social welfare and medical deficits by penal methods) but [shrug] that they have to act as if they are. And it was in obedience to that 'as if' philosophy that the staff at Optima Prison were spending a considerable amount of time and money designing programmes for 'accreditation' when they already knew that the population for which the programmes were being designed was no longer in the frame; and also making 'evaluation' plans to measure levels of a 'reintegration' which they already knew was certainly not happening, and which, they claimed, was unlikely to happen in the future. In short, the staff at Optima continued to act 'as if' they were working in a therapunitive prison designed for reintegration via programming and appropriate back-up outside the prison when everyone involved, from basic grade prison officers up to Corrections Headquarters administrators knew that the prison's whole concept of reintegration was 'imaginary' insofar as it was posited upon imaginary prisoners (they were short-term remand rather than sentenced), imaginary programmes (they were not running), and imaginary 'back-up' in the 'community' (neither 'back-up' nor 'community' existed). But it was an imaginary penalty that was having real effects in that it was incurring financial and social costs, influencing sentencing and providing a rationale for the existence and perpetuation of short-term imprisonment and more prisons. Thus, whereas exposé criminology took its name from the primary task of exposing the gap between rhetoric and reality, *the concept of imaginary penalities presupposes that the rhetoric has become the reality.*

And I suspect that this 'as if' penality may have become endemic to criminal processing and penal policies wherever governments partly contrive, and partly attempt to meet, popular demands for punitive sentencing at the same time as trying both to justify the increases in imprisonment with promises of in-prison programmes directed at recidivism reduction, and to control the outcomes of such programmes by denying all discretion of interpretation and action to prisons' staff, criminal processing workers and researchers. This is not to say that professionals cease to use their discretion. As we saw with the modification of Optima's reintegrative objectives, professionals have to use discretion in order to manage imaginary penalities, maintain professional identity and keep their jobs. For all public information purposes, however, criminal processing professionals working to managerialist audits are forced to converse within the limits imposed by governments determined to win electoral success by manufacturing (via self-fulfilling audits of imaginary successes in meeting impossible objectives) paper representations of the risk-crazed levels of control, discipline, deterrence and audit which can popularly be presented as having the capacity to reduce crime (see, for instance, Fitzgibbon (2007) on risk assessment in probation). It is under such conditions, also, that: sentencers feel justified in sending

5

more and more low-level recidivist offenders either to prison (and for longer) or on to impossibly demanding non-custodial programmes; there is a transfer of resources from the community to the prison; the overcrowded prisons cannot cope with inmate populations totally inappropriate for the programmes on offer (or vice versa); once released from prison (ex)prisoners are returned to the same, or worse social circumstances than they were in before; and any change that the in-prison programmes might have effected is negated by the insuperable difficulties inherent in the prisoners' histories of poverty and abuse and present ex-prisoner status. Concomitantly, some criminal processing and penal personnel partly see through the 'imaginary penalty' and, in attempting to reduce its contradictions, meet audit demands, and keep their jobs and professional self-respect, replace the official imaginary penalty with an imaginary penalty of their own and then, because the official story that 'prison works' is thereby vindicated, prison populations rise even faster. Yet, although this imaginary turn in penal practice may be a new (or repeat) reconfiguration of some older penalties, it is not exceptional. In autumn 2005 Optima was a local site of just one instance of what may be an internationally prevalent facet of contemporary risk-crazed governance: imaginary penalities. In the rest of this essay, I want to look at the characteristics of imaginary penalities and also at the risk-crazed conditions which have given rise to them in the UK.

Imaginary penalities

The concept of imaginary penalities as used in this chapter has a very specific meaning and refers neither to 'imagination', nor to an occupational psychology of intent, mendacity or hypocrisy. Instead, it tries to identify a specific structure of institutional worker-consciousness wherein:

- agents charged with the authorisation, development and/or implementation of a system of punishment address themselves to its principles and persist in manufacturing an elaborate system of costly institutional practices 'as if' all objectives are realisable;

- at the same time as presenting their reflexively audited actions as evidence of the effectiveness of the project;

- at the same time, also, as being aware that, when they act, they must also address themselves to an Other, oppositional but operational, penality with a material reality always and already subversive and, logically, destructive, of the objectives of the official penology.

Thus, although Althusser (1971) employed the concept of the 'imaginary' to describe a mode of knowing which he described as 'unscientific and non-theoretical', the concept is being used here to denote an ideological form of knowing (*not* knowledge) which is forced to suppress some forms of knowledge (the Other) in order to make sense of the anomic contradictions between the demands of governance and the social conditions in which those demands can be met (compare with Merton on anomie 1968/1949). However, this Other can never be totally suppressed because it is always and already implicated in the social conditions which have given rise to the demand for governance in the first place. By way of illustration, let us go back to the story of Optima.

The main question troubling me when I was interviewing at Optima was: how could prison personnel tell me that all their reintegrative efforts within the prison were, on the prison's own criteria, a waste of time when, at the same time, they were also telling me that they were working their socks off to compile a confetti of paperwork claiming just the opposite? Certainly their overt pessimism about the likely outcomes of this 'as if' operationalism was not that of constructivist psychology, based on Vaihinger's philosophical tenet that by trying out different realities we may indeed help to realise them (Vaihinger 1924/1911). The staff had no doubt that because of the rehabilitation deficit outside the prison there was no chance of the institution's rehabilitative objectives being met. Yet, their pessimism could not be explained by any lack of ideological commitment to the institutional objectives either; the administrators interviewed had all been involved with Optima's policy blueprints, and the discipline and therapeutic staff had been specially chosen for their commitment to Optima's rehabilitative ideal. So, the explanation that I eventually crafted was that the organisational consciousness of the staff had been constituted within the space between the material structural conditions constitutive of the rehabilitation deficit and the organisational cultures of audit and appraisal which demanded that the rehabilitation deficit be both recognised and denied. In other words: given all the organisational demands of audit and appraisal, the Other which Optima staff had to acknowledge was that there were no rehabilitative facilities outside the prison, that assessing the levels of reintegration was well-nigh impossible and that the deep-rooted problems of many of the women were not going to go away

7

during a short spell in prison. At the same time, for the purposes of getting on with their day to day work, they had to suppress that knowledge and act 'as if' these material problems did not exist. And maybe in previous eras prison workers would have been allowed or even encouraged to suppress that knowledge completely.

Certainly, different types of organisational and governmental regimes around the world have been known (variously) to cajole, demand or force their workers or adherents to deny policy failure. Today, however, under different structures of governance involving both disciplinary auditing procedures (Power 1997) and coercive silently silencing techniques (Mathiesen 2004) such straightforward denial of policy failure is more difficult. Staff are required to measure (and make public) their levels of achievement and because measurement can only be made against static and clearly defined objectives there is no room for the questioning or modification of objectives. However justified Optima staff themselves might have felt in replacing unrealistic rehabilitative objectives involving the world beyond Optima (over which they had no control) with more realisable institutional objectives of their own (over which they did have some control), faced with programme accreditation, programme evaluation, personal appraisals and other managerialist techniques of audit and quality control, they had to take both the formal objectives of rehabilitation and reintegration and the Other which had occasioned them (that is, conditions outside prison such as the rehabilitative deficit and the freedom of movement which makes monitoring of ex-prisoners impossible) back into the official evaluative frame. At such times, when the prison authorities and staff were forced simultaneously to accept (for the purposes of audit, institutional identity and self-identity) and deny (for the purposes of audit, institutional identity and self-identity) the saliency of both the prison's formal objectives and the material conditions outside the prison on which both designation and achievement of those objectives depended, the maintenance of an imaginary penality became more challenging. For then prison staff had to confront the fact that if the conditions necessary to rehabilitation had actually existed in 'the community' the prisoners whom they were charged to rehabilitate (and who also constituted the institution's *raison d'être*) most probably would not have been sent to prison in the first place.

Thus it is that, when the imaginary is called to account within the symbolic order of the wider society, the Other, far from being suppressed, is recognised as being both the genesis and the nemesis of the imaginary. Under risk-crazed modes of governance, the over-emphasis on positivistic social accounting procedures (Power 1997) and scientistic reflexivity (that is, finding the evidence to support the policies: Hope 2004, following Beck 1992, and Chapter 2 of this book) simultaneously demands and creates an illusion of certainty of policy realisation. In turn, the risk-induced demands that policy realisation be conflated with policy statements result in less and less discretion being granted to professionals.

Yet why would professionals require discretion to deal with actuarial (imaginary) classes of prisoners – in Optima's case, the imaginary population of sentenced prisoners which Optima had never had? Discretionary powers are granted in recognition of difference and the need to act in individual situations not covered by existing rules. Actuarialism only recognises differences between classes and, in any case, positivistic accounting grids always already have a rule to cover every case. Criminal processing professionals, therefore, in the blame-driven cultures which risk-crazed modes of governance spawn, tend to acquiesce in the pursuit of impossible institutional goals (imaginary penalities) set by the various political and management agendas, at the same time as knowing that they are acquiescing in (and thereby promoting) an imaginary order, the perpetuation of which renders those goals more and more desirable as they become less and less likely of achievement.

Imaginary, ideological, substantive and symbolic penalities

In a general and formal sense imaginary penalities are as partially ideological as any other form of knowledge. Yet, whilst most grand theories of ideology are concerned with the partiality of ideology as opposed to 'truth' (for example, Mannheim 1960/1936) or, less frequently (as in the work of Althusser 1971) with ideology being a necessary component of new knowledge, imaginary penalities are here being theorised very specifically as the complex unintended ideological processual products of the interplay of some contemporary conditions and modes of governance: economic insecurity; governance through auditing and actuarialist techniques to produce a mountain of hard copy testifying to responsible and effective government; and the official essentialisation of knowledge about crime and punishment. In short, it is the conjunctural partiality and reflexive closure of imaginary penalities which is being emphasised – although it is not denied that they are also constitutive of new knowledge in the Althusserian sense nor that such knowledge has effects at the level

9

of criminal processing. And this is a position which is very similar to that of Vaihinger (1965/1924) whose treatise entitled *The Philosophy of As If* defines 'fictions' as having at least two of the attributes which are here also attributed to imaginary penalities: consciousness of a fiction and instrumentalism. However, another of Vaihinger's features of fictions involves contingency: the fiction will be overthrown if and when it has ceased to be useful. What is distinctive about imaginary penalities, however, is that their usefulness is always both open to question by those who have to implement them, and not open to question when the livelihoods of those very same people also depend upon the premises and promises of imaginary penalities being favourably purveyed and/or audited. As a result, imaginary penalities are all the more likely to follow the same career path as Vaihinger's *still useful* fictions: fiction becomes hypothesis; hypothesis becomes dogma (Vaihinger 1965/1924: 126).

At the present time, in order to function as being both punitive and legitimate, risk-crazed governments tend explicitly to make at least two claims: that empirically tested stiff punishments can be used to produce measurable reductions in recidivism; and that the penal system is not just about punishment, but can also be a tool for the reduction of social inequalities. The implicit promise of imaginary penalities is that crime and social risk can ultimately be abolished. For the people charged with implementing penal policies, however, the tantalising 'as if' of imaginary penality breaks down once other realities of present-day prison populations and present-day social inequities are confronted and acknowledged for the purposes of managerialist audit and evaluation by the reintegration industry's own public relations machinery. With audit and evaluation in mind, a process of official recognition and denial gets underway: images of present-day relationships between punishment and inequality have to be recognised for the purposes of legitimating the imprisonment of relatively minor offenders on the grounds that their in-prison programming will turn them away from crime; but then these inconvenient cognitions have to be driven out as the unwelcome 'Other' undermining an (imaginary) integrative penality. In short, the same inequities which provide justifications for the reintegrative programmes also completely undermine them. Accordingly, the whole prison and reintegration business is a prime example of the power of the imaginary to create acquiescence in the absurd: with its actuarial constructs of offenders; with its circular and self-serving evaluations and audits of ideal prisoners; with its non-existent or ineffective programmes both inside and outside prisons; and with personnel who, in order to keep their jobs, are required by the terms of their employment to act 'as if' the imaginary is both attainable and measurable while, at the same time (in order to keep their sanity, professional self-respect and resist accusations of either incompetence or hypocrisy) they must also insist that they can hardly be expected to redress social injustices from a penal base.

Imaginary penalities are distinguishable from both substantive and symbolic penalities. Substantive penalities have traditionally been justified on the grounds that they aspire to reduce crime either via deterrence of potential lawbreakers or via a mix of welfare, punitive or disciplinary strategies aimed at actual lawbreakers. The substantive claims of imaginary penalities to reduce crime are fundamentally flawed by the closed order of knowledge of crime and lawbreakers which is created at the present time in the UK by imaginary penalities' defining conditions of existence: actuarial constructs of offenders; government-backed populist-positivist conceptions of crime and punishment; and centralisation of knowledge about criminal processing issues.

Imaginary penalities also differ from the symbolic penalities which aspire to mark a society's moral boundaries (Durkheim 1995/1896) because, by pandering to the inelastic demand for punishment by criminalising more and more behaviours previously seen as being matters of civil dispute rather than as signs of criminal transgression, imaginary penalities are often more accurate indices of a society's insecurities than they are of their moral sensibilities.

Most penal policies have had aspirational symbolic or substantive objectives which have been open to modification in the light of changing knowledge and circumstances, and both symbolic and practical penalities do indeed tend to evolve according to changing material and changing ideological conditions, resulting in their constant reconfiguration and transformation. It is not, therefore, because their objectives are sometimes modified that imaginary penalities are different from symbolic and substantive penalities.

Contemporary imaginary penalities are distinctive because:

- Imaginary penalities actuarially target imaginary criminals so that, as De Giorgi (2006: 107) says, 'concrete individuals and the social interaction in which they are involved tend to be replaced by the production of classes and categories that are 'simulacra' of the

11

real' and therefore the policy can neither succeed nor be modified; it is irrelevant.

- Imaginary penalities contradictorily imply that 'crime' can be abolished[5] at the same time as defining more and more behaviours as illegal – thus creating the conditions of both their impossibility and their perpetuation.

- Knowledge is centralised and essentialised and critique is negated via incorporative (Carlen 2002a) and other silencing techniques (Mathiesen 2004).

- Professionals working within the criminal processing and penal systems are constrained both to know and not to know that official promises of crime reduction via rehabilitation are impossible of realisation without a full recognition of other conceptions of social and criminal justice, unofficial conceptions which, because they remain unlegitimated, make the official claims and promises simultaneously necessary, desirable and impossible.

From risk governance to risk-crazed governance of crime

In arguing that imaginary penalities have been constituted within a risk-crazed governance of crime, I am not arguing that a governmental play on risk has nowadays displaced all other forms of governance. I am more inclined to agree with those commentators who argue that risk has manifested itself in a variety of terrains of governance both created by, and creating anew, ever-changing regimes of fear and uncertainty (compare with O'Malley 2004). Nor is it being argued that attempts to reduce uncertainty via calculations and predictions of risk are themselves impossible of realisation. I am arguing that, as far as crime is concerned, governments in the UK (and possibly elsewhere) have in the last 40 years made many more grandiose claims about the possibilities for reducing (rather than merely punishing) crime than has previously been the case; and that these claims have been rendered crazy (that is, impossible) because the development of a supposedly risk-proof technology of continuous crime-reduction (and, by implication, crime eradication) has also created the very conditions (transfer of community resources to overcrowded prisons, inelastic demand for increasingly punitive measures) which have made those claims impossible of realisation and (because of their imaginary characteristics) difficult to penetrate and critique. Moreover, in identifying some of the risk-crazed conditions of contemporary imaginary penalities, I am not claiming that they are necessary conditions, just that they are those which have been conducive to the fabrication of contemporary imaginary penalities. The risk-crazed preconditions for today's imaginary penalities in the UK have been: social and ontological insecurities (see Young 2007); populist criminal governance; actuarialist constructions of criminal risk and crime control; and the centralised control of surplus sociological knowledge via disciplinary audit and the silencing of critique (De Giorgi 2006; Mathiesen 2004).

Insecurities

Much has been written about the multiple anxieties constitutive of post-modern high risk societies characterised by rapid social change, new demographics of employment and unemployment, increased individualistic consumerism alongside a decline in collectivist welfare provision, and increased warnings from governments that the state can do less and less for citizens who nowadays must expect increasingly to look to private insurance and private security firms for their protection from (often undefined) threat (see, for example, Beck 1992; Stenson and Sullivan 2001; Pratt *et al.* 2005). Yet, as an eminent German historian has observed, from the fifteenth century onwards, there has also been a more stark and perennial, an older and more fundamental, anxiety about the risks attendant upon economic inequalites, about the risks incurred by the many (Jutte 1994) as a result of the social exclusion of the few, as well as, contradictorily but significantly, a concern about the costs to taxpayers of inclusive measures.[6] Thus, writing about poverty and crime in early modern Europe, Jutte reminds us that 'for early modern governments and magistrates, the poor were mainly a problem of public order, and only to a lesser extent public relief (Jutte 1994: 194–5). And, although a postwar consensus in the UK about the proper responses to crime maintained a predominantly liberal stance until the law and order politics of the 1980s (Loader 2006), at the end of the 1980s the rightwing American pundit Charles Murray (1990) found a ready following in the UK when he used the concept of 'underclass' to argue that insofar as welfare payments encourage unemployed people to self-exclude from work and family responsibilities, the welfare state was partly to blame for the rising numbers who were currently being defined as socially excluded.

The Conservative Thatcher governments and the New Labour Blair governments which succeeded them both chose to play upon the old mythical distinction between the lawabiding majority and the criminal minority (see Karstedt and Farrall 2006), as well as between the deserving and undeserving poor. Any ethical concerns about the observable over-imprisonment of poorer and ethnic minority people were replaced by 'bottom line accounting procedures'. Accordingly, and at a time of heightened social insecurities when discourses on both lawbreaking and responses to it were (and still are) framed in the language of economic threat and security risk, it is not surprising that a political party without an ideologically principled agenda, but obsessed with the fear of not being re-elected after its first term of office after 18 years in Opposition, sought and won popular support for tougher and tougher law and order measures. Now, in 2008, however, it can be argued that in light of continuing popular demand for, and government promises of, impossible levels of security and supervision in relation, for instance, to mentally ill offenders, sex offenders, released prisoners, 'migrant' workers and 'young people' in general, the UK government has been hoist with its own petard, as the tidal demand for tougher and tougher punishments and surveillance continues to increase. It is a demand which was fired, and is continuing to be stoked, not only by the government's own law and order rhetoric, but by the imaginary policies which have been another of its results. Thus, although by 8 February 2005 the Labour governments had created 1,018 new criminal offences and the prison population had risen by 25,000 in the ten years since they came to power, the significantly titled paper *Rebalancing the Criminal Justice System In favour of the Law-Abiding Majority* published in 2006 still evidenced a need to present the government as being 'tough on crime', the word 'tough' (or variations thereon) being used 33 times to describe the government's latest policy intentions in relation to criminal processing (Home Office 2006)[7].

Populist criminal governance

The attributes of a populist punitive approach to criminal processing have been well documented (for a most recent discussion see Pratt *et al.*, 2005). The popular appeal of an apparently increasingly punitive response to lawbreaking depends not only upon perceptions that there is a criminal threat but also that such threat has reached dangerous proportions because of the failure of governments to develop effective deterrents and responses to crime. When contemporary responses to crime neither reduce the actual amount of lawbreaking nor slow down the rate of increase in fear of crime, the next usual step has been to create folk devils (young people, most frequently, but historically, as well as more recently, the poor, the stranger and the unconventional) as bearers of extraordinary criminal threat. Finally, when that strategy also fails, blame for the apparently parlous state of criminal governance is politically displaced from central government policies on to the national and local agents of law enforcement and social discipline: civil servants, courts, police, prisons, social workers, schools, families, parents (compare with Garland 1996). Concomitantly, while professional knowledge based on expertise, experience and learning is downgraded, the 'will of the people' is presented as being sovereign. English criminologist Rod Morgan reminds us of the tone of UK's prime-ministerial law and order rhetoric in 1997: 'Law abiding citizens are, the Prime Minister said, "our boss".' The public want "a say in how they are policed. They want to be in charge. Our proposals do that" ' (Morgan 2006: 93). Unfortunately, and as Morgan went on to point out in the same article, when 'the public' become 'boss' they are likely to be rather selective in their assessments of a government's achievements, and are more likely to be worried by the definite increase in violent crime than relieved by a decrease in property crime. Moreover, the 'citizen boss's' perceptions and fear of crime are likely to be much more influenced by their proximity to low level acts of disorder in their local neighbourhood than by a close reading of complex official statistics with their less than reassuring footnotes on ever-changing counting rules and inclusion criteria. As a result, in the UK, the New Labour governments have had continuously to prove their toughness on crime to a 'boss' who, in reply to official claims that the fight against crime is being won, effectively replies that 'seeing is believing'. Gradually, in such a situation, on the one hand the popular demand for crime reduction via government action becomes inelastic and remains the same whatever the government does while, on the other, government rhetoric about the culpability and ineffectiveness of every criminal processing agency begins to imply that once all the agencies have been sorted, audited and 'made fit for purpose' crime will not just be reduced but could actually be eradicated.

It is when the fear of crime and rhetoric of risk-containment lead to an astonishing increase in criminal legislation and when, too, centralisation of crime control is increasingly out of proportion to the specific threats being posed, that criminal governance can appropriately be called 'risk-crazed'. Just one very small and localised example of such risk-crazed governance can be selected from the many to be found in the history of the Anti-Social Behaviour Order (ASBO), a civil order introduced into England and Wales by the 1998 Crime and Disorder Act but, significantly, backed up by criminal sanctions.

> In 2005 magistrates granted an anti-social behaviour order (ASBO) against a woman who had attempted suicide four times. She was banned from jumping into rivers, canals or on to railway lines. The 23-year-old had been rescued three times from the River Avon in Bath in 2004 after trying to take her life. She had also been found hanging from a railway parapet and police had had to stop trains to rescue her. The magistrates sentenced her for three public order offences after deciding that throwing oneself into a river did constitute disorder. Although an ASBO is a civil order, the woman would be imprisoned if she broke the order. The ASBO sought to prevent her doing anything which could cause alarm or distress to the public. (Adapted from BBC News, 25 February 2005. http://news.bbc. co.uk/1/hi/england/somerset/4297695.stm)

Actuarialist constructions of criminal risk and crime control

The influential work of Feeley and Simon (1992) in the early 1990s, raised awareness of a strand of penality – risk-based responses to crime – which has certainly been implicated in policing and sentencing since the nineteenth century. Police knowledge about high crime areas and sentencers' informal calculations about risk of recidivism were not, however, elevated into a science of actuarialism until the last third of the twentieth century. And, as O'Malley and Hutchinson (2007) have recently shown, even though actuarialist mathematical models had long since been used in the insurance industry, they were not applied to crime prevention until much later. Until the ascendancy of actuarial tables of risk of recidivism, therefore, the authorised agents of the state (for example, judges, magistrates, probation officers and social workers) were empowered to make sentencing decisions and supervisory recommendations on the basis of their professional knowledge and experience. The assumption was that as the conditions for change constantly change, the best that governments could do was to reduce uncertainty via the development and deployment of professional knowledges which, though they would be rule-governed, would be constantly open to revision in light of both experience and new scientific knowledge. Most importantly, neither policy nor sentencing were to be influenced by 'untutored public emotion towards crime and punishment' (Loader 2006: 582). Once, however, crime control became a major electoral battlefield, a diminution of professional knowledge and an elevation of popular beliefs about the relationships between crime and punishment became the order of the day. To ensure that professionals could no longer exercise a discretion which might put electoral promises of punitive rigour at risk, disciplinary audit of criminal justice and penal professionals was introduced with the aim of not only controlling the professional knowledge which was surplus to the supposedly vote-winning objectives of a populist penal policy but also with the intention of distancing the government of the day from any perceived deviations from the populist and punitive project. Privatisation of selected areas of criminal justice served the same 'distancing of the Executive from criticism' purpose, while the enforced employment of actuarial tables by probation officers and prison governors carried the political advantage of allowing any future recidivism scandals to be attributed either to system fault or professional indiscipline, rather than to policy failure. Meanwhile, and internationally, spread of the culture of actuarialism in criminal justice significantly advanced the growth of imaginary penalities, as 'concrete individuals and the social interaction in which they are involved [were] replaced by the production of classes and categories that are "simulacra" of the real' (De Giorgi 2006: 107).

Control of surplus knowledge

A main theme of De Giorgi's book, *Rethinking the Political Economy of Punishment* concerns the structural problems faced by control societies seeking to replace the disciplining of individuals with the actuarial constructions of classes and categories of risk-bearers which may turn out to be dangerously reductive approximations of the lawbreakers that actuarialism claims to pre-empt. One problematic issue concerns the management of knowledge.

[The] strategies of preventive control cannot escape a structural contradiction: ... they pretend to establish a regime of preventability, anticipation and categorisation, but the post-Fordist productivity is based exactly on the opposite principles – flexibility, innovation, creativity and inventiveness. (De Giorgi 2006: 88)

17

Thus, while technological advances create some (unskilled and no-longer skilled) workers who are surplus to production requirements, they also create increased numbers of (knowledge and professional) workers with greater powers of individualistic control over their access to information, ideas and innovation (Aas 2005). These new configurations of knowledge are both necessary and surplus to the control requirements of risk-crazed governance with its propensity to create imaginary penalties. However, attempts to control the surplus-to-requirements knowledge of dissenting criminal processing professionals, researchers and campaigning groups have themselves been innovative, and have included: the incorporation of radical critique into official discourse (Carlen 2002a); the disciplining of professionals in the criminal justice system via privatisation threats, public shaming tactics and constant managerialist audit and inspection; the creation of a wider and more general culture of acquiescence via a variety of 'silencing' techniques (Mathiesen 2004); and the suppression of academic critique via the selective promotion of only those research methodologies and research results most likely to be seen as being reflexively supportive of official depictions of criminal risk, its causes, and the strategies necessary for its governance (Beck 1992; Hope 2004).

Imaginary penalties observed

The story of Optima with which this article began could easily be represented as being nothing more than another routine account of goal modification in the light of experience. Except for one thing: the commitment both to act 'as if', and make public representations of the prison's rehabilitative/reintegrative functions as if the goals had *not* been modified, at the same time as also acknowledging (sometimes by word of mouth, sometimes by actions which speak even louder) that they are unrealisable, is a characteristic feature of imaginary penalties born of a risk-crazed governance. None the less, this article, being concerned primarily to define the contemporary pre-conditions and processual characteristics of imaginary penalties, has so far not given examples other than that of Optima. This penultimate section, therefore, now cites two other examples, this time from the UK.

Prisongate: The Shocking State of Britain's Prisons and the Need for Visionary Change (Ramsbotham 2003) is both a demonstration that, and an exploration of why, prison policy in England and Wales appears to have little influence over prison conditions. At one level it is an exposé criminology that reveals an almost total gap between stated prison policy and actual conditions in the prisons. At the same time, at least two major features of English prison governance encountered by the Chief Inspector of Prisons for England and Wales make it a prime candidate for imaginary penality status: the circular and self-fulfilling measurements of programme success; and the apparent lack of official concern or surprise about the parlous state of prisons as revealed in the Inspectorate's reports.

The Chief Inspector was repeatedly puzzled by the self-referential standards of measurement used by the Prison Service in auditing the success of its prison programmes: the practice of focusing on procedures rather than outcomes; and the teleological and closed focus on inputs instead of a concern about outputs and effective achievement of objectives – the latter of which is what most of the public would understand by any published judgment that a prison programme had been a 'success'.

The Prison Service has a curious way of measuring the success of its Sex Offender Programmes. In keeping with its obsession with targets and performance indicators, it only records the numbers completed in a year. (Ramsbotham 2003: 140)

Prisons are judged on targets that require annual reduction in the number testing positive. How honest are the reported results? One day I saw nine certificates on the wall of a prisoner's cell. ' What are those for?' I asked. 'Testing negative on mandatory testing. They know I don't use, so they test me every month. I'll have ten if you come in two weeks' time.' (Ramsbotham 2003: 84)

Similarly, Ramsbotham was increasingly taken aback by what appeared to be the insouciance on the part of government ministers in response to the Inspectorate's regular reports of gross shortcomings in the running of prisons:

Inspection report after inspection report sent to the Home Secretary, after being accepted as correct by the Director General, contained yet more evidence of what needed to be done if the Prison Service was to achieve its own Statement of Purpose. Presumably, the published aim of helping prisoners to lead good and useful lives in prison and on release was fact and

19

not just spin? However, in prison after prison, we continued to find numerous prisoners locked up all day because there were not enough activities to provide this help. The consistently high re-offending rate did not appear to be viewed with any embarrassment. Invariably the same old response was trotted out – 'We do not recognise all that was reported x months ago; significant change is under way.' (Ramsbotham 2003: 214)

And though in informal conversations English Prison Service management were prepared to allow that Ramsbotham's criticisms were justified, in interview with this author, such admissions by Prison Service and Home Office functionaries were usually followed by the silencing tactic of implying that anyone taking the Inspectorate's criticisms seriously was neither 'sound' nor 'knowledgeable' about the criminal processing system. For while 'everyone knows' that the Chief Inspector was only 'doing his job', 'everyone else knows' that in-prison programmes and decent regimes are almost certainly not in themselves going to reduce offending by released prisoners and even if they did, it would be well nigh impossible to get firm evidence that they had. So why lose credibility (or your promotion, or even your job, if you are a prison officer or prison governor) by continuing to say what everybody else always and already knows? If you are an academic, why risk offending a major source of UK criminology funding by refusing to pretend that an imaginary penalty works?

In 1999 Tim Hope was co-ordinator of a team which accepted a grant from the UK Home Office's Reducing Burglary Initiative, a programme primarily interested in 'what works' in crime prevention. But when the results of his research were less than favourable to the Home Office's plans of discovering 'what works',

The Home Office published its own pre-emptive analysis of the impact of the projects ... Through various manipulations of the data, the Home Office method [did] what it [could] to capitalise on chance, producing much more favourable findings overall. (Hope 2004, 2005)

As Hope (2004, 2005: 4) himself points out, 'given the power of politics, it is not rocket science to predict what will happen when evidence gets in the way of a good policy'. Yet maybe it should be more difficult to predict such unashamed manipulation of data when the government of the day is purveying a penality whose watchwords are 'evidence-based policy', 'partnerships' and 'the public is boss'.[8] The sentiments conveyed by the rhetoric are unexceptional, and certainly not impossible of realisation. However, in the context of a risk-crazed governance, the message behind the music is: 'We need your scientific evidence, partner; but only up to a point. Keep your surplus knowledge to yourself.' (See Hope in Chapter 2 of this book.)

Contesting imaginary penalities

Still, let us not disarm, even in unsatisfactory times. Social injustice still needs to be denounced and fought. The world will not get better on its own. (Hobsbawm 2002)

Imaginary penalities are contemporary structures of governance which have effects in terms of their heavy social and economic costs even though they are known not to achieve the successes in terms of crime reduction which, at one and the same time, are both claimed for them and denied to them. I have conceived of imaginary penalities as the unintended products of the interaction of some socio-political processes (imaginative and visionary social policy, risk avoidance, crime reduction policies, public and democratic accountability strategies, and the utilisation of scientific process in the formation and evaluation of policy) some of which in themselves might be well-conceived responses to crime and which may well deserve better outcomes than are presently being achieved. I will therefore conclude by suggesting that today's imaginary penalities should be contested on two main fronts: harm reduction versus crime reduction; and democracy versus populism.

Harm reduction versus crime reduction

Several innovative and radical challenges to imaginary penalities already exist in the UK. They are to be found in the work of Paddy Hillyard and his associates (Hillyard *et al.*, 2004) who first argued for the replacement of 'crime reduction' policies with those of 'harm reduction'; in the researches of theorists like Dave Whyte (2007) and Mike Levi (Levi *et al.* 2007) who focus on the crimes of governments and corporations, and in the research reports of Susanne Karstedt (Karstedt and Farrall 2006) and others whose work on the everyday crimes of the 'lawabiding majority' challenge dominant but very narrow conceptions of crime from several entirely different perspectives. It is not possible to do justice to all these innovative writings here. But it seems to me that, in the context of the fundamental and false implication of imaginary penalities in risk-crazed societies that, via increased punitivism, crime will one day be much reduced and virtually eradicated, academics have a duty to remind politicians and public of a fundamental sociological truth – that deviant behaviour will never be eliminated and it is neither desirable nor possible that it should be (Durkheim 1995/1896). The policy implications of such a reminder being taken seriously would be at least twofold. On the one hand, it would then behove responsible governments to encourage citizens to tolerate higher levels of social difference and deviant behaviour and to stop playing on people's insecurities to such an extent that there is an exponential demand for increasingly punitive criminal legislation and processing. On the other, it would have to be accepted that the urge to legislate against more and more types of behaviours and categories of people must be curbed until there has been a much more informed debate 'about priorities and resources' (Hillyard and Tombs 2005: 17). Even more importantly, substitution of 'harm reduction' for 'crime reduction' might at last put paid to the recurring myth that the criminal processing system can promote justice through punishment (see Hudson 1987). A great deal of work has already shown that welfare models of criminal processing can be used in support of either more or less severe sentencing (Hudson 2002; Carlen and Tombs 2006). Recently Mascini and Houtman (2006) convincingly argued that the ideology of rehabilitation has, in any case, never been part of a progressive approach to crime. Conversely, the most up-to-date research on the relationships between punishment and welfare spending found that

> countries that spend a greater proportion of GDP on welfare have lower imprisonment rates and that this relationship has become stronger over the last 15 years. The consistency of these findings across the United States and the other 17 countries studied makes it difficult to believe that this relationship is co-incidental. (Downes and Hansen 2006:1)

Democratic accountability versus populist punitiveness

Several commentators on contemporary criminal control cultures have warned that, in deploring some of the present excesses of punitivist populism, critics should not seek merely to fashion an élitist and 'liberal' criminology in denial of often well-founded popular fears and insecurities (Loader 2006: 564, 582; Ryan 2005: 146). But élitism is not the necessary alternative to populism. 'Populist punitiveness' is a political strategy designed to win votes, rather than to engage with the populace in hammering out a policy based on an informed and comprehensive review of all social harms, including those committed by employers (Tombs *et al.* 2007), corporations (Levi *et al.* 2007) and governments (Whyte 2007). And it seems to me that a truly democratic structure of competing knowledges of, and competing interests in, harm prevention and criminal processing policy-making should also once more give to workers involved in policy implementation the day-to-day discretion on how to achieve the objectives set by policy makers (compare with Wacquant 2008).[9] Policy makers themselves should have to demonstrate (via published evidence) that their policies have taken into account all known and competing knowledges (for example, academic, professional and victim-based: see Sim 2008 forthcoming for an interesting discussion of democratic accountability and crime processing). For, insofar as they keep open a space for the production of new knowledge (that is, discursive intervention), competing knowledges are the greatest threat to imaginary penalties.

Contesting imaginary penalties will not be easy and those who attempt it will always be at risk of replacing one set of imaginary penalties with another (see Edwards and Hughes, Chapter 4). The main purpose of this essay has been merely to identify, analyse and contest a dominant paradigm of crime-knowledge-processing which, because of the other knowledges of crime and social harm which it represses, is fundamentally flawed and incapable of fulfilling its false promises of crime reduction. But I have certainly not been arguing in this concluding section that responses to crimes and harms should be without ideal goals and aspirations, nor that a more democratic approach to criminal processing would necessarily be less punitive. What I have been arguing is: that the machinery of punishment cannot be justified as a means of reducing social inequality; and that aspirations towards a non-punitive social justice should resist all silencing attempts by the false promises of imaginary penalties.

Notes

1 I am grateful to all those who either discussed with me, or provided written notes on, this chapter. In particular, I thank: Jamie Bennett, Kit Carson, Chris Hale, Tim Hope, Susanne Karstedt, Mike Levi, Joe Sim, Alex Stevens, Jacqueline Tombs, Jock Young, Sandra Walklate, and all participants at the Scandinavian Studies of Confinement Research Network working group meeting 'Multidisciplinary perspectives on prison research' 14–15 May 2007, Copenhagen.

2 'Substantive penalities' refers to agendas of substantive measures designed to respond to lawbreaking; symbolic penalities refers to criminal laws which attempt to define a society's moral boundaries via the range and severity of their prohibitions and punishments.

3 The research objective was to analyse staff views of the extent to which the prison was meeting the prisoners' needs. Optima is a pseudonym: a condition of the research was that the prison's anonymity should be protected in any publications based upon the research.

4 The staff interviewed were: four headquarters staff; three senior management; six senior corrections officers; ten programmes staff; one industries staff.

5 This is never the explicit claim. The argument is that when governments criminalise more and more behaviour which was previously not criminalised, the implicit message is, ironically, that criminalisation will eventually abolish crime. This is, of course, the height of imaginary thinking.

6 Indeed, as recently as 2002, the Social Exclusion Unit (2002) in England justified the call for greater reintegration of ex-prisoners primarily in terms of the heavy social costs incurred when they reoffend.

7 Ian Loader (2006: 578) notes: 'Between 1997 and 2004, the Home Office passed (by my count) 49 Acts of Parliament dealing with aspects of crime, disorder, policing, criminal justice and punishment. Since being returned to office in 1997, the Labour government has created – as of 8 February 2005 – 1,018 new criminal offences (answer to parliamentary question asked by Mark Oaten MP).' At the latest count, 30 November 2006, there had been 60 pieces of legislation relating to criminal justice since Labour came to power. http://news.independent.co.uk/uk/crime/article2026812.ece).

8 Roy Coleman and Joe Sim have done an immense amount of work on 'partnership' ideology in the UK. For just one example see Coleman and Sim (2005).

9 It has been suggested to me that some of the more liberal penal policies are deliberately undermined by prison staff who want prisons to be more punitive. I accept that this is so, and has been so for many years. But this essay has not been about political mendacity, professional hypocrisy or policy sabotage though I recognise that all may play as much part in

penal policy-making as in every other area of social life (See Sim, Chapter 7). This chapter is about those workers who are trying to realise policies made elsewhere and who approach their jobs with commitment.

Chapter 2

Imaginable insecurities: imagination, routinisation and the government of uncertainty post 9/11

Pat O'Malley and Philip D. Bougen

Introduction

Responding to questions about imagination, Foucault (1991: 64) asked 'Where does the boundary lie between the history of knowledge and the history of imagination?' Explaining the many imaginative formulations and modifications that had helped shape the history of knowledge, Foucault declined to confine the practice of imagination to the margins of significance. In *Madness and Civilization* he wove together a multitude of extraordinary yet consequential strands to construct a history of the dividing of madness and reason dependent upon the imaginative accomplishments of assorted contributors, as the insane journeyed from the leprosarium to the asylum (Foucault 1988). He argued that the uncertainties of what constituted madness, how it might be anticipated and prevented, were subjected to imaginative formulation and modification. Imagination succeeded in creating knowledge of the anticipation of madness that linked images together into speculative hypotheses and associations. Uncertain signs of madness once defined by 'the image ... of animal spirits in the nerves was frequently replaced by the image ... of a tension to which nerves, vessels and the entire system of organic fibres were subject' (Foucault 1988: 126). 'Without the support of an image, no observation succeeded in transforming the evidence of succession into a symptomatic structure that was both precise and essential' (1988: 133). To establish an association of symptoms it was an 'imaginary landscape of qualities which was decisive' (1988: 143). These landscapes reached a scientific status as 'what some imagined or supposed' others imaginatively 'proved, numbered, named' (Foucault 1988:.128). Through the invention of ways of seeing, counting, sorting and grading, seemingly bizarre and fanciful images of madness became transformed into 'objective' and 'factual' knowledges of symptomatic profiles which could then be acted upon in the name of medicine and science.

Uncertainties about the prevention of madness similarly relied upon imagination. A doctor 'whose imagination was as moral as it was medical' prescribed 'water as the unique beverage' (Foucault 1988: 167). Rather than the imbibing of water another doctor recommended that 'all those who need to fortify their temperament install baths in their house' (1988: 168). Either as an alternative or supplement to water, madness also came to be treated by the consumption of iron filings. The virtues of iron were promoted such that 'an imagery of wonder-working iron governs discursive thought and prevails over observation itself' (1988: 162).

However extraordinary these knowledges might now seem, imagination proved essential as the workings of the mind were incrementally exposed, analysed and 'understood'. Foucault's analysis offers an historical perspective of relationships between imagination and knowledge creation in the context of uncertainty. While uncertainty has ever haunted modernity, of late its presence has become more than usually pervasive and much more than usually salient. Borrowing heavily from Ulrich Beck's (1992; 1998; 2000) highly influential thesis on the 'risk society', Francois Ewald (2002) has argued that fears of insecurity which emerged towards the end of the millennium perhaps marked a paradigmatic shift in our approach to security. Previously the metrics of risk calculation appeared to provide all manner of calculable securities, perhaps epitomised by the use of actuarial science in the development of large scale private and social security. Now, such knowledges and technologies that have been relied upon to 'tame chance' have been overtaken by incalculable threats. As Beck (1992: 55–83) also noted, these new events or 'modernization risks' emerged in ways that evaded risk's reach. Risk requires that events follow an historically repeated pattern, such repetitions allowing the accumulation of data from which correlations may be calculated and predictions computed. It is precisely the regularity, over lengthy periods of time, of rates of disease, traffic and industrial accidents, of weather events and economic cycles, that make the calculation of their future behaviour feasible. However, modernisation risks are profoundly uncertain, in the sense of being incalculable by such means. In some cases – such as holes in the ozone layer – this is because the events have not occurred before or occur very rarely and are strangers to scientific knowledge. In other instances it may be because the rate of development of the risk outpaces the capacity to accumulate data and calculate risks, as with certain new genetic technologies. In still others which we focus on, it is because the growth of communication and related technologies has transformed the imaginative capacities of a relative handful of individuals into risks of global proportions. As Beck (2002) has argued at length, these latter risks are epitomised by the activities of emergent terrorist groups, and their potential is in turn epitomised by the events of 9/11. Because the nature of the threats they pose is only limited by the limits to terrorists' imaginations, we now enter an era in which significant risks to existence are neither statistically calculable and tamable through risk technologies, nor readily to be discounted once imagined.

The threats posed by international terrorism thus open up a new dimension in the governance of security, in which radical uncertainty becomes a normal security issue: in which that which is only remotely foreseeable becomes the subject of governmental concern. Such developments do not only strain and begin to break the firm hold that risk technologies once had on the provision of security. Familiar techniques that use non-probabilistic calculation to govern the future are also shaken, for these threats challenge the core assumptions on which liberal governance itself is based. According to Jeremy Bentham, security was the primary object of government precisely because it 'necessarily embraces the future' (1962: 302). Security appeared to him as the condition of existence upon which rests rational calculation of the future and all that follows from this.

> In order to form a clear idea of the whole extent which ought to be given to the principle of security, it is necessary to consider that man is not like the brutes, limited to the present time either in enjoyment or suffering … The idea of his security must be prolonged to him throughout the whole vista *that his imagination can measure*. This disposition to look forward, which has so marked an influence on the condition of man, may be called expectation – expectation of the future. It is by means of this that we are able to form a general plan of conduct. (Bentham 1962: 308 emphasis added)

Bentham regarded this 'yoke of foresight' (1962: 307) as the foundational attribute of the liberal subject; but in practice neither Bentham nor the liberal legal institutions that grew up around this vision anticipated that the 'whole vista' of imagination should take in the improbable. Prudence required that subjects should guard themselves and others against those vicissitudes that are 'reasonably foreseeable'. Thus contract law, the central legal institution of liberal legal order, required of contractors only that they take into account possibilities 'such as may fairly and reasonably be considered as arising naturally, that is, according to the usual course of things ...' (*Hadley v Baxendale* [1854] 156 ER 145). As was later argued 'everyone, as a reasonable person, is taken to know "the ordinary course of things"' and this represents the extent of what is *reasonably* foreseeable (*1 Victoria Laundry (Windsor) Ltd v Newman Industries Ltd* [1949] 2 KB 539). Thus while we may readily recognise that imagination has always been central to liberalism, now governance has to take account of the remotely possible, not merely that which is 'reasonably foreseeable'. Thus, when Ewald (2002: 286) argues that 'in the future, it will be necessary to take into account what one can only imagine', the scope of the imaginative grasp has to be widened in ways that have not been traditionally expected of subjects or governments. Unlike the prudence that characterised so much liberal thought, now precaution 'invites one to anticipate what one does not yet know ... one must be wide open to speculation, to the craziest imagined views' (Ewald 2002: 288–9). This is the moment of imagination of which Foucault writes so vividly. It would appear that we live in a time that – while not uniquely so – has catapulted the need for speculative imaginings into pivotal arenas of government in order to deal with uncertainties and insecurities that seemingly threaten everything from Western civilisation to the continued existence of the species.

Yet even this suggests just that imagination is important only in moments of inventing the imaginaries that shape our visions of phenomena and problems. It seems clear, however, that once threats are imagined, imagination must be put to work: to render them calculable or at least estimable; to make them containable; to minimise or eliminate the harms they can deliver. In short, precisely because the threats are recognised and given their shape through acts of imagination, then imagination will also be central to the act of rendering such merely imaginable threats *governable*. For Foucault this was perhaps an issue of secondary interest. In his view, the science of the asylum proved less transformative than the knowledges invented to delineate mental conditions: 'what is constitutive is the action that divides madness, and not the science elaborated once this division is made and calm restored' (1988: ix). However, while there is much of value in this view, it rather assumes that the two processes are readily distinguishable. We could say, rather, that threats believed to be impracticable and that are discounted as matters for intervention mostly will be those we cannot imagine controlling. Conversely, those that appear practicable and plausible are very likely to be those that imagination could conceive of as capable of being governed. Each act of imagination may shape the other. For example, the development of what Ewald (1999) terms 'insurance imaginaries' helped the transformative re-imagining of such problems as individual 'negligence' in workplace accidents into a property of 'industries' which were 'seen' to have durable and distinctive 'rates' of accidents (O'Malley 2004). Thus the process of imagining and identifying risks will be influenced by imaginable technologies: technologies that are conceivable as 'practicable' solutions to the imaginable problem.

Bureaucracy and imagination after 9/11

Of course, in key ways, this had been a problem that had also attracted Weber's attention in his discussions of charismatic authority. Weber (1947: 358) proposed that the charismatic leader might derive authority from the display of 'exceptional powers or qualities', or what he more prosaically termed as the 'rule of genius' (1947: 362). Like Foucault, he contended that 'charismatic authority may be said to exist only in the process of originating' and with a 'character specifically foreign to everyday routine structures' (Weber 1947: 363–4). His subsequent discussion of transitions from charismatic to bureaucratic administration, or the 'routinisation' of exceptional powers, stressed the necessity to introduce alongside the charismatic some element of order to organisational processes:

> one of the decisive motives underlying all cases of routinisation of charisma is naturally the striving *for security* ... the objective necessity of adaptation of the patterns of order and of the organization of the administrative staff to the normal, everyday needs and conditions of carrying on administration. (Weber 1947: 370 emphasis added)

Such processes, in the aftermath of 9/11, are the focus of this analysis. Wonder-working images of knowledge to anticipate and prevent misfortune shaped post 9/11 US domestic security policy. Images were created that were as extraordinary in their own ways as those that determined Foucault's history of madness. Technological images of networked databases of flows of communication, money and people. Images of identifiable faces, body parts and kinetics. Also forewarnings from Tom Clancy novels, images of a financial futures market under terrorist attacks, a million people radiated, destroyed General Motors plants and contaminated water supplies. These images in conjunction with speculative hypotheses and associations proved as influential for the mediation of the uncertainties of security policy as nervousness, water treatments and iron filings did for madness. Furthermore, consistent with Foucauldian analysis of the unfolding trajectories of government practices, the security programmes outlined by imaginative initiatives developed intrinsic rationales with 'their own specific regularity, logic, strategy, self-evidence and "reason" ' (Foucault 1991: 75). In slightly different terms, increasingly institutionalised security practices became shaped by, and gave shape to, images of the merely possible – as security became imaginatively proved, numbered and named.

The Final Report of the National Commission on Terrorist Attacks Upon the United States (henceforth, National Commission) was made public in 2004. Convened to investigate 'facts and circumstances, relating to the attacks, the Commission reviewed 2.5 million pages of documents, interviewed 1,200 people and heard testimony from 160 witnesses' (National Commission 2004: xv). One question posed by the Commission assumed salience: 'how did the US government fail to anticipate and prevent it?' (2004: 2). The Commission concluded: 'the most important failure was one of imagination' (2004: 9). The theme of imagination recurs throughout the report. Its central hypothesis was that 9/11 had occurred because 'across the government, there were failures of imagination' and it was recognised that 'the possibility was imaginable, and imagined' (2004: 9, 345). While acknowledging that 'imagination is not a gift usually associated with bureaucracies', the Commission recommended 'institutionalizing imagination', arguing that 'it is therefore crucial to find a way of routinizing, even bureaucratizing, the exercise of imagination' (2004: 344).

The routinising or bureaucratisation of imagination was employed to generate knowledge about security. In establishing the boundary conditions between bureaucracy and imagination, boundary conditions were created between other security requirements. Boundaries between security and insecurity, between risk and uncertainty, and between insurance and misfortune prevention were determined by this alignment of routinised organisation and imagination. Knowledge was generated to establish the boundary conditions between security and insecurity by creating an apparatus of determinability connecting advanced technology research, the networked architecture of social and economic relationships and financial risk management. In doing so, routinised imagination also created knowledges establishing boundaries between calculative risk metrics and the uncertainties associated with security. Insurability against misfortune and a precautionary concern that misfortune be prevented, also became implicated in this emerging security paradigm.

In the view of the 9/11 Commission, uncertain images of the disaster had lurked in the recesses of the US intelligence community. The Commission noted numerous 'telltale indicators' which had drawn little official attention (National Commission 2004: 339–46). Imaginative scenarios had also been ignored: 'the North American Aerospace Defense Command imagined the possible use of aircraft as a weapon', and 'one prescient pre 9/11 analysis of an aircraft plot was written by a Justice Department trial attorney' (2004: 346). Other images too had gone unheeded: 'Richard Clarke [National Counterterrorism Coordinator] told us that he was concerned about the danger posed by aircraft … But he attributed his awareness more to Tom Clancy novels than to warnings from the intelligence community' (2004: 347). While the Commission documented failures of capability and management, it also convinced itself that the risks had been imagined and were containable so that the problem shifted ground: '*how* those things [failures] happened becomes harder to re-imagine' (2004: 339, emphasis in original). Governing the merely imaginable now appeared as obviously necessary and the failure to do so as bordering on unintelligible.

The 9/11 Commission sought the security that any future uncertain yet exceptional images of possible misfortune would be subjected to routine administrative attention. It established a further complementary linkage between administrative authority, imagination and knowledge. While not precluding the possibility of exceptional individual inventiveness, the Commission also believed that appropriate bureaucratic applications of systematic and routine analysis of data would provide a greater number of images relating to security. Again to discourage inattention to imaginaries, bureaucratically determined responsibilities would be assigned for investigative purposes. Importantly, it believed that clearer images of security might be obtained by filtering visions of possible misfortune through a lens of bureaucratic protocol. In what followed after the findings of the 9/11 Commission, uncertain images of threats became 'proved, numbered and named' by the capacity of contributors to explain why their images, speculation and associations, however extraordinary, were plausible foreseeabilities. Indeed, a key role for the routinisation of imagination was to provide a justificatory schema for sorting and selecting imaginary scenarios. The 9/11 Commission believed this could be accomplished by transforming uncertain images into risk-based knowledges and calculative metrics. Individual judgments of appropriateness were considered neither sufficiently reliable nor robust for practical security purposes.

Post 9/11 security policy endorsed aspects of these precautionary imperatives. Published weeks after the disaster, the Department of Defense's Quadrennial Defense Review acknowledged the uncertainties of security:

9/11 highlights a fundamental condition of our circumstances: we cannot and will not know precisely where and when America's interests will be threatened, when America will come under attack ... We can be clear about trends, but uncertain about events ... We should try mightily to avoid surprise, but we must learn to expect it. (Quadrennial Defense Review 2001: iii)

The 9/11 Commission's preoccupation with imagination also resonated with Ewald's argument of the importance of imagination for security in situations of uncertainty. In addition, the precautionary principle that uncertain misfortunes be prevented, co-existed with a persistent anxiety that insurance mechanisms be in place to address the financial ramifications of any misfortune. However, US policy foresaw the alignment of imagination and knowledge, risk and uncertainty as having a further dimension: within Ewald's framework, how to establish the boundary conditions between precaution and insurance.

To make operational a security paradigm of both precaution and insurance, legislators wrestled with the problem of surmounting knowledge deficiencies. Imagination again proved necessary. While conceding the uncertainties surrounding security, precautionary images needed to be assessed on a fantasy or whim criterion and translated into risk-based knowledges. Routinised imagination provided the knowledge to move the somewhat nebulous concept of precaution into a set of operational security practices. Similarly, while the uncertainties surrounding security did not readily translate into insurance protocols, risk-based metrics were required to introduce the insurance component of the emerging security paradigm.

Precautionary images generated the knowledge to shape reassembled insurance practices. It is these reworked concepts of routinised imagination, precaution and insurance to which we now turn.

Programming routinised imagination

In 2002 the Total Information Awareness (TIA) programme (subsequently renamed Terrorism Information Awareness) established a legislative linkage between administrative authority, imagination and knowledge. Congress located the programme within the Defense Advanced Research Program Agency (DARPA), a research arm of the Pentagon. This location rather than, for example, a newly established or another existing security agency immediately signalled a key direction of how the routinisation of imagination would proceed. DARPA had been created in response to the 1957 Soviet Sputnik launch and had been charged with 'imagining and developing new innovative technology solutions to difficult national security problems' (Poindexter 2003). The mission statement for TIA was to: 'imagine, develop, apply, integrate, demonstrate and transition information technologies … useful for preemption, national security warning, and national security decision making' (DARPA 2003: 1).

TIA sought to routinise imagination by the accumulation and analysis of data. New information technologies of risk assessment and measurement were to transform precautionary images of suspicious uncertainties into speculative hypotheses of threats, algorithmic associations and scientific knowledge. A technological infrastructure was to provide the rational schema to evaluate whether images of insecurity were merely fantasy or whim. In 2003 DARPA detailed various TIA projects: experimental methods were to be devised to prove, name and number threats to security.

One group of projects was designed to discover clusters of data or speculative hypotheses relating to the nature of possible threats to security. Here, the purpose of bureaucratised imagination was to provide a greater number of images of possible misfortune. Algorithms were then explored to identify and connect clusters of data into sequential associations, or to provide a greater degree of focus to images. Data of any and all sorts about the individual fell under the rubric of potential relevance. As Ewald (2002: 289) noted, with precautionary logic, unlike that of liberal prudence, 'all that can be excluded is that nothing should be excluded'. Insecurity became defined as emerging from threats by people otherwise engaged in routine social and economic behaviour, yet whose patterns of behaviour could be identified as suspicious by the application of intensified technological systems of social and economic inspection. The appropriateness of images or the judgmental criterion of whim or fancy was to be determined technologically, as was the assurance that images would not be ignored.

A representative, although not exhaustive, list of projects included: Evidence Extraction and Link Discovery (EELD) '... to develop a suite of technologies that will automatically extract evidence about relationships among people, organizations, places, and things from unstructured textual data'; Scalable Social Network Analysis (SSNA) 'to model multiple connection types (e.g., social interactions, financial transactions and telephone calls) and combine the results from these models'; and MisInformation Detection (MinDet) 'to detect intentional misinformation and to detect inconsistencies in open source data with regard to known facts' (DARPA 2003: 7, 9, A-17).

Another group of projects focused on the physicality of those who threatened insecurity. Threats were now constructed as deriving from people defined by a unique assemblage of body parts. Routinised imagination was now to provide embodied images of possible threats, with their investigation determined by the faithfulness or clarity of images. Technological methods of video, infrared, multispectral sensors, power radar and radio frequency tags would collect images to construct a physical or biometric signature of insecurity. Human Identification at a Distance (HumanID) would 'develop automated, multimodal biometric technologies with the capability to detect, recognize, and identify humans at a distance ... with a focus on body part identification, face identification, and human kinematics'; Next Generation Face Recognition (NGFR) offered 'a systematic development and evaluation of new approaches to face recognition ... experimentation on databases of at least one million individuals; and collection of a large database of facial imagery'; Activity, Recognition and Monitoring (ARM) would 'develop an automated capability to reliably capture, identify and classify human activities' (DARPA 2003: 10–12).

These projects created wonder-working images of 'a counterterrorism information architecture' of 'sharing data that can be easily scaled ... focused warnings within an hour after a triggering event occurs or an articulated threshold is passed', of 'support, collaboration, analytical reasoning and information sharing' (DARPA 2003: 3–4). Such techniques and knowledges created boundary conditions between uncertain images of security and methodologies of risk.

Bureaucratised imagination was intended as a robust rational schema to evaluate whether images were fantasy or whim. As Foucault observed, however, the knowledges to determine madness proved more important than the sciences elaborated once the determination had been made. The delineation of security is similarly underdetermined. Data mining projects generate redundant and random associations, 'false positives'. Tests of prototype systems in Florida identified 120,000 people statistically considered as potential threats (CNN online law center 2004). Biometric authentication of an individual is also prone to error. Pose, illumination, distance and image resolution have been discovered to impact system performance (Woodward *et al.* 2001). Yet TIA was premised upon the principle that images, speculative hypothesis and association constituted the basis of new knowledge creation. Images which when proved, numbered and named allowed the imaginative formulation of a security policy on the basis of risk. A boundary was also established between images being appropriate or merely fantasy or whim.

In 2003 Congress enacted Public Law 108-7 terminating funding for TIA. Not called into question, however, was the epistemological basis of knowledges anticipated from this particular exercise of routinised imagination. Instead, as Ewald (2002: 98) noted, uncertainty and the practice of precaution introduce unfamiliar judgments into the policy arena. TIA ended as legislators argued against the use of 'technology to pick regular Americans up by the ankles and shake them to see if anything funny falls out' (Congressional Record 2003: S2432). Yet images of the merely possible continue to generate increasingly institutionalised security practices and develop their own specific logics and rationalities. In 2004, federal agencies reported the existence of another 199 either planned or operational data analysis projects. The Departments of Defense and Homeland Security both reported inventories of such projects, as did another 23 agencies including the Departments of Commerce, of the Interior, Justice, State and Treasury (Government Accountability Office 2004a). Debate continues as to whether other programmes within TIA continue as 'black-bag' accounts with budgets not requiring Congressional approval (Hampton and Thompson 2004). So too do debates about a national biometric identification programme.

TIA also sought to bureaucratise imagination by harnessing of exceptional – almost 'charismatic' – powers or qualities. This involved the creation of external mechanisms for the accumulation and analysis of data. Here, the objective was to utilise the imaginative endeavours of individuals outside of federal agencies. Security while still formulated as an issue of data analysis became modified by a concern that public databases might not contain all available existing information as regards possible future threats (Poindexter 2003). Accordingly, a process for accessing and evaluating open sources of data was required. Futures markets applied to prediction (FutureMAP) were designed to use markets and market prices for this purpose. FutureMAP was intended as a virtual financial futures market from which to discover knowledge about security. Contracts would be traded reflecting combinations of security policy, military strategies, and geo-political trends. As a single statistic, price and price movement of financial futures contracts routinely summarise available information as regards financial market expectations. The prices of security futures were anticipated to summarise market assessments of the likelihood and sources of possible threats. The 2002 DARPA solicitation of research proposals (Hanson, n/d) explained the rationale:

the FutureMAP program at DARPA is investigating the use of markets and market-like mechanisms in aggregating information from diverse multiple sources … Composite securities provide a participant, who has insight into interrelations among basic securities, with a means of expressing this insight and benefiting from the expression if correct.

In resituating security into a virtual world of Internet traders, routinised imagination became framed by a philosophy premised upon the efficiency of private markets to process information. The evaluation of images as fantasy or whim would now be bureaucratised or rendered routine not by administrative process but by the routine outputs of transactions undertaken by external market participants. Speculative hypothesis became transformed into financial speculation, association into combinatorial futures contracts and knowledge into market prices. Financial investments in security risk were to valorise the images produced by security traders. Weber (1947: 369) noted 'for charisma to be transformed into a permanent routine structure, it is necessary that its anti-economic character should be altered'. Future-MAP endorsed the relationship between routinisation and economic incentives. Again, however, policy judgments proved problematic for the practice of precaution. Legislators questioned: 'will terrorists attack Israel with bioweapons in the next year? Surely, such a threat should be met with intelligence gathering of the highest quality – not by putting the question to individuals betting on an Internet website'. (Wyden and Dorgan 2003).

Imagining insurance

The images that created the Terrorism Information Awareness programme were complemented by another image: the programme itself might prove ineffective and as a consequence insurance arrangements should be in place to address the financial ramifications of possible misfortune. Ericson and Doyle (2004) illustrated how the insurance industry imaginatively assembles risk networks of improvised calculative practices to make insurable essentially uncertain events. These networks provide actuarial and financial matrices within which projected insurance cash inflows and outflows are calculated. The new boundary conditions created by the routinisation of imagination for security purposes demanded that imagination fulfil a further role for insurance practice. The insurability of what became known as terrorism risk required that images informed by precaution and uncertainty 'prove, number and name' this risk, thereby shaping its insurability.

Post 9/11 reports appeared of disruptions to business activity as a result of interruptions to the supply of insurance for terrorism risk. Legislators conceded, 'virtually nothing could happen in the American economy without insurance' (Congressional Record 2001: H8573). Financial security became formulated as the possibility of future attacks on uninsured property and the continued viability of insurance-dependent economic projects. Imagination was again an issue. Legislators heard from representatives of the insurance industry that 'the idea of two fully fueled 767s hitting both towers was unimaginable' (US House 2001: 125). The American Academy of Actuaries cautioned that the 'new risk of terrorism emerged from an event that had never been imagined by insurers or insureds' (US House 2001: 181). Before 9/11, terrorist attacks had been sufficiently unimaginable that terrorism insurance was provided at no cost and as a routine addendum to other coverage.

Insurance interruptions were largely attributed to the absence of insurance risk metrics due to the singular nature of what had transpired. The capacity of insurance to transform selective uncertainties into insurable risks has become an established feature of insurance practice. However, the insurance nexus between risk and uncertainty or the feasibility of actuarial risk quantification becomes disturbed by the absence of data regarding the nature, likelihood and severity of misfortune. Insurance protocols relating to coverage specification, policy pricing, reserve accumulation and the retrocession of risk are all compromised. Unknowable potential financial losses simultaneously encompassing different lines of coverage also compromise the pooling and distribution of risk to provide adequate compensatory funds.

The insurability of catastrophic events has a wider dimension beyond that of terrorism risk. A defining element of Beck's (1992) thesis of the emergence of a risk society is the non-insurability of an increasing number of catastrophic events. A similar argument has been forwarded by Giddens (2000: 137), again stressing the incalculability of risk assessment. Giddens (2000: 139) extended the argument by considering the non-insurability of catastrophic events leading to the undesirable role of the federal government as the 'insurer of last resort'. US legislators acknowledged both the unease of insurers with terrorism risk and the urgency of insurability as a matter of national economic necessity. However, rather than either fatalistically conceding the incalculability of terrorism risk or unequivocally accepting full federal responsibility for financial losses, a strategy for insurance was shaped by some form of federal involvement in the insurance industry. Imagination again proved indispensable to realise aspirations to organise an insurance paradigm involving both federal and insurance industry compensation.

Legislated images

In the legislative hearings to assess a rearranged insurance paradigm, two related issues dominated proceedings. Firstly, what impact any federal involvement might have upon the future independent capability of the insurance industry to insure against terrorism risk. Secondly, what might be the financial details of any immediate involvement. With respect to the first issue, a ranking member of the legislature noted 'we must sunset the program ... we should not disrupt the development of new products' (US House 2001: 73). To the Secretary of the US Treasury, legislation would provide a period 'to allow the private sector to establish market mechanisms to deal with this insidious new risk' (US House 2001: 80). The theme of transition was continuously repeated as legislators hoped the insurance industry might begin to imagine its own risk metrics for the previously unimaginable threat. One aspect of the routinisation of imagination was intended to take the form of the insurance industry generating sufficient knowledge about terrorism risk to allow the future creation of risk metrics such as those that existed in other areas of insurance practice. In discussions as to whether any legislation would mark a permanent federal presence in the insurance industry, a committee chairman observed, 'now you are scaring me' (US House 2001: 14). The legislative crafting of the financial details of federal involvement would reflect this concern.

The financial details of involvement, however, required another form of imagination. Legislators themselves embarked upon a process of imagination as they tried to create precautionary images of what they did not know, what they should know and what they dreaded about security. Without existing risk metrics for terrorism, legislators created their own images of future security and considered what these images implied from an insurance perspective. Speculative hypotheses were associated with the financial implications of possible misfortune both for the national economy and for federal involvement, as imagination became necessary to generate knowledge for a rearranged insurance paradigm.

The events of September 11 had cost insurers approximately $40 billion. Legislators imagined what type of future attacks might occur and the extent of future financial obligations: 'very easily [it] could end up being a nuclear stockpile, a waste facility ... then we have ... $300 billion and a million people killed or radiated ... If the General Motors plant gets wiped out, it may be a $10 billion, $20 billion disaster' (US House 2001: 37–8). Future insurance arrangements needed to consider the occurrence of such cataclysmic events as nuclear, biological and radiological attacks. It also became necessary to determine the level of financial loss at which federal intervention would be triggered, any upper limit to compensation and whether monies disbursed under a scheme should be recovered.

Legislators also considered the effects of different types of attacks on the scope of insurance coverage. 9/11 had targeted commercial property. Future arrangements required an assessment of whether coverage should encompass residential as well as commercial property. While one legislator worried 'we are going to be in litigation for the next 50 years', legislators imagined a scenario where: 'if I am in your home and I drink contaminated water, I have a claim against you ... and I can paint a scenario that maybe a water company, their wells get contaminated, and now you have a significant number of homes that have contaminated water' (US House 2001: 67).

A series of associations then connected mandatory homeowners' coverage to other insurance issues. Informed by the insurance industry that 'most personalized carriers write personal automobile and also write homeowners' policies', legislators became 'concerned about the volume. If we cover private passenger automobile coverage

... that is a big volume of claims' (US House 2001: 67–8). Images of destroyed automobiles from attacks, extensive litigation and the potential financial implications helped formulate security either as a solely commercial or also residential issue.

Insurance operates more effectively the wider the risk-sharing base. The magnitude of possible future liabilities remained unknown. Legislators became concerned that terrorism insurance might only be purchased by owners of property believed either specifically at risk of attack, 'trophy targets', or those located in geographic regions considered vulnerable. Legislators discussed whether all commercial entities should be required to obtain mandatory terrorism coverage. Legislators imagined possible targets: 'if there's a port in your state, you're affected. If there's a bridge or tunnel in your state, you are affected. If you have an airport or railway system in your state, you are affected. If you've got an NFL, NBA, NHL or Major League Baseball stadium or arena in your state, you're affected.' (Congressional Record 2002: S5477).

Allowing commercial entities to choose whether to acquire terrorism coverage would spread the losses associated with any future attack across a smaller base of insureds. Entities perceived to be at greater risk, a process of adverse selection, would also constitute a disproportionate number of policyholders, reducing the effectiveness of risk sharing.

The prevention of misfortune and its impact upon insurance arrangements was also imagined. The insurance industry had questioned the capacity of insureds to prevent misfortune (US House 2001: 66). Legislators considered the importance of incentives to deter negligent institutional behaviour, tangentially raising the issue of tort law and financial damages. They discussed whether individuals should be permitted to seek punitive damages from institutions that had been attacked but whose own actions had contributed to misfortune. They imagined circumstances where 'medical laboratories specializing in nuclear medicine might know that their security system is broken ... So it stays broken for months ... What is going to be the incentive for that corporation that failed to fix their security system?' (Congressional Record 2002: S5497).

The Terrorism Information Awareness programme had sought to routinise imagination by the accumulation and analysis of images relating to potential threats to security. Knowledge was to be derived to transform uncertain precautionary images into operational security risk metrics. For insurance purposes, however, a greater number of more focused images could not be immediately created by the application of technological invention. Neither the insurance industry nor legislators believed they had access to sufficient data to routinise imagination in such a way. Yet, the connection of precautionary images to risk metrics was still considered paramount to make terrorism risk insurable. Instead, in a highly practical manner, precautionary images themselves now constituted knowledge about security. From a Weberian perspective, legislators were required *to cultivate their own exceptional powers to create images of security*. It was hoped that the subsequent routinisation of imagination would be transferred to the insurance industry.

While the above scenarios might seem to include the craziest imagined views, their significance should not be underestimated. Legislators in imagining possible situations were exploring the contours of future insurance arrangements. The images were thought of as neither fantasy nor whim in terms of their impact upon future insurance details. Possible targets, the extent of financial commitments, funding formulas, the scope of future coverage, opt out provisions, issues of prevention and punitive damages constituted important insurance details with significant financial implications. All became associated with images of possible threats. Knowledges as operationally significant as those envisaged from TIA were being created. Imagination again provided the connection between speculative hypothesis, association and knowledge.

Security imaginaries

In his classic paper on insurance and risk, Ewald (1999: 198–9) refers to the importance of what he termed 'insurance imaginaries'. He suggests that the positive form taken by insurance, its actuarial accuracy and proven capacity over several centuries to manage uncertainty, gives rise to a sense that risk technologies have a necessary shape that is geared to the real. Consequently what has emerged as insurance more or less had to take the form familiar at the end of the twentieth century: there is little sense that things could be otherwise. Ewald suggests to the contrary that the technology of risk is so abstract, that we can never regard existing forms of insurance as 'the' expression or instantiation of risk, but always as only one of an infinity of possibilities. Insurance technology and actuarialism, he argues, 'did not fall from the mathematical skies to incarnate themselves in institutions' (1999: 198) but have always been mobilised and developed in ways that take account of the social and political conditions. But this does not lead to some form of sociological explanation: that a given institutionalisation of risk can be logically 'read-off' from its social milieu. The variability of form in insurance, he argues, does indeed take these into account, but there is more to this than tends to meet the sociological eye:

> This variability of form, which cannot be deduced from the principles of either technology or of institutions, relates to the economic, moral, political, juridical, in short to the social conditions which provide insurance with its market, the market for security. These conditions are not just constraints; they can offer an opportunity, a footing for new enterprises and policies. The particular form insurance technology takes in a given institution in a given moment depends on an *insurantial imaginary*: that is to say, on the ways in which, in a given social context, profitable, useful and necessary uses can be found for insurance technology ... So one has an insurance technology which takes a certain form in certain institutions, thanks to the contribution of a certain imaginary. (Ewald 1999: 198, emphasis in original)

As the outcome of imaginative work, imaginaries of security certainly reflect their social and political conditions, for the development of security – of which insurance is but one branch – does not emerge from a world of pure fantasy. For this reason, we have accepted that the world in the wake of 9/11 is not simply the same, that it is not business as usual. It does appear, as Beck, Ewald and others have argued, to be a world in which radical uncertainties have marched uninvited onto centre stage. But it is the work of imagination that transforms these events into governable phenomena: that constitutes them in a fashion that can be dealt with by existing or imaginable techniques. Indeed, as we have seen, such imaginings may transform technologies such as insurance where it is imagined that risk metrics as they stand can no longer govern the threat to security and must either be transformed or abandoned in favour of more uncertain and speculative ways of governing the imaginable.

This chapter should not therefore be read as an attempt to render security post 9/11 as a ridiculous form of madness resting upon baseless suppositions about the phantoms of a certain kind of political delirium. Foucault's point in highlighting the wild imaginings of those who envisaged a nervous system populated by wild animals was, of course, not that we have arrived at the truth and can only now look back and heap scorn and mockery on the foolishness of another age. It is to destabilise the idea that what we now take as truth is anything other than another imaginary with an associated science founded upon the reality that this created. Hence we are not claiming to know the truth that would reveal post 9/11 security imaginaries as merely ridiculous and phantasmagoric products of fevered imaginations. Our aim is to stress that if we can recognise that imagination is *always* a critical element in the formation of governance then we make clear that things could be otherwise than they now are. Social conditions do not make necessary specific techniques for dealing with security problems: the security techniques and institutions that exist are created by security imaginaries that constitute threats in terms of a certain image and render them into forms that become governable. They are thus available to be re-imagined.

The first casualty: evidence and governance in a war against crime

Tim Hope

Among the calamities of war may be jointly numbered the diminution of the love of truth, by the falsehoods which interest dictates and credulity encourages.

(Samuel Johnson 1758)

Pat Carlen's concept of *imaginary penality* draws our attention to how artificially constructed rationales for the criminal justice system are supplanting the substantive and symbolic justifications that have hitherto featured in public discourse. Whereas the latter are widely understood, and amenable to empirical and moral challenge, these imaginary penalities create aims and objectives that bind criminal justice agencies into performance criteria that, despite their commonsensical appearance are, for the most part, unattainable and immeasurable. Yet they also provide governments with popular political mandates. The assertion that government initiative alone can reduce crime and thereby create community safety – thus rendering re-electable those governments that claim to have done it – is one such imaginary. The task for an incumbent government, then, becomes that of sustaining these penalities in the popular imagination, which may mean a greater readiness to resist contrary claims and sceptical challenge, particularly if the stakes are high, and there is an opportunity to get away with it.

For the 'New Labour' Government of the United Kingdom, the happy circumstance of having enunciated particularly strident and ambitious crime reduction plans whilst in opposition, winning a landslide election in 1997 (in part on the basis of such promises

(Downes and Morgan 2002)), promulgating programmes and legislation once in office (Home Office 1999), and thence presiding over year-on-year reductions in the official indicators of crime, must have seemed sufficiently incontrovertible evidence. Yet, except on a few occasions (some of which will be recounted here), ministers have been reticent about claiming success; let alone crowing over their achievements. One explanation is that they have been content to let the record 'speak for itself'. In appealing to the popular imagination, the causal logic seems inescapable: government says it is going to reduce crime; it says it is undertaking activities that it claims will reduce crime; the official record shows crime going down; *ergo* a tremendous government achievement. And why should we demur? Governments have great assets as purveyors of truth: they tend to have a political and resource-based monopoly over the generation of the relevant information; and the capacity to scrutinise the evidence requires not only access to government data but possession of expertise and inside knowledge that is not normally accessible to the general public. Perforce, the public is obliged to trust the reliability and validity of their Government's claims, with the democratic compact between governments and governed as its sole guarantor.

Such trust is presumably what the then recently appointed Home Office Minister Hazel Blears, MP must have relied upon when she announced in July 2003 a '... tremendous impact on burglary rates', reported in a press release headed 'Groundbreaking Projects Crack Burglary' (Home Office Press Release 177/2003, 25 June 2003, 10:45). The Minister was drawing upon '... early findings on burglary reduction' from its Reducing Burglary Initiative (RBI). The RBI comprised a major part of the New Labour Government's '... crusade [sic] against crime' preached by the then Home Secretary (the Rt Hon. Jack Straw, MP) in his encyclical foreword to the Government's *Crime Reduction Strategy* (Home Office 1999). The RBI itself was a flagship component of the Government's Crime Reduction Programme (CRP): '... the most ambitious and innovative programme for tackling crime so far attempted in the western developed world' (Homel *et al.* 2004: 1). According to officials, the CRP was intended to find long-term, sustained reductions in crime through implementing 'what works', promoting innovation into mainstream practice, generating significant improvement in the crime reduction knowledge base, and delivering real savings through crime reduction and improved delivery (2004: 1). As the Home Secretary told Parliament in July 1998, the CRP was also unprecedented in being inspired by criminological research evidence (Goldblatt and Lewis 1998); while HM Treasury had also required the Home Office to conduct a large-scale programme of independent, social scientific evaluation of the CRP (Homel *et al.* 2004).

Evidence from social scientific research was thus to play an important role in the CRP. The evidence cited by the Minister in her announcement drew upon an accompanying Home Office research report *Findings 204* (Kodz and Pease 2003). This was based on Home Office officials' analysis of data collected by consortia of university-based researchers under contract to evaluate the impact of local crime prevention projects comprising a first-phase of the RBI. In my capacity as co-ordinator of one such consortium (Hope *et al.* 2004), I had been sent a draft copy of *Findings 204* prior to publication (none of our consortium had been involved in any of the data analysis presented therein). I expressed considerable misgivings about its methodology, concluding '... I would rather you did not publish these Findings in this form ... failing that, please note that ... if asked publicly, I shall feel compelled to disassociate myself from it' (letter 16 May 2003).[1] Whether coincidence or not, *Findings 204* was published while the British Society of Criminology was holding its Annual Conference at the University of Wales, Bangor; and I did disassociate myself when it was presented by Home Office officials at a panel which we shared in the company of my professional peers. Having voiced my misgivings, I published them subsequently in an academic peer-reviewed journal: my article replicated the method of *Findings 204* on data from our own consortium's research, and compared its conclusions, case-by-case, with those based upon our own methods, with a much less favourable prognosis for the RBI than the Minister's, to say the least (Hope 2004). The bases of each method were also discussed and the results compared. Following a protracted review process, an online-only report of our evaluation was finally published by the Home Office, unchanged, over a year after the Minister's announcement (Hope *et al.* 2004). Trustingly, we had left the selection of a title to the Home Office, though the one the officials chose – 'Strategic Development Projects in the Yorkshire and the Humber, East Midlands and Eastern Regions' – unlike those chosen for the other consortia's reports, seems quite a good way of 'burying bad news', at least from the gaze of Internet search engines.

Some while later, I published a similar, perhaps more accessible, account of the disagreement with the Home Office in an article for the journal *Criminal Justice Matters*, which also voiced some concerns about the way in which the Home Office assessed crime trends for performance purposes (Hope 2006). This was submitted in May 2006 as part of the written evidence of the Centre for Criminal Justice Studies to the House of Commons Science and Technology Committee Enquiry into Scientific Advice to Government (STC 2006, Ev 145), to which I also gave evidence in person (STC 2006, Ev 38). The publication of the Committee's report (STC 2006) evoked concern in the media. Thus the *Guardian* (8 November 2006) headlined its coverage with '… MPs accuse Ministers of twisting science for political purposes: evidence distorted to give fig leaf of respectability'. Gratifyingly, we, the social scientists, had been accepted as purveyors of truth, both by parliament and the press.

Yet, the nature and grounds for the disagreement between our findings and those of the Home Office are not so simple. Particularly, they cannot, or ought not to, be accepted on teleological grounds alone. Just because Ministers have 'political purposes' in accepting some kinds of evidence, and rejecting others, does not in itself damn the evidentiary basis of their selectivity and bestow righteousness upon our own. After all, despite the cant, politicians only act politically, and that is what the electorate expects, so long as they stick by the rules and principles of democratic trust. Instead, what I hope to suggest in this chapter is that a much more pernicious process had been at work: namely, an effort involving the collusion of the 'official' social science community within, and closely associated with, government to 'fix' the bases and criteria upon which 'evidence' for policy and practice would be constructed in order to bias results in favour of politically congenial outcomes. And this comprised the basis of our disagreement with the Home Office.

Yet, the constitutional imaginary of ministerial responsibility should equally not be taken literally as a convenient fiction whereby ministers appear to be personally cognizant of the operations of their officials – such a fiction is collusively self-serving of both politicians and theorists alike, particularly those of the latter persuasion who wish to denote super-ordinate powers to 'the State', that any empirical, institutional-political account of policy-making ought instantly to dispel (see Rock 1990; Windlesham 1993). However, like the general public itself, and despite the rise of the junior minister as a departmental micro-manager (another consequence of the new public management – see Rhodes 1997), ministers still have to trust their officials in the governance of their departments. In fact, although our own side of this particular disagreement has remained constant, that of the official side has not. The true history, and explanation, of the events surrounding the evaluation of the CRP lies within the interstices of the New Labour Governments over the period. Yet while collective cabinet responsibility and the political subservience of civil servants also remain convenient constitutional imaginaries, it would appear that, in the demise of the CRP, there had been a general falling-out between ministers, on the one hand, and Home Office officials (particularly the researchers), on the other, with the latter seeking to put their own spin on the proceedings (Davies 2003). In what follows, it is apparent that all sides of the disagreement about 'evidence' and the CRP are not just concerned about selectivity of data but disagree about the epistemology of the evidence itself. And to prosecute such a disagreement necessarily requires constructions of the 'imaginary' as well as the 'real' *on all sides of the conflict.*

Evidence-based policy and practice

Under the leadership of its first Home Secretary (Straw), New Labour put in place conceptual apparatus that would, in practice, stack the odds in favour of coming up with success. Central to this endeavour would be the co-option of social science into the machinery of governance of crime reduction. The over-arching rubric was to be that of Evidence-Based Policy and Practice (EBPP). New Labour's successful election pitch to be the better managers of crime than the incumbent Conservatives – alongside a buy-in to the prevailing rhetoric of the New Public Management (NPM) – meant that the Labour Government of 1997 was susceptible to a seemingly rational, business-like approach to crime prevention – already being practised by the Conservatives (Hope 2005) – as its own goal, albeit re-branded as Crime and Disorder Reduction (Home Office 1999). In order to identify crime prevention priorities, targets and methods, the recommended approach should be to conduct a 'crime audit' or 'crime profile', primarily based on statistical data. Concerning the framing of prevention strategies, the approach would ignore not just local professional agency expertise and practice but also most forms of political intelligence in favour of a new information-based, expert technology of decision-making. This emerging what works 'knowledge-base' would direct both noviciate local authorities and the professional police – who were to be brought into formal partnership by the Crime and Disorder Act (1998) – apparently towards a more scientific, yet 'realist', approach to crime control (Goldblatt and Lewis 1998).

In contrast to the 'nothing works' message perceived as stemming from much previous social scientific evaluation research, newer, practically-oriented 'crime sciences', emerging from the Home Office Research, Statistics and Development Directorate (RDS), were now promising useful and applicable techniques for the utilisation of information-based intelligence for policing, crime prevention and offender-management programmes within the community (Tilley and Laycock 2000). Not surprisingly, on gaining office after 18 years in opposition, and with manifesto pledges to deliver, New Labour Ministers would be highly susceptible to a technology that not only promised to hand them the prize of crime reduction, and was consistent with the performance-oriented NPM that they saw as central to their 'modernising agenda', but also would give a politically incontrovertible aura (because it was rational and scientific) to the otherwise muddling and uncertain reality of crime prevention; thereby redeeming their electoral hostage to fortune, while constructing a non-ideological criterion of accountability – that which 'works'.

Statistics and research findings have played a central role in this endeavour. Thus, more than 10 years later, the Home Office RDS Directorate was still describing itself as providing:

> ... information, research and statistics on topics that relate to Home Office responsibilities such as crime, the justice system and immigration. Home Office ministers and policy-makers, *who need to make decisions based on evidence*, then use these research findings and statistics to inform their decisions. (http://www. homeoffice.gov.uk/science-research/RDS/17 July 2008 emphasis added)

It goes on, in rather elementary fashion, to describe

> ... how we use research to make policies ... For example, by accurately measuring burglary levels over time we can find out whether our burglary-reduction strategies are working or not: if we found levels of burglary were dropping, we could develop the successful strategies further; if we found levels stayed the same or increased then that would be evidence that our anti-burglary strategies weren't working, so we would then change and improve them.

Aside from a dubious *faux-naïveté*, this is false, or imaginary, in two respects: first, clearly, as a depiction of the realities of policy-making and practical decision-making; but second, as an uncritically *realist* depiction of the evidentiary political process that was actually followed by the Home Office during this period. In this respect, the above statement is as much a deception about the Home Office attitude towards 'evidence' as it is about the use of 'evidence' in policy-making.

Jack-in-the-box

Periodically, the Home Office RDS has invested in statistical analysis to forecast trends in crime and punishment. Obviously, since we have no information on the future, forecasts are *projections* based upon prior, known information. In policy-analysis, they serve not in any mystic way but as an hypothetical or *counter-factual* – that is, a conjectural (imaginative) projection of what would happen if what may be about to happen were not to happen. Such projections are of greatest value retrospectively, since we can then assess what actually had happened against our estimate of what might have happened, had what happened not happened. Many applications of the techniques of econometric time-series forecasting are concerned with estimating reliable counter-factuals based on past performance to be used to assess the actual performance of policy interventions. The explanatory, causal role of counter-factual reasoning finds its best imaginative representation in Dickens' *A Christmas Carol* or Capra's film *It's a Wonderful Life* (1946). Just as Scrooge and George Bailey, respectively, are brought to appreciate the value of their lives by virtue of ghostly and angelic devices that project visions of a present and future without them, statistical modelling in policy analysis is intended to achieve the same effect.

Ironically, the first effort at what in later years was to become known as the 'Home Office model' – a statistical model of the long-term crime trend – was carried out below the political horizon by the then Home Office Research and Planning Unit (Field 1990). When brought subsequently to his attention by the media, it caused considerable consternation to the Home Office minister-of-the-day, largely because it suggested, contrary to government thinking, that crime trends were susceptible to economic factors, over which his government claimed to have some influence.[2] Since it implicated government economic policy as a cause of crime, the Labour Party in opposition had used the model as a stick to beat the Conservatives in its successful campaigning over crime.

One of New Labour's chief electoral pledges in 1997 was to put government spending itself upon a more rational, evidence-based footing. To that end, the Chancellor of the Exchequer initiated the first, triennial Comprehensive Spending Review (CSR), reporting in 1998. The CSR not only set out spending plans for the forthcoming period but also had required spending departments to estimate the need for the expenditure. Ostensibly, the substantial funds for the CRP were released on the basis of the case submitted by the Home Office.[3] The requirement to have the effect of the expenditure evaluated independently was part of the conditions of funding imposed by the Treasury (Homel *et al.* 2004). As part of its case, the Home Office produced a revision of its model of the crime trend: much of the post war period had seen sustained growth in the rate of crime, and until then the model seemed to produce a good fit to the trend (Field 1999).[4] However, forecasts based upon the model predicted, at best, a 26 per cent *rise* in burglary for the period 1998 to 2001 (Dhiri *et al.* 1999), projections emerging just at the time the Government was launching the Reducing Burglary Initiative (Home Office 1999). This must have posed something of a dilemma for the Home Secretary: on the one hand, the forecast demonstrated the need for the RBI; on the other hand, if it turned out to be true, it did not augur well for its prospects.

Undaunted, the Home Secretary, Jack Straw, set about making a virtue of the forecast's counter-factuality:

> ... There is nothing inevitable about the trend in the model. Halfway through this period there is good evidence we are in fact bucking the projected trend. Burglary in the first two years of this period is down, not up; and vehicle crime is down, not up. This research therefore underlines the relative success achieved so far, but also the scale of the challenge we must face. (Quoted in *Guardian*, 30 November 1999)

As the *Guardian* helpfully went on to explain (presumably steered by the Home Office Press Office):

> ... The resulting projections are based on a forecast of what will happen if current demographic and economic trends continue *without any impact from crime reduction measures taken by the police and the government*. (Emphasis added)

Disingenuously, however ... officials said the last two years (that is, since the election in 1997) had seen property crime fall by 12 per cent when their model predicted it would rise by 6 per cent. This conveniently over-looked the fact that crime trends, including burglary, had been declining since around 1995, prior to Labour gaining office (Walker *et al.* 2006, Figure 6.2), in effect giving the Home Office four years worth of confidence in their trend-bucking assertions, while also inserting a new, politically advantageous Year Zero into the trend. Even more advantageously, the briefing suggested that this was 'an indication that the historic link between crime and the economy might be breaking down'.[5] Be that as it may, how convenient would that possibility be for a Crime Reduction Strategy consisting primarily of deterrent, support and control measures aimed at individual victims and offenders (Home Office 1999)? So, we have the Home Secretary offering a political wager. Yet unlike previous governments' hostages to fortune (Downes and Morgan 1994), this time he had taken the trouble not only to calculate the odds but also to set up the terms of the wager. And he seemed to have won his bet with the electorate – residential burglary recorded by the police declined by around 20 per cent (Walker *et al.* 2006, Table 2.04) during this specific period. Since 1995 there has been a 62 per cent decline in burglary reported to the British Crime Survey (Walker *et al.* 2006, Table 2.04); *ergo*, a tremendous government success, contributing to a favourable climate that produced two further election victories.

Sauce for the goose is sauce for the gander

Just as the Home Office had engaged in counter-factual reasoning, so too did we in our effort to evaluate the impact of a number of the pilot Strategic Development Projects (SDPs) of the RBI. Details of how we measured project impact and the specific methods of our statistical (time-series) evaluation model are contained in Hope *et al.* (2004).[6] The grounds for the divergence between our results and those of the Home Office (Kodz and Pease 2003) are published in Hope (2004). But why was it that the Home Office felt so compelled to repudiate our results? A clue is contained in the implications of our analysis, as set out in Table 3.1 (from Hope *et al.* 2004). Column A lists the percentage change in the number of burglaries per month occurring in each of the SDP's target areas during the period that they were in receipt of the first phase of Home Office funding. Column B provides an estimate of the change in burglary that our methods suggested could be attributed solely to the specific, measured outputs of each of the SDPs. This is a hypothetical estimate provided by our model of what would have been the impact of the project alone, net of all the other changes going on in each area that would have affected the areas' observed burglary rate (Column A). So, by subtraction, Column C represents an estimate of the contribution of all these other things, net of the project. In our statistical model, the test of significance of the estimate of change attributable to the project is evaluated by comparing an estimate of the change that might be due to our measure of project impact (our designated 'factual') against a projection of the trend prior to the initiation of project activities, net of the impact of the project. This is the total of 'counter-factual' possibilities, of which the residual change (Column C) is an alternate, observed 'factual' representing the influence of all the other (counter-factual) things that were not produced specifically by the factual projects.

Table 3.1 Impact of projects on burglary

Project	A Change in target area	B Change in target due to project (modelled)	C Other change in target (A – B)
Group A			
A1	−36	−49*	13
A2	−40	−43*	3
A3	−47	−37*	−10
A4	−3	−35*	32
A5	−29	−27*	−2
A6	−20	−4*	−16
Group B			
B1	−40	−27	−13
B2	−42	−21	−21
B3	−24	−20	−4
B4	−2	−15	13
B5	13	−10	23
B6	−32	−7	−25
B7	−37	−6	−31
Group C			
C1	−47	4	−43
C2	−16	6	−10
C3	−36	6	−42
C4	29	11	18
C5	−14	12	−26
C6	13	34	−22
C7	14	39*	−25

*statistically significant at p.<.05. Reproduced from Hope *et al.* (2004).

Despite burglary declining in all but four of the 20 project areas studied, there was 'tremendous' variation in the degree to which the reduction could be attributed to the project rather than to 'other things'. Some projects (mostly in Group A) appeared to be out-and-out successes, apparently dominating the trend and reducing burglary in their areas. Other projects (mostly in Group C) also dominated their local burglary trend but in the opposite way, appearing to be making things worse (Group C), often despite what might have been an otherwise favourable downward trend. The remainder appeared to be battling against the impact of 'other things': sometimes heroically (seemingly keeping a rising tide of crime at bay), sometimes ineffectually, and sometimes negligibly. Fortunately, in the context of generally declining crime rates, such 'failures' might be overlooked. But all these local struggles were smoothed over by the officials' method (Kodz and Pease 2003) which, in all cases where our results disagreed, attributed observed changes to the effect of the projects, rather than attributing them to the effect of other things (Hope 2004). Unless the experience of our projects was totally different from those studied by the other consortia,[7] then the same smoothing-over of local experience allowed the Minister the evidence needed to claim success overall, in anticipation of the remainder of the RBI to come.

Wriggle room at the Home Office

Of course, in the higher, political scheme, this kind of local detail probably does not matter very much, especially in a state such as the UK where power is highly centralised. If what counts for re-election purposes is a national reduction in crime, then it does not really matter how that came about; after all, government can always imply that it had a hand also in many of the 'other things' that could have brought about the crime drop. One obvious escape route would be to attribute the national reduction in crime to the general impact of the government's economic and social policies, including its specific programmes for local regeneration and tackling social exclusion. But for the Home Office that would mean not only giving away a success to other ministries but also a restoration of the 'historic link' between crime and the economy, which it had sundered previously.[8] The Home Office also ventured another imaginative way of wriggling out of the problem by claiming that substantial reductions could be attributed to an *anticipation of benefits* effect (Smith *et al.* 2002), whereby observed reductions locally were imagined to have been brought about by the

55

mere announcement that crime prevention activity was about to take place, presumably scaring away the local burglars.[9] Unfortunately, the evidence put forward in support of this fancy (Bowers and Johnson 2003) is as flawed as the methodology employed to support it (Hope 2004; Hope et al. 2004).

In any event, Home Office officials had sold the idea of the CRP as a set of locally based, practical crime prevention projects (Homel et al. 2004) specifically intended to find out and implement 'what works, for whom, and in what circumstances'. Certainly, all the Strategic Development Projects had had their plans inspected, revised and approved by a group of Home Office consultants prior to being granted funds (Tilley et al. 1999). However, with evidence mounting of massive and widespread implementation difficulties, certain Home Office officials, their associates and consultants, evidently started to brief against the ministerial line, especially that of the Treasury. Strangely, at the same time as officials seem to have been briefing the Minister about the tremendous success of the RBI, they were also telling the Guardian journalist Nick Davies about how ministerial actions had undermined the likelihood of success of their Crime Reduction Programme (Davies 2003).

The essence of their critique was repeated in a subsequent, supposedly objective, review of the implementation of the CRP (Homel et al. 2004). One of their central arguments is that the aspiration of the CRP to be an experimental exercise in EBPP was countermanded by ministers (obviously for political purposes), who shifted projects away from being experiments towards being expected to reduce crime, also shifting the management of the CRP away from the evidence-based crime prevention professionals at the Home Office, who were prevented from having a hands-on, directive involvement with local projects. It was further alleged that, following Treasury guidelines, Home Office officials had been instructed (against their wishes) to advise the independent consortia hired as evaluators not to provide projects with evidence on their progress. Thus, local projects were denied an opportunity to find out how they were doing, could not adjust their implementation plans in the light of initial difficulties, and so were not able to deliver anticipated crime reduction. The implicit argument is that had the CRP management access to the progress of projects, and had the local projects access to information in a timely fashion, the apparently massive implementation failure of the CRP could have been avoided (see Bullock and Tilley 2003).[10] Still, although plausible, and certainly self-serving, this excuse has another great advantage as an 'imaginary': since it is *post hoc ergo propter hoc* fallacious, it cannot be put to the test.

Nevertheless, from a contracted evaluator's perspective, this line is also factually untrue. I would imagine that all evaluators' contracts had required them, as ours did, to evaluate process as well as impact, but I do know that we were obliged to provide regular project monitoring evidence to the Home Office (including costs and use of resources) from an early stage. Indeed, it almost seemed that our purpose, as our contract managers appeared to interpret it, was primarily to collect data that would be fed into their own analysis – as indeed happened publicly with *Findings 204* (Kodz and Pease 2003; see also Hamilton-Smith 2004). Importantly, right from the start we were obliged to collect monthly totals for the number of burglaries recorded in the target areas for each of the projects, sending these each quarter as a return to our Home Office research managers – two of whom were also the authors of Homel *et al.* (2004). Further, arrangements for project accountability were also in place throughout via the regional government offices. Thus, Home Office programme managers (and presumably ministers) did have feedback on the implementation of the CRP from an early stage, and did have an inclination about the reality of how the projects were working.

Questions then arise as to what was done with this early evidence, and what its impact was on the management and progress of projects and the CRP itself: to what extent did Home Office officials feed this information back to projects, and did this information have any effect – if not, what then accounts for implementation failure? Notwithstanding whether ministers' expectations of the CRP were realistic (nor how they might have formed these expectations), how did Home Office officials themselves react to the 'evidence' that many aspects of their programme were facing major difficulties? Crucially, did their advice on the early evidence of implementation difficulties, assuming it was given, have an effect on subsequent ministerial decisions? Indeed, we do know, from the report of the *Guardian* journalist Nick Davies in 2003 (Davies 2003), that the decision to devolve management of the remainder of the CRP to newly appointed Crime Reduction Directors, based in the regional government offices, was taken in this context. So, was this a political move by Home Office ministers to wriggle off the hook of the CRP; and, far from bucking the trend, was this an effort to pass the buck to the hapless local projects, via their regional Crime Reduction Director patsies? Or is that another teleological account of political purposes?

Shooting the messenger

Finally, when all else fails, why not resort to that well-known practice of shooting the messenger? A convenient and revealing means of recounting this process is provided by reference to a Home Office email correspondence of 9–15 August 2006: the subject matter is entitled 'RE: Politics of Criminological Research' which appears to have been prompted by the submission of a 'draft chapter' by its authors, whom we shall call X and Y.[11] In the correspondence with X and Y that occurred three months after I had given my evidence to parliament, officials said, with reference to *Findings 204*:

> ... It was important that the results from the three RBI consortia were brought together and Ken [*sic*] undertook an analysis using a standard shift-share analysis, *which is the norm for evaluations of this kind*. The findings were subject to our usual peer review processes. I have to say that I find it astounding that the authors [that is, X and Y] casually describe work by a person of ... eminence as the 'Home Office mounting a re-analysis which managed to turn failure into success'. (9 August 2006, 3:12 p.m. emphasis added)

With regard to our own research, the officials said:

> ... This [that is, our time-series method] is *a non-standard method*, and one which differed from the solution adopted by the other two consortia [involved in evaluating the RBI-Phase 1] ... We also had other external advice that suggested Tim's time-series method was weaker ... Tim may not like that conclusion ... Coupled with the independent advice we received from a range of sources, I do not think it is fair to repeat Tim's accusations as if they have credibility. (10 August 2006, 6:10 p.m. emphasis added)

Until I had sight of this correspondence I was unaware of the existence of this particular piece of external advice; nor in the course of drafting Hope *et al.* (2004) were we apprised of it; nor, needless to say, were we offered an opportunity for scientific rebuttal. Neither, if this is its view, has the Home Office sought publicly to counter the credibility of my evidence to the House of Commons, either at the time when the STC would have been able to take evidence, or in the Government's Response to the Committee's Report (STC 2007). Presumably, then, confident in the eminence of its own appointed experts, Home Office officials remain privately dismissive not only of our own, apparently more humble, scientific acumen but also of the credulity of the House of Commons.

Nevertheless, Home Office confidence in its own expert advisors might be misplaced. It was as surprising to see time-series analysis regarded as a non-standard method of programme evaluation (compare with McCain and McCleary 1979) as it was to see 'shift-share' analyses described as standard. For instance, there is no reference to this latter method in either the Green Book (HM Treasury, n/d) or the Magenta Book (Policy Hub n/d) – the standard official handbooks of policy appraisal methods intended to guide government research. Although not perhaps entirely imaginary, 'shift-share' analysis does not appear to be part of the standard official repertoire of policy-evaluation methodologies. Rather, the method resembles a form of 'change score analysis', an approach that is considered to be 'notoriously unreliable' (Judd and Kenny 1981: 123–4). Evidently though, it must have been thought sufficiently reliable to be used in the published Home Office report on the overall cost-effectiveness of the RBI-Phase 1 projects (Bowles and Pradiptyo 2004) – again applied to our consortium's data against our wishes.

The diminution of the love of truth

The techniques used by Home Office officials described here seem a good example of those discussed by Thomas Mathiesen (2004): while overt repression of opposition is unacceptable in a democracy, there are nevertheless ways in which government can set about the 'silent silencing' of criticism. A particularly sophisticated way of doing this is to promulgate evidence-based policy criteria, and then to manipulate not only the evidence employed but also its epistemology. The relationship between science and politics uncovered here stands in contrast to that famously proposed by Donald T. Campbell (1969). For Campbell, the value of the relationship lay in maintaining the *autonomy* of the two spheres of science and politics, precisely to preserve the over-arching value of accountability to the public interest that ought to govern practice in either sphere. In Campbell's view, the danger inherent in too close a coupling of science and politics resides in a powerful imperative:

... it is one of the characteristics of the present situation that *specific reforms are advocated as though they were certain to be successful.* For this reason, knowing outcomes has immediate political implications ... if the political and administrative system has committed itself in advance to the correctness and efficacy of its reforms, it cannot tolerate learning of failure. (Campbell 1978: 80, original emphasis)

For Campbell, the great threat was the *trapped administrator* – those officials (elected or appointed) who are unable to resist the temptation to use political authority to manipulate the evidence they present in public to produce a more tolerable valuation. Why Campbell was committed to developing an autonomous scientific approach to policy evaluation was that he foresaw a time when officials would become sufficiently adept in the manipulation of methods as to render it impossible for the electorate to assess their claims without the aid of counter-expertise. With EBPP, it would seem that time has come. Furthermore, since this imperative has not abated, trapped administrators may now feel sufficiently emboldened to go on the offensive – to counter-attack the independent counter-expertise that resides in the Academy – at first in silence but also complicit with those 'quisling criminologists' who are prepared to do their master's bidding (Hope 2008).

As Ulrich Beck argues in his vision of the *Risk Society* (Beck 1992), the more relevant systematic intelligence has become in shaping and governing social life, the more that scientific rationality (the authority for such intelligence) has become a form of governance. But governance does not supplant politics. So, as science comes to shape politics, it becomes itself a site for politics, losing its monopoly as a unitary method, and opening up opportunities for the legitimisation of contending methodologies and epistemologies about the nature of science, its conduct and its criteria of validity. As political life becomes scientised, and *vice versa*, the structures of authority in each of the spheres lose their autonomy; science can now legitimately guide politics, but *quid pro quo* politics now has a say in science – what it endorses, what it encourages and how that which it supports is to be conducted. The value of science ceases to be derived from its methodology alone and is now also to be derived from its promise of utility.

The emergence of the *regulatory state* (Braithwaite 2000), of which New Labour's strategy for the governance of crime would seem a good example, further problematises the epistemology of evidence, since not only politics but now also public administration comes to rely upon scientised evidence, notably in the shape of EBPP. Yet again, far from avoiding politics in some imaginary world in which regulation and accountability become subsumed into technical expertise, the short-run political advantages to be gained from EBPP may rebound upon those who seek to profit by it, for as Jasanoff remarks:

> ... if it is seen that science cannot provide definitive answers to questions about risk, then policy-makers cannot fall back on unassailable technical justifications for their regulatory choices. (Jasanoff 1987: 225)

Yet it would seem that the policy-makers' answer would be to make sure that science is indeed *seen publicly* to be providing definitive answers. Nevertheless, since recourse to the conjectural (hypothetical, counter-factual) imaginative is a method by which science evaluates its own evidence, to engage with scientific evidence so as to eradicate its indeterminacy and contestability paradoxically involves imposing, instead, a political imaginary, including a 'politicising' of scientific methodology.

Some ways of regulating disputes and resolving conflicts about scientific evidence take place in public. In the regulatory state, one mode is to treat scientific evidence like other forms of public evidence, subjecting disputes ultimately to the scrutiny of the courts or other quasi-judicial regulatory bodies (Jasanoff 1987). For scientific communities themselves, the institutions of peer review aim to serve a self-regulatory purpose; offering a public guarantee as to the reliability of the evidence produced, and a guide to the grounds upon which disputes subsist.[12] However, the calamitous imagery of warfare provides government with the excuse it may need for evading public scrutiny: allowing it the right to abrogate the public interest to its own, to select information for the greater good, and to construct its evidence in secret. In his Godkin Lectures at Harvard University, nearly half a century ago at the height of the Cold War (though referring to certain calamitous science-based decisions of the previous global conflict, including the 'carpet-bombing' of German cities) C.P. Snow said that 'almost all secret scientific choices are something like pure closed politics' (Snow 1961: 56).[13] Away from public gaze, decision-making is shaped by the *habitus* of government bureaucracy: where skill in committee, the inertia of decision-making, and the efficacy of what Snow called *court politics* (having the ear of the minister) all predominate; and where players adept at their manipulation, or servile to their protocols, can command attention and influence. As Snow suggests, such conditions give greater rein to certain kinds of science, and scientist, than to others. Though it remains moot as to whether it is the politician that influences the scientist, or *vice versa*, it would seem that the imaginary of secret scientific warfare that evidently still pervades government science, nevertheless has real consequences, for both politics and science.

Notes

1 The Home Office obliged by removing reference to our consortium from the Acknowledgements to *Findings 204* (Davies 2003).
2 When appraised of the implications of the model, at a press conference held by the minister (John Patten) to account for a recent rise in crime, he reacted, apparently impromptu, by disparaging the researcher (and hence the research) *ad hominem*, along the lines of 'isn't he the one that wears the earring' (for a full account see Brake and Hale 1992). This was an 'imaginary' in another sense too because he wasn't (although another colleague was). Aspersions about attire seem to be part of the imagery constructed in British political life when it suits (as it were) to denigrate specialist expertise, *viz*:
    Mr Glass: '... I remember in the Treasury the geekier economists were referred to as 'v-necks'. These were people who came to work in v-neck sweaters and obviously were not entirely reliable!' (STC 2006, HC 900-II, Q1003)
    Professor Hope: 'As I said, I served in what was once the Home Office Research and Planning Unit. It was not a directorate. I was certainly proud to be a geek or a v-neck and I may even have worn denim at some point during my career.' (STC 2006, HC 900-II, Q1004).
3 Around £250 million for the initial Crime Reduction Programme, with an additional £150 million to support local CCTV installations (Homel *et al.* 2004).
4 As noted below, the subsequent behaviour of the crime trend in England and Wales has differed markedly from that predicted by the model. The scientific response would be to undertake further research to come up with a better-fitting model that also accounts for the decline in officially recorded crime rates over the past ten years (Hope 2007; Lewis 2003).
5 As just indicated, this had scarcely been acknowledged officially as an 'historic link' before it was sundered again.
6 While we introduced an innovative way of measuring specific project impact – the construction of a measure of the *intensity* of project impact

using both qualitative and quantitative data – all the 'raw' data we had collected and used to construct our measure had been approved by, and carried out on instruction from, the Home Office RDS (see Bowles and Pradiptyo 2004). Of course, our epistemology is 'realist' in the sense that it assumes that our measures validly represent a reality, net of measurement error itself.

7 The information that would allow an evaluation of this possibility remains in the hands of the Home Office, though it does not look likely (Bowles and Pradiptyo 2004).

8 Members of the public have been told repeatedly through the media about the internal Labour Party conflict and competition between Tony Blair (the Prime Minister) and Gordon Brown (the Chancellor of the Exchequer). Within the imaginary of collective cabinet responsibility, it was alleged that some policy issues, such as crime, and some ministries, such as the Home Office, were the fiefdom of the PM, while others, such as economic policy and the Treasury were those of the Chancellor. While it must remain a matter of speculation as to its reasons, the apparent tension between the Home Office and the Treasury over matters surrounding the governance of the CRP must remain an important part of the backdrop.

9 A book of essays published in honour of one of the originators of this idea is entitled *Imagination for Crime Prevention* (Farrell *et al.* 2007).

10 The Home Office has not released information that would afford an assessment of the extent of this failure.

11 A copy of this exchange has been released to me in response to a 'subject access request' under the provisions of the Data Protection Act, 1998. Information regarding the identity of individuals was 'redacted'. A fuller account of this correspondence is contained in Hope (2008).

12 I elaborate elsewhere on the concept of peer review in relation to these events (Hope 2008).

13 I am grateful to my colleague Philip Stenning for coming across Snow's book in a second-hand bookstore in New Zealand.

Chapter 4

Inventing community safety

Adam Edwards and Gordon Hughes

'security' is therefore something we imagine, and what we imagine shapes our mentalities and practices of governance. (Wood and Shearing 2007: 6)

We should also beware of confusing narratives, of any kind, with what they are about (even in cases where they are about other narratives); this is an 'epistemic fallacy' which has plagued hermeneutics. (Sayer 2000: 141)

Introduction

What is a criminological imagination for? The orthodox response to this question, to better represent the causes and/or meaning of crime, has been challenged by advocates of a performative understanding of criminological thought. Performative accounts are concerned with the ways in which narratives bring into being, or 'instantiate', the very objects they then seek to explain.[1] Whether or not any particular instantiation is a more or less accurate representation matters less than what it does in producing particular ways of understanding whilst obviating others (Rose 1999). It has been argued, for example, that American society is increasingly 'governed through crime', wherein problems of government, such as the transition from adolescence to adulthood, are instantiated as problems of criminality and disorder requiring criminal justice interventions rather than as problems of health and welfare implying social policy responses (Simon 2007). In the UK, similar arguments have identified the 'criminalisation of social policy' in 'neo-liberal' rationalities of rule, in which welfare is justified primarily in terms of its contribution to the reduction of crime and disorder rather than as an end in itself (Crawford 1997).

The performative approach has been celebrated for liberating criminological thought from the burdens of better representing 'reality' to instead, 'provide resources to think beyond what already exists' (O'Malley 2006: 193). This approach has been particularly influential in studies of 'governmentality' in criminology, which seek to diagnose 'the intellectual, linguistic and technical ways in which phenomena are constituted by government as governable problems' as a basis for questioning 'how not to be governed thus' (O'Malley 2006: 192 193; Smandych 1999). Realist arguments, for example over 'what works, what doesn't and what's promising' in crime prevention (Sherman *et al.* 1997) and allied attempts by organisations such as the Campbell Collaboration to arbitrate useful and valid criminological knowledge, particularly on methodological grounds (http://www.campbellcollaboration.org), are criticised for failing to escape the problematic of government, 'the task of making us into something else, to govern us better, on the basis of a superior regime of truth' (O'Malley 2006: 193). For social science orthodoxy this rejection of producing knowledge that can better represent the past and present, is nihilistic. For its advocates, performative studies are better placed to promote an open-ended, future-oriented and democratic contestation of government than intellectual traditions that proscribe what can be thought; they prioritise imagination and political choices over methodological censure and other forms of theoretical closure (O'Malley *et al.* 1997).

Conversely, our contention is that re-defining the purpose of the criminological imagination in terms of the production of performative rather than representational concepts misrepresents their interdependence. Performativity is dependent on existing representations as we necessarily stand on the shoulders of existing narratives in bringing into being new concepts. Performative criminology is also dependent on representational criminology insofar as it aspires to translate its visions of crime and control into practice. Beyond an anarchistic desire to 'destabilise rule' (O'Malley 2006), the imagination of desired futures will not be translated into action unless they effectively represent an originating state from which this alternative future is projected. In the terms of discourse analysis, successful narratives of change are those that convey a convincing story about an original state ('where we are'), a desired end state ('where we need to be') and decisive interventions ('how we get from here to there') (Hay 1996: 157 n16). As such criminological futures are instantiated *through* representations of the present.

It is in these terms that we use the notion of 'invention' to refer to this process of imagining criminological futures through representations of the present. The idea of invention also alerts us to the anterior conditions of criminological thought which mediate any one imagined future. These conditions can include other, competing, criminological narratives as well as the concept-independent conditions of the criminological imagination, particularly the unequally allocated political, economic, organisational, informational and constitutional-legal resources available to proponents of competing futures.[2] This anteriority has further implications for understanding the different purposes of the criminological imagination. Apropos the introductory quote from Wood and Shearing (2007: 6), above, we may imagine security in terms of various wars on crime, drugs, terror and so on, or in terms of more egalitarian, solidaristic, socially just polities. Such imagination also *shapes* our political rationalities of rule, insofar as imagination is required to instantiate governable phenomena, but governing *practices* cannot be reduced to the imagination. To do so is to grant imagination too much power, to commit the 'epistemic fallacy' referred to in the other headline quote (Sayer 2000: 141). Confusing any one criminological narrative with what it is about provides no grounds for contesting its knowledge claims.[3] In relation to this, the epistemic fallacy obscures how any one particular criminological narrative exists in an anterior relationship to the particular social contexts in which it is produced and deployed.

The invention of community safety provides a useful illustration of the interdependence of performative and representational criminology both because of its polyvalence and because of the specific geo-historical contexts in which it has been produced and deployed. This concept has proved to be a fertile ground for the criminological imagination in Britain, acquiring a following amongst an increasing volume of policy-makers and practitioners of local governance. The concept has also produced a growing body of academic research and debate, including the establishment of specialist journals, *The Community Safety Journal* and *Crime Prevention and Community Safety: an international journal*, a number of textbooks, research monographs and edited collections (Gilling 1997, 2007; Crawford 1997, 1998; Hughes 1998, 2007; Hughes and Edwards 2002; Hughes *et al.* 2002, Matthews and Pitts 2001). It has been variously defined as, 'a synonym of crime prevention with fluffy overtones added' (Pease and Wiles 2000), a feel good word marked by extreme vagueness (Gilling 1997), and a 'capacious phrase' signifying security against harms from all sources, not just those proscribed by criminal law (Hughes 2006). In turn, the international transferability of the concept, particularly around the non-Anglophone world, has been limited by its ethnocentricity, reflecting its origins in the very particular politics of control in British localities since the early 1990s (Stenson and Edwards 2004; Edwards and Hughes 2005) and the limited export of the concept around fellow Commonwealth countries (Carson 2007).[4]

This polyvalence has accommodated a number of competing narratives. In the remainder of the chapter, four in particular are selected as a means of exemplifying the interdependence between representational and performative criminology. They are those that depict community safety as a progressive 'third way'; a repressive state apparatus; a neo-liberal political rationality; and as an 'arboreal vision of control'. Each are structured around representations of the original state of community safety from which desired futures are projected.

A progressive 'third way'?

An obvious point of departure is the uses to which the concept of community safety has been put by governmental advisors, policy-makers and practitioners. Notwithstanding scepticism amongst some academics over the imprecision and utility of the concept, it has acquired a substantial following amongst police officers, local government employees and voluntary and commercial organisations since its popularisation in British public administration through the publication of a report by the Home Office Standing Conference on Crime Prevention (colloquially known, after the chair of the committee producing the report, as 'the Morgan Report') in 1991.[5] A National Community Safety Network (NCSN) providing support to those employed as community safety officers by local authorities and constabularies was established shortly after the publication of the Morgan Report and currently has members covering the vast majority of CSPs across the UK.[6] The Morgan Report itself was also heavily influenced by representatives of local government, particularly the Association of Metropolitan Authorities representing large urban authorities in England and Wales that tended to be run by the Labour Party. This social democratic influence on the Morgan

Report, established to review developments in multi-agency crime prevention since Home Office circular 8/1984 on the need to adopt a more preventive approach to crime, can be discerned in its content definition of community safety in terms of a 'portfolio of activities' (Home Office 1991: 32). These activities extended beyond measures to reduce the opportunities for crime, for tackling specific types of crime and assisting victims to a focus on 'Tackling the causes of crime', through 'family support initiatives, youth programmes, community development programmes and neighbourhood initiatives, pre-school programmes, alcohol and drug misuse prevention schemes, education and school based programmes, work with offenders and their families, employment and training programmes, debt counselling.' (Home Office 1991: 32).

As such the Morgan Report used the concept of community safety to retrieve the gamut of dispositional theories of crime causation that constitute the principal sociological and psychological contributions to governmental criminology. These had been eschewed during the previous decade by a national Conservative administration critical of the social determination of crime and concerned to promote neo-classical principles of deterrent penal regimes for rational offenders. The unsurprising rejection of the Morgan Report's recommendations for community safety by this administration provided the Labour Party, then in opposition in Westminster, with a basis for reformulating its approach to 'law-and-order', specifically through Tony Blair's now renowned concept of being 'tough on crime and tough on the causes of crime'.

The political importance of Blair's reformulation of crime control policy, during his tenure as opposition spokesperson on Home Affairs, both for his personal political career and for the subsequent electoral fortunes of the Labour Party, has been the subject of much analysis and commentary (Downes and Morgan 2002; Matthews and Young 2003; Tonry 2004). Our point is that the concept of community safety enabled the Labour Party, both at the national and municipal levels, to re-assert the social democratic association of crime control and social policy whilst accommodating more immediate, palliative, measures for reducing crime and addressing the needs of victims. It therefore provided a means of loosening the 'hostages to fortune' that had characterised the Labour Party's depiction, by its political opponents, of being 'soft' on crime, tolerant of civil disorders, particularly those associated with disputes undertaken by the industrial wing of the labour movement, and more concerned with the welfare of offenders than the rights of victims (Downes and Morgan 1994; Gilling 1997, 2007; Crawford 2001).

From its origins in the political dynamics of national and local government in Britain, the very imprecision of community safety as a concept proved useful in instantiating the problem of crime as a composite of social causes, to be addressed through policies on family support, employment and training, education and youth work, situational opportunities, remediable through household security, environmental design and planning, support for victims. In these terms, the intellectual coherence and internal consistency of the concept is less important and less interesting than its capacity to outflank and out-think more reductionist narratives about crime control through enforcement of the criminal law, punitive deterrence or social policy interventions.

This imprecision is confirmed in the evolution of the concept in official discourse about crime and disorder reduction from the uses made of the Morgan Report by the Labour Party whilst in opposition to its more muted expression in the blizzard of legislative and policy initiatives passed by Labour in government since the general election of 1997. The plasticity of the concept was signalled almost immediately in one of the white papers that preceded the omnibus Crime and Disorder Act 1998, in which reference was made to 'community safety orders', subsequently renamed Anti-Social Behaviour Orders (ASBOs), concerned with tackling incivilities and restoring moral authority within blighted communities. Following protests from the growing population of community safety workers who, apropos the Morgan Report, saw themselves more in the mould of welfare professionals-come-technicians of crime prevention than arbiters of moral authority, the concept was dropped. Instead of being redefined more in keeping with the sentiments of the Morgan Report, reference to community safety was replaced altogether with an emphasis, instead, on 'crime and disorder reduction'.[7] The Crime and Disorder Act placed a statutory obligation on both district local authorities and constabularies to establish multi-agency partnerships and implement preventive strategies. It is argued that this provided a 'politically satisficing' solution of getting elected local government to assume responsibility for crime reduction without antagonising the police or threatening their operational autonomy (Hope 2005).

From this compromise over both the institutional responsibility for leading local crime control and the allied nomenclature of 'crime and disorder reduction' rather than community safety, through to the current Home Office Reform Programme for the statutory partnerships, there persists a 'politically satisficing' ambivalence over what the concept of community safety can and should signify (Hughes 2007:

42–8). It is notable, for example, that in the context of devolution, the statutory partnerships in Wales are officially known as 'community safety partnerships' and that the overwhelming proportion of funding received by these partnerships comes from programmes for youth crime prevention and tackling substance misuse administered by the community safety division of the Welsh Assembly Government's Department for Local Government and Social Justice (Edwards and Hughes 2008a, 2008b). Here the nomenclature of community safety partnerships is deliberately counterpoised to that of 'crime and disorder reduction partnerships' employed in England whilst the location of community safety work within a department explicitly concerned with *social*, not criminal, justice matters in relation to the broader politics of devolution and attempts to differentiate Labour in Wales from Labour in Westminister. Specifically the Assembly Government has dismissed the high volume use of ASBOs in certain English localities as typical of a 'low-trust' politics that further undermines the relationship between public authorities and the general public (Drakeford 2005). In place of this the Assembly Government uses the concept of community safety to privilege a more social democratic preoccupation with crime prevention through youth work and rehabilitative drug treatment regimes.

Whether this articulation of community safety within the politics of devolution translates into discernible, systematic, differences in practice between Welsh and English multi-agency partnerships remains a moot point for research. The point here is that, as a concept, community safety has been used in official discourse over the past decade to signify moral authoritarian interventions against 'anti-social behaviour' and social democratic measures for promoting socially just, 'high-trust', polities. The polyvalence of the concept is further demonstrated through research on community safety officers about the meanings they attribute to their own work (Hughes and Gilling 2004; Edwards and Hughes 2008a). This suggests a complex admixture of understanding, including in one, admittedly atypical, case a community safety manager describing himself as an 'unreconstructed Marxist-Leninist' who welcomed ASBOs, not as an instrument for the class oppression of the usual suspects but as a means of protecting law-abiding working class communities from a feral lumpen proletariat in a context in which they have been deserted both by the market and by liberals more concerned with the civil liberties of actual and 'at risk' offenders than with the multiple victimisation of already disadvantaged communities (Edwards and Hughes 2008a).

That such a practitioner of community safety could deploy concepts associated in academic criminology with, *inter alia*, Wilson and Kelling's 'right realist' broken windows thesis, Ken Pease's notion of repeat victimisation, Lea and Young's 'left realist' concern with the vulnerabilities of the working class to criminal victimisation and Reiner's recent invocation of a social democratic political-economy of law and order, demonstrates the scope for invention admitted by the concept of community safety. It demonstrates the distance there often is between the relatively 'smooth' narratives of academic criminology and their messy adaptation in criminological practice. The messiness of the social life onto which social science often imposes a specious conceptual order is a major theme in broader methodological debates (Law 2004); here the implications for understanding the actual and prospective interrelationships between criminological imagination and practice can be explored further through reference to self-consciously academic accounts of community safety.

A repressive state apparatus?

Counterpoised to the bricolage of criminological ideas found in official, particularly, practitioner narratives on community safety, some commentators working within the tradition of critical social science have offered an altogether smoother interpretation of this concept and what it signifies. Drawing inspiration from the Althusserian and Gramscian Marxist analyses of an earlier generation of critical criminologists (Hall *et al.* 1978; Scraton 1987), these commentators identify community safety as a set of particular practices that form part of a repressive state apparatus whose function is to regulate the conditions for capital accumulation (Coleman *et al.* 2002; Coleman 2004, 2005).

Using findings from local case study research, such as a study of the Safer Merseyside Partnership in the North West of England, this narrative identifies the preoccupation of community safety work with urban regeneration strategies concerned with the civic boosterism of attracting inward capital investment and increased consumption, particularly in the retail sector: 'This project is underpinned by a logic of social and economic regeneration that attempts to forge and disseminate a market oriented and entrepreneurial inspired notion of the "public interest"' (Coleman *et al.* 2002: 97). Having problematised community safety in terms of places that are safe for business, it follows that challenges to safety are those that threaten capital accumulation requiring, in turn, measures to contain or expunge such threats. In these terms, CCTV technologies are deployed alongside more aggressive, 'zero tolerance', street policing to cleanse the commercial centres of cities of unproductive labour and populations that deter consumers, particularly beggars and those consuming alcohol on the streets (as opposed to in the bars and restaurants).

In this narrative community safety is imagined as a set of repressive, 'revanchist', policing practices aimed at retaking public space for the purposes of capital accumulation whilst obviating alternative conceptions of safety, such as youth work within disadvantaged neighbourhoods. Further, the narrow conception of community safety amongst urban elites obviates action on other threats to public health, such as toxic waste disposal, traffic pollution and allied corporate crimes that are excluded from the purview of community safety work: 'these inclusionary and exclusionary practices can be understood as part of a wider social ordering strategy which is legitimated by the moral and intellectual project of social and economic regeneration' (Coleman *et al.* 2002: 96).

Interest in capturing the concept of community safety and using it to signal the need for public protection against a variety of harmful activities perpetrated by corporations against vulnerable working class communities has increased amongst critical criminologists (Croall 2004; Tombs *et al.* 2007). Again, this demonstrates both the polyvalence of the concept and its focus for political contestation over the definition of 'safety' for different communities of interest. Our particular interest here, however, is in the relationship between the performative and representational aspects of this critical narrative and, in turn, what this tells us about the criminological imagination. In problematising community safety as an exercise in securing the conditions for capital accumulation strategies (such as the regeneration of post-industrial cities such as Liverpool around retail consumption during the daytime and alcohol consumption at night), this narrative instantiates community safety as a repressive apparatus and channels the vision of the social researcher onto those policing practices that fit this initial problematisation. To what extent this imagination also provides an accurate and exhaustive representation of community safety in the case study area in question as well as further afield is questionable. It is questionable precisely because of the messy, inchoate and often disorganised conceptions of community safety revealed through research into the dispositions of community safety workers (Edwards and Hughes 2008a,b) and into the practice of partnerships in other localities in England and Wales (Hallsworth 2002; Stenson 2002; Foster 2002).

What this alternative research alerts us to is the doubly hermeneutic character of the criminological imagination; it must place an interpretation on the interpretations of the workers, organisations and practices it envisages. As such, there is ample opportunity for slippage between the performative and representational claims of criminological knowledge; is the depiction of Liverpool as a 'revanchist' city an exhaustive representation of community safety in that locality or a product of the very imagination of those employing an Althusserian/Gramscian lens through which to view it (Hughes 2007: 172–6)? This needn't matter if, apropos O'Malley's (2006) promotion of the diagnostic and destabilising role of criminological thinking, there is no pretence at making superior truth claims about the world as it really is. Where the purpose is, however, precisely to imagine real-world conditions further conceptual work is needed to negotiate the various problems of reductionism and determinism that can debilitate representational knowledge. That a healthy scepticism toward self-consciously academic narratives should be cultivated as much, if not more, than the distrust shown towards those offered by the subjects of these narratives (Clegg 1993) – to community safety workers and policy-makers for example – is further reinforced by the existence of competing academic theories of community safety. Reference to two of these will suffice in making the point that representations of community safety belie the capacity of any one, smooth, narrative to adequately capture its multi-faceted causes and consequences.

A neo-liberal political rationality?

Whereas critical criminology was, at one time, synonymous with the kind of Marxist political-economy advocated by Coleman and his colleagues, it now accommodates the work of those influenced by a very different intellectual tradition associated with Foucault's study of power, particularly his concept of governmentality which examines the role of political rationalities in defining objects of control and proscribing how these objects so defined should be interpreted and acted upon (Foucault 1991; O'Malley 1992; Stenson 1993; Garland 1997; Smandych 1999; Rose 2000).

In Britain, arguments about the meaning of crime prevention and community safety have provided a focal point for this tradition of thought, in particular David Garland's thesis about the contradictory political rationalities at play in 'late-modern' strategies of control. Specifically, the episodic bouts of 'punitive display' by sovereign states anxious to legitimate their authority through various wars on drugs, crime, terror and so forth, exist in tension with the *sotto voce* admission that state authorities lack the effective capacity to govern crime and disorder alone. This limit to the sovereign state and the normality of high crime rates in Britain provides the real world conditions to which governing strategies must adapt by 'responsibilising' citizens and other private actors to more actively participate in their own governance. Central to this adaptation is the promotion of measures for identifying and reducing the opportunities for crime and disorder generated through the everyday routines of citizens (Garland 1996, 2001).

In these terms, community safety is counterposed to various forms of punitive display, such as zero tolerance policing, anti-social behaviour orders, child curfews, parenting orders and so on, and allied to a new logic of prevention and risk management that,

> instead of pursuing, prosecuting and punishing individuals ... aims to reduce the supply of criminal events by minimising criminal opportunities, enhancing situational controls, and channelling conduct away from criminogenic situations ... Community safety becomes the chief consideration and law enforcement becomes merely a means to this end. (Garland 2001: 171)

Community safety is consequently allied to a certain neo-liberal political rationality in which state intervention, even in the core competence of order maintenance, is rolled-back as private citizens are required to act as individualised prudential actors better insuring themselves against future risks of criminal victimisation (O'Malley *et al.* 1997). What, for Garland, is eclipsed in this interplay between punitive criminologies of the other and adaptive criminologies of the self, is the social democratic criminology that had prevailed in the mid-twentieth century under the influence of Merton's strain theory, the Chicago School's ecology of social disorganisation and Cloward and Ohlin's subcultural theories of delinquency, privileging welfare state interventions, particularly those aimed at the education, training, employment and recreation of young people.

As noted above, however, community safety has been regarded, notably by community safety workers themselves, as a means of resuscitating a more Fabian vision of control (Edwards and Hughes 2008a). The elision of community safety with neo-liberal politics has also been challenged for obscuring the increasing accommodation of punitive strategies within community safety work, most notably through the pressure put on multi-agency partnerships to use ASBOs and other coercive powers, which was present at the outset of the local statutory partnerships in 1999 and further intensified following the passage of the Anti-Social Behaviour Act 2003 (Allen 1999; Hughes 2007).

Again, the capacity of the concept of community safety to escape any neat and coherent association with any particular political rationale, like the difficulties of associating it with the function of regulating capital accumulation strategies, reiterates its polyvalence. It should be clear that community safety is a floating signifier with no fixed referent and a multiplicity of significations capable of being aligned with a broad spectrum of political positions on crime and disorder. As such the criminological imagination of Garland or O'Malley, no less than Coleman *et al.* cannot be equated with an effective representation of community safety *per se*, albeit the performative effect of these academic narratives has been significant in bringing into being new perspectives on its political uses and, by contrast, clarifying the often implicit aetiologies of crime and disorder buried in the bland managerialism of local community safety strategies and action plans. The question remains, does this diagnostic role for criminological thought suffice? Presumably critics of community safety bother to criticise because, having imagined social order otherwise, they wish to translate this imagination into effect?

An arboreal vision of control?

The fourth and final narrative on community safety is, in many regards, the most provocative and de-stabilising exercise in criminological imagination of all those considered here. It draws its inspiration from the work of the post-structuralist philosophers Gilles Deleuze and Felix Guattari (1987), whose broader critique of western philosophical traditions challenges the common preoccupation with producing 'arboreal' knowledge, as exemplified by the historical device of genealogical or family trees. They use the family tree as a metaphor for a recurrent philosophical tendency to seek total, exhaustive, knowledge of a phenomenon and to do so using clearly delineated conceptual boundaries and hierarchies employing, in turn, unidirectional notions of causality, as in the lineage of a family with roots that branch out in binaries of spouses – children – spouses and so on. For Deleuze and Guattari this is a specious exercise which misconceives the more inchoate, protean, multi-directional and unpredictable qualities of social relationships, which are better envisaged in terms of the botanical metaphor of the rhizome. This metaphor captures the heterogeneous mutation of social relationships and their osmosis into one another, creating in turn further mutations, for example in the assemblage, breakdown and re-assemblage of non-nuclear families. The point of the metaphor is that it expresses the kind of thinking that is needed to apprehend the dynamic qualities of social relationships and how this thinking has been debilitated by the rigid conceptual hierarchies and categorisation associated with, for example, modern social science.

This opposition between arboreal and rhizomatic thinking has been imported into criminological thought by those interested in innovations in the control of crime and disorder often associated with community safety. Two key examples will suffice, Haggerty and Ericson's (2000) study of the 'surveillant assemblage' and Hallsworth's (2008) interpretation of violent street worlds. These demonstrate the dissonance between the problem-solving activities which community safety workers are asked to undertake, to render problems of crime and disorder intelligible and measurable for the purposes of their subsequent remediation, and the protean qualities of these problems which escape precise definition and calibration. Arboreal visions of control are subverted both by the rhizomatic qualities of control itself and by the rhizomatic qualities of the street crime and disorder that are the focus of much control. This narrative suggests a basic contradiction in community safety work, the struggle to delimit the limitless.

Haggerty and Ericson (2000) for example, describe the proliferation of CCTV as part of a broader 'surveillant assemblage' of technologies and practices geared toward the generic surveillance of the population. This is contrasted with the narrower images of Orwell's 'big brother' or Foucault's discussion of the panopticon, which thought of surveillance in terms of particular technologies employed by the powerful to discipline specific groups or individuals (the political rebel, the inmate of a penitentiary, and so on). Whereas much analysis of surveillance is preoccupied with discrete technologies, such as the deployment of CCTV, and their cumulative impact on civil liberties, such as the rights of 'non-productive' or 'under-consuming' populations to move freely about the commercial city, Haggerty and Ericson focus instead on the underlying logic of surveillance, which they argue is, driven by the desire to bring systems together, to combine practices and technologies and integrate them into a larger whole. It is this tendency which allows us to speak of surveillance as an assemblage, with such combinations providing for exponential increases in the degree of surveillance capacity. (2000: 610)

Haggerty and Ericson (2000: 616) use the concept of 'assemblage' to describe the ways in which surveillance technologies mutate, feed off one another, become integrated into a limitless and multi-directional apparatus whose current deployment, much less future usage, cannot be deduced from a singular cause.

No single technological development has ushered in the contemporary era of surveillance. Rather, its expansion has been aided by subtle variations and intensifications in technological capabilities, and connections and other monitoring and computing devices. (2000: 616)

For example, CCTV has become integrated with computer systems, radio-links and other telecommunications in order to monitor general populations, such as retail consumers, as well as track particular suspect populations. These technologies are now, in turn, being linked-up with computer programmes such as Geographical Information Systems (GIS) not only to identify 'hot-spots' of offending and victimisation but also for 'data mining' exercises in which information held on previously discrete databases (for example, school attendance records, health records, police recorded crime, fire service data, financial records, even retail intelligence on consumer spending patterns and so forth) is cross-referenced in an attempt to reveal the dynamics producing threats to community safety (Hirschfield 2005). This kind of 'partnership intelligence' gathering and analysis is now promoted as the appropriate basis for the strategic assessments that community safety partnerships are now required to undertake on an annual basis[8] (Edwards and Hughes 2008b).

For Haggerty and Ericson (2000: 618) this kind of mutation amongst surveillance systems is accompanied by the development of their multi-directional foci. Contrary to Orwellian and Foucaultian images of the top-down exercise of surveillance by the powerful against specific groups and individuals, the surveillant assemblage subverts this hierarchy of observation enabling the spread of surveillance to cover wealthier and more powerful cohorts of the population. Indeed, the wealthier and more powerful a person is, the greater their surveillance will be, given their entry into credit card databases, private as well as public healthcare records, more intense use of the Internet and other communications and information technologies and passage through passport checks and other transport termini and so on. Neither are the powerful only subject to surveillance by the powerful but, in Mathiesen's (1997) phrase, 'synoptic' technologies, such as mass media coverage and live streaming of data through the Internet, render government decision makers, celebrities and other elites more visible to the general population. Further, the development of portable and affordable technologies such as digital cameras facilitates a democratisation of surveillance including, in some instances, political activists and trades unions recording the policing of their demonstrations and industrial protests to deter their unlawful suppression. The idea of the surveillant assemblage therefore challenges any simple representation of control in terms of a particular interest group or function or political rationality. For whilst surveillance technologies may be differentially applied, as in the tracking of suspect populations through commercial city centres (Coleman *et al.* 2002), this does not exhaust the multiple uses to which they can be put. As such the concept of the rhizome subverts the over-homogenous imagery of control whether in the dreams of public authorities or the nightmares of libertarian critics.

Just as discrete control technologies can mutate and be used in ways not originally envisaged, so their objects of control defy neat delimitation. Hallsworth (2008) extends the concept of the rhizome further to analyse how the chaotic qualities of street violence escape the arboreal visions of 'gang talk', by which he means a certain intellectual tradition of American criminology exported to the UK and other European countries in the wake of growing official concerns about the increasing use of guns and knives in acts of inter-personal violence:

> ... gang talkers typically impose onto the street the kind of arboreal structures that best define the bureaucratic world in which they normally dwell. A world, that is, which is orderly, hierarchical, discernible, measurable, predictable and thus containable by thought. In effect, gang talkers are tree thinkers and interpret gangs like trees in an urban forest: there they are, this is how many there are, they have this structure, this hierarchy, this cluster of risk factors and so on. This arboreal tendency ... leads them to over order the inherent contingent amorphous volatility of street life. And this is why I am always

suspicious when I hear people evoke the gang in terms of lieutenants, wanabees, soldiers etc. (Hallsworth 2008: 6)

This kind of 'mirror imaging' in which public authorities project their own ways of thinking and organising onto their subjects of control is prevalent within community safety strategies and action plans employing the repertoire of the problem-solving approach (Read and Tilley 2000; Bullock and Tilley 2003), and in Home Office injunctions to formulate interventions that are 'Specific, Measurable, Achievable, Realistic and Timebound' (SMART) (Home Office 2003). In these terms community safety offers an arboreal vision of control in which feral populations of street criminals can be tamed and order restored through the promise of 'SMARTer' intelligence. For its Deleuzian critics this project is designed to fail insofar as it imposes a specious conceptual order on social relationships that cannot be understood from the standpoint of public authorities' own categories and measurement of behaviour.

Beyond 'gang talk', the problems of mirror imaging can be discerned throughout the 'intelligence-led', problem-solving approaches which community safety officers are required to undertake by the statutory duty to return annual strategic assessments of their work. The predominant intellectual traditions underpinning the analysis of crime patterns in these strategic assessments are those of rational choice, routine activities theory and situational crime prevention and these delimit street crime in terms of discrete 'events' that can be enumerated and mapped to reveal their concentration in time and place (Clarke and Eck 2003; Hirschfield 2005). In doing so, the antecedent conditions of these events are forgotten and the meaning of street violence for its 'rational' protagonists is obviated (Young 2004). Conversely, using findings from his own empirical research programme on street violence in London, Hallsworth identifies different 'ecologies' of violence, possessing their own rules of engagement, some of which may evolve into those associated with the purported cultures of the 'American street gang' (Klein 1995), but many of which do not. Indeed, Hallsworth argues that, contrary to the highly structured image of gang violence in the United States,

The problem of violent street worlds in the UK is, in part, a problem of the lack of organised gangs. What we tend to have is more loosely affiliated gangsters … and this is why the violence they do takes the explosive form it does. This … is because the violence rules they are beholden to over-affirm violent escalation while unfortunately not proscribing rules that might delimit the violence they do. (2008: 11)

If the 'hot-spot' analysis of crime patterns facilitated by GIS imposes an arboreal vision of control upon inherently rhizomatic processes of crime and disorder, it follows that other intellectual traditions are required for the cultivation of a rhizomatic imagination. To this end, Hallsworth identifies the promise of the phenomenological methods of cultural criminology (2008: 13). In place of 'voodoo statistics' qualitative research methods are required that render intelligible the 'ecologies' of street crime, the rules of violence as understood by protagonists themselves (Young 2004; Hallsworth 2008: 8ff).

The broader salience of this Deleuzian influence on the criminological imagination is that it disturbs the impulse in much critical, as well as governmental, criminology to police the conceptual as well as methodological boundaries of how crime and disorder should be represented. For the inclination to reduce explanations of community safety to the regulation of capital accumulation or the effects of political rationality are as 'arboreal' in their delimitation of criminalisation processes as the problem-solving paraphernalia of Home Office research. In these terms, Deleuzian criminology is performative *par excellence*, preoccupied as it is with deconstructing the over-rationalised, patterned and structured imagery of crime, disorder and control found in official and some critical social science as a means of promoting an alternative rhizomatic vision of control.

It is clear, however, that Haggerty and Ericson's notion of the 'security assemblage' and Hallsworth's 'violence ecologies' are also offered as *superior representations* of crime, disorder and control, superior that is to the official and critical criminologies they have first deconstructed and dismissed as 'arboreal'. It is questionable, however, whether it is possible to ever escape arboreal representations of social life; does a non-arboreal representation of the 'inherent contingent amorphous volatility of street life' or the 'rhizomatic expansion of surveillance' imply an inherently contingent amorphous and volatile or rhizomatic method of inquiry and argumentation? How can the mutable, open-ended, quality of the social relations signified by the idea of community safety be represented in ways that avoid the structuring devices of social science, including, ironically, those of *post*-structuralist thinkers? For whilst the 'smooth' narratives of modern social science have been challenged for necessarily traducing the complexity and messiness of the very objects they seek to represent (Law 2004), it is notable these challenges are themselves invariably articulated through smooth, structured, and coherent narratives.

Conclusion

In summary, this diagnosis of four alternative narratives about community safety demonstrates how both official and academic accounts are performative in bringing into being ways of thinking about crime, disorder and control that were hitherto unimagined. Whether conceived as a progressive, problem-solving activity, a repressive state apparatus, a political rationality or an arboreal vision of control, however, each of these accounts also makes claims about the limits of other narratives as, for example, misrepresentations of political choices as matters of technical measurement or of volatile practices as structured and rational action. In turn this alerts us to the necessary, rather than contingent, relationship between the performative and representational dimensions of the criminological imagination. Whereas some advocates of performative thinking, such as those associated with the study of governmentality, believe it possible to dispense with representational thinking in order to liberate the criminological imagination to conceive 'how not to be governed thus' (O'Malley 2006), our contention is that any diagnosis entails criticism and this entails representational claims about how the world is now as a precursor to imagining how else it could be in prospect.

Given the inescapable dependence on representational knowledge claims, criminological imagination is better cultivated through a direct engagement with, rather than circumvention of, the 'burdens of sociological realism' (Rose and Miller 1992). In these terms theories of community safety as a progressive third way, repressive state apparatus, political rationality and arboreal vision of control provide useful abstractions from geo-historically specific practices. Elsewhere we have outlined what a critical realist programme of research into such practices could look like (Edwards and Hughes 2005; Hughes 2007). Here it suffices to conclude with a call for the development of criminological imagination through research programmes into concrete, criminalised practices and their control.

Notes

1 In social science the concept of 'performativity' is associated with the linguist J. L. Austin's (1955) discussion of 'speech acts' which bring into being the objects they signify rather than just describing or representing them, for example 'I bet you ...' brings into being a wager, 'marry me', a betrothal, and so on. More recently the concept has been applied in studies of gender (Butler 1990) or markets (Callon 1998) to consider the ways in which theories of sexuality or economics don't just describe objective social relations but constitute them. As discussed below, in criminological thought, performativity is most obviously associated with the studies of governmentality which document the ways in which theories constitute the crimes and processes of control, the objects of study, which they then seek to explain (Smandych 1999).

2 As documented in research into the power of populist media representations of crime and disorder relative to the more subtle and sober representations of the academy in defining the acceptable parameters of the politics of law and order (Reiner 2007; Downes and Morgan 2002).

3 For those arguing for a performative criminology, unfettered by any need to represent 'reality', circumventing this contest is precisely the point but then, of course, one is liberated to be as cruel as one likes.

4 It may be noted that the 'export' of social crime prevention and community safety ideas and practice in Australia in the 1990s appears to have been an interesting admixture of the managerialist and social democratic pragmatism of the Morgan Report alongside an emphasis on the symbolic social inclusivist and socialist politics of social crime prevention associated with the Bonnemaison experiment in the 1980s in France (personal communication between Gordon Hughes and Adam Sutton, University of Melbourne).

5 The British crime prevention expert, Professor Ken Pease, has argued, 'It is of interest that the Morgan Committee preferred the phrase "community safety" over "crime prevention" because the latter "is often narrowly interpreted and this reinforces the view that it is solely the responsibility of the police" ... The extreme vagueness of the Morgan Committee's definition of community safety gives no confidence that the revised definition will provide a satisfactory focus for the work.' (Pease 1994: 687 n11).

6 It is important to recognise that community safety work, however defined, has had a significant institutional presence across local authorities and police forces in the UK both before and more markedly since the 1998 Crime and Disorder Act. Estimated, never mind precise, numbers of public servants engaged in community safety-qua-crime and disorder reduction work are not easy to pin down. This is of course due to the capacious character of community safety *per se* and its currently rapid expansion and colonisation of both old and new areas of local governance,

such as 'waste management', 'regeneration', 'youth inclusion', 'city centre management' and so on . However, if we restrict ourselves to dedicated community safety team members in local authorities across England and Wales, a conservative estimate would be minimally about 3,000 public servants.

7 This emphasis on crime reduction in the first instance and latterly also disorder reduction has been given intellectual support and seen the production of new governmental technologies such as GIS mapping, hot spot analyses, situational measures, and so on, the so-called 'new criminologies of everyday life' (Garland 2001) and what we may term 'anti-social/anti-sociological' crime scientists formerly associated with the Home Office and now located in the Jill Dando Institute at University College London.

8 Following the passage of the Police and Justice Act 2006, the requirement on statutory Crime and Disorder Reduction Partnerships in England and Community Safety Partnerships in Wales to return tri-annual crime and disorder audits has been replaced by the requirement to submit annual strategic assessments of threats to community safety, defined primarily in terms of 'anti-social behaviour' and those street crimes measured by the British Crime Survey.

Chapter 5

Telling sentencing stories

Jacqueline Tombs

Introduction

This essay is about contemporary sentencing policy objectives and
the impossibility of their realisation through sentencing practices. Its
primary focus is not, however, upon the disjunction between policy
rhetoric and its achievement – though that gap certainly exists. Rather
it concerns ways in which policy rhetoric has become a reality for
sentencers and how this frames their practices. It explores the effects
of recent regulatory sentencing policies, which redefine the legitimate
knowledge base for the act of sentencing and which specify, in ever
more detail, both the form and content of the information sentencers
are to use in making their decisions. It is about how these shifts in
sentencing policy have narrowed the space for professional discretion
and judgment and about how this narrowing has provoked a new
layer of imaginary penality in sentencing; imaginary in the sense that
contemporary sentencing policy has made the realisation of its own
goals through sentencing practices less likely of achievement.

Sentencing has always been an imaginative art insofar as it
involves imagination and creative ability. The construction of stories
is central to legal judgment in criminal cases in general (Bennett
and Feldman 1981) and to sentencing in particular (Aas 2005; Tata
2007). In producing coherent sentencing narratives (see Hough *et al.*
2003; Tombs 2004; Jacobson and Hough 2007), sentencers consider the
'facts' of the cases presented to them, the information provided about
the circumstances surrounding the crime and offender in question,

and create interpretive frameworks within which those facts and circumstances considered relevant are evaluated. In short, in sentencing they aim to 'tell a story' that is meaningful; that makes sense in terms of the sentence imposed. Sentencing is also imaginative in the sense that judges, for the most part, cannot know if the sentence they impose actually achieves its purpose – other than for those sentences imposed simply on grounds of denunciation, though most sentences typically involve multiple purposes. Even with strictly incapacitative sentences, aimed at public protection, in most instances offenders will eventually be released. In terms of other sentencing purposes, at the point of imposition sentencers can only imagine the impact of their sentences; they cannot know whether their sentences 'work'. They sentence because they 'hope' that something will happen; that their sentences will – at least some of the time – achieve what they want them to.

This was all clear to me whilst conducting a sentencing research project in Scotland (Tombs 2004) and during subsequent discussions with members of the Scottish judiciary.[1] But what also became increasingly clear was that something else was going on in relation to sentencing; something that narrowed sentencers' choices and inhibited them from being able to tell sentencing stories based on as textured information, as open a list of 'facts about the case' and 'circumstances of the offender', as they had been previously able to, and which, at the same time, 'compelled' them into sending more low level recidivist offenders to prison. Sentencers told me that in framing their sentencing decisions they must have regard to new legislative restrictions and (by implication at least) the policy goals they embed. Most importantly, they told me about how information presented to them in order to aid their decision-making – risk assessments, national standards, performance management regimes – had restricted their discretion. At the same time, however, in order to sentence individuals (as opposed to legal categories of offenders), they continued to draw on traditional sentencing values (for example, showing mercy) and their creative abilities in constructing meaningful stories about the crimes committed by contextualised individuals. Yet it is precisely this context that is increasingly eroded for them by current sentencing policies. And it is in the erasure of context and meaning that we find imaginary penality in sentencing (see Carlen, Chapter 1). Whereas discretion allows judges to use their judicial competence[2] to combine rules in the ways best suited to the case in hand and thereby to impose imaginative (that is, creative) sentences which are open to (that is, influenced by) the peculiarities of specific cases, imaginary penalities are not open to the peculiarities of specific cases, but rather are pre-directed at a closure engineered by a variety of (often opposed) bureaucratic rules designed not for doing justice but for controlling risk. The rest of this article then, which draws on the Scottish sentencing study, is structured around the main argument that:

i.   the managerialist project embedded in late modern attempts to structure judicial discretion in terms of new forms of accountability and within the context of punitive populism has been self-defeating because

ii. incorporation of various social accounting procedures to make the achievement of policy goals more certain has had the opposite effect as

iii. imaginative sentencing is suppressed and supplanted by an imaginary penality.

Regulating judicial discretion

Few areas of criminal processing have come under as much political, media and public scrutiny over the past few decades as judicial discretion in sentencing. Though the forms which the search to 'structure' this discretion has taken are peculiar to late modern times, the focus on the control, sometimes erasure, of judicial discretion in sentencing goes back a long way (see Thomas 1979, 2003). Commenting in the early nineteenth century on the unlimited discretion of the judges in England and Wales in deciding whether or not to reprieve an offender for execution, Romilly wrote:

If so large a discretion as this can be safely entrusted to any magistrates, the legislature ought at least to lay down some general rules to direct or assist them in the exercise of it, that there might be, if not a perfect uniformity in the administration of justice, yet the same spirit always prevailing, the same maxims left in view. (Romilly 1810: 15)

More general concerns about arbitrariness, idiosyncrasy and injustice in sentencing intensified in the latter part of the nineteenth century. These were expressed in the press, in legal journals, by government, by liberal reformers, by humanitarian groups and by judges themselves (see Thomas 1979). The apparent 'disparity' in the sentences pronounced by the judiciary on individuals was portrayed as a consequence of their unlimited discretion in making sentencing decisions. To ensure consistency in sentencing, and thereby justice, the solutions proposed to control this discretion centred on providing a 'standard' which, 'might be obtained either by Act of Parliament, by an Order in Council, or even by agreement amongst the judges themselves' (Lord Penzance, cited in Thomas 1979: 48).

Similarly, during the latter part of the twentieth century, concerns about arbitrariness, injustice and the abuse of power in sentencing (all of which were attributed to the relatively unfettered use of judicial discretion) resurfaced with a vengeance under the guise of proportionality and 'just deserts' (see Frankel 1972; Morris 1974; von Hirsch 1976). This time the proposed solutions to curtail sentencing power centred, in the United States originally but subsequently elsewhere including Britain, on the introduction of sentencing guidelines, sentencing information systems and other formulaic devices which would provide 'transparency' and 'consistency' in judicial decision-making (see Aas 2005). But here the similarity of today's sentencing concerns with the concerns about judicial discretion in the nineteenth century ends. Though there were clearly populist pressures in relation to sentencing then, changes in the political climate in the late modern period have exaggerated these pressures (see Tonry 1992, 1996; Clarkson and Morgan 1995; Rex and Tonry 2002; Tata and Hutton 2002) to such an extent that what were originally conceived as 'liberal' reforms, aimed at keeping down levels of incarceration, have had diametrically opposite effects and have fuelled penal expansion (Rothman 2003; EFF 2004; Millie *et al.* 2007). The rise of punitive populism at a global level (see Pratt *et al.* 2005; Pratt 2007), coupled with the managerialist technique of social auditing (see Carlen, Chapter 1), have given the search for constraints on judicial discretion distinctive meanings and effects in contemporary penal culture. Earlier concerns about possible individual injustices and discriminatory practices have been overshadowed by concerns about judicial accountability. But this time accountability is not to the ideal of the rule of law in the name of justice but rather to the criminal processing system itself in the name of effectiveness. As Aas has argued,

The focus of judicial activity, therefore, shifts from reflection on the concrete circumstances of a case and the legal and ethical principles involved, to communication (account-giving) concerning judges' own decisions to the system. The question is not primarily whether a decision was appropriate or just, but rather whether it follows the prescribed procedural standards and is properly accounted for. (Aas 2005: 154)

Though the 'auditing' methods adopted have differed across jurisdictions, the common aim has been to limit the discretionary powers of the judiciary so that sentencing is more transparent, consistent and predictable and the achievement of sentencing policy goals more certain. With this shift in the critique of discretion, from a focus on the abuse of judicial power in relation to individuals to a concern with accountability to the system (see Garland 1997, 2001), came new forms of managerial control to regulate the activities of the judiciary along with the other professional groups working in the criminal processing system. The United States, for example, through the introduction of detailed numerical, matrix sentencing guidelines, illustrates just how far efforts to control the judiciary through auditable procedures can go. And, even though the United States stands alone in its use of matrix guidelines, other jurisdictions (including England and Wales and Scotland) have constructed their own methods for reconfiguring sentencing accountability.

The distinctiveness of the contemporary political desire to control the discretionary powers of the judiciary lies in the way in which accountability has been institutionalised within the context of punitive populism, especially through various techniques of social auditing – sentencing guidelines, sentencing information systems, risk assessment forms, and so on. These 'technologies of mistrust' (see Power 1999; Rose 1999) undermine the earlier legitimacy accorded to the professional knowledge and judgments of sentencers. Judicial discretion is about the power to balance, to make a choice based on professional knowledge and experience between alternative courses of action in relation to contextualised individuals. Discretion is not about following already prescribed courses of action as they relate to categories of offenders. But with the new forms of accountability the professional judgment of sentencers to pass sentences open to the peculiarities of specific cases is to be informed by formulaic devices generated by statistical probabilities as they relate to whole classes of crimes and offenders. And, at the same time, through these new formats and technologies, the activities of the judiciary can be monitored more closely and evaluated in terms of system rather than professional sentencing objectives; yet another example of the self-referentiality evident throughout the criminal processing system (see Ericson and Haggerty 1997; Garland 1999, 2001).

Reconfiguring sentencing structures

As noted above, the rise of punitive populism, coupled with the managerialist technique of social auditing, have given the search for constraints on judicial discretion distinctive meanings and effects across jurisdictions. In England and Wales, since the 1990s, sentencing policy has become heavily politicised, restrictive and severe. Populist sentencing policies introduced by both the Conservative and New Labour governments (see Downes 1998), under an endless series of statutes,[3] have sought to narrow the space for judicial discretion (Dunbar and Langdon 1998; Ashworth 2001) by, for example: the introduction of mandatory minimum sentences, the raising of maximum sentences, escalating penalties for persistent offenders, increasingly punitive community orders, and the proliferation of preventive orders (Anti-Social Behaviour Orders being the most infamous). All the new community measures have been backed by prison for offenders' breaches of sentence and various new ways of reconfiguring the information to be used by sentencers in making their decisions have been established.

It was within this context that the Sentencing Advisory Panel[4] was established by the Crime and Disorder Act 1998 to advise the Court of Appeal on guidelines for sentencing particular types of offences. In giving advice, the Panel must take account of sentencing statistics, the effectiveness and costs of penal measures and must consult both with the public and an approved list of organisations. Until 1998, the review of sentences by the Court of Appeal alone,[5] since its first meeting in 1908, had provided the basis for judicial self-regulation within a relatively loose statutory framework (see Thomas 1979, 2003). Now, under the Criminal Justice Act 2003, the Sentencing Advisory Panel's function is to advise the Sentencing Guidelines Council rather than the Court of Appeal. The Council, chaired by the Lord Chief Justice, is responsible for issuing sentencing guidelines 'to assist all courts in England and Wales, to help encourage consistent sentencing'.[6] The Council receives and considers the Sentencing Advisory Panel's draft guideline, issues its own draft guideline for consideration by the Home Secretary and the Home Affairs Committee of the House of Commons, receives their comments, and then formulates what is known as a 'definitive guideline'. The Council's obligation to consult politicians before issuing a definitive guideline was designed to manage an alleged 'democratic deficit' in pre-existing sentencing procedures (see Ashworth 2005).[7] Sentencers must have regard to such definitive guidelines in individual cases and give reasons if they wish to depart from an applicable one.

The Criminal Justice Act 2003 also, according to government claims, represented a major step towards achieving sentencing consistency in setting out the purposes of sentencing in statute for the first time in England and Wales.[8] The purposes of sentencing are the punishment of offenders, the reduction of crime (including its reduction by deterrence), the reform and rehabilitation of offenders, the protection of the public, and the making of reparation by offenders to persons affected by their offences (section 142,1). *Justice for All*, the White Paper preceding the 2003 Act, argued that the aim of such statutory definition was to ensure that sentencers consider the various purposes and achieve 'the right balance' between them (Home Office 2002). Sentencers are to achieve the 'right balance' by making the assessment of offence seriousness, proportionality,[9] the main consideration in most sentencing decisions (section 143, 1). The Sentencing Guidelines Council's guideline, *Overarching Principles: – Seriousness* (2004), expands on how the right balance is to be achieved. Whilst emphasising that the proportionality principle is the benchmark, the guideline specifies when the other sentencing purposes are defensible. The purposes of reform and rehabilitation can be justified, but only after sentencers have first considered the seriousness of the offence and decided that a community sentence of a particular level is warranted.[10] Public protection, on the other hand, supersedes the principle of proportionality at the outset when dealing with so-called dangerous offenders.[11] The Act (sections 224–36) introduces three levels of sentence which the courts *must* impose where certain conditions taken to relate to the risk of 'dangerousness' are fulfilled: imprisonment for life, indeterminate sentences of imprisonment for public protection and extended sentences.[12]

The story of what this whole raft of sentencing reforms has achieved in England and Wales is complex. For, at the same time as an ever more restrictive and punitive sentencing policy has contributed to the judicial imposition of more prison sentences and for longer (see Hough *et al.* 2003; Jacobson and Hough 2007), judges themselves express considerable disquiet about governmental intervention and have felt – at least until now – under more pressure to impose severer sentences than they would have done if left alone to employ their judicial discretion, and certainly more severe sentences than those being imposed for similar crimes by Scottish judges (Millie *et al.* 2007).

During the 1990s Scotland did not experience anything like the power struggles that occurred between the judiciary and the legislature in England and Wales (Ashworth 2001). At the same time, members of the senior Scottish judiciary have been much less ready to express their views publicly on legislative changes than have their counterparts south of the border.[13] While sentencers in Scotland have not escaped a growing number of legislative restrictions on their power, they have not (yet) experienced as much political intervention as sentencers in England and Wales. The slower rate of increase in the prison population in Scotland than in England and Wales throughout the 1990s can be attributed, at least in part, to a comparative absence of political interference in sentencing matters in Scotland (see Millie *et al.* 2007). Prior to the establishment of a devolved Scottish Parliament in 1999, Scottish penal policy was made primarily by civil servants and non-governmental experts working in Edinburgh, working at a distance from their politicians based at the UK government in London. Scottish politicians played a much less important role in sentencing matters than they did in England and Wales and sentencing power remained more firmly in the judges' own hands.[14] The comparative absence of political involvement in sentencing policy *and* Scotland's common law tradition, which gives the judiciary considerable freedom to expand or restrict the law, has resulted in few rules or guidelines governing the exercise of judicial discretion (see Tombs 2004, 2005). There is no penal code and no statutory statement of the purposes of sentencing; though such a statutory statement was recommended by the now dissolved Sentencing Commission for Scotland (SCS 2006).[15] A large proportion of sentencing decisions relate to common law crimes which, with the exception of murder,[16] have no mandatory sentences. Also, there are no maximum penalties for common law crimes apart from the limits imposed by the sentencing powers of the particular court in which a case is sentenced. Maximum sentences are, however, set out in statutory offences – of which there have been many in recent years – and legislation has increasingly specified the imposition of minimum sentences.[17] Unlike England and Wales, few Court of Appeal 'guideline judgments' have been issued in Scotland and there is no system of sentencing guidelines. But this is changing. Scotland has not escaped global trends towards ever more punitive responses to crime and it has not escaped the 'dead hand of managerialism' (Carlen, Chapter 1). The shift towards greater regulation of judicial discretion, though it has come later and the degree of embeddedness may be less, is as evident in contemporary Scots penal culture as soaring incarceration rates and the obsession with risk and managerialism are in all parts of the criminal processing system.

Since 1999, when the establishment of a devolved Scottish Parliament promised to give Scotland more democratic control over Scottish matters,[18] politicians have played an increasingly direct and significant role in penal policy. Scotland's first government since 1707, a Labour-led coalition with the Liberal Democrats, set about producing a series of policy reports (see, for example, MacLean 2000; Cosgrove 2001; Bonomy 2002; Normand 2003; McInnes 2004; Scottish Executive 2000, 2004, 2006) and legislative enactments aimed at increasing efficiency and effectiveness throughout the criminal processing system. In the name of providing better public protection *and* crime reduction a series of new authorities were established.[19] At the time of writing, the story goes on with the publication of yet another review of community penalties aimed at 'reforming and revitalising' their use and effectiveness (see Scottish Government 2007). As in England and Wales, and indeed other countries, these policies have addressed putative popular demands for punitive sentencing by making increasingly extravagant claims about their public protection and crime reduction potentialities (Carlen, Chapter 1). And all, in seeking to achieve policy goals through sentencing practices, have restricted the discretion of the judges to use their judicial competence to combine rules in the ways best suited to the case in hand and thereby to impose imaginative (that is, creative) sentences which are open to (that is, influenced by) the peculiarities of specific cases. Albeit with distinctive and uneven expression and effect, imaginative sentencing has been suppressed and supplanted by imaginary penalties in sentencing which, not being open to the peculiarities of specific cases are, instead, pre-directed at a closure engineered by diverse (often opposed) bureaucratic rules designed for controlling risk rather than doing justice.

Sentencing, actuarialism and risk

Actuarially-based methodologies and techniques of risk assessment and its management have been increasingly influential throughout the criminal processing system, including sentencing (Feeley and

Simon 1992, 1994). This is not, however, to argue that sentencers' own assessments of risk have not been previously important in making sentencing decisions. Rather, it is to point out that 'sentencers' informal calculations about risk of recidivism were not … elevated into a science of actuarialism until the last third of the twentieth century' (Carlen, Chapter 1). The emergence and development of this 'science of actuarialism' in relation to penal matters paralleled shifts in the classification and assessment of 'dangerousness'. The calibration of dangerousness, previously assessed on the basis of an individual's past offending, now involved a concern with the probability of future crime to protect the public from 'dangerous offenders' – typically reconstituted as serious violent and/or sexual offenders (see Pratt 1995, 2000) – and the concept of risk became 'an orienting principle around which decisions about appropriate responses to perceived danger are conceived and organised' (Brown 2000: 93). As with governments in many other countries (Pratt 1995), the government in Scotland legislated to protect the public from dangerous offenders at the same time as actuarially-based methodologies provided potent penal strategies for predicting, managing and controlling the probability of their future crime (see Simon 1998; Feeley 2004). The penal objective of predicting the future specifically for 'dangerous offenders' soon saw its expression in a variety of forms and formats – in parole prediction tables, sentencing guidelines, and a package of risk assessment techniques – providing prototypes for predicting the likelihood of reoffending for low level recidivist offenders as well. The assessment of risk was no longer primarily to be made on the basis of sentencers' own professional knowledge and experience. Now this professional judgment was to be 'assisted', sometimes controlled, by the predictive values and scores arrived at through the use of actuarially-based risk instruments.

For example, in Scotland the 1998 legislation on extended sentences for serious sexual and violent offenders[20] requires that sentencers obtain a social enquiry report, which must include a formal assessment of the risk posed by an offender, before imposing such a sentence. Extended sentences, which comprise a period of imprisonment ('the custodial term') and a period of licence ('the extension period'), are discretionary but can only be imposed where the judge considers on the basis of all the 'facts' of the case, including the risk assessment, that the offender will constitute a threat to public safety on release. In imposing an extended sentence the judge is required to consider the actual extension period necessary to protect the public from serious harm and it is in this context that risk assessments come to the fore. Appeal Court opinions are replete with references to the levels of risk assessed and the imposition of sentences and/or extension periods have been quashed due to 'low risk' assessments and/or the failure to order assessment reports (see Brown 2007: 55–71). Similarly, the assessment of risk in social enquiry reports has been central to Appeal Court opinions in relation to supervised release orders (SROs) introduced in 1995 for those convicted of a serious offence other than a sexual offence and, though sentenced to less than four years' imprisonment, considered to present a risk of serious harm to the public on release.[21] As with extended sentences, Appeal Court opinions have quashed the imposition of SROs as incompetent because, for example, a risk assessment report had not been ordered thereby preventing the sentencer from being able to make a proper assessment of risk (see Brown 2007: 71–7).

Legislation requiring sentencers to consider risk assessments in sentencing serious violent and sexual offenders was further extended by the Criminal Justice (Scotland) Act 2003.[22] Amidst media and political claims of extreme public concern about the risks posed by such offenders, the Scottish government provided risk assessment and management with its own institutional form. The 2003 Act created a new public body, the Risk Management Authority (RMA), new provisions for the assessment and sentencing of high-risk offenders, and a new sentence, the order for lifelong restriction (OLR). The RMA[23] was constituted as a national centre for expert advice on offender risk assessment and risk management to address two alleged problems: first the lack of interagency communication and information exchange about high risk offenders whose liberty presents a risk to the public; and second, the absence of national standards and consistency in risk assessment and risk minimisation approaches. Despite the lack of predictive certainty with risk assessment methodologies and the well known fallibility of judgments of dangerousness (Brown and Pratt 2000; Monahan 2004), in the words of one of the senior civil servants responsible for introducing the RMA, 'the scientific community convinced policy makers that there is evidence to bring to bear on risk assessment and ministers are fully behind it [the RMA] … they [ministers] think the public will be reassured'.[24] The policy goals were to achieve public protection and crime reduction through 'ensuring the effective assessment and minimisation of risk' (2003 Act section 3, 1). And the RMA was to play a crucial role in relation to the new order for lifelong restriction (OLR) by providing arrangements to assess the risk posed by an alleged serious violent and/or sexual offender and for minimising any risk established subsequent to that assessment. The OLR, which can only be imposed by judges in the High Court, is an indeterminate prison sentence intended for offenders assessed as meeting specified risk criteria. Various risk assessment procedures are involved before an OLR can be imposed. First the court can make a 'risk assessment order' if a person is convicted of a sexual offence, a violent offence, an offence which endangers life, or an offence the nature or circumstances of which indicate a propensity to commit such offences and if it appears that the 'risk criteria' may be met. On a risk assessment order an offender can be remanded in custody for up to 90 days during which time a 'risk assessment report' is to be prepared by a person 'accredited' by the RMA and must follow RMA guidance. In imposing an OLR, the judge sets a punishment part and after serving this period of imprisonment, an offender's release depends on a 'risk management plan'. This plan must include an 'assessment of risk', the 'measures to be taken for the minimisation of risk, and how such measures are to be co-ordinated'; all of this to be approved by the RMA. If released, the Parole Board will set licence conditions and following release the risk management plan is to be implemented in the community. The stated purpose of the risk management plan is to ensure that an offender's risk is 'effectively managed' on a multidisciplinary basis. Agencies with statutory responsibilities such as the Scottish Prison Service, local authority criminal justice social work services and health providers are required to collaborate on the preparation of risk management plans. The agency responsible for writing and submitting the plan to RMA is known as the lead authority; the RMA can give direction to the lead authority about the risk management plan and to the practitioners involved in risk management, and plans are subject to RMA annual review and amendment. Established in 2005, the RMA has been involved with the seven orders for lifelong restriction imposed since the sentence became available in the High Court in 2006. Otherwise, it has promoted its wider remit in relation to the accreditation of risk assessors, training practitioners in risk methodologies and commissioning research.

In addition to this institutional manifestation of how deeply governmental penal policy on risk has penetrated in Scotland, sentencers are routinely presented with the information drawn from a plethora of risk assessment tools[25] used by social workers, psychologists and other professionals in the criminal processing system, not only in relation to preventive sentences of imprisonment for public protection but more widely in relation to assessing the possibility of rehabilitation through community sentences. Under national standards, local authority criminal justice social workers in Scotland have been responsible for the production of actuarially-based risk assessments in pre-sentence social enquiry reports for a wide range of offenders, low level recidivist offenders, first offenders, young offenders and so on, since the early 1990s. Similarly, in England and Wales 'risk assessment' is now central to the production of probation officers' pre-sentence reports and is generally undertaken using the Offender Assessment System (OASys) tool; a standardised, electronic process by which all offenders subject to pre-sentence reports (and other categories of offender) are assessed in terms of their likelihood of reoffending, the risk they pose to themselves and others, and their practical, social and psychological needs (see Jacobson and Hough 2007). At the time of writing, the Risk Management Authority, in collaboration with the Scottish Government, Scottish Prison Service and Association of Directors of Social Work, plan to introduce a 'national risk assessment and minimisation instrument' aimed at reducing reoffending. This instrument, the Level of Service Case Management Inventory (LS/CMI) Scotland, is an 'electronic system' combining risk and needs assessment with case management across agencies and will be used for offenders in prison and in the community (Scottish Government 2007).

Sentencers' own assessments of risk of recidivism, whether for the purpose of securing protective and/or rehabilitative sentencing aims were, and still are, based on their professional knowledge and experience, together with the knowledge about individual offenders and the circumstances surrounding specific criminal events presented to judges by other criminal justice professionals. These assessments have, however, increasingly been framed within discourses imbued with actuarially-based knowledges of risk. This is reflected in Appeal Court opinions, which are nowadays replete with discussions of the competence of sentencing decisions in light of whether or not appropriate risk assessments have been secured from other relevant criminal justice professionals prior to sentencing. The concern with risk is also evident in judges' own reports to the Appeal Court which characteristically emphasise how risk assessments have been used in arriving at specific sentences.

The foregoing detail of the bureaucratisation of risk is somewhat dense. But it is the very density and embeddedness of risk management technologies which make them unamenable to easy analysis and, in default of any transparency, imbues them with an aura of expertise and authority. The detail of the criminal risk apparatus has been presented to demonstrate the extent to which technologies of risk assessment and management have affected judicial discretion in sentencing through the restrictions and classifications embedded in the information presented to aid sentencers in their decision-making (Aas 2005). This information, routinely supplied to sentencers by other groups of criminal justice professionals, is formatted and presented in certain ways according to various modes of social accounting – compliance with national standards, performance management regimes, accreditation procedures and the like. The argument is that these methods of social accounting *and* the technologies and practices of risk have gelled with legislative regulations governing judicial discretion and that this coalescence, within the current climate of punitive populism, has provoked imaginary penalties in sentencing. These imaginary penalities have themselves contributed, in diverse yet significant ways, to more and more low level recidivist offenders going to prison thus rendering the policy goals of crime reduction and public protection ever less likely of achievement.

Sentencing imaginings and realities

Today's sentencers in Scotland and elsewhere are required to frame their sentencing decisions within legally prescribed parameters – minimum and mandatory sentences, sentencing information aids, requirements for risk assessment reports and so on. These parameters have narrowed the space for the use of discretion based on judges' own professional knowledge and experience. None the less, within that space judges still have to pass sentences in specific cases, and they still have the authority to make the sentences appropriate to the individuals in the dock. It is thus in such a context that Scottish sentencers act *as if* their sentencing decision is framed within the reality created by recent policy emphases on risk assessment, prediction and anticipatory control, at the same time as they still act within their continuing, albeit increasingly challenged, authority to individualise sentences. Though the discretionary space has been narrowed, judges still pursue traditional sentencing aims, especially rehabilitation. And, above all, they still try to sentence according to values (for example, showing mercy) that privilege their own professional knowledge and experience as judges rather than the policy goals of politicians – as the managerialist thrust in penal matters would have them do (see Bonomy 2002). And it is here, in the sentencing of specific cases within the context of a politicised managerialism, that the clash between traditionally creative, imaginative sentencing and the new imaginary penalities can be observed.

Analysis of data collected in my sentencing study (Tombs 2004) reveals several ways in which these imaginary penalities have not resulted in achieving the sentencing policy goals of reducing reoffending and ensuring public protection but instead have achieved more incarceration and for longer periods. Sentencing, as was noted earlier in this chapter, has always been – and still is – imaginative in the sense that judges can only imagine the impact of their sentences; they cannot know, with the exception of denunciation (which is not stated as a purpose of sentencing in the Criminal Justice Act 2003), whether their sentences will be effective in achieving sentencing purposes. For the most part they sentence in expectation; they 'hope' that something will work. Scottish judges, like their counterparts elsewhere, have also for many years sought to achieve multiple purposes in sentencing, for example, by arguing that public protection may be best served if the risk posed by an offender is dealt with by a rehabilitative sentence.

> The extent to which a sentence can effect a degree of rehabilitation can meet the purpose of protection of the public. (Judge 3)[26]

And all were emphatic that sentencing aims 'have to be thought out in relation to individual cases'. But sentencers were uncertain about the capacity of sentences to prevent recidivism. They emphasised that a community sentence would often be imposed in a 'borderline custodial case' because there were hopeful signs that the offender could be rehabilitated (see also Hough *et al.* 2003; Tombs and Jagger 2006). They talked about giving 'an optimistic sentence', about looking 'to see if there is a hope'. Even when they were not optimistic, they spoke about giving an offender 'a chance', particularly with young people.

> I was by no means confident that I wouldn't see him for something else before he went on the course … but anyway, I gave him a chance. I don't know what will happen, I don't know whether it will be successful or not. I hope it will. (Judge 15)

Sentencers also talked about hope in relation to the potentially deterrent effect of prison sentences.

> It is to be hoped – and that may be a rather forlorn hope – that people will be deterred [by imprisonment] … but I don't have any evidence that severe sentences do that. (Judge 1)

Even with strictly incapacitative sentences imposed to protect the public, there could be no certainty; given that offenders will eventually be released from prison, the risk to the public may re-emerge. Sentencers could not be certain, for example, that an offender would 'co-operate' with a sex offender programme offered in prison. Likewise it was impossible to predict the effectiveness (or even the existence) of any such programme in terms of preventing recidivism.

And when they had run out of hope completely with low level recidivist offenders, when 'something had to be done', it was time to impose a retributive sentence (Tombs and Jagger 2006).

At the bottom end it is this repeat, repeat, repeat offences, and eventually you just run out of options and the only thing left is a custodial sentence ... you've given them every chance and they haven't taken it, and really you have no option left. (Judge 27)

Nevertheless, judges had to believe that the sentences imposed by the courts could be 'effective'. And what gave them 'signs of hope' depended crucially on their ability to individualise sentences in terms of the 'facts' of the case and the knowledge they had of the individuals who came before them for sentence. To give someone a chance, for example, involved making meaningful assessments about the character of individuals as well as the material realities of their lives. Such judicial shrewdness, born of years of experience, local knowledge and professional values, is, however, increasingly restricted by penal policy reforms that provide 'information' for sentencing in 'predefined packages of meaning' (Aas 2005) – risk assessments, sentencing information systems, the threat of guidelines – that decontextualise individual offenders thus making the individual subject a 'collection of characteristics' rather than a whole person with a coherent identity. As a consequence, sentencers are rendered 'consumers of meaning' (Rodaway 1995) rather than its creators. Having to pass sentences in specific cases where individuals are increasingly decontextualised by formulaic risk tools makes it more difficult for sentencers to understand the meaning of the criminal event(s) in the offender's life and, at the same time, narrows the space for hope to emerge. As a consequence, and with low level recidivist offenders in particular, the time comes more quickly when 'something has to be done', where custody is imposed as 'the last resort'.

The more that sentencing policy has promoted legislation, instruments and matrices to identify those characteristics of offenders as a class that are considered relevant in sentencing aimed at crime reduction and public protection goals, the less the judges can know about who they are sentencing. The judges' stories suggest that the features of what offenders are like, their characters as well as their social and material context, are blurred rather than sharpened (compare with Clear and Cadora 2001) by the new formatted knowledges and predefined packages of meaning. Instead of clarifying what the judges want to know about in sentencing, knowledge of the offender is now buried beneath the weight of all the managerialist apparatus and a 'hyperactive frenzy of legislation' (Loader 2007/8: 41). Scottish judges expressed considerable frustration with the amount and speed of legislative change (see also Jacobson and Hough 2007) in relation to the judiciary's views on this in England and Wales) and repeatedly observed that the statutory provisions in relation to sentencing had become 'hugely complex' and that though there were now more non-custodial sentences, 'the more rules, the less we can use them'. They argued for 'simplifying the whole procedure' in relation to sentencing in general and non-custodial sentencing in particular.

It needs to be made easier for us to impose the non-custodial option. There are a lot of hoops ... There are statutory matters that you've got to explain ... there'll be some judges who'll be sitting there, thinking, 'I'll need to look up how I impose one of these things', so they don't bother imposing it ... they kid themselves on the proper thing to do is just to jail the guy because that's easy. (Judge 14)

Punitive sentencing as a consequence of more rules and increased complexity was seen to be compounded by the self-referentiality inherent in performance management systems and national standards used to audit the success of criminal justice professionals in meeting system generated targets. For example, the sheer volume of cases coming before the courts (attributed by judges to performance measurement regimes for procurators fiscal, Scotland's public prosecutors), meant more prison sentences.

The trouble is they [public prosecutors] are just doing things according to particular policies and formulae. They've had stringent new targets imposed on the time it takes to report cases

... work is coming flooding into the court ... there's no time to give proper consideration to community penalties. (Judge 33)

Sentencers also argued that national standards for the provision of pre-sentence social enquiry reports had significant implications for what they conceived of as a 'good' social enquiry report from criminal justice social workers.

The national standards seem to be getting more and more complicated. They're being followed, I think, for social workers to protect themselves rather than give a good report ... there's always the temptation with national standards for a person to take their eye off the problem and focus on the rules. (Judge 16)

In sentencers' estimation then, social workers' concerns about disciplinary audit, about adhering to the rules rather than producing a 'good report', made a prison sentence more likely.

If all they [local authority criminal justice social work departments] do is improve delivery against a set of ideal nationally driven standards and performance indicators there's no guarantee ... that local judges are going to use their non-custodial disposals any more. (Judge 27)

The new rules and formats for the presentation of information to sentencers prior to sentence made it more likely that they would impose a prison sentence in other ways. Sentencers typically conceived of a 'good report' in terms of how much it was able to tell them about an individual offender and the circumstances surrounding the criminal event(s). However, given the emphasis on risk assessment in national standards, judges' knowledge of all the factors they typically consider in passing sentence in specific cases was disappearing. The 'traditional emphasis' of social enquiry reports on 'rehabilitation and helping offenders' had been replaced by an emphasis on non-transformative risk management and control. A Scottish judge, with sentencing experience stretching back 30 years, has commented on the significance of this shift for sentencers.

In their social enquiry reports, social workers were [increasingly] asked to report on the offender's attitude to his offending, on his empathy or lack of it with his victims and to assess the offender's likelihood of re-offending. Somehow, the individual offender got lost in all this, and social enquiry reports stopped telling us what an offender was like. (Scott 2005: 24)

Similarly, several sentencers who were critical of the formulaic nature of the risk-based instruments used by criminal justice social workers to measure risk of reoffending, who argued that these devices were 'too rigid' and used pre-defined criteria in a 'pseudo-scientific manner' (as Jacobson and Hough (2007) found with judges in England and Wales), also mentioned that their knowledge of the individual had been 'lost'. This erasure of contextualised individuals through their assignment to 'risk categories' had the effect of restricting sentencers' discretionary power to individualise sentences; particularly in their decisions about sentencing in cases considered as on the borderline between custodial and non-custodial sentences.

Some sentencers[27] argued that the 'business' of risk assessment itself had made the imposition of a prison sentence more likely.

All that risk assessment stuff reduces the options. We get [social enquiry] reports saying things like 'there is no focus here for probation'. Social workers are not as flexible as they were. (Judge 8)

This 'tendency to risk inflation' in social enquiry reports (see also Fitzgibbon (2007) on pre-sentence reports in England and Wales) increased the likelihood of a custodial sentence being imposed. Similarly, the requirement for sentencers to obtain additional risk assessments in some cases meant that more people were in custody on remand for longer periods.

When I come to sentence, and he's been in custody all this time, and the reason he's been in custody is that in this type of case … nowadays, you've got to call for a report from a chartered psychologist and for a social enquiry report … all these risk assessments nowadays draw out the whole process. (Judge 26)

Several sentencers further observed that the risk assessment business reduced their options insofar as it consumed resources that might otherwise be devoted to community sentences.

I despair of this Risk Management Authority … and the only thing it doesn't do is manage risks. It's all about setting standards

... and you can bet their five million pound budget will be coming out of the same budget for the people who are actually doing the work with offenders in the community. (Judge 18)

More generally, sentencers argued that government policies, including the contracting out of public services, adversely affected the implementation of community sentences in ways that made it more likely that a prison sentence would be imposed. This was noted, for example, in relation to supervised attendance orders, which may be used instead of either imposing a fine or imposing a prison sentence for fine default.

The supervised attendance order scheme ... it's a piecemeal sort of thing ... what happened was that they [the local authority social work department] thought there weren't enough referrals to continue to contract it out in financial terms ... so they took it away from Apex and said they would supervise it themselves. But then they found they couldn't do it. (Judge 39)

In particular, sentencers doubted the rehabilitative and reparative potentialities of inadequately resourced community sentences.

If these disposals are not properly supported and resourced then I, as a judge, and no doubt my colleagues, lose confidence in them, and decide that these things are not effective. (Judge 22)

And not infrequently, when they had wanted to impose a non-custodial sentence, notably community service, they had imposed prison instead. This judges attributed to the unacceptable waiting periods before such orders could be implemented due to increasing resource constraints on those criminal justice practitioners responsible for implementing sentences in the community.

If you make a community service order they [the local authority social work department] say they won't be able to start it for four months ... this waiting period alters judges' opinions. I take the view that community service can't be provided so I'm going to send someone to prison. (Judge 16)

Similarly, the strict criteria of eligibility for a drug treatment and testing order (DTTO) meant that judges were unable to impose such sentences instead of prison.

We have got the situation where if somebody is remanded in custody he won't be accepted for the DTTO because he has stopped taking drugs. He's not now bad enough to be on a DTTO, and we say 'Well, we can't really send him out and say "go on, commit a few more crimes so that I can get you on a DTTO." ' (Judge 12)

Given the perceived lack of appropriate community sentences due to inadequate resourcing and 'crazy rules', and even though they expressed uncertainty about programme effectiveness, in hoping for 'something to work',[28] sentencers were very open to the rhetorical claims about the rehabilitative and reintegrative potential of in-prison programming and activities. This had an impact not only on sentencers' decisions to imprison but also on their decisions about the lengths of prison sentences.

And that – twelve months in prison – we were told is about the shortest meaningful sentence you can impose in terms of making any impact. If you serve six months then that's about the shortest prison sentence ... that will have a rehabilitative effect on an offender by way of having time to put them on one of these programmes. (Judge 8)

We've been told by senior people in the Scottish Prison Service that they can't organise any courses for people serving short sentences. They can't offer any rehabilitation. (Judge 17)

None the less, even when they sentenced people to custody 'in hope' that programmes would effect rehabilitation or 'in despair' because the offender's past 'failure' on community sentences and chaotic lifestyle meant that there was no other option (Tombs and Jagger 2006), and even when they 'knew' that desistance from offending had little, if anything, to do with their sentences, especially prison sentences, the maintenance of hope was central to their ability to do their jobs.

You're always hoping optimistically that the accused will not return, that in some way the sentence you impose on that occasion for those crimes may be the turning point ... it probably will be factors totally outwith our [sentencers'] control that may lead to them changing or slowing down in offending if they do so ... after 30 years I still don't know if the sentences I've imposed ever had any effect. (Judge 4)

So, what the judges' narratives about sentencing reveal is that in spite of the legislative and other restrictions on their discretion, in order to do their jobs, they held onto the hope of rehabilitation. At the same time they acknowledged that, with the offender increasingly buried beneath the weight of a politicised managerialism, and with that managerialism itself diverting more resources from community sentences to meet self generated performance goals, prison sentences were more likely. All of this detracted from rehabilitative sentencing in the community, thus making the achievement of sentencing policy goals more and more unrealisable.

Sentencing prospects

The new regulatory forms imposed on sentencing decision-making – risk assessments, national standards, minimum sentences, increased maximum sentences, protective sentencing, and so on – have clearly not achieved sentencing policy goals to reduce reoffending and provide improved public protection. So, instead of looking at this failure, instead of modifying policies, the Scottish government plans to introduce more regulations on sentencing power in pursuit of the same policy goals. Though Scotland is behind England and Wales in terms of the restrictions placed on judicial sentencing discretion, at the time of writing, the introduction of a sentencing guidelines system is under consideration. Before being dissolved in 2006, the Sentencing Commission for Scotland, in its final report on *The Scope to Improve Consistency in Sentencing*, recommended the introduction of an Advisory Panel on Sentencing in Scotland (APSS). Its purpose would be to produce draft guidelines to submit to the Appeal Court. The power to approve or decline to approve any sentencing guideline would rest with the Appeal Court (SCS 2006). Though in comparison with other guidelines systems this model still leaves the judiciary in control, Scottish sentencers viewed such a proposal as the first step on the way to something much more restrictive. While sentencing guideline judgments from the Appeal Court (of which there are presently only a few) were fully consistent with the tradition of judicial self-regulation enshrined in Scotland's common law approach, judges expressed concern about recent political and public 'interference' in sentencing and argued that this threat to judicial independence would intensify with the introduction of a guidelines system.

> There is considerable resentment from the judges at so-called advice from the Scottish Executive on sentencing … it is compromising judicial independence. I see guidelines as more interference. (Judge 35)

> Pressure groups are much more influential. That would become stronger with guidelines. (Judge 12)

The introduction of guideline systems undoubtedly opens up possibilities for more managerial control and surveillance over the judiciary and over how they exercise their sentencing power (Aas 2005). Scottish sentencers are resistant to this challenge and frequently made reference to the disciplinary effects of guidelines, especially 'strict guidelines' that 'tie you down'.

> Sentencing guidelines will become more than guidelines and be referred to on appeal and form a kind of straitjacket for the sentencer. (Judge 14)

More than this, they viewed the 'tick box approach' as an 'improper way to administer justice'.

> One of the dangers with [having] guidelines is that you end up with the judge trying to make sure the Appeal Court knows you followed the guidelines rather than do justice to the case … you then get tangled up with the rules; demonstrating that you've read the guidelines. (Judge 21)

> You've got to do justice to the individual case. Highly structured guidelines remove the flexibility necessary for the individual case. (Judge 3)

Above all, sentencers argued, the introduction of strict guidelines would subvert the interests of justice by further reducing their ability to individualise sentences. Time and again they observed that sentencing is 'more of an art than a science', a 'balancing exercise' between rules and values, where professional experience, intuition and subjective judgment are central. Guidelines attempted to 'quantify the unquantifiable', to narrow the space for 'discernment and discretion'. Such a formatted conception of what is deemed necessary in sentencing is clearly at odds with judicial conceptions of every 'case' – offender and offence – as unique and contextualised (Aas 2005). Without exception, Scottish sentencers were emphatic about the need to maintain their ability to individualise sentences without being 'haggled by guidelines'.

> Every case is different and every individual accused is different, and broadly speaking the judge should have the chance, untrammelled by guidelines ... of reflecting that diversity. (Judge 10)

The need to take account of a wide variety of factors in arriving at a 'just sentence' in individual cases required 'flexibility' not guidelines. And the search for transparency in sentencing through guidelines was, for Scottish sentencers, yet another policy manifestation of mistrust in their professional judgment. It could only be taken as an indication that they were 'not to be trusted in sentencing people'.

> For [guidelines] to be introduced here would inevitably lead to a supposition that sentencers were not to be trusted to do their job properly and in particular not to be trusted to do what they wanted. The constitutional implications of this should not have to be spelled out. (Lothian 2006: 21)

If and when a guidelines system is introduced in Scotland, on the basis of what has happened in other guideline jurisdictions, it is likely that more and longer prison sentences will be the result (Rothman 2003; EFF 2004; Millie *et al.* 2007). The impact of the restrictions on knowledge for sentencing provoked by risk-based assessment techniques and national standards has already narrowed the space for judges to consider the very wide range of circumstances surrounding the offence and the offender that they have traditionally taken account of in arriving at a 'just sentence' in specific cases. Judges are concerned with justice. While the consequences of sentences in the past might have been unknown (that is, in the sense of achieving specific sentencing purposes), government policy nowadays, by suppressing traditional judicial concerns about justice in its promotion of accountability to the system, curtails what the judges can know about who they are sentencing and about the material realities of their lives. This throws judges back onto what it is possible to know, and having to imagine more, about what the offenders they are to sentence are like. And the less they know about the offender and the circumstances surrounding the criminal event, the less likely it is that they will know about factors they consider relevant to personal mitigation (compare with Jacobson and Hough 2007), and the factors they consider relevant to opting for a community sentence in cases 'on the borderline' between custodial and non-custodial sentencing (see Hough *et al.* 2003; Tombs 2004), thus making a prison sentence more likely.

In this chapter it has been argued that the managerialist project embedded in late modern attempts to structure judicial discretion in terms of new forms of accountability within the context of punitive populism has been self-defeating. The incorporation of various social accounting procedures to make the achievement of policy goals more certain has had the opposite effect. Audit methods and the technologies and practices of risk have gelled with legislative restrictions on judicial discretion to narrow the space for imaginative sentencing, where judges are able to use their creativity and judicial competence to combine rules in the ways best suited to the peculiarities of specific cases. Imaginative sentencing has been suppressed and supplanted increasingly by an imaginary penalty, where sentencing is not open to the peculiarities of specific cases but rather is pre-directed at a closure engineered by a variety of (often opposed) bureaucratic rules designed not for doing justice but for controlling risk. And this imaginary penalty in sentencing, which has resulted in more incarceration and for longer periods, has made the sentencing policy goals of crime reduction and public protection less rather than more likely of achievement.

Notes

1 The research was conducted in 2004 and involved extended interviews with 40 sentencers throughout Scotland – with five Judges of the High Court, 34 Sheriffs and a Stipendiary Magistrate – hereafter referred to collectively as judges. All Sheriffs were also asked to provide information about how they had made decisions in four cases that they considered lay on the borderline between custodial and non-custodial penalties – two of which went to custody and two of which went to community sentences. The main object here was to understand sentencers' logic-in-use when they made decisions to imprison. Follow-up discussions about recent developments in sentencing policy, including proposals to establish an Advisory Panel for Sentencing in Scotland and sentencing guidelines were held with individual judges at Judicial Studies Committee Refresher Courses from 2005–7.
2 See Carlen (1976: 10) for this technical use of 'competence'.
3 Mandatory minimum sentences were first introduced by the Crime (Sentences) Act 1997. Other provisions were contained in the Crime and

Disorder Act 1998, the Youth Justice and Criminal Evidence Act 1999, the Proceeds of Crime Act 2002 and, most recently, the Criminal Justice Act 2003.

4 The Panel includes three judicial, three academic and three lay members with no background in criminal justice, and others experienced in policing, probation, prisons and magistrates' courts.

5 Court of Appeal guidance takes a variety of forms amongst which are guideline judgments, which set out a general approach to be taken in relation to a certain type of offence; interpretation of sentencing legislation; settled lines of decisions, that is, where a series of individual decisions, generally on a point of principle, acquire authority; pronouncements on general sentencing policy, usually in relation to custodial sentencing for certain types of offender; Attorney General's References under the 1998 Criminal Justice Act which allows for appeals against sentence on the grounds of leniency; and ordinary sentence appeals (see Ashworth 2005).

6 The Council has a judicial majority (seven members) with four other members drawn from prosecutors, police, defence lawyers and victim services – see the Sentencing Guidelines Council website: www.sentencing-guidelines.gov.uk; see also Tonry 2002.

7 Once sentencing becomes 'a tool in the hands of politicians', in the name of 'democratic crime control' there are, however, no limits to punishment so long as the majority are not affected (Christie 1993: 191).

8 Part 12 of the Criminal Justice Act 2003, which contains a wide range of provisions on sentencing, is now the most significant statute within sentencing law for England and Wales.

9 Proportionality has been long established as the fundamental guiding principle of English sentencing law (Jacobson and Hough 2007; see also Home Office 2001, 'The Halliday Report'). For commentaries on proportionality or 'just deserts' as a fundamental objective of sentencing see von Hirsch 1976, 1986 and 1993; von Hirsch and Ashworth 2005.

10 In relation to community sentencing, the 2003 Act introduced a generic community sentence to which sentencers can attach one or more of a very wide range of different conditions and requirements. The Act also introduced three new disposals combining sentencing in the community as well as in prison. 'Custody plus' involves a prison sentence of up to three months followed by a licence period of at least six months, to which conditions are attached; intermittent custody allows custody to be served on weekdays or at weekends; and 'custody minus', a new form of suspended sentence where the custodial sentence can be suspended for a period of six months to two years, during which time community requirements can be imposed.

11 Sections 224 to 236 of the Criminal Justice Act 2003 introduce 'an entirely new regime for the sentencing of offenders described as dangerous' (Ashworth 2005: 210).

12 An extended sentence differs from the extended sentence under the Powers of Criminal Courts (Sentencing) Act 2000. The new extended sentence comprises a minimum one-year custodial sentence, from which the offender may be released at the half-way point on direction from the Parole Board, followed by an extended licence period of up to five years (for violent offences) or eight years (for sexual offences). Imprisonment for public protection is an indeterminate sentence, for which the judge must set a minimum custodial term. The offender can be released only when the Parole Board is satisfied that the offender no longer poses a risk to the public. Then the offender will be placed on licence for life, unless the Parole Board determines that the licence can be revoked.

13 The judges in England and Wales, for example, argued publicly and strongly against the limitations placed by government on their discretionary powers though the introduction of various mandatory and minimum sentences in 1997. This is not to argue that judicial discretion does not have its problems in terms of individual idiosyncrasy and discrimination (see, for example, Hood 1992; Hedderman and Gelsthorpe 1997) if it is not well structured and monitored (see Hudson 1998). The argument here is that the managerialist thrust of late modern attempts to structure discretion in terms of new forms of accountability and within the context of punitive populism are self-defeating.

14 See Doob and Webster (2006) for a similar argument in relation to Canada.

15 The Sentencing Commission for Scotland was a judicially led body, set up by the Scottish Executive under its policy statement 'A Partnership For A Better Scotland'. The Commission, which was launched in November 2003, had the remit to review and make recommendations to the Scottish Executive on the use of bail and remand; the arrangements for early release from prison, and supervision of prisoners on their release; the basis on which fines are determined; the effectiveness of sentences in reducing re-offending; and the scope to improve consistency of sentencing – see www.scottishsentencingcommission.gov.uk.

16 The Murder (Abolition of Death Penalty) Act 1965 prescribes a mandatory sentence of life imprisonment for murder.

17 In particular, section 287 of the Criminal Justice Act 2003 prescribes minimum sentences of three years' detention for those aged 16 to 20 years and five years' imprisonment for those aged over 20 years convicted on indictment of illegal possession or distribution of firearms. Section 205B of the Criminal Procedure (Scotland) Act 1995 prescribes minimum sentences of seven years' imprisonment for those aged 18 years or more convicted in the High Court of a Class A drug trafficking offence where the person has previously been convicted in any court of two other Class A drug trafficking offences, unless there are specific circumstances relating to the offences of the offender which would make the sentence unjust.

18 Scotland has maintained its own separate legal system since the Act of Union in 1707.

19 These include the Risk Management Authority to manage the risk posed by serious violent and sexual offenders, Community Justice Authorities to reduce and manage the risk of reoffending more generally, and the establishment of the now dissolved Sentencing Commission for Scotland to, amongst other things, make recommendations on the scope to improve consistency in sentencing (SCS 2006).

20 The Crime and Disorder Act 1998 (section 86, 1) introduced a new section 210A into the Criminal Procedure (Scotland) Act 1995 which deals with extended sentences. Solemn courts imposing terms of imprisonment for serious sexual offences (of any length) or violent offences attracting a term of imprisonment of four years or more have a discretion to place the offender on licence when the judge considers that the offender may pose a serious threat to public safety after release. Section 210A (4) imposes an obligation on the sentencer to obtain a social enquiry report assessing risk before imposing an extended sentence. A 'violent offence' is defined as an offence inferring personal violence other than a sexual offence. A 'sexual offence' is defined by reference to the particular offences set out in the statute and includes rape, indecent assault and lewd, indecent and libidinous behaviour or practices (in effect, child sexual abuse).

21 Supervised release orders can be imposed under the Criminal Procedure (Scotland) Act 1995, section 209 (1). The order must not exceed 12 months after the date of release and must not be longer than the date by which the entire term of imprisonment specified in the sentence has elapsed. During the order the offender is to be supervised by a criminal justice social worker of the relevant local authority and must comply with requirements imposed by the court and any requirements reasonably specified by the supervisor.

22 Part 1 'Protection of the Public At Large', sections 1 to 13 and schedules 1 and 2 of the 2003 Act specify in considerable detail arrangements to assess the risk posed by serious violent and sexual offenders and for minimising any risk established subsequent to that assessment. The legislation establishes risk criteria for sentencing which are that the nature of, or the circumstances of the commission of, the offence of which the convicted person has been found guilty, either in themselves or as part of a pattern of behaviour, are such as to demonstrate that there is a likelihood that the offender, if at liberty, will seriously endanger the lives, or physical or psychological well-being, of members of the public at large (section 210E). It also sets out procedures for risk assessment through the use of a 'risk assessment order' (section 210B). Such orders are not subject to appeal. The scope and remit of the risk assessment report are also defined, allowing allegations as well as convictions to be considered and enabling the assessor to express an opinion on the level of risk. Risk assessment reports are subject to challenge by counsel

and an alternative report can be commissioned by the accused (section 210C). The purpose of the OLR is to replace, in most cases, discretionary life sentences.

23 The Risk Management Authority has a board of seven members, chief executive and 12 staff – see www.rmascotland.org.

24 This quote is from one of six interviews I conducted with government officials in 2005 immediately prior to the establishment of the RMA.

25 For example, the Violence Risk Appraisal Guide, the Historical Clinical Risk-20, the Sexual Violence Risk-20, the Risk Matrix 2000, ASSET.

26 The 40 judges interviewed in the sentencing study (see note 1 above) are numbered individually to protect their anonymity.

27 Most of this paragraph is taken from Carlen and Tombs 2006.

28 Most of this paragraph is taken from Carlen and Tombs 2006.

Chapter 6

The 'seemingness' of the 'seamless management' of offenders

Anne Worrall

Styal prison and young offender institution, Cheshire, as part of a joint initiative aimed at cutting reoffending, has distributed prison keys to probation officers. ... The scheme aims to break down barriers between prison officers and the probation service and provide *seamless support* to female offenders. Prisoners have welcomed the changes for providing greater continuity, and staff say they have a better understanding of those they are caring for (Public Service Awards nominee, *Guardian*, 28 November 2007, emphasis added)

The concept of 'seamlessness' in the management of offenders has emerged as a defining penal imaginary of the twenty-first century in England and Wales. In this chapter, I examine the emergence, development and maintenance of this concept through the legislation, policy, organisation and practice of supervising (or 'managing') prisoners and ex-prisoners. Although I base my arguments on the specific legal, social and political configuration of criminal justice in England and Wales in the period from the mid 1990s, the features of 'seamlessness' that I identify here have universal applicability, insofar as they invoke a vision of cohesive social control that is not only impossible to achieve but also undesirable.

The aspiration that every sentenced offender should be allocated a personal manager to supervise and monitor their progress through prison and following release into the community (otherwise known as 'one sentence: one manager' (NOMS 2006)) sounds eminently sensible and uncontroversial in principle. Indeed, it could be argued that this ideal has underpinned the work of probation officers for decades. The term 'through-care', common since the 1970s, described the role of the probation officer in ameliorating the 'pains of imprisonment' by supporting the prisoner through the latter part of their sentence and back into the community. But, as Hudson *et al.* (2007: 631) argue, the notion of 'seamlessness' is very different and implies 'one essentially indivisible sentence' in which the *constructive* work commenced in custody is continued in the community. Hudson *et al.* identify the Criminal Justice Act 1991 and the introduction of the *automatic conditional release* of prisoners serving sentences of between 12 months and four years as being the first official example of a 'seamless sentence', insofar as the period spent in custody and the period of supervision after release were to be planned as a coherent whole. The first version of the Probation Service National Standards, produced in 1990, describes the 'seamless sentence' as:

A wholly new concept, namely that of a sentence served partly in custody and partly in the community with the offender being liable to recall to custody right up to the end of the sentence. (para. 8.6 cited in HMI Prisons and Probation 2001: 29)

Seamlessness became a fully-formed imaginary in the discourse of penalities in England and Wales after The Carter Review of Correctional Services (Carter 2003; Home Office 2004). Carter did not use the term 'seamless sentence' but is credited with coining the phrase 'end-to-end offender management'. Carter proposed, and the government accepted, the creation of one National Offender Management Service (hereafter NOMS) that would take responsibility for managing the supervision of every offender 'regardless of whether they are serving their sentences in prison, the community or both' (Home Office 2004: para. 42). Carter argued that there was a need for a 'new' approach to managing offenders that would break down the silos of the two services in the interests of reducing reoffending. He was concerned about the poor co-ordination of services for offenders between prison and probation and his solution was to promote what later became known as the 'four Cs' of the National Offender Management Model:

- Continuity (of care/treatment and, where possible, relationship)
- Consistency (of message, behaviour and, where possible, person)
- Consolidation (of learning of new behaviours)
- Commitment (of staff to the process) (NOMS 2006)

While the call for 'end-to-end' offender management was considered the least controversial of his recommendations at the time (Hough 2006) it cannot be considered out of the context of Carter's – and the government's – two other concerns. These were the 'modernising' of correctional services (and, in particular, the introduction of what Raynor and Maguire term the 'fifth C' of 'contestability'[1]) and the desire to bring the rapidly increasing prison population under control through greater transparency, consistency and targeting in sentencing (Hough 2006; Raine 2006; Raynor and Maguire 2006).

Although the implementation of such a model might be fraught with difficulties, the ideals of continuity, consistency, consolidation and commitment in the management of offenders, as in the rearing of children, are regarded as undeniably 'good' principles by which to be guided. 'Seamlessness' is a goal – a state of perfection even - to which all policy-makers and practitioners should aspire.[2] In contrast, I want to argue that 'seamlessness' is not only impossible to achieve but is also undesirable because it denies the 'pains of imprisonment', the restricted availability of the more constructive aspects of contemporary prison regimes and the existence of legitimate conflict or tension between the various agencies and personnel involved in dealing with offenders. In so doing it creates the 'prisobation officer',[3] as described in the Public Sector Award nomination above who regards the extension of the power to lock and unlock as being synonymous with the provision of seamless support, continuity and 'better understanding' (see also Gough 2005). The absence of appropriate seams, edges and boundaries means that the field of intervention (in this case, imprisonment followed and/or preceded by community supervision) cannot be divided into manageable, accountable sections. Thus, when something goes wrong (as it inevitably does – sometimes in a routine way, sometimes more spectacularly), it is impossible to locate, isolate and mend the weakness in the fabric (darn a hole or apply a patch) because the whole garment is ruined and has to be replaced. Hence the never-ending need for innovation – 'new' legislation and 'new' approaches.

I want to argue for the replacement of the concept of 'seamlessness' with that of 'patchwork', which, according to Chouard (2003) is 'an art of juxtaposition, governed by the principles of heterogeneity, [following] the rule of fragmentation that favours contact, contrast, and difference'. 'Patchwork in criminal justice' may initially appear an inappropriate metaphor, conjuring visions of 'make do and mend' second-handedness and jumble. Better by far, surely, is the analogy of pristine fabric with the potential for 'wraparound' (pashmina?) services to offenders? But patchwork is a sophisticated art form:

Multiple, polymorphous, variegated, the paradigmatic motif of patchwork generates the weft and the weave of the meaning of .... kaleidoscopic text and sets it squarely in the .... domain of 'le pele-mele des possibles' (Lachaud 1991, cited in Chouard 2003).

Chouard interprets 'le pele-mele' as 'the pile up', but a more accurate translation is 'the pell-mell' of possibilities. 'Le pele-mele' has connotations of labyrinths, kaleidoscopes, collage, quilting and patchwork. Moreover, in some parts of Europe, the phrase also refers to a frame, within which a collection of pictures might be arranged and re-arranged.[4] In other words, the possibilities of order and boundaries are embedded within the concept of disorder and jumble. Patches may be stitched together or held in place by a frame, offering a degree of stability and integrity while, at the same time, allowing for the possibility of re-arrangement without wholesale destruction.

In this chapter I am aiming to develop the argument that the threadbare imaginary of seamlessness is founded on five sewing metaphors: the 'warp and weft' of NOMS; the 'cloth' of the Criminal Justice Act 2003; the 'catwalk' of discretionary release; the 'wear and tear' of licence compliance and, finally, the 'recycling bin' of recall.

The warp and weft of NOMS and end-to-end offender management

In August 1998 the Home Office launched what might, facetiously, be termed a new national game called 'Rename the Probation Service' (Worrall and Hoy 2005). It invited suggestions for a name that 'is capable of inspiring public confidence in the work of that Service' and, while expressing 'no strong preference', provided a number of suggestions to stimulate ideas. These were:

The Public Protection Service
The Community Justice Enforcement Agency
The Offender Risk Management Service
The Community Sentence Enforcement Service
The Justice Enforcement and Public Protection Service
The Public Safety and Offender Management Service
The Community Protection and Justice Service

(Home Office 1998: para. 2.14)

The call to rename the probation service, despite the acceptance by the Home Office that probation 'is a long established concept, well understood internationally' (1998: para. 2.13), arose from the determination of the new Labour government to abolish any terminology that might be 'misunderstood' or 'associated with tolerance of crime' (1998: para. 2.12). None the less, the proposal that a service with (then) 7,200 probation officers and a total of fewer than 15,000 employees (including clerical and administrative staff) could provide 'public protection' was difficult to take seriously (Worrall and Hoy 2005: 91).

The Prisons-Probation Review had been set up in July 1997, shortly after the new government took office, and was intended to explore the possibility of integrating the prison service and the probation service. The consultation document reporting on the review was entitled *Joining Forces to Protect the Public* (Home Office 1998). The review rejected a merger of the two services, partly for reasons of principle (that there was insufficient overlap of responsibilities) but predominantly, one suspects, for reasons of cost (delicately phrased as 'disruption to staff and difficulties of renegotiating major IT initiatives' [para. 2.38]). In fact, very few of the review's recommendations affected the prison service. The probation service, however, as well as being renamed, was to undergo a major restructuring. Of most significance was the proposal to create a unified national service with national leadership directly accountable to the Home Secretary. This proposal, of itself, could go a long way towards remedying the perceived shortcomings and lack of credibility of the service. That the new leadership would not be leading a recognisable probation service, however, rather undermined the gesture.

The desire of the government to erase the concept of 'probation' from the collective conscience was the surface manifestation of a more fundamental desire to blur the boundaries between freedom and confinement and extend the disciplinary effects of imprisonment wider and deeper into the community. As the review put it, 'we are interested in looking at ways of replacing the present cut-offs with a more flexible set of sanctions based on a continuum of loss of liberty, reparation in the community and correction of offending behaviour' (1998: para. 1.8). Community-based sentences were no longer to be viewed as alternatives to custody (as they were in the 1980s as a response to prison overcrowding and the decarceration debate) or as sentences in their own right (as in the Criminal Justice Act 1991, which sought to reduce the prison population directly by limiting the powers of sentencers) but as part of a continuum which allows smooth and easy movement between prison and the community. The state of tension – indeed of healthy conflict – that had hitherto been assumed to exist between advocates of imprisonment and advocates of community-based penalties had been rendered redundant. As John Patten had predicted a decade earlier, we were all in the same business now – the business of punishment – with no differences of principle:

> The fact is that all probation-based disposals are already in varying degrees forms of punishment … It is bizarre to scratch around to find polite euphemisms for what is going on. (Patten 1988: 12 cited in Worrall and Hoy 2005: 32–3)

Retribution, deterrence, restoration and rehabilitation could be fitted neatly together within a politically constructed consensus about the purposes of punishment. The only differences were those of approach and even the differences of approach were being eroded. Thus Patten's speech marked the start of a desire to eject the Other of penal pluralities from official discourse about law and order (see Burton and Carlen 1979: 21).

By December 1999, the government had decided on the name 'The Community Punishment and Rehabilitation Service'. The change received no support from any probation organisation and probation officers feared that offenders would quickly find a mischievous (if admittedly inaccurate) abbreviation that would soon make it the subject of ridicule (CRAPOs working for CRAPS!). Following Early Day Motion No 346, the government reconsidered and, to everyone's delight, abandoned the name change. But the more serious business of changing the culture of the probation service continued apace (Worrall and Hoy 2005: 92).

In 2001, the National Probation Service for England and Wales was created, with a national director who set out her strategy in a document called *A New Choreography* (NPS and Home Office 2001). The strapline of the National Probation Service changed from the traditional 'Advise, Assist and Befriend' to the more aggressive 'Enforcement, Rehabilitation and Public Protection' and its aims were to be:

- Protecting the public
- Reducing reoffending
- The proper punishment of offenders in the community

- Ensuring offenders' awareness of the effects of crime on the victims of crime and the public
- Rehabilitation of offenders

(NPS and Home Office 2001: iv)

These aims are now incorporated into The Offender Management Act 2007[5] which 'signals an unambiguous expectation by Parliament that the management of offenders in custody and the community will change permanently' (Edwards 2007).

It might be argued that all these developments, while affecting managers and policy-makers in the service, would still leave the grass-roots probation officer with his or her professional autonomy in respect of individual cases. But that would be to fail to take account of National Standards and their implications for the training of probation officers.

From 1989 onwards, the Home Office compiled a series of ever more prescriptive National Standards directing practice in relation to all aspects of probation service supervision. They cover not just broad policy guidelines, but detailed instructions about the administration of orders. They cover frequency of contact, record-keeping, rules about enforcement and the taking of breach action, and the content of supervision sessions.

There were some good professional justifications for the National Standards, and few disputed the need to standardise some very variable and inconsistent practices across the country and between individual officers. Professional autonomy had undoubtedly been used in the past as an excuse for poor practice. Also, if anti-discrimination was to be taken seriously, then there had to be an attempt to ensure minimum standards of service delivery.

However, National Standards must also be seen as the government's attempt to make individual probation officers more accountable to management and management more accountable to the government. The overriding point about the introduction of National Standards was that they limited the discretion of the individual probation officer and focused on the management of supervision rather than its content or the supervisory relationship. And it followed that the need for probation officers to undertake two years' training as social workers, when all the procedures they would ever need to follow were now laid out in a glossy ring-bound folder, must be open to question.

By 1996 the Conservative government was threatening to abolish university-based training for probation officers altogether. The new

Labour government reversed this, but insisted on the introduction of a new Diploma in Probation Studies, which combines a two-year undergraduate university degree with a NVQ Level 4 award. The award is employment-led and run by consortia of probation services and higher education institutions. There is little doubt that probation training as it now exists is extremely demanding but there is disquiet among some who deliver it that the specificity of the roles and tasks for which trainees are equipped may not produce the flexible, reflexive and creative employees that are needed to work imaginatively with offenders in the twenty-first century (Bailey *et al.* 2007).

The emergence of the National Offender Management Service in 2004 can thus be characterised by the desire of the government to eradicate the concept of 'probation' from the nation's psyche and erode the professional identity of probation officers, while at the same time creating a narrative of 'joined up' penal thinking and cost-effective delivery of both public protection (through risk assessment) *and* services to offenders (through contestability). The Offender Management Act 2007 introduces the concepts of 'the probation purposes' and the 'officer of providers of probation services'. The role of 'the probation officer' no longer exists in legislation – only a series of services to fulfil 'the probation purposes' that may be delivered by an authorised 'officer of providers'. Edwards (2007) describes the change as evolutionary rather than revolutionary but some might disagree. A revolution that takes ten years to come to fruition may still be a revolution.

Cutting one's coat to fit one's cloth: Criminal Justice Act 2003

The Criminal Justice Act 2003 did for the sentencing of offenders what the creation of NOMS did for their post-sentence management. It has been described as:

> a wide-ranging, labyrinthine and controversial initiative to win public confidence in criminal justice, attempting to embrace crime prevention and public protection in sentencing in tandem with proportionate punishment (Stone 2007: 71)

Unlike the Criminal Justice Act 1991 which gave pre-eminence to offence seriousness and the principle of proportionality, the 2003 Act attempts to reconcile every conceivable aim of sentencing: punishment, deterrence, rehabilitation, public protection and reparation. Additionally, it recognises the concept of 'persistence' and regards previous convictions as aggravating factors. In an attempt to counter the 'revolving door' of short-term imprisonment, the Act reintroduces the suspended prison sentence with community-based conditions attached and community penalties themselves become generic, with a menu of conditions from which sentencers can choose. As Stone points out, the 'inflationary potential' of these options is 'obvious' (2007: 72).

But the most significant contributions of the Act to seamlessness are the Extended Sentence and the Indeterminate Public Protection (IPP) sentence, both of which are imposed in cases of serious 'specified' violent and sexual offences where the judge concludes that there is a significant risk that the offender will cause serious harm to members of the public by committing a further 'specified' offence. The Extended Sentence is a version of a determinate sentence and is imposed where the maximum sentence is less than ten years. The sentence consists of a 'normal' custodial sentence (typically one to two years) followed by an 'extended' period of supervision in the community. No extended sentence prisoner can be released automatically before the end of the custodial period, but they become eligible for parole consideration halfway through. The IPP is an indeterminate sentence imposed where the maximum sentence is more than ten years. It is effectively a life sentence but with a short 'tariff'. Once the tariff (typically one to two years) is expired (and bearing in mind that many such offenders will have served much of their tariff while on remand), the offender has to be considered for release by the Parole Board. The problems confronting the Parole Board are considered in more detail later. At this stage suffice to say that the use of IPPs has far exceeded expectations – 2,500 within two years of the introduction of the IPP sentence in April 2005 (Parole Board 2007a).

The effect of the Extended Sentence and the IPP has been to create a blurring of the boundaries (a seamlessness) between determinacy and indeterminacy at the sentencing stage among a far wider proportion of offenders than would previously have been expected to receive indeterminate sentences. While some might argue that the IPP is no more than an extension of the old 'two strikes' automatic life sentence, Nichol (2007) points out that the list of qualifying offences for the old life sentence was 11 and required two convictions before its imposition. By contrast, the list of qualifying offences for an IPP numbers 153 and the sentence can be triggered by the first offence.

The use of Extended Sentences and IPPs serves the imaginary of seamlessness by imposing an apparently relatively short period of custody followed by an extended period of supervision in the community. Thus the sentence promises both punishment and rehabilitation, the relative proportions of which depend on the prisoner's progress. In reality, as we shall see later, the prisoner will inevitably be unable to demonstrate that it is no longer necessary for the protection of the public that they should be confined (which is the test the Parole Board is required to apply).

Walking the catwalk for discretionary release

Prior to the full implementation of the Criminal Justice Act 2003, the process of release from prison, except from life sentences, was relatively straightforward. Those serving sentences of less than four years were released automatically at the halfway point; those serving longer sentences could be considered for discretionary release (parole) at that stage but would otherwise remain in custody until the two-thirds point of their sentence. Various lengths of supervision (licence) in the community followed, during which time, prisoners were liable for recall to prison if they reoffended or failed to comply (breached) the conditions of their licence (Padfield and Maruna 2006).

The Criminal Justice Act 2003 has complicated matters considerably insofar as all determinate sentence prisoners, of whatever length of sentence, will now be released automatically at the halfway point. However, all prisoners subject to Extended Sentences or IPPs, however short their custodial term or 'tariff' must now be considered by the Parole Board before they can be released. This, it is argued, uncouples the (common sense?) relationship between offence seriousness, dangerousness and sentence length and allows the Parole Board to focus on those prisoners deemed 'dangerous' by the courts (Shute 2007).

Applying for parole has always been something of a fashion show, in which the prisoner displays all the couture garments they have acquired in a bid to impress the Parole Board that their 'risk of reoffending has been sufficiently reduced to be manageable in the community'.[6] The full wardrobe of garments consists of: remorse; victim empathy; good prison behaviour; a portfolio of (preferably designer-label) offending behaviour programmes; support from prison-based and community-based probation officers; an OASys risk assessment score in the 'low' or 'medium' range; a 'robust' release plan, including (in the case of violent or sexual offending) Multi-Agency Public Protection monitoring. Here are two entirely

fictional examples of the written reasons[7] given by the Parole Board
for releasing and not releasing respectively two prisoners:

John Smith is serving six years for offences of conspiracy to supply
Class A drugs (cocaine) and Class B drugs (amphetamines). He
was one of a group of six men, who received lengthy prison
sentences. He has a history of entrenched drug misuse and
his involvement in supplying enabled him to finance his own
drugs. His involvement was driving a vehicle and dropping off
drugs to buyers. He accepts full responsibility for his part in the
conspiracy which he says was triggered by a family death. He
has an extensive criminal record, including some violence, but
mostly offences related to theft and driving. He has breached a
number of community sentences.

In prison, Mr Smith's behaviour has been excellent. He
has no adjudications or failed mandatory drug tests and he
has progressed through the system to open conditions. He is
currently engaged in full time work in the community from
Monday to Friday. He has also successfully completed a number
of town visits and home leaves. He has undertaken numerous
educational and vocational courses, as well as drug awareness,
offending behaviour and assertiveness courses and the Think
First programme. Having previously spent a number of years
in prison, reports suggest that he has made a determined effort
to use his time constructively on this sentence. His OASys risk
assessment summary weighted score is 70 out of 168, placing
him in the medium category. Both probation officers support his
application, believing that the offending behaviour work he has
undertaken and his time in open conditions will have reduced
his risk of re-offending sufficiently to make it manageable in the
community.

On release, Mr Smith intends to return to live with his partner
and their children and this address has been assessed as suitable
by the home probation officer. The panel has to weigh the
seriousness of the index offence, Mr Smith's criminal record and
his past history of drug misuse against his maturing attitude,
offending behaviour work and his good progress through the
prison system. On balance, the panel is of the view that Mr
Smith has made every effort on this sentence to reduce his risk
of re-offending and to change his lifestyle. Consequently, parole
is granted with conditions to protect the public and ensure
compliance with supervision.

Paul Jones is serving six years for offences of conspiracy to supply Class A drugs (cocaine) and Class B drugs (amphetamines). He was one of a group of six men, who received lengthy prison sentences. He has a history of entrenched drug misuse and his involvement in supplying enabled him to finance his own drugs. His involvement was driving a vehicle and dropping off drugs to buyers. He claims he had no choice but to act in the conspiracy and says that his judgment was clouded by a family death. He has an extensive criminal record, including some violence, but mostly offences related to theft and driving. He has breached a number of community sentences.

In prison, Mr Jones's behaviour has been mixed. He has two adjudications for failed mandatory drug tests but he has progressed through the system to open conditions. For a period he was engaged in full time work in the community from Monday to Friday but was withdrawn from this after returning late to the prison on two occasions. He successfully completed a number of town visits but was returned to closed prison conditions after admitting drinking alcohol on one visit. He has undertaken a number of educational and vocational courses, as well as a drug awareness course, but he has not undertaken any other offending behaviour work. Having previously spent a number of years in prison, reports suggest that he has made more of an effort to use his time constructively on this sentence. His OASys risk assessment summary weighted score is 110 out of 168, placing him in the high category. Neither probation officer supports his application, believing that his limited offending behaviour work and his failure in open conditions will not have reduced his risk of re-offending sufficiently to make it manageable in the community.

On release, Mr Jones intends to return to live with his partner and their children and this address has been assessed as suitable by the home probation officer. The panel has to weigh the seriousness of the index offence, Mr Jones's criminal record, his past history of drug misuse and limited offending behaviour work against his reasonable progress in prison and his satisfactory release plan. On balance, the panel is of the view that, while Mr Jones has made some effort on this sentence to reduce his risk of re-offending, it is not yet a sufficiently low level to be manageable in the community. Consequently, parole is refused and conditions will be added to his non-parole licence to protect the public and ensure compliance with supervision.

With the implementation of the Criminal Justice Act 2003 has come an increase in the number of Extended Sentence and IPP cases being considered by the Parole Board. IPP cases are subject to the same procedures as life sentences, which involves periodic reviews and oral hearings. Thornton (2007) argues that this procedure is

> ill-suited to the needs of automatic and IPP lifers whose minimum terms are too short to allow for a satisfactory progression in the approved manner. Indeed it is not possible at present for any lifer to obtain release within less than three years of his sentence even though many IPP minimum terms are less than that period. (2007: 128)

A similar problem faces the Parole Board when considering Extended Sentence prisoners as can be seen in the following case:

Dave Brown is serving 12 months with two years' extended licence for an offence of unlawful wounding (s.20). The offence arose from an argument in a supermarket that escalated into violence when Mr Brown produced a penknife from his pocket. The victim received a wound requiring stitches. He has an extensive criminal record, mostly for offences related to theft, drugs and driving but including a number of convictions for assault and possession of weapons. His record of compliance with court orders is poor, having breached community sentences on a number of occasions, but he is said to have completed previous custodial licences successfully.

In prison, Mr Brown's behaviour has been satisfactory, despite a couple of adjudications for relatively minor matters. He is regarded as a good and trusted worker in the prison. Because of the short time he has been in prison, he has been unable to undertake any offence-related work, although he is said to be willing to do this in the community. His OASys risk of reconviction weighted score is 71 out of 168, placing him in the medium category. The prison probation officer does not support the application because he considers it too early in the sentence to be able to provide a suitable release package and risk management plan.

On release, Mr Brown proposes to return to live with his partner and daughter and this address is assessed as suitable by the home probation officer. He also has good prospects for returning to his previous employment. The home probation officer supports early release with strict licence conditions, including non-contact with the victim and an exclusion zone. The panel has carefully considered the evidence supporting early release but has to weigh this against the serious nature of the index offence, Mr Brown's criminal record, which includes similar offences, and his failure to undertake any offence-related work so far in prison. On balance, it is not satisfied that his risk of re-offending and harm has yet been sufficiently reduced to justify release at this time. Parole is refused and conditions will be added to his future licence to protect the public and ensure compliance with supervision.

Increasingly, however, such prisoners are becoming aware that they are being dressed in cheap high street garments made in sweatshops and being pushed out onto a catwalk to be judged by couture standards. In recent judicial reviews of the cases of *Wells v the Parole Board* and *James v the Parole Board* (Parole Board 2007b) judgments were made that it was unlawful to detain IPP prisoners when prison overcrowding meant that they could not gain access to offending behaviour courses to demonstrate to the Parole Board that they were no longer a danger to the public.[8]

An even greater challenge to the concept of seamlessness has come from the case of *Brooke & Ter-Ogannisyan v the Parole Board* in which four prisoners successfully argued that their right to a fair hearing in respect of their release had been violated because of the close link between the Parole Board and the government, through its former sponsoring agency, the Home Office (the *Guardian*, 8 September 2007). The court found that the perception that the Board was an instrument of government policy was not without foundation and cited two instances of the government interfering with the independence of the Board. The first of these was the refusal of the Home Office to fund interviews with prisoners applying for parole; the second was the former Home Secretary, John Reid's, lecture to the Parole Board in May 2006, promising to change the composition of the Board by appointing more victims of crime as members.

Another way in which prisoners are subverting seamlessness is by insisting on oral hearings, which have increased from 500 cases in 2002/3 to 2,500 in 2006/7 (Parole Board 2007a). A European Court of Human Rights judgment (Stafford) in 2002 and House of Lords judgment (Smith and West) in 2005 have given prisoners more rights to request face-to-face hearings with members of the Parole Board, rather than accepting paper-based decisions. The Board estimates that an oral hearing costs around £1,200 more per case than a paper-based panel (Parole Board 2007a). Whether or not this increase in oral hearings has anything to do with the near-abolition of routine parole interviews is hard to say (oral hearings are not applicable to exactly the same range of cases as interviews were) but, on the basis of cost alone, one suspects it would have been more economical in the long run to retain interviews, which had at least an appearance of greater fairness.

The wear and tear of resettlement and licence compliance

It is not my intention to argue that most released prisoners are not in dire need of well co-ordinated support from a variety of statutory and voluntary agencies if they are to stand any chance of reducing their risk of re-offending, nor to dispute that there has been progress in this regard in the past decade (Maguire 2007). My argument is that NOMS and seamlessness are not primarily concerned with the resettlement or rehabilitation of ex-prisoners. They are about the *management* of those ex-prisoners – about compliance, enforcement and public protection. Nowhere is this more clearly demonstrated than in the claim that multi-agency programmes for prolific offenders are 'win/win' programmes. If offenders reduce their offending, that is success; if they don't, then they are returned to prison and that is also success (Worrall and Mawby 2004; Farrall *et al.* 2007).

Recent research on the relationship between probation officers/ offender managers and offenders stresses the significance of continuity (Farrall 2002; Trotter 1999; Rex 1999; Partridge 2004; Robinson 2005). While one (official, imaginary) interpretation of this might be continuity of *offender management* both in custody and in the community, another interpretation might be that of continuity of relations, providing committed support (creating patchwork out of pell-mell) while the offender 'zig-zags' their way to desistance (Burnett 2004). There is little evidence that the rhetoric of NOMS will accommodate a tolerance of 'zig-zagging'. Nevertheless, in reality, there is no alternative. If the custodial door is set to revolve, as it seems to be under current sentencing legislation and practice, then the only choice is whether or not we attempt to set in place sufficient support networks in the community to encourage offenders to remain 'out' for a little longer each time. Yet, while some may choose to call this war of attrition 'seamlessness' and misrepresent the eventual prison 'burn out' experienced by some persistent offenders as success for reduction in re-offending strategies, let us not pretend that returns to prison are anything other than setbacks or 'interruptions' on the path to desistance for many others (Farrall *et al.* 2007: 373).

But sometimes things go spectacularly wrong and the hubris of 'win/win' turns into the nightmare of 'lose/lose'. In 2006 NOMS was dramatically exposed to the kind of media scrutiny and vilification previously reserved for social workers following inquiries into the deaths of children whose previous neglect or abuse had been overlooked or inadequately addressed. A series of killings by offenders being supervised by the probation service, some of them following release from prison by the Parole Board, has been described by a former Home Secretary as being 'a dagger at the heart of public confidence in the probation service'. Two cases resulted in independent reviews by HM Inspectorate of Probation (2006a and b), which make for salutary reading. The two cases are the murder of John Monckton by Damien Hanson and Elliot White and the murder of Naomi Bryant by Anthony Rice. The two inquiries tell, I think, two rather different stories about NOMS.

In November 2004, a London business man, John Monckton, was murdered in his own home by Damien Hanson, who was on parole from a 12-year prison sentence, and Elliot White who was subject to a Drug Treatment and Testing Order both supervised by the notoriously under-resourced London Probation Area. The conclusion of the inquiry was that there had been overall failures and specific deficiencies in the management of the two men.

> The key theme that runs through this report is that people can perform poorly when they are unclear about their responsibilities within a process, and this can put them and their employers in an indefensible position when a dreadful crime takes place (HM Inspectorate of Probation 2006a: 2).

While Elliot White was poorly supervised in a rather mundane way, mistakes and failures to communicate – and sheer incompetence – were more significant in respect of Damien Hanson. In prison, Hanson appeared to make relatively good progress, undertaking offending behaviour courses and generally convincing staff that he was being rehabilitated. Unfortunately, a crucial risk assessment score of 91 per cent likelihood of re-offending was never made available to the Parole

Board. On top of this, bungled release arrangements and downright incompetent supervision were, in the view of the Inspector, unlikely to have 'inspired the respect, credibility and confidence that one would be seeking from this difficult offender'. The review concluded that there had been a *collective failure* to manage Hanson and White. Serious mistakes and deficiencies could be identified and lessons could be learned. Four probation officers were suspended, though later reinstated, the union claiming that they had been scapegoated.

The inquiry into the case of Anthony Rice is, in my view, of a different and altogether more depressing order. In August 2005, Rice murdered Naomi Bryant, a woman he had met a few days earlier. He was on life licence, having served 16 years for attempted rape (and having previously served seven years for rape) and he had reported to his probation officer only hours before he committed the murder. In this case, everyone was only too well aware of the risks involved and everyone was attempting, in a thoroughly professional and humane way, to balance the need to support and encourage the offender against the need to protect the public. Rice had been turned down twice for parole before being released. He was subject to extremely strict licence conditions and multi-agency monitoring in Hampshire Probation Area. He appeared to be making progress and gradually earned a relaxation of his restrictions. Although it was possible with hindsight to identify mistakes and errors of judgment – what the Inspector this time called *cumulative failure* (HM Inspectorate of Probation 2006b: 4) – there was no suggestion of incompetence or of anyone taking their responsibilities less than seriously. And yet, and yet …. The key conclusion pounced on by the media was that those involved had paid too much attention to the possible contravention of Rice's human rights by disproportionate restrictions on his movements and activities at the expense – fatal as it turned out – of public protection (Whitty 2007). The popular press demanded to know 'what about victims' rights?' and called for the abolition of the Human Rights Act.

It is one thing to criticise probation officers for not doing their job properly – as in the Hanson and White case – but it is quite another to say, as in the Rice case, that the job itself is outdated and irrelevant. The implication of the report of the Rice inquiry, as I read it, is that we might as well give up the balancing act. The stakes are too high and the only safe serious offender is an imprisoned one. Those involved in the Rice case had tried to work seamlessly but they had failed.

The recycling bin of enforcement and recall

The creation of NOMS in 2004 was intended to provide 'seamless' sentencing and supervision with continuity of responsibility for the offender from custody to community – though too frequently also back again. The revolving door of re-offending and, in some ways more worryingly, technical licence and supervision violation (for example, failing to keep appointments, leaving approved accommodation, contacting prohibited associates or victims) has meant that the element of traffic flow controlled by the Parole Board is considerably stronger into prison than leaving it. In the past five years, the numbers of prisoners recalled to custody for breaching licence conditions has risen by 350 per cent from just over 3,000 in 2000 to just over 11,000 in 2005. (In 2006, the Parole Board dealt with 14,669 recall cases.) Of these, research suggests that only a third had re-offended (HM Inspectorate of Prisons 2005), while the remainder had breached other conditions of their licence. As some writers have put it (Maruna 2004a; Padfield and Maruna 2006) this is not so much an offender management service as an offender 'waste management' service – but a costly, discriminatory and ineffective one.

The Criminal Justice Act 2003 removed the discretion from probation officers to institute breach proceedings when an offender fails to attend an appointment or otherwise to comply with their licence on a second occasion (Hedderman 2006). Setting aside for the moment the argument that this level of compliance is unrealistic for the kind of offenders who are subject to it (Padfield and Maruna 2006), the aim of these provisions was to give probation officers a 'flexible risk management' tool (Thompson 2007). When probation officers were sufficiently concerned that an offender was about to re-offend, or their risk of causing harm seemed to be increasing, they could have them recalled to prison to 'cool off' for a short while. The Parole Board, which is required to consider every recall case, could then re-release them after a suitable period, chastened and more willing to co-operate with the probation service. One might think that this is another example of seamlessness, especially as the Secretary of State's Directions to the Parole Board (under section 239[6]) of the Criminal Justice Act 2003) set out a 'presumption that the Board will seek to re-release the prisoner in all cases where it is satisfied that risk can be safely managed in the community. In reality, however, the Parole Board has become increasingly risk averse and very rarely re-releases a prisoner at a first post-recall panel. Most cases are set for further review at a future date that can be anything up to a year ahead. Thompson (representing the probation service) plaintively remarks, 'the Parole Board has not been re-releasing offenders in the numbers envisaged' (2007: 150).

As Thompson continues to explain, this sets up a kind of vicious circle in which the Parole Board and the probation service strive to outdo each other in risk aversion, with probation officers losing confidence to recommend re-release and the Parole Board criticising the absence of 'robust' release plans. Instead, she calls for practitioners to reclaim their professional judgment and

> Consider whether a failure to comply with licence conditions represents an *unacceptable* failure: whether the act of recall would increase the offender's risks by destabilising him/her, interrupting what is otherwise positive compliance with the sentence plan, or by losing accommodation or employment or the support of family and friends. (Thompson 2007: 153)

Compliance, as Bottoms (2001) has argued, is a complex process and is as dependent on incentives, routines and sense of social obligation as it is on deterrence and coercion (Hedderman and Hough 2004). The apparent seamlessness of enforcement, recall and re-release (or, more frequently, non-re-release) takes little account of these subtleties and continues to assume that the solution lies in the *management* of the process rather than the development of professional practitioner skills to support and motivate offenders to comply with their licence conditions (Raynor and Maguire 2006; Hudson *et al.* 2007).

The importance of seams

The imaginary of seamlessness has five core components:

- An official law and order discourse that, in seeking to eject the Other of unofficial versions, misrecognises a unitary image in which all purposes of sentencing are compatible and achievable;

- The legal construction of indivisible sentences where the boundary between the inside and the outside of prison becomes irrelevant and/or dissolved in the interests of public protection and flexible individualised treatment;

- In the name of a 'holistic' approach, the creation of the 'prisobation' officer who is afforded greater 'freedom' to support offenders by acquiring more of the trappings of imprisonment, such as prison keys, risk assessment tools, executive recall procedures;

- An 'independent' body that decides release and re-release on the basis of 'objective' assessment about a very narrow and prescribed range of factors deemed relevant (within official law and order discourse) to the prediction of risk of re-offending and of causing serious harm, but for which many prisoners may not – and indeed could not – have been prepared (see Halsey, Chapter 11; Hörnqvist, Chapter 9);

- The provision of 'wraparound' post-release services, tailored to the needs of each individual ex-prisoner and delivered locally by co-ordinated multi-agency projects and arrangements in 'win/win' strategies, where returning the persister to custody is as much a measure of success as is claiming credit for the desister's change of heart.

What all these components have in common is an inability to deal with the inevitability of 'loose ends'. The appearance of seamlessness requires that 'loose ends' be tied up and hidden on the 'wrong' side of the material, never to be visible on the 'right' side.[9]

The imaginary of seamlessness is threadbare – thin and tattered because the 'loose ends', refusing to be hidden away, unravel. Carter's belief that 'end-to-end' offender management would reduce re-offending and thus reduce the prison population has been exposed as having quite the opposite impact. Of course, Cohen wrote about 'iatrogenic feedback loops' 20 years ago: 'control leads to more control … new systems being created to deal with the damage done by the old systems, but then inflicting their own kind of "damage"' (1985: 171–2). What, if anything, has changed in those 20 years? Managerialism and the New Penology notwithstanding, perhaps the only difference is that we now *know* Cohen's analysis. As Carlen argues in the Introduction to this book, policy-makers and practitioners *know* that concepts such as seamlessness do not, and cannot, be implemented, but that is no longer significant. What matters is that the concept binds together all decent people in a version of Durkheim's collective conscience. It is sufficient for the system to 'stand for' seamlessness because that defines the 'kind of society' we wish to believe we live in.

In a review of Raynor and Vanstone (2002), Nellis (2003) warns against embracing the concept of seamlessness too readily, arguing that:

So long as the idea of community penalties as something distinctively different from prison existed, at least the possibility of penal reductionism remained alive: without that distinctiveness even the possibility slips away, and imprisonment is normalized. (Nellis 2003: 479)

We need to remind ourselves that there *is* a boundary between custody and the community, that probation officers are different from prison (and police) officers, that resettlement is different from licence compliance, that a determinate sentence is different from an indeterminate one, that rehabilitation is different from risk assessment and that recall to prison is *not* a 'useful management tool'. All these mechanisms of control have their place but they cannot – and should not – be woven into a seamless fabric. Together they form the jumble, or pell-mell, from which a modest patchwork of support and, conceptually separately, control might be stitched. Patchwork

... fits together pieces of varying size, shape and colour and plays on the texture of the fabrics ... an amorphous collection of juxtaposed pieces that can be joined together in an infinite number of ways ... (Deleuze and Guattari 1987/2004: 526)

Notes

1 'Contestability' refers to the government's desire to open up the provision of services for offenders in the community to the private and voluntary sectors.
2 The acronym ASPIRE features in the National Offender Management Model: Assess, Sentence Plan, Implement, Review, Evaluate (NOMS 2006).
3 For a discussion of the emergence of the 'prisi-polibation' officer (the result of the blurring of boundaries between the police, prison and probation services) see Mawby, Crawley and Wright 2007.
4 I am grateful to Ronnie Lippens for these insights.
5 www.opsi.gov.uk/acts/acts2007/20070021.htm
6 As a former member of the Parole Board, this was the phrase I used most commonly when summarising my reasons for recommending (or not) the release of a prisoner.

7 Although these three case studies are based on real cases for which I drafted reasons while a member of the Parole Board, they are all presented here in a fictional form with no identifiable characteristics.

8 As I write, Lord Carter has produced a new report on the future of imprisonment in which he acknowledges the problems posed by IPPs and calls for a review of this sentence (Carter 2007).

9 The temptation to extend sewing metaphors is great. Many sewing terms – bias, easing, interfacing, stitching, for example – could illuminate aspects of criminal justice.

Chapter 7

Pain and punishment: the real and the imaginary in penal institutions[1]

Joe Sim

The state is invisible. It must be personified before it can be seen, symbolised before it can be loved, imagined before it can be perceived. (Walzer, cited in Neocleous 2003: 4)

Loyalties do not grow simply in complex societies: they are twisted, invoked and often consciously created. (Hay 1977: 62)

The imaginary and the fantastic have become deeply embedded in the political culture and popular consciousness of England and Wales. The subtitle of Larry Elliott and Dan Atkinson's book, *Fantasy Island*, neatly, but pointedly, sums up the direction of the authors' analysis: *Waking Up to the Incredible Economic, Political and Social Illusions of the Blair Legacy* (Elliott and Atkinson 2007). As the subtitle suggests, Elliott and Atkinson are concerned with deconstructing the legacy of Tony Blair and, in particular, Blair's fantasy that 'Britain under his stewardship is well on its way to becoming "this other Eden"' (2007: 26). In a similar vein, Simon Critchley has noted how '… it is through the fantasy of the enemy that the fantasy of the homeland is constituted. Politics has arguably always been conducted at the level of fantasy; the image and the spectacle, but it is particularly egregious at the present time' (Critchley 2007: 134).

The fantasies discussed by Elliott and Atkinson, and the egregiousness identified by Critchley, have been particularly evident with respect to Blair's interventions into the debates concerning law and order. From his time as Shadow Home Secretary, when he linked the abduction and murder of two-year-old James Bulger by two ten-year-old strangers to the apocalyptic breakdown of the social order (despite the fact that the majority of children murdered are killed by relatives and friends), through to the identification of 100,000 known offenders who, he argued, were responsible for a disproportionate number of crimes, Blair's 'rhetorical compulsion'[2] as Prime Minister was pre-eminent in articulating a very definite and precise image of criminality. In a Gramscian sense, his compulsive rhetoric was pivotal in tutoring and educating the wider society into, if not embracing, then at least seriously accommodating, commonsense definitions of social harm and criminality. In turn, his reductive evocations were underpinned by an excoriating, evangelical positivism that demanded interventions into the lives of the socially mendicant, those identified as depraved, deprived, desperate and dangerous.

In making this case, Blair, his government ministers and many in the mass media inevitably, and arguably deliberately, ignored the compelling evidence concerning a range of crimes and social harms – domestic violence and murder, rape, deaths at work, deaths on the roads, racist and homophobic abuse, attacks and murders, income tax evasion, deaths in custody and state crime – whose impact on particular groups was, and is, often more severe and deleterious than the conventional crimes with which he was concerned. These harms, while occasionally being recognised by politicians and policy makers, have not broken through the commonsense rhetoric governing crime in England and Wales. It was (and is) a commonsense which was not only redolent of Einstein's definition of the term as 'the collection of prejudices acquired by age eighteen' (cited in Thomas 2007: 28) but was one which the government appeared either unwilling or unable to transcend. This, in turn, allowed specific images (and imaginaries) to dominate and lead the cultural and political debate despite the availability of competing data and research evidence which provided a more complex picture regarding the risk and nature of victimisation that different groups, especially those on the economic and political margins, faced in their everyday lives (Hillyard et al. 2004).

Furthermore, Blair, both as Shadow Home Secretary but, particularly as Prime Minister, articulated his own version of what Stuart Hall has termed 'regressive modernisation' (Hall 1988: 2). While Blair constantly argued for the modernisation of the institutions of British society in order to face the challenges of the globalised free market, crucially, he did so by invoking a sepia-tinted, idealised view of the past in which community cohesion was built on respect and responsibility and where crime was held in check by informal mechanisms of social control which magically and mysteriously produced a pluralistic, consensual social order. In a key speech in June 2006, he discussed the world as it was before the Second World War. Here, 'the men worked in settled industrial occupations. Women were usually at home. Social classes were fixed and defining of identity. People grew up, went to school and moved into work in their immediate environs' (Blair 2006: 3). For Blair, while there was 'something both comforting and suffocating about these communities', it was the informal mechanisms of social control which operated within them which provided the heartbeat which pumped the life blood of order into them and the lives of those who lived within their idealised boundaries:

The disciplines of informal control – imposed in the family and in schools – are less tight than they were. The moral underpinning of this society has not, of course, disappeared entirely. That is why our anti-social behaviour legislation, for example, has proved so popular – because it is manifestly on the side of the decencies of the majority. It deliberately echoes some of the moral categories – shame, for example – that were once enforced informally ... these communities were very effective at reproducing informal codes of conduct and order. *They contained a sense of fairness and honour, what Orwell habitually referred to as 'decency'.* (2006: 3–4, emphasis added)

This 'imagined community' (Anderson 1983) and, in particular, the reassertion of informal social controls, was central to Blair's vision of the moral and social order he envisaged as operating in twenty-first century Britain. However, his golden beacon of idealised communitarianism mystified an altogether grimmer picture of communities in which the lives of many women and children, living within their patriarchal boundaries in the first half of the twentieth century, were scarred as they faced an often brutal reality of domestic violence and incest from which the informal mechanisms of social control offered little protection. The communities which Blair so idealised were often based on a culture of masculinity which not only kept this violence hidden but was also overtly hostile to outside state intervention (White 1986; Hague and Wilson 1996). None the less, despite this evidence, the imaginary community remained central to Blair's sense of governance to the point where a document published by New Labour in 1998 could argue that:

137

In the past the large factories and pit villages produced their own stable social conditions. In particular, they helped to foster the transition from adolescence to adulthood. Economic deregulation has led to the breakdown of these community ties. As communities have disintegrated all too often levels of crime and disorder have increased. (Labour Party, cited in Sim 2000: 331)

In addition, New Labour (and Blair's) imaginary world was, and remains, built on a classic juxtaposition between, and categorisation of, individuals into the law abiding, decent majority and the feral, amoral minority. As Foucault constantly pointed out, such juxtapositions have been central to the development of intrusive measures of surveillance and control since the birth of the prison at the beginning of the nineteenth century and legitimated their subsequent dispersal into the social body of the disciplinary society he saw emerging at that time (Foucault 1979). This juxtaposition reached its zenith in July 2006 when the Home Office published *Rebalancing the criminal justice system in favour of the law-abiding majority* (Home Office 2006). This caustic document contained a foreword by Blair, and an Executive Summary by his flint-edged, hard-line Home Secretary John Reid. Again the document was underpinned by implicit and explicit categorical juxtapositions: the law-breaking minority and the law abiding majority; the victim and the offender; balance and imbalance; the communitarian past and the anomic present; and the formal and the informal. The second and third paragraphs of the Introduction set the tone for what was to follow:

We are a pioneering nation in criminal justice. Our court system is one of the oldest and most highly respected in the world. We pioneered policing, and our police forces are reckoned among the finest in the world. And we also led the way in prison reform and in the development of the probation service, making sure that our penal system was about rehabilitation as well as about punishment, so that it protects the public in the long term as well as in the short term.

This is a proud history. But we must make sure that, as well as having a long pedigree, our system is fitted for the modern world, and that we continually challenge it to make sure that it supports its fundamental purpose of delivering justice which keeps citizens safe. (Home Office 2006: 9)

It follows from this argument that the criminal justice system, its institutions and the state servants who manage and run them, are particularly imbued with, and underpinned by, symbolic representations which are themselves imaginary, fantastic and, indeed, often delusional. In the case of England and Wales, these representations have been central to the maintenance of a deeply divided social order since at least the beginning of the eighteenth century (Hay 1977).

This is the context within which I want to set the discussion in this chapter which is concerned with a related, though more circumspect issue: investigating the imaginary prison. In focussing on the prison as an imaginary entity, the chapter is concerned with analysing how the official rhetoric of the institution, based upon the essential benevolence, justice and accountability of its everyday operations, ideologically mystifies the grim reality faced by many of the confined. The chapter focuses on penal policy under New Labour, and the social construction of the institution as an imaginary place for the healing of the socially and economically marginalised. It utilises prison officers as a case study in imaginary penality as it is they, and their powerful union representatives, who, historically and contemporaneously, have been a deeply embedded ideological and material presence in building a hegemonic consensus around the difficult nature of their occupation and the subversive dangerousness of those whom they confine, who themselves are ideologically constructed as determined by some malevolent psychological or biological programming which propels them to disengage with the rehabilitative benevolence on offer. However, the often physically grim, psychologically lacerating and spiritually withering reality of prison life is quite different from the imaginary, inclusive prison. It is a reality where violence, and the threat of violence, are often embedded in the very fabric of prisoners' lives to be mobilised at any point in the day or night if the macro collective order itself is threatened or the micro order of prison officer authority is challenged or subverted by prisoner insubordination. Thus, the imaginary prison, and the socially constructed world of prison officers, forecloses debate about the actuality of penal practices as they are directly experienced by the confined.

At the same time, this imaginary world is not hegemonic; it is often undermined by, and riddled with, its own internal contradictions. Therefore, the chapter is also concerned with the challenges to, and contestations around, the imaginary prison which have come from prisoners' rights organisations and prisoners themselves. These challenges transcend this imaginary world of the present, and instead imagine a future built around a different penal reality, underpinned by different possibilities for responding to offenders not as 'lesser breeds outside of the law' (Gilroy 1987: 72) but as individuals who share a common, though fractured, humanity with those beyond the prison walls. Therefore, the concept of the imagined (as distinct from the imaginary) as utilised here is ideologically disruptive in that it operates to expose the desperate reality of prison life. It thereby stands in direct opposition to official discourse and its underpinning rhetoric of progressive, ameliorative reform. The imagined is also politically transgressive in that it provides the ideological parameters for thinking about and developing progressive interventions which both recognise the corrosive dangers of state incorporation and which are also future orientated: in the case of the prison towards fundamentally questioning and radically transforming the process of confinement *and* the wider inequitable social and political arrangements which provide the meaning for, and give legitimacy to, the institution's existence. It is to a consideration of these two intertwined issues that the chapter now turns.

The twenty-first-century imaginary prison: more prisons, less crime

One key imaginary element in official discourse is built on the fallacy that more prisons equals less conventional crime and more public tranquillity. Politicians, in particular, have been central to the articulation of this argument. In his classic text *Prison on Trial*, Thomas Mathiesen pointed out that politicians justify their position as governors of social reality by engaging in continuous social action which invariably and inevitably involves expanding the number of prisons:

> By relying on the prison, by building prisons, by building more prisons, by passing legislation containing longer prison sentences, the actors on the political level of our own times ... obtain a method of showing they act on crime as a category of behaviour, that they do something about it, that something is presumably being done about law and order ... No other sanction fulfils this function as well. (Mathiesen 1990: 139)

As the room for political and ideological manoeuvre has become increasingly circumscribed so politicians have fallen back on a penal mentality where the prison has become both the starting point *and* the finishing point for the debate around crime control. Consequently, social action in and around the prison involving building more prisons and refurbishing existing institutions, has set the parameters for the debate about law and order, as well as giving meaning to the career prospects of the politically upwardly mobile in a law and order society. Mathiesen's point is directly relevant to the politics of New Labour's law and order policies. Between 1997 and 2007, successive New Labour administrations spent approximately £187 *billion* on law and order 'services' (Solomon *et al.* 2007: 18).

More particularly, in 1995, total penal expenditure for the year was over £2.84 billion; by 2006 this had risen to over £4.3 billion. At the end of 2007, there were 139 institutions holding just over 81,500 prisoners. Between 1995 and 2007, the prison population had increased by 60 per cent, or more than 30,000 prisoners, while the projected figure for 2014 was over 100,000.[3] The Carter review, conducted for the government by Lord Carter of Coles and published in December 2007, recommended that a further 6,500 prison places should be added to the ongoing prison building programme which was already adding 8,500 places to the system. The majority of these places would be constructed and developed inside three mysteriously termed 'Titan' prisons which for Carter were to be '... a key part of the strategy for the modernisation of the prison estate. Each Titan prison would provide up to 2,500 places, comprising five units of approximately 500 offenders all holding different segments of the prison population' (Carter 2007: 38).

Thus, the prison remains central to the law and order discourses, plans and objectives of the New Labour government (and indeed to the law and order objectives of their Conservative opponents). It also remains deeply embedded in the popular and political consciousness of the society despite 200 years of crisis, contestation and conflict and its failure (at least in terms of its overt goals) to deliver redemption by way of the rehabilitated offender. And yet the institution has not only endured but, as the data outlined above indicate, it is on an expansionist course that will move England and Wales up to the next rung on the international ladder of imprisonment with respect to the rate at which the country imprisons the Queen's subjects. Imagining that the prison, through this rate of imprisonment, will contribute to the stabilisation of a deeply unstable and unequal social order with its desperate cultural, synoptic obsession with the cult of celebrity (Bauman 2002; Mathiesen 1997) is built on the search for the magic bullet of reform which will progressively lead the institution away

141

from the lurching crises that bedevil its everyday existence towards a penal nirvana that is organisationally stable and progressive and, above all, offender friendly as it and its workers pursue programmes and policies built on the benevolent normalisation of the confined. However, as Foucault has noted, the discourse of reform, and the imagined benefits it will bring, has been central to the idea of the prison since its inception at the end of the eighteenth century: 'word for word, from one century to the other, the same fundamental propositions are repeated. They appear in each new, hard-won, finally accepted formulation of a reform *that has always been lacking'* (Foucault 1979: 270, emphasis added). I will return to the discourse of 'lacking' below and its relationship to the imaginary prison. For the moment I want to pursue the issue of reform further by looking at the current penal situation in England and Wales for it is here that the idea of the reformed prison has reached its zenith through the arrival of the highly genderised 'working prison' (Carlen 2002b; Sim 2005).

Making the institution work

Since 1997, New Labour governments have argued that prisons can be made to work, at least in theory:

not by pursuing [Michael] Howard's policy of bleak austerity but through committing staff and resources to developing a range of different programmes specifically designed to change attitudes, challenge behaviour and lower the rate of recidivism. Programme delivery was to be achieved through the construction and consolidation of a web of *partnerships* operating *between* criminal justice and local authority agencies in order to provide a *'joined-up'* response to crime and punishment. (Sim 2004a: 253, emphasis in the original)

How were these partnerships to be achieved? In the twenty-first-century prison, the traditional custodians of the confined, the prison officers, have been joined by a phalanx of criminal justice workers, new 'judges of normality' (Foucault 1979: 304), who together have reinforced the view that the prison is *the* place to redeem the deviant. From the 'chaotic' drug addict to the 'determinedly' unemployed, from the educationally and emotionally 'illiterate' to the parental 'failure', there will be a programme that fits the risk profile of these individuals which in turn will normalise them and their behaviour. In the last ten years there has been a proliferation of these 'judges of normality' moving into the prison either as creators of new fields of discipline such as health promotion or as representatives of the old disciplines such as psychology whose field of disciplinary influence has been extended through the sheer number of its practitioners employed in prisons. Additionally, the role of psychologists in supervising psychological assistants, enlisting the support of prison officers trained in the basics of psychology and extending their reach into the post-prison community has reinforced this disciplinary influence still further. Between 1999 and 2002, the number of psychologists doubled to over 600 which made the prison service 'the largest single employer of applied psychologists' (Towl, cited in Sim in press). In 2004 alone, more than £150 million was spent on cognitive skills programmes (Ford, cited in Carlen and Tombs 2006: 344).

There are, however, two fundamental criticisms that can be made of this brave new world of penal 'community, identity and stability'.[4] First, the new partnership programmes demonstrably individualise broader social and structural issues so that it is the offender's distorted and twisted viewpoint which needs the intervention of experts. Women are particular targets for individualised intervention and attention where the goal is to change 'their *beliefs* about the world; the problem is in their heads, not their social circumstances' (Carlen 2002b: 169, emphasis in the original). Second, Carlen and Tombs have noted that:

> therapeutic programming in prison is always buttressed by all the old punitive and security paraphernalia of previous centuries of creative penal governance; and that such an accretion and layering of disciplinary modes of containment strategies effortlessly produce the mixed economy of the therapunitive prison. (Carlen and Tombs 2006: 339)

Carlen and Tombs' argument is important for the purposes of this chapter in that they are pointing out that the punitive was, and remains, central to the deployment of containment strategies behind the walls of penal institutions.

Thus, from the perspective of prisoners, violence, and the threat of violence, are visibly embedded in, and welded to, these containment strategies, while simultaneously remaining marginal and invisible to those who perpetuate the imaginary myth of a revitalised prison service built on a raft of sanctified, Zen-like principles of toleration, respect and understanding. At a fundamental level, as Robert Cover has noted:

... most prisoners walk into prison because they know they will be dragged or beaten into prison if they do not walk ... The 'interpretations' or 'conversations' that are the preconditions for violent incarceration are themselves implements of violence ... The experience of the prisoner is, from the outset, an experience of being violently dominated, and is colored from the beginning by the fear of being violently treated. (Cover 1986: 1607–8)

Nicos Poulantzas made a similar point less than a decade earlier when he noted that 'the institutional materiality of the state' (Poulantzas 1978: 49) is not just reproduced by physical violence and repression but it is also reproduced by 'something about which people seldom talk: *the mechanisms of fear*' (1978: 83, emphasis in the original). For Poulantzas, these mechanisms:

are inscribed in the labyrinths where modern law becomes a practical reality; and while such concretization is based on the monopoly of legitimate violence, we must go into Kafka's Penal Colony in order to understand it. (1978: 83)

Recent reports by the Chief Inspector of Prisons, and her team, support Poulantzas' argument. Despite the endless calls and demands for reform and change from liberal prison reform groups and academics, and despite the appeasing rhetoric articulated by successive governments, the prison remains a dangerous place, physically and psychologically for the confined.

In Pentonville in 2006, 'only 43% of prisoners ... believed that most staff treated them with respect' (HM Inspectorate of Prisons, cited in Sim 2007: 192). Furthermore:

Fewer prisoners than in 2005 felt at risk from other prisoners: but many more felt at risk from staff: 40% (compared with 29% last time) said that they had been insulted or assaulted by staff ... Some prisoners told us that they were reluctant to complain formally about ill-treatment by staff, in case of reprisals; and the one formal complaint we saw had not been investigated properly. Use of force was high, and recording of how and why it was used was insufficiently precise. (Sim 2007: 192)

The punitive prison culture is also differentiated by 'race'. In 2005, the Prison Inspectorate interviewed 5,500 prisoners in 18 prisons and found that it was Asian prisoners who faced the greatest bullying and abuse with 52 per cent indicating that they felt unsafe 'compared with 32% of white prisoners and 18% of black inmates ... while Asian prisoners face[d] most racist abuse from other inmates, black prisoners felt they were least likely to be treated with respect by staff' (*Guardian*, cited in Sim 2007: 192–3).

The situation at Wormwood Scrubs prison between 1992 and 2001 provides a scorching example of the issues around violence in prisons. In early 2007, the former prison governor Peter Quinn, who co-authored a review of the prison, indicated that there were 'almost 40 officers [who] were each involved in assaulting three or more prisoners, often on many occasions' (Letter to *Private Eye*, No 1175, 5-18 January 2007). Quinn went on to provide a damning indictment of the regime with respect to one prisoner in particular:

> ... there was the disturbing inquest into the death of John Boyle who was found hanging in his cell and who had injuries inconsistent with hanging. There was no Prison Service investigation into this suicide, as there should have been. This becomes all the more sinister in the context of those whose cases I reviewed, who had been threatened that they would be hanged by staff who said they had got away with it before. One prisoner misheard them to say that the prisoner they had killed was 'John Ball'. There were many more allegations of staff brutality that fell outside my terms of reference.

Finally, and in keeping with the analysis developed below, those staff who attempted 'to ameliorate things' were faced with 'a campaign of personal vilification characterised by attacks on their property, qualifications or sexuality'.

The issues discussed above raise serious theoretical and political questions about the role of prison staff in the imaginary prison. It is this question to which I now turn.

Imaginary prison staff

While violence, and the fear of violence, remain central to the lives of the modern prisoner there is a further dimension to the role that prison officers perform which further enhances the imaginary prison. Put simply, prison officers often do not believe in the policies that they are supposed to implement to change prisoner behaviour. Indeed, in concentrating on the gap between rhetoric and reality, media correspondents, government ministers, liberal reformers and many academics mystify a profound issue and concern, namely that the often vituperative, feral attitudes that underpin the everyday interactions that many, though not all staff, have with prisoners, *is* the reality on the landings, particularly in the local inner city prisons that remain locked in an atavistic time warp that emphasises solidarity with fellow, basic grade officers, no matter what their managers might say, and punitive degradation for the confined, no matter what official policy might indicate (Sim 2007).

Thus, while the state (in this case, prison officers as state servants, aided and abetted by their union representatives, the Prison Officers' Association) 'never stops talking' (Corrigan and Sayer 1985: 3), this 'state talk' is incessantly focussed on an imaginary 'lack' – lack of resources, lack of time, lack of managerial support, lack of public and political sympathy for the difficult nature of their everyday work. Concentrating on the politics of 'lacking' obscures the fact that the majority of prison officers as state servants are acting as if they *believe* they can, and indeed, *want* to deliver on the promised benefits of the prison if only more time, more resources, more managerial support and more public sympathy were forthcoming for the difficult job they do in quarantining the disreputable away from the respectable. The unofficial strike by prison officers in August 2007 provides a perfect illustration of what prison staff see as their beleaguered position, a position that they have constantly and incessantly articulated to the point where this has now become accepted as a key starting point and a dominant 'truth' for the debates about the problems besetting the contemporary prison. In a press release – *Union Pays Tribute to British Press* – which was sent to all political and industrial correspondents, leaders of the Prison Officers' Association (POA):

> placed on record their thanks to the British press and media for the fair and accurate way in which they reported the events pre and post the National Strike of prisons in England and Wales on Wednesday 29th August 2007. Colin Moses National Chairman said: 'It is pleasing to see that the British Press gave a fair and balanced synopsis of the events surrounding the POA's fist [sic] National Strike in its 68 year history. The general public's view was that the action by prison staff was both right and justified.' Brian Caton General Secretary said: 'It is not very often that a

union pays tribute to the press and media, but on this occasion it is only right and proper that we acknowledge our fellow union members, who work for a variety [sic] press and media organisations and gave a fair and accurate report to the British public.' (Prison Officers' Association, 2007)

In the aftermath of the dispute, a further imaginary 'truth' was disseminated, namely that prison staff are the regular victims of systemic and uncontrolled violence. Thus in October 2007, the POA demanded that their members should be able to use batons against 15-year-old detainees:

Glyn Travis, assistant general secretary of the POA, said there was a need for staff at young offenders institutions (YOIs) to protect themselves. His members, he said, had sustained fractures, bitten off ears or injuries to the face with a pen in assaults by inmates classed as children or juveniles. Assaults on staff rose 'well in excess of 100 per cent' over the past three years. Mr Travis added there was a 'serious problem' with the criminal justice system and if staff were allowed to carry the batons, 'juveniles will think twice about picking up a pool cue'. (www.telegraph.co.uk. Accessed 23 October 2007)

What has been created here is the image of the prison officer as the central figure in a benevolent web of penal supplication, the guardian and protector of the body and mind of the prisoner and of a penal social order that is fragile and beset by the morally and socially feral. Reinforcing this 'truth' is the deeply embedded discourse of the prison officer as the victim of the pathological other – the atavist and the amoral. There are a number of important points to be made about the social construction of the prison officer as victim which I have discussed elsewhere (Sim 2004b). For the purposes of this chapter there are two specific points I want to make. First, violence against prison staff is treated as if it were the norm and that they face an everyday battle to avoid being bullied and bludgeoned by the feral other. In reality, violence against staff:

operates through a dialectical process sustained by *exaggeration* in relation to the numbers who are assaulted and murdered and *overdramatisation* in relation to the seriousness of the violence against them. At the same time, violence committed *by* state servants is also mystified ideologically through a process of *individualisation* and *circumspection* ... this means focusing on the few 'bad apples' allegedly responsible for institutional violence while narrowly defining the nature and extent of violence against those who are in the care of the state. This dialectical process has allowed powerful interest groups such as the POA and the Police Federation virtually to monopolise the debate about the violence and danger faced by their members. In a Gramscian sense, this accreditation, consecrated and blessed by the vast majority of the mass media and political spokespersons, has been integral to the commonsense, populist discourse concerning what state servants do and *what is done to them* on a daily basis. (Sim 2004b: 126, emphasis in the original)

Second, accounts by those staff who are committed to creating an empathic and empowering environment for prisoners indicate that they are embedded in a culture that not only systematically traduces them but behaves as if it is *they and their efforts* that are at fault, that it is they who lack the basic instinct for ensuring that prisoners do not rise above their status as less eligible subjects in the barren, psychologically lacerating regimes that the majority of the confined are subjected to on a daily basis and which many find difficult, sometimes impossible to cope with, hence the desperate rates of suicide, attempted suicide and everyday mutilation that pervade the penal estate in England and Wales. Yet, despite the traducing of these officers, and the systemic difficulties they face as individual workers alienated from the punitive penal environment, it is the 'imaginary community' of prison officer culture in which empathic staff are supported and encouraged in their efforts at redeeming the confined which remains the dominant ideological lens through which the role of these officers is understood. The alienation and stress of their everyday existence is subsumed under a powerful ideology of cultural benevolence and prison officer respectability. This image, too, pervades the commonsense understanding that prison officers have of their jobs. Again, in practice, the reality for those staff who do want to provide empathic support can often be grim and unforgiving, especially towards women officers and minority ethnic staff. In the latter category, such staff are more likely to leave the prison service than white staff. Why? An imaginary explanation would conclude that such staff cannot deal with the pressure of being prison officers. Consequently, their inability to cope can be explained through a positivist, often racist, discourse and lens that emphasises constitutional, psychological, family or environmental factors that differentially and pathologically propel minority ethnic staff away from 'doing their time' as prison officers. However, as Marcia Thomas has noted, in reality minority ethnic staff are confronted by the structural issue of institutional racism as well as a series of cultural practices which impact detrimentally on them. These cultural practices – the solidarity of white prison officers towards each other, the banter within prison officer culture and the quasi-military structure of the culture (Thomas 2007: 27–30) are intrinsic to the operation of the prison and are 'responsible for the negative experience of BME prison officers' (2007: 31).

Given the situation outlined above, in the final part of this chapter I want to turn to the strategies which have been developed to respond to the imaginary prison in order to combat and compete with its nefarious impact on contemporary politics and culture.

Contradicting the imaginary

… competing knowledges are the greatest threat to imaginary penalties. (Carlen 2007: 19)

Amy Myrick has made the point that the power of the 'carceral's objectifying gaze' will always be confronted by the 'living, breathing criminal' (Myrick 2004: 107).[5] She develops this point through an exploration of the writings of American women prisoners in the first decade of the twentieth century. For Myrick, and contrary to Foucault's arguments about resistance, prisoners' writings allowed them to resist the carceral panopticon, not by rebelling through 'storm[ing] the Panoptic tower' (2004: 108). Rather:

Prisoners who consciously mirrored a conservative audience chipped away at the carceral. By making appeals that "mirrored" their audience, prisoners obscured their individual identities behind formulaic reflections of 'normality' … their writing defied labelling as 'normal' or 'delinquent'. It did so by obfuscating the data needed for elites to make that call. Writers ceased to be individuals. Instead, they hid behind a 'mirror' of a 'normal' American public, even while officials were projecting very different standards, which, if accepted, they claimed, would bring greater rewards. (2004: 107 and 109)

Myrick raises some important issues regarding the challenges that prisoners developed to undermine the gaze of panoptic power through constructing themselves as the reformed individual, a figure who was so integral to the bourgeois imagination of nineteenth-century American (and indeed British) penal reformers. Central to this strategy, as she notes, was the obfuscation of data which in turn subverted the power of elites to categorise, and hence, control the confined.

In writing books, poetry and articles, prisoners have clearly developed one mechanism for generating alternative 'truths' and 'competing knowledges' which stand in sharp contrast to the accounts articulated by those who are charged with managing and running prisons; accounts which inevitably involve the hagiographic documentation of the interpersonal skills and progressive policy designs they, and their colleagues possess, *whether they believe in them or not.* This development, what Foucault termed the 'insurrection in subjugated knowledges' (Foucault 2004: 7), has a long and important history in British prison culture because these 'subjugated knowledges' expose the often desperate gap between official rhetoric and the grim reality of punishment, an issue which, as Carlen notes, also has a long history in penal politics (Carlen 2007).

Thus, since the early 1970s, a body of alternative knowledge has emerged which has made the invisible visible. This has taken place in the context of the lamentable failure of democratic class politics and politicians to make any kind of worthwhile and serious intervention into the prison system by way of challenging the antediluvian, embedded structures of power that dominate the institution's everyday practices. Although referring to the general political situation regarding the institutionalisation of mendacity in political discourse, the point made by Leo Panitch and Colin Leys has specific applicability to the prison question and the construction of an alternative penal 'truth'. As they have noted:

..the degeneration of public discourse is neither unchallengeable nor irreversible, even if the structural condition that underlies it could only be removed by a thoroughgoing democratic revolution. For the present the important thing is to help make the problem and its causes as visible as possible. (Panitch and Leys 2005: viii)

In England and Wales, radical prisoners' organisations such as the National Prisoners' Movement (PROP), Radical Alternatives to Prison,

Women in Prison, INQUEST and more recently No More Prison, have been crucial in challenging and contesting dominant state discourses through making the invisible visible not only by taking prisoners' accounts seriously, but perhaps, more significantly, by *taking seriously what happens to them inside:*

> ... visible strategies of contestation have included demonstrations outside prisons to draw attention to deaths in custody and the deleterious impact of vulpine, prison regimes on the lives of those who have taken their lives inside. These demonstrations have challenged the traditional invisibility of the prison and its 'circumscribed and specific' role as a 'place of memory' within capitalist modernity (Auge 1995: 78). Instead, public protest renders the prison visible, and makes it part of contemporary, collective thought as opposed to existing on the forgotten margins of a culture which, in the words of Zygmunt Bauman, is built on *'disengagement, discontinuity and forgetting'*. (Bauman 2004: 117, emphasis in the original, cited in Sim in press)

INQUEST'S work around deaths in custody has been pivotal in challenging and transgressing the social construction of those who die in the 'care' of the state as generating their own deaths through their pathological inadequacies. This positivist discourse is a central plank in the political and popular imagination and, in turn, has distracted attention away from the deeply embedded cultural practices of punishment and humiliation that have remained central to the delivery of many penal regimes and which provide the structural underpinnings to the decisions made by individual prisoners to take their own lives. In December 2007, in the case of 20-year-old Louise Gilles, who committed suicide in Durham prison, an inquest jury heard that:

> ... she was a prolific self harmer and during her time at Durham there were 23 reported incidents of self harm. In the last week of Louise's life she had been downgraded to 'basic' regime, staff having removed her television and radio despite knowing that these had been a major distraction from the voices telling her to harm herself ... Prison staff appeared ignorant of her condition and interpreted her as being 'lazy, dirty and idle'. To downgrade her to basic regime was in effect to punish her for behaviour she couldn't help. (INQUEST 2007: 2)

The desperation felt by the confined has extended to beyond the prison walls. Despite the rhetoric of 'joined-up' government which has been central to the discourse of New Labour in the last decade or so, and which again has been endemic to the government's imagined modernisation of the criminal justice system, the community has not provided the protection to ex-prisoners that this modernisation discourse would claim. On the contrary, death remains central to their post-prison experience to the point where the Prisons and Probation Ombudsman has maintained that 'sadly there are far too many deaths occurring in the immediate period following release from custody for me to be able to look into all but a few of them' (Shaw 2007: 1). He has also noted that in a study conducted by the Home Office in 2003 'in the week following release, prisoners ... were about 40 times more likely to die then [sic] the general population' (2007: 1).

There is a final, desperate irony around the imagined modernisation of the contemporary prison, and the never-ending, government-driven focus on the need for the powerless in particular to be responsible for their actions and activities. According to Eric Allison, INQUEST has investigated over 2,000 deaths in custody since 1995. Contrary to the idea that the system is moving benevolently forward and, indeed, becoming more responsible and hence more accountable, many of the deaths highlight:

> ... issues of negligence, systematic failure to care for the vulnerable, institutional violence, racism and abuse of human rights. Yet, despite a pattern of cases where inquest juries have found evidence of unlawful or excessive use of force or gross neglect, *no prison officer, at individual or senior management level, has been held responsible.* This even applies to the 10 cases, where 'unlawful killing' verdicts have been returned. (Allison 2007: 13, emphasis added)

Conclusion

What conclusion can be drawn from the arguments outlined above? Imaginary penal politics remain a key conduit for both legitimating, maintaining and indeed intensifying authoritarian law and order policies. In imagining (and sometimes inventing) a plethora of internal (and external) enemies – from the young to the single parent, from the criminal to the terrorist – both Conservative and New Labour administrations have been at the heart of the state's authoritarian advance in the last three decades (Sim in press). Making this point does not mean dismissing the impact that conventional crime has had, and continues to have, on those on the political and economic margins of a deeply divided, exploitative social order. Clearly, for these groups, crime can have a deleterious social and psychological impact that is neither imaginary nor transitory. Recognising the detrimental and destructive forces unleashed by conventional criminality, and the victimisation that this engenders, therefore challenges the glib assertions made by politicians that those who present a critique of criminal justice and penal expansionism cannot empathically conceptualise what life is like on the margins for the poor and the powerless.

More fundamentally, such critics are often imagined and constructed as being pro crime and anti victim (a discourse which has its roots in the often baleful assertions made by self-proclaimed left realists in the 1980s). Their views are deemed as unworthy and dismissed in favour of ideas that are in touch with the 'real' feelings and experiences of 'ordinary' people. The valorisation of common sense, and the dismissal of ideas that are outside of the world experiences of an imagined and glamorised working class community, was perfectly epitomised by David Blunkett in his time as Home Secretary. His modernising agenda was straightforward. It 'was built on a nostalgic idealisation of a past in which informal social controls controlled crime and generated a respectable and acquiescent social order. Blunkett then mobilised this "communitarian past" and juxtaposed it with a "vision of an apocalyptic present" which was "then used to justify an authoritarian future based on a further clampdown on civil liberties and legal rights"' (Sim in press).

However, like any social process, what appears to be a relentless, unforgiving drive towards social authoritarianism in general, and penal authoritarianism in particular, is an exercise that is not only contradictory and contingent but is one which often generates unforeseen and unwelcome outcomes for those pursuing such policies. Furthermore, the imaginary can also be socially constructed in different, directly empowering ways. It is, for example, perfectly feasible to imagine a more utopian response to crime which transcends the punitive drive towards repression and retribution. This is an immensely difficult strategy to pursue in the current, febrile, political climate where the merest hint of utopian thought is constructed as the meandering ramblings of individuals who are out of touch with the 'real' feelings, aspirations and desires of the wider population for whom politicians such as Blair, Blunkett, Brown and

Cameron presume to speak with their emphasis on pragmatic (and cost effective) solutions to social problems. And yet, the articulation of an idealistic utopianism on the one hand, *and* the development of pragmatic policy interventions and reforms on the other, are not irreconcilable opposites. As Russell Jacoby has noted:

> the choice we have is not between reasonable proposals and an unreasonable utopianism. Utopian thinking does not undermine or discount real reforms. Indeed, it is almost the opposite; practical reforms depend on utopian dreaming – or at least utopian thinking drives incremental improvements. (Jacoby 2005: 1)

Following Jacoby's argument, it is therefore possible to imagine, develop and implement a penal politics that is not regressive and repressive. Imagining an alternative penal realm that transcends the merely repressive, *and* intervenes to change the terms and direction of the policy debate around prisons, are two sides of the same political coin. Indeed, it is important to remember that repressive ideologies, policies and practices have not achieved hegemony despite the desperate and vituperative emphasis placed on them by those in power, not just in the last three decades, as a result of the rise of the neo liberal, new right, but arguably since the birth of the modern prison at the end of the eighteenth century (Sim in press).

Indeed the intensification in the punitive mentality, and the flood of punitive rhetoric that has transpired since the mid 1970s, has not washed away the belief in redemption and rehabilitation, even in the most desperately poignant social situations. This was manifested by the example of Anthony Walker's mother, who, in the midst of unimaginable grief after her son's brutal racist murder in July 2005, talked openly about forgiving his racist murderers. Where were the voices of politicians in this case? While they condemned Anthony's murder as an act of racist barbarism, they were much less forthcoming regarding his mother's plea for forgiveness and redemption. Why? Simply put, her sentiments did not chime with the retributive philosophy articulated by successive New Labour ministers and their Conservative opponents. *Their* imagined victim was one whose family desired vengeance and revenge. This, in turn, meant that the discourse of the victim was socially constructed in very particular ways to the point where those who have been, and continue to be, victims of corporate criminality or who have suffered violence at the heads, hands and feet of state servants, were (and are) not considered as 'real' victims in need of empathy, support and justice. *Their* needs remain on the political and criminal justice margins, subservient and subjugated in the drive to create an image of respectable victimisation that is then used to legitimate a further increase in the authoritarian powers of the state.

Importantly, therefore, despite the power of the imaginary (and the symbolic), and the influence it exerts on criminal justice personnel and policies, crime control in the form of the prison still remains a contested area in the context of an institution which is not only beset by internal contradictions, conflicts and contingencies but is also, as Pat Carlen has noted, part of a 'dominant paradigm of crime processing which ... is fundamentally flawed and incapable of fulfilling its false promises of crime reduction' (Carlen 2007: 19). This then turns the question back to what the alternative might be, a position perfectly articulated by Arthur Waskow, whose words, although written in 1972, arguably have even greater resonance in the twenty-first century as a bulwark against the toxic and insidious influence of an imaginary penal politics that enslaves the imagination and reduces social and political action to the level of pragmatic and often unprincipled expediency:

the only full alternative is building the kind of society that does not need prisons: A decent redistribution of power and income so as to put out the hidden fire of burning envy that now flames up in crimes of property – both burglary by the poor and embezzlement by the affluent. And a decent sense of community that can support, reintegrate and truly rehabilitate those who suddenly become filled with fury or despair, and that can face them not as objects – 'criminals' – but as people who have committed illegal acts, as have almost all of us. (cited in Davis 2003: 105)

Situating Waskow's poignant, inspirational yearning within the theoretical and strategic context of Thomas Mathiesen's concept of 'the unfinished' (Mathiesen 1974: 13–36) provides a very different vision and starting point for thinking critically about law and order. It is a vision that imagines an alternative penal *and* social reality built on empowering and protecting the many at the expense of the few thereby both reversing existing political and penal arrangements and transgressing the crushing entombment of the human spirit that currently prevails both inside and outside the walls of the modern prison.

Notes

1 This chapter is dedicated to the late Ken Murray who, as a prison officer in the Barlinnie Special Unit, not only imagined a different world for prisoners and prison staff but through his leadership put his vision into practice.
2 This was a phrase used by Anthony Beever on BBC Radio 4 News on 20 October 2007. It seemed to me to capture perfectly Blair's rhetorical flourishes.
3 These data are taken from various points in the Carter review. (Carter 2007)
4 This was the motto of the World State, as described by Aldous Huxley in the dystopian *Brave New World*, first published in 1932 (Bradshaw 1993: unpaginated). The contemporary relevance of the motto, especially in New Labour thinking, is striking.
5 Thanks to Roy Coleman for pointing out this article to me.

Thanks to Pat Carlen for her helpful and supportive comments on an earlier draft of this chapter.

Chapter 8

Imaginary reform: changing the postcolonial prison

Andrew M. Jefferson

Introduction

This chapter analyses the imaginaries that animate attempts to bring about changes in postcolonial prisons in Nigeria.[1] The penality under consideration is imaginary reform. The concept of the imaginary which both informs the analysis and is further developed by it refers to a process with two defining features: an authoritative agenda based on an assumption of the universal applicability of human rights and western penal norms; training programmes which in their top-down didacticism deny recognition to local practices, local people and local knowledge. The chapter's main arguments are that:

1 Reform projects animated by transnational flows of normative and normalising discourses on human rights and imprisonment are routed through standardised pedagogical practices which, in the main, fail to recognise and address the embedded experiences of the people and institutions targeted for reform.

2 Although the agents of reform fail to recognise the material conditions which are inimical to the success of the reform interventions, they none the less continue with training programmes both as though they *can* succeed and as if the continued repetition of the same programmes all over the world is evidence that they *have* succeeded.

3 One consequence of attempting to implement prison reforms via the unquestioned and repeated use of cross-national training programmes is that the very fact of them happening may be

mistaken for evidence of human rights implementation – even though the preconditions for human rights implementation in the prisons are never discussed in the training sessions.

4 A concomitant consequence of refusing to recognise both local conditions and the lived experiences of the prison officers who work in them is an imaginary reform – featuring imaginary prisons, imaginary guards and imaginary prisoners. The tragedy is that such sequences of imaginaries can lead people to believe that problems have been addressed, or are being addressed, without the status quo being changed.

The chapter is divided into three main sections and a conclusion.

Human rights and penal reform

The chapter's arguments are illustrated by observations and analysis of two penal reform training events in Nigeria: one of these, a course on aftercare, was instigated from within the Nigerian Prison Service (NPS); the other, on Standard Minimum Rules (SMR) was sponsored externally. But whilst the SMR training was obviously part of human rights discourse, the concept of aftercare for prisoners is a more direct import from western penal philosophy. None the less, it is also the case that flows of penal norms from the West to the South have become integrally connected to flows of human rights discourse and practice (compare with Piacentini (2006) in relation to Russian prisons). The advocacy work of the International Centre for Prison Studies (ICPS) in London (perhaps best exemplified by their manual, *A Human Rights Approach to Prison Management* (Coyle 2002) which has been widely translated and circulated around the world) is a good example of this fusion of rights and norms. The book is jointly sponsored by ICPS and the British Government's Foreign and Commonwealth Office as part of the export of 'good governance', a commodity of the development industry which is regularly portrayed as going hand-in-hand with democratisation and human rights. Certainly the Nigerian trainees themselves interpreted the aftercare training as being about prisoners' rights, one of them remarking: 'This course is really an eye-opener. Even in my dream last night I saw myself treating every inmate as a unique person with rights and privileges to be pursued by me. I shall leave no stone unturned in trying to actualise this noble course.'

Now one might be tempted to say that the Standard Minimum Rules (the subject of the second training event observed) are not about human rights either; they are rules and guidelines for prison practice. Yet, given their dissemination by Prisoners Rehabilitation and Welfare Action (PRAWA), it is reasonable to argue that the SMR are also seen as part of a human rights discourse. The manual on which the training was based is explicit on this (Agomoh 2000a: 2). The Controller General of Prisons, Alhaji Ibrahim Jarma, writes in the foreword:

I commend the effort of PRAWA for organising the training of trainers workshop on Good Prison Practice and International Human Rights Standards which I believe is focused on ways of instituting internal checks and balances within the prison service to facilitate observance of human rights standards …

And further,

I believe the programme epitomises a genuine and practical assistance from a human rights voluntary organisation towards ensuring that the observance of human rights becomes a reality within our prisons …

In addition, PRAWA themselves frame the SMR in terms of the 'history of human rights in prisons', the main topic of the training's opening address. Part II of the manual is called 'The development of human rights and the need for human rights'. It discusses the relevance of human rights and the 'role of prison officers in the implementation of human rights instruments' (Agomoh 2000a: 15). Also it explicitly states on page 22 that 'The SMR training is an intervention in the Prison administration system aimed at integrating human rights philosophies in prisons.' PRAWA's own institutional identity as a human rights organisation with observer status with the African Commission of Human and People's Rights and the Director's position on the National Human Rights Commission further establishes the link between training in the SMR and human rights discourse, while another of their publications (Agomoh 2000b: 23) refers to the SMR as pertaining to the 'Right to: Life, integrity, freedom from torture, health, respect for human dignity, due process of law…'.

I have wanted to make explicit, at the outset, the links between human rights discourses and penal reform interventions in Nigeria because throughout this chapter, I will be arguing that training for penal reform in Africa today is played out under a (global) human rights 'umbrella' discourse which authoritatively, and silently, effectively silences protest that local conditions must be taken into account if cross-national or international reform-interventions are even going to begin to succeed (compare with Mathiesen 2004). The local linking of penal reform and human rights serves also to authorise imaginary reform discourse through an insistence on the universality of human rights and their enshrinement in law. Both the reform agenda and the mode of delivery of the SMR training are animated by a pervasive pedagogy about the universality of rights and their global impulse. Whilst the aftercare training is facilitated by Prisons Headquarters, it, like the SMR training, is an example of penal norm export (Jefferson 2007a). Under the auspices of justice sector reform, explicitly introduced to improve prison conditions, training programmes about prisoner classification, rehabilitation and aftercare, together with new prison buildings, are being sponsored by government development agencies and the United Nations. But, rather than reforming prisons, the importation of such an assemblage of Western prison governance strategies may well be lending a spurious legitimacy to Nigerian, and other African, penal systems.

Training aftercare officers, rights discourses and changing minds

In October 2002, as part of eight months' ethnographic fieldwork amongst prison officers in Nigeria, I participated in, and evaluated, a training course for newly deployed aftercare officers held at the Prison Staff College in Kaduna. For five days I observed and made notes of the proceedings and towards the end I distributed a very simple questionnaire which all 42 participants completed. Most participants had had very little daily contact with prisoners. They were either based at state or zonal headquarters offices, and were part of the rather bulky administrative apparatus that serves the prisons. The survey asked about their hopes for their new role, their fears for that role, whether their expectations of the course had been met and how they would put into practice what they had learned.

The course consisted mainly of lectures by senior staff from Prisons Headquarters (HQ) who had special responsibility for the welfare division of the Nigerian Prisons Service (NPS). Question and answer sessions were also part of the programme. My first impressions on reading through the responses to the survey were that the trainees were a well-informed group who were able to articulate what was expected of them. Their replies to questions highlighted both their hopes and fears about the likelihood of being able to implement what they had learned on the course. In lecturers' answers to questions from participants, the novelty of the task ahead was recognised primarily in terms of the need to improvise and introduce innovations. Respondents were clear that aftercare would enable them to contribute to fulfilling the aims of the NPS by rehabilitating, reforming, and reintegrating offenders. Enlightening and enabling the community through liaison, public relations, and going out and meeting people and agencies were all mentioned, as were relating to colleagues and managing resources.

Levels of motivation appeared to be high. Officers wrote of their desire to work well, to show dedication, to live up to expectations, to strive to be role models for colleagues, to be determined, and to show zeal and full commitment to carrying out their new duties. At the same time they believed their new role would help portray the NPS in a good light, improve staff morale, and help reduce recidivism. In responding to the questionnaires the trainees described themselves as being motivated, determined, encouraged, prepared, enriched, informed and confident. They described the course as opening their eyes, awakening them, opening them up, exposing them to new knowledge, arming them with information, enabling them to relate to others, equipping them, and empowering them. In terms of practicalising what they had learned, they spoke of the need to: be resourceful; reach out to inmates, colleagues and communities; negotiate to get things done properly; appoint liaison staff; and to involve others. In sum, they made statements of intention. They did not for the most part indicate much by way of *how* they had been equipped to fulfil these tasks nor how the knowledge they had acquired related to the everyday reform practices they imagined they would be carrying out.

Participants praised the course – the survey form did not really allow them to criticise it – and declared their intention to do all in their power to put into practice what they had been taught. I did not doubt their sincerity. Neither did I question the sincerity and good intentions of the course facilitators. Their training discourse was persuasive and compelling. The need for change in the Prison Service, the need for effective supervision of prisoners on discharge, the need to educate society and improve the image of NPS were all made quite clear.

However, even at this stage, some respondents voiced fears about impediments to reform, focusing mainly on lack of funding and materials, possible resistance from colleagues, prisoner suspicion of prisons personnel, community resistance to welcoming back ex-prisoners, big workloads and having staff of the right calibre for reform implementation. Although training staff appeared to accept these worries as being legitimate, they also implied that if officers had the right leadership qualities they would be able to overcome all obstacles to reform. During the closing ceremony a number of suggestions were made from the participants which were fielded by a Deputy Controller General (DCG) from Headquarters, present for the ceremony. Officers asked about the provision of vehicles, the need to publicise aftercare services and the need for refurbishing offices. The DCG responded by saying that he would go straight back to Headquarters and follow up the issues raised. But he also encouraged participants themselves to make a 'passionate sentimental submission' for case work allowances – before adding that Internal Affairs – the ministry responsible for prisons – had unfortunately not been allocated sufficient funds to meet existing costs! The overall message was conciliatory rather than optimistic.

Constraints on implementing reform, then, were not hidden or covered up. On the other hand, though, there was no suggestion that any institutional attempts would be made to overcome them. Instead the responsibility for realising reform was displaced on to officers via rhetoric

official aftercare goes beyond doing your duty; it's a concern with humanity; it's a concern with national security; it's a concern with the future of our country (DCG)

and responsibilisation strategies (compare with O'Malley 1992, 1996) which implied that the success or not of any innovatory reforms would depend purely on the personal qualities of the officers themselves. For example, in the lecture on 'Challenges to Aftercare' the trainees were encouraged to be visionary and creative. In another lecture, this time on the ethical issues of practising aftercare, heavy emphasis was put on the integrity of the officer and the way the officer should use his/her 'personality in the service of humanity'. Aftercare officers were to be 'friends of the poor' from whom 'natural love must flow out'!

I turn now to the second training event. In April 2002 a Nigerian Non-Governmental Organisation (NGO,) PRAWA, ran a training workshop for a group of Nigerian and Ghanaian prison officers at the Prison Staff College (PSC) in Kaduna. The three day training was supported by Penal Reform International and the European Union.

PRAWA are a small scale but well respected national NGO working for torture victims and prisoners' rights. They have quite a good relationship with the prison authorities. During the training course they were represented at different times by their executive director, their deputy director (both women, the latter a former senior prison officer), a male co-ordinator, a female chief magistrate from the east of Nigeria and three prison officer resource persons. The delegates from Ghana were predominantly second-in-commands of local prisons. Nigerian delegates included officers in charge of local prisons as well as those serving under them. The course was aimed at officers with prisoner contact. Its focus was the United Nations Standard Minimum Rules for the Treatment of Offenders (SMR).

On the first day of the course, approximately 14 Ghanaians and 20 Nigerians were present. This was not just a sensitisation exercise; it was also a 'training of trainers' workshop, and involved didactic teaching, group assignments, question and answer sessions and role plays. PRAWA representatives and the Prison Service resource persons all took active part in the teaching. After the initial introduction the chief magistrate introduced an icebreaker and delegates were asked about their expectations of the workshop, after which ground rules for the workshop were established. The Chief Magistrate explained the purpose of the event, emphasising that what they learned was expected to impact on others, that they were, in fact, being trained to train others. She also spoke of the need to domesticate UN legislation if it was to be effective locally. The uniformed resource person spoke of how the SMR are a bottom line reference point on how to humanise the prisons system, but also acknowledged that they are worth nothing if they remain on the printed page; there is a need to practicalise them. The style of training, moreover, was presented as being 'bottom up'. As the uniformed resource person put it: 'We lecturers don't want to do the talking. We want the problems to be identified by you.'

The workshop's second day featured role plays in which delegates were asked to act out scenes featuring particular aspects of prison practice: for example, reception procedures, discipline procedures, provision of medical services. Two role play scenarios were outlined: in the first, participants were required to portray how they would normally carry out certain procedures in the prisons; in the second, they were required to act as they would expect to proceed if incorporating the new knowledge they had acquired of the SMR. By the time the role plays were being conducted the officers had been introduced to the SMR, to its objectives to 'humanise the penal system; to conform with global standards of civilised conduct; to contribute to social reform' and to the SMR's focus on human dignity and proscription of cruel, inhuman or degrading punishment.

While the plays presented me with an opportunity to get a sense of prison practice, they also presented an opportunity for trainers to get a sense of the culture into which they were attempting to intervene. But the role plays were not used in this way by the trainers. Instead they were seen solely as a means of ascertaining what the delegates had learned. Unfortunately, one of the role plays on discipline suggested that the players had made a total misreading of the intended impact of the SMR (Jefferson 2005). In both the 'before' *and* the 'after' role play the prisoner was pushed, hit, forced to squat and generally humiliated. The only change in the behaviour of the officers was in the manner in which they acted towards their superiors in the second role play: they marched more smartly and saluted more formally. In discussion afterwards, the humiliation of the prisoner was indeed commented upon adversely by workshop facilitators and, in return, the way in which the prisoner was made to squat was defended by the officers as a means by which prisoners are encouraged to show respect to the senior officer. The facilitators then suggested in reply that maybe such treatment does not engender respect. But it was here that the workshop seemed to meet its limit. When visually confronted with prison practice little more than clichéd critique was forthcoming from the facilitators. The question of *why* the treatment of the prisoner was not transformed in the second role play was not pursued in terms of the SMR.

Analysis

Analysis of the training events described above suggests that imaginary penal reform as instanced by the importation of rights discourses into the Nigerian prison scene is engendered by: a lack of inquiry into the structural and subjective worlds of prison personnel; a refusal to recognise the perpetrators of situated prison violence and investigate its local causes; a silent but operative insistence on the universality of human rights and the global applicability of western modes of training as exemplified by the failure to tailor programmes to address the specific conditions in which their attempted implementation must occur; and unquestioned assumptions about the positive relationships between human rights, international law and local justice.

Lack of inquiry into the institutional and subjective worlds of prison personnel

The Nigerian Prisons Service is a paramilitary organisation still inflected with facets of Nigeria's years under military rule, a rule which was seriously interrupted in 1999 by what many hoped would be a transition to democracy. Today, prison practice in Nigeria, as in so many other places in the world, is still characterised by military-style discipline, a punitive logic and a correctionalist ideology (Jefferson 2007b). The significance of organisational hierarchy for the governance of prison staff and everyday penal practice cannot be underestimated. It is therefore all the more surprising that trainers so blithely exhorted individual prison officers to work to change and challenge the prison system by virtue of their new knowledge and possibly by 'force of personality and leadership'. Compliance with such an exhortation would require individual officers to pit themselves against the very logic of a paramilitary prison service that presently rests not on the SMR but entirely on the military ethos of each individual officer knowing their own particular place within the organisational hierarchy. The essentially punitive logic of penal practice (applied to junior members of the service as well as prisoners) combined with a focus on discipline and the hierarchical mode of organisation, does not allow individual prison personnel to challenge the *status quo*. Position within, rather than knowledge from without, is *what matters* (compare with Liebling 2004)[2] in Nigerian prisons. In other words, everyday life in the prison is not governed by what people know but by how people are connected to one another in formalised relations of subordination. Yet, despite their awareness of their own relative powerlessness to change the existing system, the aftercare officers were still willing to buy into the optimistic imaginary of the trainers.

Both training events denied (through failure to discuss them) not only the logics and institutional structure of contemporary penal practice in Nigeria and elsewhere but also the specific and local socio-economic conditions, explicit recognition of which (as opposed to implicit recognition – see next section) might have added to a greater understanding of why both international and local practices take the forms they do. Explicit recognition and discussion of the severe constraints on the Nigerian Prisons Service, including difficulties of paying staff salaries on time, difficulties transporting prisoners to court, and general poor conditions for prisoners and staff alike might have made it more difficult for the trainers and trainees to collude in the imaginary that the three R's of reform, rehabilitation and reintegration are achievable without the requisite changes in the prisons and prison administration being made. Yet, despite the fact that the Prisons Service is dominated by security concerns and a disciplinary ethos which would make it difficult for the officers to implement what they had learned on the course, the notion of the re-integrative aftercare officer was sustained via a process of recognition and denial which displaced the responsibility for reform away from the institution and its constraints and squarely upon the imaginary freedom of action imputed to the aftercare agents.

The optimism about reform expressed by aftercare officers despite their fears about the severe constraints operating in the prisons to which they would return was a form of knowing forced upon them by the trainers' insistence that the success of the training would be dependent upon the strength of their personal leadership. Caught between external agendas for the correction of deviant states and the spread of global penal norms and the actual prisons in which these agendas are supposed to be played out, the officers were interpellated as the main agents responsible for the success of the reforms. Such responsibilisation of individuals at the same time as discussion of institutional constraints on, and impediments to, reform is minimised, feeds into the persistence of the myth that 'training' is the tried, tested and sufficient instrument for the global adoption of the imaginary that human rights and imprisonment are compatible.

Refusal to recognise the perpetrators of situated prison violence and investigate its local causes

Although the upbeat approach to change displayed by both trainers and trainees left little discursive space for discussion of the likely situational constraints upon attempts to operationalise rights discourses in the Nigerian prisons, the actual rationale for both training events observed was in fact rooted in an implicit knowledge and recognition of the poor conditions in the prisons and of the violence endemic to them. Yet the training sessions appeared to pay scant attention to local factors or to discuss their significance for the participating prison personnel. This was apparent in the trainers' response to the violence towards prisoners instanced in the role-playing session. For, in commenting on the violence exhibited in the role play, the trainers did not investigate its significance to participants as a situated meaningful activity. Instead, they treated it merely as a technical violation of an externally defined norm of conduct and a counterproductive mode of penal control. Yet a prerequisite of rights-based interventions is recognition of the existence of violent prison guards. Brought face to face with them, however, these human rights trainers chose to act as if the unnamed actors of critical human rights reports were absent even as they were present. I am not, of course, suggesting that the alternative would have been to engage in any processes of blame and shaming of the officers involved; but, if an understanding of the conditions which generate violence in custodial institutions is to be preconditional to a reduction in penal violence, then recognition and discussion of those conditions is essential.

Insistence on the universality of human rights and the global applicability of western programmes of training

Both training events described in the first section of this chapter feature an attempt to deliver and distribute new knowledge about universalisable standards which are alien to Nigerian prison practice, and about competences which are impossible of realisation while the economic and institutional conditions for their application are virtually non-existent. But the focus of the training did not actually claim to be on in-prison practice. The stated aim was to 'change minds'.

Training has always been the preferred method for bringing about change in developing countries. Since the times when the early missionaries and anthropologists embarked on educative programmes as part of attempts to share 'civilisation' with 'the natives', training them in 'our' ways has been part and parcel of north–south relations. The very taken-for-grantedness of such pedagogic agendas makes them difficult to question. Lave (Lave and Wenger 1991; Lave 1993), Dreier (2001, 2003), Nielsen and Kvale (1999) and others have argued that it is extremely difficult to examine theories of learning critically, given that the overwhelmingly dominant form of promulgating learning in the western world is through teaching. In the West we have grown up with an educational system that is built on, and reproduces, an understanding of itself as being both universal and universalisable. As a result, other modes of thinking and of transmitting knowledge become difficult to comprehend (Dreier 2001).

More importantly, as far as knowledge export to other countries and cultures is concerned, the fact of being cast in the role of cross-national trainers has also come to be taken as obvious testimony to the trainers' own excellence. Thomas (1978: 57) describes changes during the first half of the twentieth century as combining 'to make the English Prison system ... an exemplar of prison reform'. He continues:

> Vestiges of this are plentiful. For example, each year, despite the dismantling of the British Empire, groups of senior staff from the Commonwealth attend long courses at The Prison Service College, Wakefield, a practice begun in the 1930s.

The implication is that if we are training others it must be because we are really good at running prisons ourselves! And as the quality of the training is assumed to be excellent then 'training' must implicitly legitimate not only itself but also its recipients and their subsequent practice. Central to training ideology is the concept of 'the programme', and an article of faith of programming is that those who have been 'programmed' are necessarily equipped to implement the programme wherever it is required.

Recently I was asked to participate in training some Eastern European civil society groups in rights-based penal reform strategies. When I suggested that it would be reasonable for payment to be calculated so as to cover the costs of time spent tailoring the training to make it relevant to the situation and experiences of the trainees, I was told that this is not standard practice. The assumption is, apparently, that trainers already have a programme that can be delivered, and that the audience and their local context is irrelevant to its design and content. It is the message to be distributed and delivered that is the vital component. The argument that knowledge might be received differently by differently situated actors does not carry much weight. That some prison officers around the world (including the UK) have expressed views that human rights can be seen as 'getting in the way of corrections' (prison officer, Nigeria) and that closer relations with prisoners can be seen as 'putting the snake around our necks' (prison officer, India) is not taken seriously by the universal programme designers. Recipients of the training programmes, wherever they are based, are assumed to be uniformly ready and waiting to receive the good news about human rights and prison aftercare which will then endow them with the same imaginary excellent human rights record in prisons which has, as instanced by the programmes apparently, already been vouchsafed to their teachers from the West!

Human rights, international law and local justice

Marie Dembour (2006) has asked whether the problem of realising human rights lies with rights as concept or rights as practice. She identifies four 'schools of rights':[3] the natural, the protest, the deliberative and the discourse schools; and she demonstrates the extreme breadth of rights discourses and practices. Arguably the most visible rights discourse, at least in development practice, justice sector reform and in the realm of the prevention of torture and organised violence (TOV) is the natural school where rights are perceived doctrinally as tied almost irrevocably to conventions and the law.

The problem of human rights orthodoxy and the rigid binding of human rights to law is that it assumes law to be benign, to be in and of itself some kind of ultimate good. Yet laws and the systems and procedures of jurisprudence are of course the historical products of particular times and settings. Law and justice, moreover, are not synonymous.[4] For, as Hudson (2006a: 30) has pointed out, one important function of invoking the rule of law is as a means of 'reinforcing the message that dominant society is against certain behaviours'. Furthermore, in law 'claims to justice can only be acknowledged if they are voiced in the terms of the dominant group' (Hudson, 2006a: 34). And Asad (2000) puts this even more starkly when he refers to human rights discourses as being primarily 'about undermining styles of life by means of the law' (para. 307). The attempted export of 'good governance' by targeting deviant states through training in SMR involves 'othering' assumptions that Africans are 'not like us' and need help, via law, to become like us. The overall message implicit in the human rights training programmes which I observed was that though the personnel of Nigerian prisons are 'not like us' (otherwise they wouldn't 'need' the training in the first place) they (and we) should act 'as if' they are 'like us' so that Nigeria can more speedily be recognised as a legitimate player in the global market place' (compare with Young (2007) on this type of 'othering').

Conclusion

This chapter has identified the reform imaginaries constitutive of two training events aiming to sensitise Nigerian prisons personnel to rights discourses in such a way that they become agents for change upon their return to the prisons. We have seen how the two events featured processes of othering and silencing (of Nigerian prison personnel) and reductionism (of complex penal issues to the panacea of human rights principles), and how both also neglected to confront the economic and cultural conditions in which Nigerian prison personnel go about their daily jobs in the prisons. Consequently, it was argued that imaginary reform is primarily instantiated through the bracketing off of all impediments to realisation of the reformed prison officer and the reformed prison.

Imaginary reform, in this instance however, was not solely constituted via denial of situated social practices. It was combined with the authoritative voice of rights and global penal norms and delivered via the standard packaging of programming. What was absent from the reform interventions I witnessed was an understanding that structure and subjectivity are generated simultaneously in practice, that the material and the personal are constituted together.

In view of the foregoing analyses and arguments, I end this chapter by suggesting that an analytic focus on persons-in-practice (situated subjects) might point towards the way in which change could usefully be understood as an aspect of both persons and practice simultaneously. Ignoring persons and practice is certainly unlikely to foster transformation of either and is more likely to reproduce conditions of inequality and perpetuate violence. Training staff in SMR by interpellating them as being solely responsible for change, and then thrusting them back into contexts where the training appears meaningless and irrelevant and their positions untenable if they seek to put their training into practice, is likely to result in nothing more than an increase in staff alienation. As a prison officer in another West African country (Sierra Leone) recently observed, 'When the prison officer's roof is leaking he is angry with the prisoners; when he gets paid he dances with them.' Until reformers get to grips with the material worlds of prison officers little headway will be made with reform projects.

The implications of the arguments of this chapter are not that we should abandon rights or reform, nor that training interventions have no effects. The arguments of this chapter are designed to challenge reformers to think about how materiality, relationality and the logics and structures of institutional practice can (and must) be taken into account when prison reform strategies are being planned. In the absence of their local relevance and realisation, rights training interventions run the risk of reproducing by default existing conditions of inequality and injustice whenever the occurrence of formal 'training' is, in itself, wrongly assumed to have addressed a material issue. If legal scholars and development practitioners continue to insist on human rights as bound only to universalisable conventions and universalisable law, rights-based reform strategies will continue to have limited impact. The problem is not with the concept of rights. The problem inheres both in the insistence of rights activists that rights be tied to western law and the extent to which they themselves continue to be committed to western modes of education and training as the sole routes to changing institutionalised practices. Recognition, appreciation and analyses of local situations might allow a more visionary practical rights discourse to flourish. We must, therefore, move away from the 'as if' of imaginary reform from without and in its stead imagine: a concept of rights uncoupled from western law; an effective recognition of local reform spaces; and the building of democratic change from within.

Notes

1 I use the term postcolonial advisedly to remind us that the Nigerian prisons, whilst certainly adapted to local conditions, were in the first place imposed by the British as a direct result of colonial expansion and the protection of British trade interests, the first prison being built in Lagos in 1872. To refer to the postcolonial prison serves to remind us in the West that we are not free of responsibility for the criminal justice institutions that we so often criticise. It also serves as a reminder about the politics of intervening in countries to build structures and institutions that are more for the benefit of external than internal interests and of the ongoing legacies of models laid down during the first half of the twentieth century. For much of current penal ideology in Nigeria still harks back to policies and practices taught and established before independence in 1960.

2 Whilst I have some doubts about the idea of the 'moral performance of the prison', preferring to think in terms of the amoral performance of the perpetrative institution, the idea of *what matters* offered by Liebling is useful.

3 Dembour is well aware that her 'schools' are a heuristic device. In actual practice activists and scholars occupy multiple and changing positions. Her schematic representation and discussion of the variety of positions available is however incredibly useful.

4 If we are persuaded by Asad's argument this claim is resisted by the Universal Declaration of Human Rights itself. He states, '*The Declaration* assumes – problematically – a direct convergence between "the rule of law" and social justice' (Asad 2000: para. 10).

Chapter 9

The imaginary constitution of wage labourers

Magnus Hörnqvist

The prison has been a site of the productive constitution of wage labour since its inception. For two hundred years, prison inmates have been trained to become wage labourers by a combination of work and discipline. Yet the specific targets and techniques have changed over time, along with the nature of work and the requirements in the lower tiers of the labour market. In this chapter I argue that the ideal of the stress-managing service worker has replaced that of the disciplined industrial worker in the course of the last decades. The cognitive skills classroom has dethroned the factory and the focus of interventions has shifted from employment to employability. At the same time, while the labour market affects the prison, the contrary does not necessarily hold true. I will argue that the labour market-related effects of the current European prison are marginal. That claim challenges basic assumptions of penal theories associated with Marxism, governmentality studies as well as cognitive behaviouralism. Although conceptualised very differently, the impact of the prison tends to be exaggerated, with either the repressive or the productive effects on the labour market being over-emphasised. Consequently, an analysis of the penal constitution of wage labourers needs to pay more attention to its imaginary character.

Over-emphasising repressivity

During the Fordist period, treatment was the order of the day for prisoners. What stood out, for contemporary researchers, was the element of psychological treatment; 'more psychologists, psychiatrists, and social workers are being hired' (Anttila 1971: 10). In Sweden, as in other countries, many prison inmates took part in group therapy and group counselling (KVS 1967; Sundin 1970). Industrial work, however, was the primary treatment method. 'To be employed with suitable work' was considered to be the primary means for furthering the correction of the prison inmate (KVS 1967: 39). The conception of 'suitable work' reflected the industrial nature of the economy at large.

The model prisons in Sweden, constructed around 1960, were being built around factories. The factory was the heart, around which the wings were spread out, surrounded by a seven-meter high concrete wall. Torsten Eriksson, the director-general of the prison service at the time, wanted facilities that were above all factories; the penal dimension came second (Bondeson 1974: 332). Prison inmates were disciplined to adapt to the routine habits of industrial labour. In the activity report for the year 1966, the prison service states that 'for the adult normal clientele, employment has as far as possible been organised as vocational training in factories and workshops geared towards modern, industrial production'. Every second inmate was involved in 'real industrial production'. The prison service was organised in four 'production lines': mechanical industry, wood industry, construction work and 'various industries', including textile industry and laundry. Commodities such as road signs, hospital beds, uniforms, files, small boats, desks and loading pallets were produced (KVS 1966: 38f; KVS 1967: 39). In addition, one-fourth of the inmates was working in agriculture or forestry. The rest, or those described as 'lacking the prerequisites for performing at an intense working pace in a civil industrial environment', were employed with internal service and work therapy.

The work inside the prison was designed to resemble the working conditions outside the prison (Sundin 1970: 133f). Industrial work was the primary means for correction – and the goal to aim for upon release. Prison inmates were assumed to be immediately employable upon release. In relative terms, compared with the current situation, it was a small step from the forced work inside prison to the ordinary labour market. Almost half the inmates were seen to be industrial workers already; 45 per cent of the total number of inmates in the late 1960s were labelled as workers in the manufacturing or the construction industry (SOU 1971: 313).

The Fordist era, in general, was characterised by the proximity between the factory and the prison, secured through the operation of disciplinary power (Donzelot 1979; Foucault 1979; Melossi and Pavarini 1981; De Giorgi 2006). If the prison resembled the factory, it was because both institutions were part of the same disciplinary archipelago. Wage labourers were from an early age disciplined in institutions such as the family, the school, the army, the public employment service and the psychiatric care. There was 'a continuous gradation of the established, specialized and competent authorities', which 'moved gradually from the correction of irregularities to the punishment of crime' (Foucault 1979: 299). The 1960s' factory prison was at the very end of that continuum. It was moreover integrated in the ordinary economy through the mechanisms of the welfare state. The government saw as its responsibility the creation and maintenance of full employment (Meidner 1992). This responsibility also included prison inmates. The wages were determined by collective agreements, negotiated at the central level between strong trade unions and the employers' association. Prison inmates were exempted and denied to organise in the union, but when released they would share the conditions of the rest of the working class.

The social context of the current prisons is very different. The Swedish model has been dismantled (Svensson 2001), the assembly-line has gone overseas and the distance between the prison and the labour market appears to have grown. A survey in the late 1960s revealed that half of the entire prison population was employed with regular work before the prison term. At the turn of the millennium, the equivalent figure was one out of eight. Formal labour market participation had dropped from 49 per cent to 13 per cent (SOU 1971: 316; Nilsson 2005: 152). Further, inside the prison, many inmates are *currently* employed with the 1960s type of industrial production. Assembly and packaging, wood industry and mechanical industry are still very important in terms of day-to-day activities inside the prison (KV 2006a; KV 2007); equivalent work opportunities, however, are hard to find in the community upon release.

This may indicate that the role of the prison has changed in relation to the labour market. According to one interpretation, with the transition from Fordism, the prison took on a strictly repressive function. The productive, disciplining function has disappeared, and the relation to the labour market is negative. The prison has become a dumping-ground. The role of constituting wage labour has given way to that of containing non-wage labourers. The prison is seen as the central pillar of 'the government of surplus', since it takes care of a part of the population which is not required on the labour market, and which in this sense constitutes a surplus (De Giorgi 2006:

chap. 3). The surplus population is physically isolated, and barred from interfering with the operation of the market economy. Individuals who constitute part of a 'permanently dysfunctional population' are incarcerated in accordance with their levels of assessed risk (Feeley and Simon 1994: 192). Their surplus status is permanent rather than temporary. Therefore, in 'the waste management prison' (Simon 2007: 173), dangerous collectives are warehoused without any thoughts of their future labour market participation.

This does not necessarily imply that the prison no longer constitutes wage labour. On the contrary, the government of surplus-thesis is perfectly compatible with the long-standing Marxist emphasis on the crucial importance of the prison in securing a constant supply on the labour market *repressively*. The thesis of the prison as a site of an on-going repressive constitution of wage labour exists in two versions; one stresses the ideological function whereas the other concentrates on the physical aspects.

In their classic study, Georg Rusche and Otto Kirschheimer point to what could be called the deterrence-effect. The effect is repressive since it is produced by the use of force, and ideological since it comes through the perceptions of the wage-labouring majority. The prison produces *indirect* labour market effects, since it deters the members of the working class who are *not* targeted and increases their willingness to take legal employment in line with prevailing conditions on the labour market. The conditions of incarceration impact on motivation, and make the working class accept otherwise unattractive employment (Rusche and Kirschheimer 2003/1939; Rusche 1978/1933). This is also known as the principle of less eligibility. The deterrence-effect is taken for granted, or used as part of a historical narrative. It is assumed, in particular, that the prison has 'served as clear and convincing lesson for those outside who refused to adapt' (Melossi 1981: 196), and that this was important in the making of a class of wage labourers in the nineteenth century.

The physical dimensions are stressed in theories focusing on the repressive management of poverty. The social consequences of insufficient or underpaid work opportunities are contained within the institution. The containment-function comprises two aspects. First of all, the prison isolates a part of the population that is superfluous on the labour market, and prevents them from disturbing social order while incarcerated (Wacquant 2004). Secondly, it constitutes wage labour negatively, by curtailing other sources of income. Along with the police, the prison 'coercively closes off any access to any means of subsistence other than the wage' (Neocleous 2000: 70).

The current practice of incarceration signals a determination on the part of most western governments to manage the consequences of the growing inequality repressively. I do not want to contradict that. Yet it would be wrong to think of this as a strictly repressive campaign. And to the extent to which it no doubt is a repressive campaign, there is a tendency to exaggerate the prison-effect on wage labour. Both versions of the thesis of an on-going repressive constitution of wage labour in prison can be questioned on empirical as well as conceptual grounds.

The deterrence hypothesis is problematic as it only theorises perceptions. The actual performance of the prison is irrelevant, only its perceived performance matters. In this way, the deterrence hypothesis is not strictly speaking a theory on the prison. It tends to neglect what is going on in the prison, to make way for an interest in the mediated effects of prison on non-inmates. The prison is reduced to a place where people are worse off than they would be in a regular workplace in the low-wage sector. Further, the deterrence-effect is postulated rather than investigated. To what extent does the prison actually deter the working population from supporting itself through extra-legal sources of income? Research on 'the theory of general prevention', which maintains that the fear of punishment and prison makes the population at large abstain from criminal acts, cannot be cited to support the hypothesis. On the contrary, the idea of a deterrence-effect seems to be an unfounded common sense opinion (Mathiesen 2000: chap. 3).

Numbers present the main problem for the containment hypothesis. The prison population still forms a minuscule part of the total workforce, despite its growth lately. In Sweden, it constitutes 0.2 per cent of the population in the ages 16 to 64 years. Nowhere in Europe does the prison population represent a significant economic factor. Even in England and Spain, where the rate of incarceration is roughly double that of Sweden (Walmsley 2006), the size of the prison population is marginal in relation to the size of the total workforce. A successful transformation to wage labourers would affect the lives of former inmates, but not the day-to-day business of the labour market. In addition, the prison population is not only a minuscule part of the total workforce, but also, which is even more important to the containment-hypothesis, only a small part of the workforce that is not supported by waged labour. In Sweden, up to 25 per cent of the total workforce is not supported by waged labour. The group comprises long-term unemployed, persons on long-term sick leave, social assistance recipients, and recipients of disability pensions (AMS

2003; Prop. 2002/03). In economic terms, they could be considered a surplus population, since most members are not actively competing on the labour market, as opposed to being temporarily unemployed. The relation between the number of prison inmates and the part of the workforce which is not supported by wage labour is about 1 to 100 in Sweden. The ratio might differ, as the prison population is larger and the social insurance system is less generous in other European countries. Still, to speak about a substantial rather than symbolic containment-effect, one would expect significantly higher rates of incarceration. The containment-function is far from complete when around 99 per cent of the population that might be considered superfluous on the labour market is not incarcerated.

The thesis that the current prison, as opposed to the Fordist prison, would execute a 'government of surplus', bolstered by the deterrence or the containment hypotheses, can only provide a partial account of the relation between the prison and the labour market. It might be of relevance with regard to the exceptionally high incarceration rates in the US (Wilson Gilmore 2007; Western and Beckett 1999). Yet in Sweden, and probably elsewhere in Europe, the impact of the prison, taken by itself, on the labour market is negligible. Moreover, taken as a theory of the prison, the thesis ignores what is going on inside the prison, and also for this reason, it misrepresents the element of change. At least with regard to European conditions, one cannot speak of a transition from productivity to repressivity. Even the small minority of the non-working population that is sent to prison will encounter an institution that is productive and maintains a positive relation to the labour market. The relationship however appears to be one-sided. Whereas the prison does not affect the labour market, the labour market affects the prison, not in terms of the size of the prison population but in terms of the content of the treatment. Labour market demands saturate the prison and affect what happens there. That explains why industrial work was the dominant treatment in the 1960s while cognitive behaviouralism dominates today. It also explains why the factory and the assembly line moved into the prison in the 1960s, while prison inmates now encounter small-company bosses in the service economy in the form of role-playing exercises.

Reflections of the current labour market

Even if the employment opportunities for former prison inmates are significantly reduced, the labour market is no more distant to the current prison than during the height of the Fordist era. The relative distance to the world of work is apparent. The prison is still a site of productive power with intimate connections to the prevailing economic regime. What has changed is the way in which wage labour is constituted in prison. I would highlight two changes; (i) the focus of interventions has shifted from employment to employability, and (ii) the ideal of the stress-managing service worker has replaced the disciplined industrial worker.

From employment to employability

The Prison Treatment Act currently in force is a legacy of the industrial welfare approach. It was enacted in 1974 and states that special efforts should be made to provide the inmate with 'suitable employment' and 'suitable living accommodation' upon release, and obliges the prison service to meet the need for education and vocational training 'as far as possible' during the prison term. But the intentions are not being converted into performance targets or translated into administrative routines.

The unemployed status of most prisoners before and after the punishment is reflected in the current cognitive-behavioural ideology. The inmates are no longer seen to be employable. The current rehabilitative approach, the *What works* strategy, adopted in the mid 1990s, proceeds from the assumption that the inmates are different from other citizens precisely because they lack the fundamental prerequisites for employment. The theory of criminogenic needs constitutes the core of *What works*. All efforts rotate around such needs – the identification, targeting and measurement of criminogenic needs, which, by definition, are causally related to offending and can be changed.

Within the Swedish prison service, the theoretical construct is operationalised in the form employed for the individual sentence plan. The criminogenic needs surveyed cover a total of 14 areas: financial situation, education, employment, accommodation, parenthood, family, friends, leisure activities, physical health, mental health, alcohol/drug abuse, compulsive gambling, criminal acquaintances and criminal values. All of these 14 attributes of the inmate are considered criminogenic by the prison service, that is, as having an established relationship with re-offending that is supported by scientific evidence. Moreover, a single inmate may have several criminogenic needs. As studies of the Swedish prison population have shown, this is a population that, as a group, is plagued by financial problems, low education, unemployment, homelessness, health problems and drug use. In many cases, the problems are multiple (Nilsson 2002). However, the current rehabilitation strategy presupposes a specific selection of needs. It is based on the prioritisation of a set of individual attributes, which is translated all the way down from policy-oriented research into administrative guidelines and finally into the instructions embedded in the form employed for sentence plans. In the end only two of the 14 listed criminogenic needs are prioritised: criminal acquaintances and criminal values (KVVFS 2004).

The prioritisation is made with reference to research that supports the claim that offenders often exhibit deficient social skills and antisocial cognition. *The Cognitive Skills Theory Manual* concludes that 'many criminals' are marked by 'a different and distinct "thought process"' (KVV 2002: 6). The thought process is strongly correlated with offending. This claim is based on meta-analyses summarising the findings from a whole range of studies. In one such meta-analysis, Paul Gendreau *et al.* found that the strongest predictors of recidivism were antisocial attitudes, identification with offenders and antisocial personality (Gendreau *et al.* 1996). Further, those features which constitute the strongest predictors are also viewed as the most suitable targets for intervention. If criminal acquaintances and criminal values are systematically targeted, re-offending will be significantly reduced; provided, of course, that the criminal values and thinking are targeted in the correct way and with the correct techniques. The selection of criminogenic needs is intimately connected with a set of preferred interventions – namely, uniformly delivered cognitive-behavioural programmes. *The Theory Manual* asserts that correctional interventions with a cognitive-behavioural focus are the most effective in reducing offending, based on studies conducted by intellectual forerunners of the *What works* strategy such as Don Andrews, Robert Ross and Frank Porporino (KVV 2002). Other types of interventions targeting *other* types of criminogenic needs are considered ineffective. In particular, providing inmates with vocational training and work opportunities is seen as futile, in and of itself, since many of them are incapable of retaining employment. Such an effort will sooner or later be subverted by the inherent shortcomings of individuals who do not master the necessary cognitive and social skills. Instead, interventions must target the underlying inability – 'a different and distinct 'thought process' – that prevents inmates from benefiting from vocational training and work opportunities.

The goal of steady employment is by no means out of sight. On the contrary, by changing themselves and developing new types of 'skills, knowledge and thought patterns', the prison service envisions that the inmate will stop offending and will achieve inclusion into the labour market and other cycles of social life (KVV 2005). Even though the inmates are not assumed to be job-ready, they can change and become employable by learning a pre-selected set of social skills and actively pursuing social options. The focus is on the *available* non-criminal options, however restricted these options are. The inmate's position in the social structure is irrelevant. The vision is restricted to becoming self-controlled and responsible under the prevailing circumstances, and *this* change is of a personal nature. It is a vision that is typical of productive power, and involves simultaneously blaming and spurring on those who are targeted. 'In framing difficulties we encounter as the consequence of our poor thinking,' Kathleen Kendall argues in relation to the spread of cognitive behaviouralism in correctional systems, 'it individualises social problems. However, it does this in ways which appear to empower us' (Kendall 2004: 70).

Conceptually, the dominant focus is limited to individuals. Institutions and social structures never enter into the analysis (van Berkel *et al.* 2002). The response to social exclusion and unemployment is not seen to lie in structural change. More or less everything except the excluded individuals themselves is excluded from policy considerations. There are no collective solutions, only individual differences. The goal could be described as 'personalized trajectories of integration' (Procacci 1998: 74). This involves a tacit, but very specific, conception of the state's role in regulating the labour market. The state must design a solution for each and every individual, and the different responses must reflect the differences that exist between individuals in terms of employability and the motivation to work. This notion of social inclusion excludes the 'demand side' from policy considerations – neither the number of available jobs nor labour market conditions constitute an object for intervention. Jamie Peck and Nikolas Theodore have remarked that this is an example of 'supply-side fundamentalism', since the intent of the state is to 'work aggressively on the supply side to "flexibilise" and "motivate" the unemployed' (Peck and Theodore 2000: 729). The sole focus is on the unemployed as *individuals* who must be integrated into the work force via state-designed 'personalised trajectories'.

The dominant notion of employability emerged in the mid 1990s. From the outset, the concept was defined narrowly, in terms of characteristics of the individual job-seeker. A broad range of individual characteristics, however, went into the definition of employability: social skills, personal appearance, formal education, job-specific qualifications, employment history, access to transport, household circumstances (children at home), health and wellbeing, demographic characteristics (age, gender), language skills, geographical mobility and wage flexibility (McQuaid and Lindsay 2005: 209f). This may suggest – misleadingly – that employability is an intrinsic property of individuals. In fact it is always relative to the current demands of the labour market; 'employability is primarily determined by the labour market rather than the capabilities of individuals' (Brown *et al.* 2003: 110). Hence, individuals are more or less employable depending on *the match* between on the one hand the competence and the characteristics of the job-seeker and on the other hand the characteristics and competence that are valued and in demand. By implication, an individual's employability *may improve*. The skills and characteristics of the individual can be made to better correspond to labour market demands. This aspect – the dynamic aspect – makes the issue interesting from the point of view of interventions.

There is also a bottom line, namely the state in which one is considered not to be employable *at all*, as opposed to not being employable in relation to a specific job. In such a case, the immediate aim becomes creating – or restoring – basic employability. This is the point of intersection between labour market considerations and correctional cognitive behaviouralism. The assumption that prison inmates are not employable can now be qualified. First of all, it means that the prison population lacks basic employability as determined by the current labour market. Secondly, it means that they could be made employable in relation to some forms of employment by means of cognitive behavioural interventions.

There are two main aspects to the concept of basic employability. One relates to the issue of *retaining* a job. Studies of the temporary staffing business in Sweden have shown that flexibility currently constitutes a crucial aspect of employability. For the individual employee, this implies the ability to adapt to varying demands and working conditions with no apparent effort (Garsten 2004). Alongside the importance of flexibility, there is a growing emphasis on what Ronald McQuaid and Colin Lindsay call 'basic personal presentation' and 'basic social skills' – or, as they have also been termed, 'soft employability skills'. Since many entry-level jobs are found in the service sector, social competence and appearance are vital for employability in the sense of retaining one's job. Soft employability skills are also important in interview situations with potential employers. Thus social skills and demeanour are also crucial in terms of *acquiring* a job – which constitutes the other main aspect of basic employability.

Proceeding from McQuaid and Lindsay's analysis of how the concept is used, it is also possible to isolate *a more detailed notion* of basic employability, which constitutes the immediate aim of the interventions associated with first and foremost social democrat initiatives across Europe from the mid 1990s. They list the following items as 'essential attributes' under the general heading 'individual factors of employability': basic social skills, honesty and integrity, basic personal presentation, reliability, willingness to work, understanding of actions and consequences, positive attitude to work, responsibility and self-discipline (McQuaid and Lindsay 2005: 209).

This list could also be viewed as a definition of basic employability. Self-discipline, a positive attitude to work, responsibility and integrity are not job-specific skills but generic qualities required at more or less any workplace. The list could equally well be taken to define the target for cognitive behavioural interventions in the Swedish prisons.

Constituting stress-managing service workers

The prison has changed along with the nature of work. In the factory prison, inmates would 'learn to work conscientiously, respect fixed working hours and adjust to a high working pace' (SOU 1971: 70). But when entry-level jobs are mainly found in the service sector, the cognitive skills classroom has dethroned the factory. A crash course in the virtues of being on time and delayed gratification is no longer sufficient. The current prison is shot through with the norms of the service economy, as modified by considerations of social class.

Cognitive Skills, or The Reasoning and Rehabilitation Training Programme, is the most well-known of all cognitive behavioural programmes. Since the mid 1980s, it has been widely used in several countries in Western Europe and North America (KVV 2002; Vanstone 2000). Cognitive Skills comprises 38 classes, delivered over a period of 13 to 19 weeks. Like all cognitive-behavioural interventions, it is of limited duration and concentrates on a few basic skills. If successful, the programme will engender basic employability. This could be read as the core assumption of the entire rehabilitation strategy:

Many offenders display antisocial behaviour because they lack the skills to act in a pro-social way. Many have difficulties in relating positively to peers, teachers, parents, employers or other authority figures (including prison staff). The ability to act in social situations in such a way that one is *accepted* and met with positive reactions – rather than *rejected and punished* – demands that the offender develops an adequate register of cognitive and social skills. (KVV 2000: 161, emphasis added)

It is taken for granted that the position is subordinate and that the relevant situations are filled with conflicts and frustration. It follows that the actual targets for interventions are impulsive reactions in stressful situations and a failure to act responsibly in the marginal social position which prison inmates are assumed to occupy. Inmates commit crimes and are unable to maintain employment or relationships because they lack the necessary skills to cope with hardship and the expectations of their superiors. The use of the words 'accepted', 'rejected', and 'punished' are not indicative of a relationship between equals. The inmate is the subordinate party. The responsibility lies with the inmate to act so as to avoid being 'rejected' and instead become 'accepted' by 'teachers, parents, employers or other authority figures'.

The subordinate social position of the target group influenced the tactics. This is visible above all in the use of role-playing as the preferred means of intervention. Role-playing in this context goes back to the 'psychotherapy for the poor' designed by Arnold Goldstein. His books (1973 and 1976) are frequently referred to in the *Cognitive Skills* manual. Psychotherapy for the poor was developed as a response to the failure of conventional, insight-oriented psychotherapy when applied outside of the middle class. The lessons of the class-specific failure of psychotherapy would later be translated into the 'responsivity principle' of the *What works* approach, according to which all programmes must be 'consistent with the ability and learning style of the offender' (Andrews and Bonta 1998: 245). Goldstein's approach was explicitly adjusted to what was perceived to be a specific learning style among 'lower-class patients' seeking psychiatric assistance. In particular, it was considered necessary to utilise

techniques responsive to such generalisations about lower-class patients as desire for authority and direction; preference for activity, rather than inspection; desire for structure and organisation; and preference for concrete and objectively demonstrable explanations, rather than engagement in more symbolic activities. (Goldstein 1973: 17f)

The diagnosed learning style reflects the subordinate social position. 'Lower-class' psychiatric patients, and later inmates, needed to be told what to do. Their 'desire for structure and organisation', as well as their 'desire for authority and direction', *were* matched by structure, organisation, authority and direction. In a programme setting, this translates into clearly defined roles and unequivocal instructions. The idea is that the skills cannot be taught by giving lectures, reading textbooks and discussing matters which are *not* 'concrete and objectively demonstrable'. Learning requires the activity of the body rather than the mind. It is assumed that 'the best treatment for offenders' is when the individual 'directly and systematically practises the skills needed to live more effectively' (KVV 2000: 9).

Slavoj Zizek has noted that disciplinary procedures presuppose a notion of ideology as material praxis, where 'the "external" ritual performatively generates its own ideological foundation' (Zizek 1994: 13). Nowhere is this more apparent than in the role-playing associated with cognitive behavioural therapy. The classes provide a space where individuals act as flexible wage labourers, responsible fathers and responsive parolees, while being addressed as flexible wage labourers, responsible fathers and responsive parolees. The corresponding attitudes and beliefs about the world are communicated along with the behavioural instructions, and it is by actually conducting themselves as wage labourers, for example, that the inmates will start to think about themselves as wage labourers, 'in a situation which is as close to real life as possible' (KVV 2000: 212).

The crucial situations are those filled with conflicting interests and frustrations. In the role-playing exercises, all situations are fraught with trouble. Four figures constantly recur in these scenarios: 'your boss', 'your parole officer', 'your partner' and 'a friend'. The inmate must learn to handle everyday frustration in the workplace, negotiate conflicts with superiors, manage stress in close relationships and say 'no' to old friends. That is absolutely essential. The lack of conflict management skills leads to relapses into antisociality. Instead of seeking a compromise and expressing their concerns in a straightforward manner, the majority of offenders are seen to react with aggression, or inversely, to avoid conflicts altogether, and to 'instead devote themselves to different kinds of manipulative behaviours which often are illegal' (KVV 2000: 212). Any foothold gained on the road from the prison to the labour market will immediately be obliterated. Hence, the inmates must learn how to compromise and express concerns in a non-provocative way – by trying out different strategies and correcting themselves while doing so.

The prison service of the 1960s graded the prison inmates with respect to the working pace, willingness to work, attendance, and so on (SOU 1971). The problem was adjusting the inmates to the demands of industrial production; the working pace of the machinery, the 40 hour working week, and the four weeks of vacation every year. Today, it is the harsh world of the low-paid service sector that is being enacted in the scenarios. The main problem is dealing with people under stressful conditions. 'Your boss' in the role-playing exercises is consistently unsympathetic – demanding, irritated or arrogant. One scenario is: 'You want to ask your boss about a day off, but you notice that he seems tired and irritated when he arrives in the morning.' You may really need to do something else that day, but you depend on the permission of 'your boss' as well as on your ability to adapt to the mood swings.

In another scenario, the issue is more appropriate clothing at the workplace. The boss requires clothes which the inmate/employee cannot afford to buy. Among the options at hand, the successful ones involve a combination of deferring and explaining, which makes the boss forgiving to the extent that the former inmate is not fired. 'Being fired' is the natural outcome if the prison inmates mismanage the requirements of their superiors. It is assumed that no one will help them; neither the union nor fellow workers appear in the scenarios. In this way, by acting out micro-conflicts at the workplace, the course participants learn that sustained employment relies on complex negotiating and coping skills.

The general ability to deal with stress is seen to presuppose a variety of specialised skills. One of them is straightforward communication. In the manual, the first scenario designed to teach participants straightforward communication is: 'You have made a mistake at work. Your boss notices this, and yells at you that you are useless' (KVV 2000: 157). This role-play requires two actors. Both characters, the boss and the employee, are played by programme participants. The events unfold depending on the reaction of the inmate/employee, who is instructed to respond in one of three ways:

Aggressively:
You get angry and say: 'I don't like it when you criticise me! Leave me alone.'

Non-straightforward:
You say: 'I'm sorry. I was stupid. It will never happen again.'

Straightforward:
You realise that you have made a mistake and say: 'I'm sorry,
I will be more careful next time. But I don't think you need to
yell at me' (KVV 2000: 157).

All participants must perform at least six times, acting as both the boss
and the inmate/employee and experiencing what happens when they
respond – or are responded to – in each of the three ways. Afterwards
they will be asked what it felt like. When the participants are (not
acting but rather) part of the audience, they are asked to observe and
take notes – and in particular to pay attention to 'body posture, facial
expressions and gestures as well as the verbal communication' (KVV
2000: 155). The scenes are also recorded on video, making it easy
to take a closer look at details in the performance. Comments and
reflections from the participants are encouraged. The teacher will wait
until the end of the class to underline the benefits of 'straightforward'
conflict responses.

To manage stress it is essential to gain control over 'uncontrolled
emotions' (KVV 2000: 155). Anger, in particular, must be contained.
The labour market constitutes one important arena where former
inmates must learn to master self-control in the face of constant
frustration and conflicting expectations. The following self-reasoning
technique teaches anger management, in what is described as
'probably the most important exercise that you [the teacher] can have
with them' (KVV 2000: 266). The participants are asked to visualise
themselves standing in a queue for a movie. They are 'hot, tired and
hungry', when they suddenly notice a man in a suit and waistcoat,
who jumps the queue. The teacher then says:

You tell him, firmly but in a friendly tone, 'hey you, there is
a queue here!' He turns to you and says in a patronising way:
'fuck you!' (KVV 2000: 269).

The participants are told to write down how they think they would
act and think in that situation. The teacher encourages 'truthfulness',
and will in particular focus on responses involving successful use of
violence against the well-dressed man. The teacher is instructed to
argue that when the police arrive on the scene, they will be convinced
by the well-dressed man that you attacked him for no reason. 'Who
do you think the police will arrest – the guy in a suit and waistcoat
or me who is on parole? Guess!' (KVV 2000: 271). The argument is
not built on an ethical judgment saying that it is wrong to hit the man

in the suit, but on the assumption of the class-bias that characterises the work of the police. The inmates are to be convinced on their own terms, and the teacher appeals to a conception that the police will never believe them, and that for this reason this particular course of action is futile. They must concede that the class-biased nature of policing is not liable to change. In this way, the inevitability of the current social structure is tacitly invoked and used as an argument.

The training programme culminates in a series of exercises in 'creative thinking'. The opposite of 'creative thinking' is called 'cognitive rigidity', analysed as a 'lack of flexibility'. This rigidity may lead to a 'feeling of being overwhelmed', which eventually finds its expression in 'inappropriate and antisocial behaviour' (KVV 2000: 279). It is challenged in ten classes and, in each class, the inmates are taught one basic thinking skill; for instance, how to weigh up benefits and drawbacks, or set priorities. To the extent that the exercises involve 'creativity', this refers to the ability to change one's perspective. The participants are taught how to see things from another angle, to consider other people's point of view, or to start thinking about laws and other rules 'from a broader and more balanced perspective' (KVV 2000: 288). This will improve flexibility and help the participants become more adjustable:

> through critical analysis of their own reasoning, they will become more flexible and more willing to adjust to new circumstances and situations, and consider them to be challenges rather than further evidence of the unfairness, injustice and misfortune which come their way and which are beyond their control. (KVV 2000: 354)

Practising the skills in creative thinking will enable the inmate to respond to changes on the local labour market and to other non-criminal options. The prevailing social conditions are re-imagined as 'challenges rather than further evidence of the unfairness, injustice and misfortune'. The programme ends on a positive note – everyone can become a winner. The same message was delivered in the introductory one-to-one meeting between the teacher and the inmate. Success, it was stated, did not only depend on 'education and social class' or 'access to labour market opportunities'; instead, the crucial difference was that 'successful individuals' were able to 'master a set of thinking and reasoning skills' (KVV 2000: 17). Therefore, learning the skills of the cognitive skills programme is *more* important for success than class background and access to labour market opportunities. The uneven nature of the playing field is acknowledged and simultaneously denied. If the harsh world of low-paid service jobs is affirmed during the exercises, it is denied as the prison inmates are motivated to programme participation.

Over-emphasising productivity

The cognitive skills programme relies on voluntary participation and individual responsibility, appeals to self-interest, and empowers the individual in certain respects. At the same time, it contains elements of the opposite: coercion, imposed objectives, close monitoring and limited competence. It targets behaviour, but speaks of thinking skills and values. The aim is to produce basic employability and stress-managing wage labourers. But is that also the outcome? Just as with the theorisation of the repressive dimension of the prison, there is the risk of over-emphasising its *effects*. In this case, the effects are related to productive rather than repressive interventions.

The thesis of the prison as a *productive* constitution of wage labour exists in two versions; one concentrates on the impact on recidivism whereas the other stresses the citizenship effect. The first version is associated with the official prison ideology. *What works* was built on the claim that 'this works!' to change the rate of re-offending. That is, it would affect the actual behaviour of formerly incarcerated individuals. Several studies have been performed with a straightforward focus on re-offending. Some of them have failed to show that the cognitive-behavioural programmes are effective in terms of reducing re-offending (Robinson 1995; BRÅ 2002; Falshaw *et al.* 2003). One recent meta-analysis shows moderate effects on re-offending (Wilson *et al.* 2005). Taken together, as Simon Merrington and Steve Stanley have commented, 'the evidence from rigorously conducted reconviction studies suggests that we are unlikely to see a major impact on reoffending rates, as promised by the "What works?" literature, from programmes alone' (Merrington and Stanley 2004: 18).

Such discouraging results have not affected the belief in the effectiveness of the cognitive-behavioural programmes. What has been affected, however, are the routines of quality assurance. Programme effectiveness is established independently of re-offending rates. Auditing bodies have pointed out the incomplete nature of the follow-up routines. The Agency for Public Management has noted the absence of performance targets framed in terms of re-offending.

Although reducing re-offending is 'probably the most important goal' of the prison service, according to the auditors, 'the statistics on re-offending have not been developed to follow the rate of re-offending on a continuous basis and to relate this to the measures taken by the prison service' (Statskontoret 2003: 43). The National Audit Office re-stated the demand for performance indicators, as well as follow-up routines, focused on the re-integration of former inmates, which could form the basis for policy-level action (Riksrevisionen 2004). There are currently no follow-up routines covering subsequent behaviour or social inclusion. The rate of unemployment of former inmates is of little relevance to the operation of the prison service since the internal system for ensuring quality does not consider employment or other indicators of legal income.

As recidivism and employment data cannot be used to ascertain success, other standards have been found to ensure the quality of the programme. The preferred standard in this regard is pro-social attitudes and values. The success of the programme is ascertained through instruments focusing on self-reported values, rather than on behaviour. The Cognitive Skills programme contains its own follow-up routine. The overall purpose is to detect pro-social change, operationalised as that which is measured by three types of questionnaires. In this respect, programme participants have shown improvements in the context of before and after tests (BRÅ 2002). The test results are seen as reliable indicators of programme effectiveness. In 2000, following five consecutive years of measurement, the national cognitive skills co-ordinator in the prison service self-confidently asserted that 'today, we can demonstrate with such certainty that it [Cognitive Skills] works' (Chylicki 2000). And in 2003, the Cognitive Skills training programme was formally approved by a central accreditation panel consisting of university professors and prison officials, who rated programme delivery and quality (KV 2006b: 25). Accreditation meant that the programme, 'based on the available research, can be expected to reduce re-offending, on the condition that it is correctly delivered' (KVS 2004: 3).

The questionnaires can only supply information on the self-reported perceptions and dispositions of the inmates. Nothing can be said about whether the taught skills are transformed into habits, as intended. Yet although the measures themselves are far removed from conduct, they are theoretically linked to pro-social behaviour. The stated opinions of the inmates are said to 'mirror personality traits and attitudes' that are positively, or negatively, correlated with criminality (BRÅ 2002: 18). This chain – answers which are assumed to indicate personality characteristics, which are assumed to underlie criminal conduct – enables the prison service to uphold a connection with the goal of reduced re-offending, which is not visible in the reconviction data. In this way, as Pat Carlen states (Chapter 1) 'an elaborate system of costly institutional practices' has been created in which the prison employees act *as if* the objectives are realisable while they are in fact not.

The second version of the thesis of the prison as a site of an on-going productive constitution of wage labour comes from the governmentality literature. If the first version focused on the minimum requirements for wage labour, namely non-involvement in criminal trades, the second version takes aim at the maximum requirements, and advances the idea of a citizen-effect. As Mary Bosworth has noted, there is wide-spread consensus in contemporary Foucauldian analysis that productive power produces citizens. The interventions are seen to be 'a primary means of creating accountable and thus governable and obedient citizens' (Bosworth 2007: 68). Training programmes similar to Cognitive Skills have also been defined as 'technologies of citizenship' through which 'individual subjects are transformed into citizens' (Cruikshank 1999: 1). As a consequence, training programmes are considered successful to the extent that individuals 'come to experience themselves' as 'active citizens' (Dean 1999: 32).

This no doubt mirrors the assumptions as well as the ambitions of the prison service itself. According to the assumptions underlying *What works*, a specific type of personality is projected to underlie the criminogenic needs (KVV 2002:15). Antisocial values, attitudes, thinking patterns, emotional reactions and social skills are enduringly linked together into an antisocial personality. At the other end of the spectrum, indicators of self-control and responsibility point towards an individual, embodying all the values, sentiments and predispositions to act associated with an imagined model citizen. This figure is the very opposite of the antisocial personality of the typical offender. This basic conception of difference between the inmate and the citizen has been taken over in the Foucauldian tradition, along with a preoccupation with personal transformation.

But the citizen is not visible in the interventions. The cognitive skills programme teaches basic skills related to the labour market and rudimentary reproductive functions. Turning criminals into citizens transcends the aim of the exercises. The competence produced by the cognitive-behavioural interventions may be important to finding and retaining work in the lower tiers of the labour market. Yet basic presentational skills and self-control in stressful situations are less essential for citizenship in a more inclusive sense. The curriculum does not include being able to take part in political life, form associations, plan one's own work, engage with other parents, or to act in other arenas which might also be considered constitutive of citizenship. To borrow an expression from T. H. Marshall, the programme will not lead the inmates 'to be accepted as full members of society, that is, as citizens' (Marshall and Bottomore 1992: 6). Rather, the successful completion of the programme involves the accomplishment of a state of citizenship, which is reduced to the ability to follow the instructions of superiors, and at the same time hold a relationship together, pay the bills on time and raise children. This bundle of features, however, is more reminiscent of Marx's figure of the wage labourer than of Marshall's notion of the citizen. The inmates may well turn into responsible and active citizens. But strictly speaking, that does not constitute part of the programme. At the same time, and in line with the complex character of productive power in general, there is an inherent tension between the constitution of the wage labourer and the citizen. Citizens are mobilised not simply as labour power but as stakeholders in a common endeavour. Despite the focus on elementary skills, the Cognitive Skills programme is presented to the prison inmates as the way back into society, and participation is linked to their aspirations of social inclusion. However, because of the necessary institutional constraints inherent in imprisonment, the self-governing citizen maintains a presence only as the imaginary other in an ideal of interdependency around which the interventions are organised, but which all aspects of the prison violate (compare with Mark Halsey, Chapter 11).

Conclusion

Contrary to the thesis of a transition from productivity to repressivity, the power exercised by the prison does not – or at least not in Sweden – appear to have undergone any fundamental change since the 1960s. The prison is still a site of productive power, connected to the world of work through the use of disciplinary interventions, even though the employment rates of prison inmates have dropped significantly. The continuity is striking. Nowadays, as in 1790, when the 'means of extracting labour' was a central preoccupation in the panopticon (Bentham 1995: 66ff), inmates are trained to become wage labourers by a combination of work and discipline. Yet the specific targets and techniques of the discipline have changed over time. In the course of the last decades, the ideal of the stress-managing service worker has replaced that of the loyal industrial worker and the focus of interventions has shifted from employment to employability.

The relationship between the prison and the labour market appears to be mainly one-sided. Prison treatment changes along with the nature of work and the requirements in the lower tiers of the labour market, whereas labour market-related effects of the prison are marginal, at least in Europe. This conclusion contradicts the tenets of very different scholarly traditions such as Marxism, governmentality studies and cognitive behaviouralism. Although they conceptualise the process differently, the mainstreams of all three traditions agree that the current practice of incarceration affects the constitution of wage labour. Yet, no matter how the constitution process is conceived – as deterrence, as containment, as improved social skills or as citizen-training – the effect must be considered negligible.

The idea of a deterrence effect on the workforce is a common sense opinion that has yet to be substantiated. The containment effect is contradicted by the small numbers of non-wage labourers in prison, relative to the total number of individuals in the workforce who rely on sources of income other than the wage for extended periods of time. The non-effect on behaviour related to labour market participation is moreover consistent with the nature of repressive power in general. The repressive aspects of incarceration do not produce specific acts. Instead, they reduce the competence to act, or provokes disobedience (Hörnqvist 2007). Neither of these effects is positively related to employability – or citizenship.

While the prison is crammed with productive disciplinary interventions, there is no reason to assume a citizenship-effect. The target of interventions is basic employability rather than citizens. Further, as suggested by the employment and the reconviction rates of former prison inmates, the programmes are rarely successful in terms of behavioural change. It follows that the constitution of the wage labourer is imaginary rather than real. The prison is not a site where wage labourers are actually constituted; it is a show room for the type of labour market opportunities and demands which await the inmates upon release. This also implies that the attempt at the penal constitution of wage labourers is imaginary rather than merely unsuccessful. It is an ideological projection of an ordered microcosm of obedient wage labourers into the perceived chaos of unemployment and criminality.

Chapter 10

Re-imagining gendered penalities: the myth of gender responsivity

Kelly Hannah-Moffat

In the late 1980s, correctional organisations worldwide began an important re-evaluation of their approaches to offender management. From this, a new emphasis on efficient, effective, evidence-based correctional programme strategies and resource management developed, which contributed to an international restructuring of correctional services. Risk, need and responsivity (RNR) principles, originally developed by Andrews *et al.* in 1990, have become a central component in this ongoing restructuring. The RNR model evolved out of an influential practitioner-driven research agenda that rejects the popularised 'nothing works' claim, seeks to determine 'what works', and strategically deploys 'effective', targeted correctional interventions. The RNR model identifies the risk-need factors associated with recidivism (for example, criminogenic needs[1]) and matches offenders to 'evidence-based' programmes designed to target these needs, with the aim of lessening the likelihood of re-offending. Although the RNR framework has recently been challenged by scholars in an effort to produce alternative regimes (Ward and Maruna 2007; Mair 2004; Sorbello *et al.* 2002), it continues to inform and organise prevailing correctional practices. In Canada, RNR principles remain the central approach to correctional treatment under its revised system.

The vast research literature on RNR has only recently considered the implications of this model for women and, to a lesser extent, ethno-cultural and racialised groups. Feminist scholars have offered strong theoretical and empirical critiques of the RNR model for failing to attend to gender differences (Bloom 2003a 2003b; Hannah-Moffat and Shaw 2001; Kendall 2002 2004; Kendall and Pollack 2003; Chesney-

Lind and Pasko 2004). But RNR advocates maintain that men and women share similar risk and need factors and that gender need only be considered within the context of *responsivity*, which refers to the matching of styles and modes of service to the learning styles and abilities of offenders (Andrews *et al.* 1990: 20). The RNR model does not distinguish between racialised or ethno-cultural groups of men and women: as with gender, culture, ethnicity and race are relegated to consideration only within the context of responsivity. How these axes of diversity intersect with gender and/or influence risk and need principles remains unexplored.[2]

There is no doubt that, over the last 30 years, substantial gains have been made in correctional research, policy development and programme design for women and girls. Researchers from multiple mainstream and critical perspectives have convincingly demonstrated gendered demographic differences and that men and women commit different crimes, have different pathways into crime, do prison time differently and experience social economic worlds differently.[3] More recently, the literature posing the question of 'what works' for women has led to the development of 'gender responsive' guiding principles for women offenders (Bloom and Covington 1997; Bloom 2003a; Bloom *et al.* 2003) and a plethora of feminist research on female offenders' risk, need and responsivity factors. The identified need for gender appropriate programming is gaining momentum in the academic community and at the institutional level. A recent national survey of American female prison wardens demonstrates widespread support for the adoption of gender appropriate correctional models (van Wormer and Kaplan 2006). Corrections Canada, which has a long-standing institutional commitment to 'women-centred' programming, recently adopted the language of gender responsivity. British and Australian penal systems have also adopted the language and ideals of gender-informed[4] penal policies (Carlen 2002a). Arguably, gender responsive discourses are rising to ascendancy alongside RNR principles. Yet the extent to which these discourses capture the feminist principles of gender responsivity discussed below is questionable.

Feminist-inspired gender responsive models view the importance of gender, race and culture differently from the RNR version of gender responsivity. The former argue for a holistic, contextualised understanding of women's needs and treatment requirements. In the feminist-inspired gender responsive model, women's 'risk' is firmly positioned within a gendered socio-economic and political context. Although some aspects of the RNR model and the feminist-inspired model overlap (that is, concern about assessment and treatment efficacy) these models have distinct genealogies, beginning with different assumptions about gender, structure, agency and oppression. Despite such important differences, these two templates for correctional programming are being integrated in correctional research policy and programming with increasing regularity. National and international evidence suggests that the logic of RNR is being superimposed on women's regimes and, in some cases, actively merged with the principles of gender responsiveness (Hubbard 2007; Byrne and Howells 2002). Canada's 2004 programme strategy for federally sentenced women, which provides a framework for programme development and implementation for federally sentenced women, is one example of the merging of these two logics (Fortin 2004). Yet scholars have not examined how these two models are being connected in research and practice nor considered the implications of organising punishment around precarious assemblages of 'gendered responsivity'.

In this chapter, I focus on the blending of the RNR with feminist-inspired gender responsivity within Canadian corrections. First I examine the logics of responsivity as operationalised in the RNR, show how this logic positions gender, and how it is applied to female offenders. Next, I review the feminist-inspired gender responsivity model and show how it is selectively combined with RNR in Canada's 2004 *Program Strategy for Women Offenders*. In so doing, I trace the development of 'women-centred' corrections in Canada, beginning with correctional reforms sparked by the crucial 1990 report of the Task Force on Federally Sentenced Women, *Creating Choices*, which established Canada as an international leader in women-centred penality. Finally, I examine unresolved difficulties associated with the newly configured ideal of gender responsivity currently operating in Canadian corrections.

Risk, need and responsivity

Risk, need and responsivity[5] are widely recognised as the three key principles of correctional classification and are considered central to the delivery of 'effective' correctional treatment programmes (Andrews *et al.* 1990: 19). Effectiveness in the RNR model is explicitly defined as achieving reductions in recidivism (Andrews *et al.* 1990: 19). Within the RNR model, the *risk principle* is an endorsement of the premise that criminal behaviour is predictable and that treatment services need to be matched to an offender's level of risk. Thus, offenders who present a high risk are those who are targeted for the greatest number of therapeutic interventions. The *needs principle* pertains to the importance of targeting criminogenic needs (those empirically linked to the risk of recidivism) and providing treatment to reduce recidivism. Here, 'treatment' often means cognitive behavioural interventions that claim to teach and not 'treat', as previous rehabilitative connotations suggest. The *responsivity principle* expands this premise. Andrews and Bonta (1998: 245) suggest that '... treatment be delivered in a style and mode that is consistent with the ability and learning style of the offender. Offenders are human beings and the most powerful influence strategies [correctional interventions] available are behavioural/social/learning cognitive behavioural strategies'. Thus, the current convention in risk assessment and classification is to use the principles of risk and need to systematically bring together information about an offender's history and needs to develop a treatment plan and assign levels of supervision (Bonta 2002); the responsivity principle is used to establish the most suitable intervention. In the RNR model, responsivity is integrally linked to, and contingent upon, risk and need. It is one element of the RNR trilogy, and so discussions of responsivity are difficult to separate from risk and need.

RNR-inspired research has yielded a series of risk-need assessment and classification instruments (that is, the *Level or Service Inventory – LSI*) that are now widely used in many international correctional jurisdictions to link offenders' risk-need to rehabilitation (Maurutto and Hannah-Moffat 2005). This research has also produced a plethora of programme evaluation literature seeking to determine which programmes most effectively and efficiently target criminogenic factors. Although questions of programme and classification effectiveness are important in determining the direction of correctional reform, for correctional treatment providers responsivity has been positioned as a fundamental concern,[6] and yet it has received far less critical scholarly attention than risk and need (Andrews *et al.* 2006; Ward and Maruna 2007: 50; Hubbard 2007).

Responsivity requires attentiveness to how diverse populations respond to various treatment options and to the specific responsivity factors that may facilitate or impede an individual's response to intervention (Ogloff and Davis 2004: 233). Although scholars differ in their categorisation and definitions of responsivity factors, most refer to *general* and *specific* factors. *General responsivity* suggests that 'in general, optimal treatment response will be achieved when treatment providers deliver structured behavioural interventions[7] in a warm and empathetic manner while simultaneously adopting a firm but fair approach' (Blanchette and Brown 2006: 116; Andrews *et al.* 1990; Gendreau *et al.* 2004). According to Bonta and Andrews (2007: 1), *specific responsivity* is the 'fine tuning' of the cognitive behavioural approach in consideration of internal and external responsivity factors. *Internal responsivity* emphasises individual factors such as intellectual functioning, motivation, emotional and mental health, self-esteem and other specific personality traits. Internal responsivity requires that practitioners attend to individual circumstances and a particular array of causes, while cautioning against a 'one size fits all' approach (Ward and Maruna 2007). *External responsivity*, on the other hand, refers to a vague and eclectic range of factors including gender, culture, life circumstances, staff characteristics, therapeutic relationships, environmental supports and programme content. *Specific responsivity* is the matching of service with internal and external factors (Andrews *et al.* 2006).

It is within the context of specific responsivity that the extensive literatures regarding gender- and culturally-specific programming introduced in the next section are recognised as important. However, the literature pertaining to gender, race, culture and responsivity is typically characterised 'as largely unevaluated in terms of its responsivity effect' (Andrews *et al.* 2006: 19); meaning (within RNR logic) that gender and, to a greater extent race and culture, have yet to be empirically established as statistically related to treatment outcome. Gender, however *is* considered to impact the personality and learning style of women offenders. Further, because an 'effective matching of offenders' and counsellors' "styles", as well as intensity of intervention is central to an individual's motivation and readiness for treatment [treatment responsivity]' (Kennedy 2000: 50) gender-based considerations are important to the type and structure of correctional intervention. Culture, which is also listed as a 'responsivity factor' by Andrews *et al.* is not explored in the RNR literature. The silence on race and culture is a continuation of the marginalisation of research on race, ethnicity and culture in mainstream penology.[8]

Researchers have recently taken issue with the empirical research supporting RNR principles. It is almost exclusively based on white male correctional populations, and yet RNR principles are routinely used to assess women and non-white populations and to legitimate correctional programmes. Such applications fail to recognise that risk and need differ among, and between, gendered, stratified and racialised groups. Critiques further focus on the RNR model's reliance on standard risk-need assessments in identifying treatment targets and developing programmes for individual offenders, regardless of gender or other diversity factors. The majority of research on gender in the context of RNR investigates gendered factors associated with a male–female binary. Such a binary approach rests on specific assumptions about the nature of 'gender'. Hannah-Moffat and O'Malley (2007) argue that the insistence on viewing risk (or need or responsivity) as a neutral statistical category limits our understanding of how 'gender' constitutes what we define as risk, and the categories used to identify and assess levels of risk. By design, statistical actuarial techniques used to determine 'effectiveness' cannot address the multiplicity and complexity of differences between, and among, groups of men and women primarily because they operate at the level of the aggregate. Within RNR-informed research, gender unconsciously becomes a uniform category of difference that applies narrowly to how women respond to various styles and delivery modes of treatment, and perhaps more broadly to treatment content. The relevance of gender relates to how being male or female is perceived as impacting treatment and the 'effectiveness' of treatment; not to the identification of 'needs', the gendered pathways to crime, or the experiences of criminalised women. Evoking the responsivity principle in this context necessitates adopting the logic of the RNR model, wherein priority is given to aspects of a woman's life that are empirically shown to contribute to recidivism. Needs, even when modified to include gender relevant variables, are constructed within narrowly defined parameters. Criminogenic needs are not necessarily linked to a woman's perception of what she requires, but are thought of in terms of risk reduction and treatment targets. Treatment programmes are designed, accredited, delivered and evaluated on the basis of their effectiveness at reducing criminogenic needs, and not women's self-reported needs – many of which have yet to be empirically linked to recidivism.

Gender-informed researchers from a range of fields have increasingly indicated that gender-specific risk-need factors exist, that the RNR model requires 'gender specific definition, measurement and focus', and further, that non-criminogenic needs may play an important role in treating women (Sorbello et al. 2002: 199; also see Holtfreter and Morash 2003; Hollin and Palmer 2006; Belknap and Holsinger 1999; Moretti et al. 2004; Reisig et al. 2006). Although evidence of gender differences raises responsivity considerations with respect to different treatment delivery styles for women (Pelissier and Jones 2005), how gender differences should impact correctional treatment and services, especially as they relate to risk and need, remains unclear. The positioning of gender within the RNR model stands in marked contrast to the feminist-inspired gender responsive models I explore next. These models do not construct gender (or race and culture) as variables to be controlled for in a statistical analysis: they are not simply responsivity considerations. Gendered and racialised experiences are considered fundamental in shaping women's identities, opportunities, and experiences as well as the societies in which they live. As critical race theorists aptly illustrate, it is impossible to treat individuals fairly if they are treated as abstractions, unshaped by the particular contexts of social life. Gender responsiveness in the context of the RNR model focuses on quantitative measures of 'effectiveness', individual deficits or sex differences. It fails to capture the nuanced complexities of 'difference'. Alternatively, proponents of gender responsive penal approaches begin from a more holistic premise of qualitative difference, which places considerable emphasis on context.[9]

Gender responsive programmes and services

Proponents of gender responsive approaches, unlike RNR researchers interested in gender as it relates to responsivity, begin from the premise that men and women are qualitatively different in terms of their level and type of risk and need. They argue that gender responsive approaches 'require an acknowledgement of the lived realities of women's lives, including the pathways they travel to criminal offending and the relationships that shape their lives' (Bloom and Covington 2003: 2). Theoretically, this acknowledgement applies to the continuum of correctional intervention from risk assessment and needs identification through to the development and delivery of treatment programmes and services. Proponents of gender responsive approaches argue that policies, programmes and procedures that reflect gender-based differences can make the management of women offenders more effective, increase resources, improve staff turnover and prevent sexual misconduct, improve programme delivery, decrease the likelihood of litigation against the criminal justice system and improve the gender responsiveness of services and programmes (Bloom et al. 2003: vi).

In 2003, the US National Institute of Corrections published a document titled 'Gender responsive strategies: research, practice and guiding principles for women offenders' that outlined the prevailing research on women offenders and presented clear guiding principles for correctional practice (Bloom et al. 2003). This document represented a significant transition in women's penality, in which principles of gender responsive programming were envisioned as an alternative to mainstream gender-blind penal regimes. It advanced the concept of gender responsiveness and used it to create a set of best practices in women's corrections, which are refined in subsequent articles (Bloom 2003a; Bloom *et al.* 2003; Covington and Bloom 2006). Although other countries, including Canada, had a longer institutional history of 'women-centred corrections'[10] this document was one of the first 'empirically grounded' templates for women's correctional management inspired by feminist research.

Chapter Four of Bloom *et al.*'s (2003) report presents a set of six guiding principles and supporting 'empirical evidence' for the development of a gender responsive criminal justice system. The guiding principles are: (1) acknowledge that gender makes a difference; (2) create an environment based on safety, dignity, and respect; (3) address substance abuse, trauma and mental health issues through comprehensive, integrated and culturally relevant services and appropriate supervision; (4) develop policies, practices and programmes that are relational and promote healthy connections to children, family and significant others; (5) provide women with opportunities to improve their socio-economic conditions; (6) establish a system of community supervision and re-entry with comprehensive, collaborative services (Bloom *et al.* 2003). These principles, together with the new vision, are characterised by the authors as 'building blocks', 'blueprints' and 'cornerstones' for improving the management and supervision of women within the criminal justice system. In contrast to the RNR model, these principles firmly position gender as a central organising principle for correctional reform. Gender responsive scholars argue that their approach is based on empirical gender differences. In this way, the gender responsive model is similar to the RNR model. However, unlike the RNR model's reliance on statistical categories, the gender responsive model draws its evidence from studies that use diverse methodological approaches including qualitative interviews, surveys and ethnographies. The gender responsive vision of penal reform is not narrowly linked to concerns about 'effectiveness' in terms of targeting and reducing recidivism. Instead, its theoretical foundation allows for consideration of the complexity and multiplicity of diverse women's experiences.

The gender responsive model is predicated on four related theories: relational theory, pathway theory, trauma theory and addiction theory. Relational theory maintains that women are relational and that 'the primary motivation for women throughout their life is the establishment of a strong sense of connection with others' (Covington and Bloom 2006: 16). Relational theory also maintains that women and men's psychological development differs. Relationships are portrayed as fundamental to women's sense of identity and self worth. Pathway theory signals the importance of gender-specific adversities in producing and sustaining women's criminality, namely histories of abuse, mental illness tied to early life experiences, addictions, economic and social marginality, homelessness and relationships (Bloom 2006: 16). According to pathway theory, the profound differences between the lives of men and women shape their patterns of criminal offending. Trauma and addiction theories are both used to underscore the importance of ensuring that gender responsive penalities are 'trauma-informed' (Steffensmeier and Allan 1998: 17). To be trauma-informed requires service providers to shift from a logic of security and control to a logic of caring treatment. This shift avoids triggering trauma or re-traumatising the individual and requires that counsellors and other staff adjust their behaviour to encourage the coping capacities of the prisoner, enabling them to manage their trauma symptoms. This focus on enabling women is extended in the model's conceptualisation of addictions treatment, which proposes a holistic approach emphasising competencies, self-reliance and strengths, rather than calculations of risk and need.

This conceptual framework provides the foundation for what Bloom and colleagues (2003) refer to as a two-tiered gender responsive approach to treatment programmes and services that focuses on (a) structure and (b) the content and context/environment of treatment. Structural aspects of the model include:[11] emphasising women's competencies and strengths and promoting self-reliance; using women-only groups, especially for primary treatment (for example, trauma, substance abuse); hiring staff members to reflect the client population in terms of gender, race/ethnicity, sexual orientation, language (bilingual) and ex-offender and recovery status; and using gender responsive assessment tools and individualised treatment plans, with appropriate treatment matched to the identified needs and assets of each client. Content and context/environment factors include the argument that services/treatment should address women's practical needs, such as housing, employment, transportation and childcare, regardless of whether they can be empirically linked to recidivism (Bloom et al. 2003: 89).

The gender responsive theoretical framework is different from the 'psychology of criminal conduct' (PCC) (Andrews and Bonta 1998) that informs the RNR model. Within the RNR model, gender responsiveness is contingent upon the paradigmatic logics of RNR, which postulates that treatment should target criminogenic factors and focus on the highest risk offenders. RNR and gender responsive approaches position gender differently at a very fundamental level. Feminist-inspired gender responsive approaches place gender at the centre of their analysis. They argue that gender fundamentally shapes the reality and contexts in which women live and that it is important to recognise biological and demographic sex differences as well as how society and institutions are gendered (Bloom *et al.* 2003). Sexism (and racism) has become embedded in correctional practices through the uncritical use of programmes and policies declared 'genderless' or 'gender-neutral' that are, in fact, 'male-based' (Bloom *et al.* 2003; Hannah-Moffat 2001b). Gender responsive approaches attempt to ameliorate these deeply entrenched inequalities by placing women's experiences at the centre. The RNR model acknowledges gender but considers gender as an element to be added to the principle of responsivity. The principles of risk and need purportedly remain 'gender-neutral'. Traditional areas of criminogenic need (marital/ family, substance abuse, personal emotional issues, employment/ education and associates, and attitude) are seen as 'valid' for both men and women. This empirical claim fails to recognise how gender operates differently in each of these generic categories and how issues not captured in traditional categories are relevant to the production of a gender-informed model of assessment and treatment.

These conceptual differences have resulted in feminist researchers arguing that gender responsive treatment modalities are not compatible with the RNR model. Particular concerns are raised about the concept of responsivity because it stresses cognitive behaviouralism, which, some feminists argue, individualises and decontextualises women's experiences (Kendall 2002 2004; see discussion in Blanchette and Brown 2006: 126). Recall that RNR researchers explicitly state that specific responsivity is the 'fine tuning of cognitive behaviouralism'. In spite of such logical inconsistencies, however, the RNR model and the feminist-inspired gender responsive model are merged in Canada's 2004 programme strategy for federally sentenced women. In the next section, I use the example of Canada's strategy for federally sentenced women to demonstrate how principles and discourses of gender responsiveness have evolved in practice and policy in response to emerging literatures on RNR and gender responsive corrections. I demonstrate how, with their basis in different assumptions about the nature of gender, the RNR model and feminist-inspired model of gender responsiveness produce different outcomes regarding the centrality of gender to women's penality.

Assembling gender and responsivity in policy and practice: Canada's strategy for federally sentenced women

In the early 1990s, Canada undertook a significant restructuring of women's prisons in response to the renowned report of the Task Force on Federally Sentenced Women, titled *Creating Choices* (1990). This reform was meant to redress a long history of sexism and neglect in women's corrections through the development of an alternative women-centred correctional model that focused on the unique needs and experiences of women (Hannah-Moffat 2001b; Hayman 2006). The initial adoption and creation of women-centred prisons was hasty, poorly conceptualised and based on only the scant amount of theoretical and empirical research on how gender should inform penal programmes available at the time. Although well-intentioned, the labels 'gender sensitive' and 'women-centredness' were attached to a wide range of improvised and poorly adapted programmes and managerial processes, without real consideration of *how* gender should be operationalised.

With the publication of Bloom *et al.*'s report in 2003, gender responsive discourse began to spread throughout North America with surprisingly little resistance or debate in the academic community.[12] Premised on the notion that an 'effective' system for female offenders has to be structured differently from a system for male offenders, it was compatible with Canada's broader correctional vision for women's prisons set out in the 1990s. The ideal of gender responsiveness, similar to the Canadian concept of women-centredness that came before it, was intended to mark a conceptual shift in women's penality, an alternative approach to treatment and programme development for women. To some extent, these logics have altered penal regimes, but not necessarily as expected, with the Correctional Services of Canada (CSC) remaining philosophically and organisationally committed to the RNR model, but also to the development and implementation of women-centred correctional programmes.[13]

In 2004, CSC updated its 1994 *Program Strategy for Federally Sentenced Women Offenders*.[14] The 2004 strategy represents a significant departure from previous women's programme documents by clearly positioning the treatment of women prisoners within a gendered version of the RNR. The programme strategy begins with a concise summary of the

RNR and its relevance to women's correctional treatment. Within this strategy, gender responsive 'ideals' and research on gender responsive treatment are modified to conform to RNR principles, with a focus on efficacy of treatment as measured by risk of recidivism. This is an expected outcome in regimes occupied with concerns about efficacy of treatment, where there is a competition for, and need to protect, scarce treatment dollars, and where there are gaps in knowledge and contestations about how gender matters to correctional assessment and treatment.

After laying out the importance of the RNR principles and choice, the strategy articulates its commitment to the principles of women-centredness, a holistic approach, a supportive environment and diversity, which captures a vast, ambiguous range of differences. These are consistent with the principles of gender responsiveness and aligned with some of the therapeutic ideals of responsivity scholars, but absent from the current strategy is a clear focus on how these broad principles can be incorporated into programming. Instead, the programme strategy introduces a narrow understanding of gender and its relevance to programming. *Creating Choices*, which arguably was the first penal document to espouse a gender responsive correctional alternative, stated that such narrow definition 'mitigates against a holistic understanding of women's experiences and needs; an understanding which encompasses physical, emotional, psychological, spiritual and material needs, as well as the need for relationships and connectedness to family and others. If needs are not understood in the context of past, present and future life experiences, if a woman is not seen and treated as a "total person", programmes and policies designed for federally sentenced women will continue to be inadequate and dehumanizing' (TFFSW 1990: 61). This emphasis on holistic treatment, which forms the basis of feminist-inspired gender responsive penal reforms, is not as apparent in the 2004 programme strategy. Instead the strategy defines a holistic approach as follows: 'programs designed for women must recognize the importance of understanding the link with all the areas of a woman's life such as her own self-awareness, her relationships with significant others, her sexuality, and her spirituality' (Fortin 2004: 6). The failure of the 2004 strategy to capture the complex and intersectional character of women's problems demonstrates the difficulty in merging the ideal of holistic treatment with the RNR model's risk-needs prediction, which seeks to hierarchically isolate and treat primarily criminogenic needs.

By 2004, Canada's programme strategy for women had become squarely focused on the RNR model and repositioned gender along with other axes of inequality as a 'responsivity factor' (Fortin 2004: 6 and 8). In the RNR model only some needs are legitimate correctional targets. As previously established, the criminogenic needs to be targeted by correctional programmes are those which are statistically co-related to recidivism. By default, this definition of need categorises needs that are not statistically significant as illegitimate targets or 'lacking in criminogenic potential'. Technical correctional definitions of need are legitimated and authorised by a bureaucratised version of science, not by individuals' lay assessment of their circumstances. Consequently, policy makers and researchers are engaged in a definitional politics that seeks to construct not only a legitimate or 'intervenable need' that is a legitimate correctional target, but by default, also categorises some needs as illegitimate targets or 'lacking in criminogenic potential'. Ironically many of the needs that women prisoners and feminist researchers consistently identify as being meaningful to treatment and change do not fit with the RNR's scientific conceptualisation of need or responsivity. Because responsivity is conceptually linked to principles of risk and need, prior assumptions about need are embedded in the model.

By positioning gender as a responsivity factor, but not central to risk-need assessment (crucial to identifying programmes and their content), gendered concerns are compartmentalised, de-legitimated and only superficially addressed. The RNR is principally concerned with issues of offender management (Ward and Maruna 2007). Bureaucratised scientific knowledges such as the RNR are influential and frequently used to silence competing knowledges,[15] organise institutional practices and to legitimate or de-legitimate a diverse range of correctional programmes. As scholars have observed, RNR in many ways conflicts with gendered, racialised understandings of women's needs and alternative models of correctional treatment (compare with Ward and Maruna 2007). Canada's deeply rooted institutional commitment to RNR limits its ability to meaningfully address gender-based concerns.

Pre-existing assessment practices are used to identify the criminogenic aspects of women's lives and to filter women into relevant programmes. In the 2004 strategy, the gender-informed assessment practices advocated by proponents of the gender responsive model are not even mentioned. Although the report acknowledges a list of factors that feminist scholars have identified as relevant to women's crime and that shape the social, political and cultural contexts of women's lives (dependency, poor educational and vocational achievement, foster care placement, living on the streets, prostitution, parental death at an early age, low self-esteem and suicide), little is said about the relevance of these factors to assessment, or more concretely to programme delivery or content.

The assessment process, which is not presently gender-informed is, however, cited in the report as central to the process of determining to which programmes/interventions women are referred 'to reduce the risk to re-offend' (Fortin 2004: 7). Information obtained through an intake assessment is used to devise a correctional plan that 'incorporates the full spectrum of individual needs and choices, including cultural and spiritual needs' (2004: 7). The issue here is not with the practice of assessment, but rather with the positioning of gender within this process. A programme strategy that purports to identify a template for identifying and 'treating' cogent aspects of a woman's life should use an assessment process that is gender informed in the criteria it uses to assess and identify areas requiring intervention. In Canada, assessment technologies have not incorporated the knowledge of women's crime because traditional criminogenic factors are considered equally salient to both men and women. Gender is repositioned in this regime as important to the delivery and mode of treatment and in how 'women's personalities' impact treatment, but not to the identification of treatment needs or programme content. The continued use of this practice is puzzling in light of feminist critiques of gender-neutral assessment techniques and, by default, of correctional models, which do not build gender-informed assessment tools for women from the ground up (Blanchette and Brown 2006; Thigpen et al. 2004; Hannah-Moffat and Shaw 2001; Zaplin 1998). RNR and feminist-inspired gender responsive scholars agree that the appropriate assessment of needs is crucial to programming. Needs assessment by definition compartmentalises and prioritises women's needs. This issue is complicated by the introduction of concerns about the statistical relevance of needs to recidivism. If a commitment to holistic interventions is to be maintained, programme strategies such as this must reconcile the contradictions that emerge when RNR definitions of criminogenic need are embedded into gender-responsive correctional programming models.

The emphasis on targeting traditional criminogenic needs presents a distinction between programmes that are characterised in the programme strategy as correctional programmes versus social programmes. *Correctional programmes* are defined as 'interventions which address the multiple factors that contribute directly to criminal behaviour' (Fortin 2004: 7). Ironically, the strategy states:

There is international support for the development and implementation of correctional programs that are gender specific. In the past decade, the Correctional Service of Canada has set standards of practice that are based on research that is sensitive to the unique situation of women offenders. Consequently, the practice of delivering non-gender specific programs to women offenders is dissipating. Studies based on women offenders highlight the range and density of presenting difficulties. *Not all difficulties are criminogenic though, and while it is recognized that to be effective, institutional and community interventions must focus on factors that contribute directly to offending, for women offenders there are important responsivity issues to take into consideration (e.g. victimization issues).* (Fortin 2004: 7, emphasis added)

The distinction of non-criminogenic versus criminogenic further informs the programme strategy for women by characterising correctional programmes into treatment categories including: substance abuse; sex offender therapy; reasoning and rehabilitation (cognitive skills training revised); and anger and emotion management programmes. Comparable programmes are offered to men. The extent to which these programmes have been re-conceptualised for women is unclear. As this quote shows, 'effective' gender responsive programmes are re-imagined as modifications to generic programmes designed to target criminogenic needs. The range of interconnected issues that are not easily disentangled or measured against recidivism but that affect women are not programme priorities. These are precisely the concerns that lead feminist-inspired, gender responsive scholars to advocate for holistic interventions and attentiveness to structural, environmental and context-specific factors.

In spite of its silence on gender-informed assessment, the 2004 programme strategy recognises that women are different from men and that gender-specific programming must 'reflect the psychological development of women'. To accommodate gender difference, the programme strategy draws selectively on the feminist-inspired gender responsive model's use of relational theory to reaffirm that relationships play a central role in women's lives and are central to change. It notes:

Although some basic elements of effective correctional programming may apply to both men and women offenders, there are some elements that differentiate the two. Gender-specific programming must reflect an understanding of the psychological development of women. Current thinking in this area suggests that women place great value in the development and maintenance of relationships. Consequently, 'situational pressures such as the loss of valued relationships play a greater role in female offending'. While social learning theories and cognitive behavioural interventions have proven effective with offender populations of both genders, some academics believe that relational theory is an approach that adds effectiveness to programming for women. Relational theory focuses on building and maintaining positive connections and relationships. The main goal is to increase women's capacity to engage in mutually empathic and mutually empowering relationships. To enable change, women need to develop relationships that are not reflective of previous loss or abuse. (Fortin 2004: 5)

This quote draws explicitly on Bloom *et al.*'s 2003 template for gender responsive programming. The focus on relationships fits with the traditional set of criminogenic needs (for example, marital/ family, personal emotional and associate domains) that RNR scholars emphasise as key correctional targets. This combination deliberately positions women's relationships and relational capacities as criminogenic (Hannah-Moffat 2007). The necessity of focusing on relationships is portrayed as important to the treatment of women only and it is framed as being gender responsive. Left under-explored are the 'assumptions' about women, the punitive and regulatory emphasis on women's relationships, and the latent essentialism of this interpretation of relational theory.

Gender and mental health

Within the programme strategy, mental health programmes are also seen as a priority, with women being considered as in particular need of these programmes. The description of responsivity isolates mental health as a particularly salient concern:

One major concern with women offenders is the prevalence of mental health needs. Similarly, the needs of low functioning women who need assistance in daily living skills must be addressed. Also, given the added stress associated with prolonged incarceration, timeliness of program participation is of great importance for women serving long term sentences (10 years and over). (Fortin 2004: 6)

Here, mental health and long-term incarcerations are positioned as responsivity considerations and implied gender differences. The strategy devotes considerable attention to mental health programmes. Interestingly, it is within this context that abuse and trauma are discussed. Concerns about gender and treatment focus on and prioritise mental health needs and the needs of 'low functioning women'. They also note that: 'programs for women must use an approach that is relevant in dealing with the multi-faceted needs of women offenders as opposed to narrow windows of issues. Women need to address emotional regulation issues which underlie other needs such as cognitive functioning and/or substance abuse' (Fortin 2004: 8). This psychologisation of women, along with the use of dominate correctional cognitive behavioural and RNR models for incarcerated women, is the subject of extensive feminist critique (Pollack 2006; Kendall 2002; Pollack and Kendall 2005; Maidment 2006). Although salient, the emphasis on mental health in the context of responsivity reinforces a gendered pathologisation of criminalised women that is largely uncontested in terms of its gendered representations and regulatory effects.

Gender and programme evaluation

Criminogenic needs are linked to the capacity to evaluate the 'effectiveness' of interventions provided to women. Empirically-based programme evaluations play a central role in the legitimation and justification of correctional programmes. The programme strategy advocates the evaluation of women's correctional programmes against traditional measures of effectiveness. It notes that programmes need to include:

… a framework to evaluate the program's effectiveness. Areas of evaluation include, at a minimum: recidivism, reintegration of participants, and assessment of change against program targets, participant satisfaction, rates of participation and attrition, and influence of participant responsivity on outcome. As an element of correctional programs, pre and post assessment batteries are made up of measures that have been validated with offender populations. (Fortin 2004: 25)

Although an evidenced-based approach is laudable, this statement of evaluation fails to appreciate that neither gender-based responsivity factors (Hubbard 2007), nor treatment targets that should measurably reduce women's recidivism, have been conclusively determined. Further, adopting a holistic approach would render such evaluations difficult, if not impossible.

Correctional agencies are to be commended for both their attentiveness to gender and for their concern about evidence-based practices. Nevertheless, vigilant analysis of these principles and subsequent correctional initiatives are important. Increasingly, programmes are being accredited, resources are being allocated, and women are being assessed and managed with criteria derived from a hybrid gendered responsive and RNR archetype. The cycle is vicious – to accredit a programme (gender responsive or otherwise) it must be assessed against responsivity criteria (CSC 2003). Yet these criteria for women remain vague and unspecified.

Gendering responsivity within the RNR

Canadians Blanchette and Brown (2006), feminist supporters of the RNR model, are at the forefront of a recent research initiative that seeks to determine how feminist therapy can be integrated into the RNR. They endorse the RNR model and emphasise the importance of developing a gender-*informed* responsivity model that is only *partly* informed by feminist therapy. They note: 'the existence of widespread cultural support for feminist philosophies sufficiently justifies its inclusion in the (tentative) reformulated gender-informed responsivity principle provided that we can empower women to lead pro-social lives' (Blanchette and Brown 2006: 120). However, they also specify that while cogent, there are few empirical evaluations of feminist therapy that demonstrate its 'effectiveness'[16] in achieving measurable reductions in recidivism.

Blanchette and Brown's (2006) comprehensive analysis of the research on women offenders' assessment and treatment argues that RNR and gender responsive treatment models are compatible. Their research carefully examines current research on women, feminist critiques of the RNR model, and current conventions in feminist therapy; they conclude that feminist theories and relational theory 'dovetail seamlessly' with responsivity (Blanchette and Brown 2006: 136). They state:

... general responsivity is a multidimensional construct that complements rather than opposes seemingly, divergent theories (i.e. Relational theory) or applications (i.e. enhance self-efficacy). [...] The true spirit of the responsivity principle is much broader [than cognitive behaviouralism], encompassing social learning principles as well as relational aspects of therapeutic alliance (e.g. mutual respect, warmth, empathy, firm but fair use of authority). Moreover, *these general responsivity elements dovetail seamlessly with relational theory* (Covington 1998). Recall that, consistent with feminist philosophies, relational theory posits that women in particular are significantly interested in feeling connected to other human beings. Additionally, the theory asserts that connectedness is achieved via empathic, empowering and mutually contributing and respectful relationships. *Thus as stated, the responsivity principle and relational theory can co-exist peacefully. We believe we have already taken the first step towards reconciliation by explicitly incorporating the concept of empowerment into the proposed reformulated responsivity principle.*

Blanchette and Brown 2007: 129 (emphasis added)

Power dynamics aside, what is missing from their analysis is attention to the other theoretical pillars of gender responsiveness, in particular pathways and trauma theory that Bloom *et al.* (2003) posit as central to the structure and context of the gender responsive model. On the surface, RNR and gender responsive models can co-exist peacefully and even employ similar therapeutic strategies (that is, cognitive behaviouralism[17]), but taken as a whole these models are not internally compatible.

The absence of empirical evidence supporting the 'effectiveness' of alternative feminist approaches to assessment, treatment and programming places managerially-minded correctional agencies in a quandary as to how gender 'ought to matter'. Gender is officially acknowledged as important, but an understanding of how to use gender to redesign correctional assessment remains limited. The claim by researchers such as Blanchette and Brown that empirically-based alternatives that depart from the RNR model are absent has led researchers and policy makers to a continued consideration of how gendered considerations can be integrated within the RNR model. This has primarily focused on isolating the factors relevant to women that are empirically linked to offending and recidivism; although consideration is also given to non-criminogenic (that is, not empirically linked to recidivism) factors as they relate to responsivity.

The feminist literatures that speak to 'responsivity' specifically highlight differences in the importance of relationships (Bloom *et al.* 2003, 2005; Covington and Bloom 2006; Dowden and Andrews 1999; Andrews and Dowden 2006), victimisation, empowerment[18], and self-esteem (Hubbard 2006) as 'promising' gendered responsivity factors. Feminist proponents of the RNR model ague that the operationalisation of responsivity should be able to account for empirically established gendered learning and communication styles, as well as a host of non-criminogenic responsivity factors that may impede or facilitate correctional treatment outcomes including child care, protection from abusive partners, physical and mental health care, safe and affordable housing, transportation and access to staff after hours (see Blanchette and Brown 2006: 120–6 and Messina *et al.* 2006). The identification of gendered risk-need and responsivity factors often accompanies an attempt to quantify and test the importance of 'known gender-differences', so as to shift the status of differences from non-criminogenic to criminogenic where possible. In short, the feminist correctional literature embraces the possibilities of a gender-*informed* RNR approach that recognises, empirically 'tests' and incorporates into treatment 'relevant' qualitative and quantitative differences between men and women.

Gender, responsivity and therapeutic context

The discussions of responsivity that filter into penal policy discussions focus on individual factors not structure. A neglected element of responsivity as laid out in the RNR pertains to the penal environment and the 'delivery of programs'. Both the RNR model and gender responsiveness visualised a penal environment that provides a warm, empathic, empowering therapeutic milieu with the intention of mitigating aspects of distrust and disempowerment inherent in punishment. Yet there is little discussion in either literature about the contradictions inherent in the penal therapeutic context. Many penal scholars have warned us about the dangers of 'carceral clawback' (Carlen 2002b) and about how the gender-based reforms succumb to the material and legal realities of inherently punitive environments (Carlen 2002a, 2001b; Hayman 2006; Hannah-Moffat 2001a, 2001b). Clearly there are limits to what can be achieved in a penal context and, while the ideals of responsivity and gender responsive programming are laudable, there is little discussion of how therapeutic interventions are impacted and shaped by the carceral context. The punitive and involuntary nature of prison is different from other therapeutic contexts. This context can differentially impact 'responsivity' factors such as motivation and readiness for treatment. Unlike the feminist-inspired gender responsive model, the bulk of the RNR research focuses on the individual *not* the penal-therapeutic context. There is little exploration of the understandable reasons why some women resist well intentioned intervention in prison, even if it is meant to 'empower'.

In this context, Birgden (2004), who subscribes to many of the tenets of the RNR model, astutely recognises that change within corrections is coerced by law, and so argues for 'a serious consideration of the external responsivity principle in offender rehabilitation'(2004: 293; also see Birgden 2002). She suggests an emphasis on staff as well as the offender 'in terms of staff motivation to support a cultural shift towards rehabilitation and the skills to assist offenders to engage in rehabilitation programmes' (Birgden 2004: 283). This discussion is consistent with Covington and Bloom's (2007: 23) presentation of how 'the development of gender responsive services needs to include the creation of a therapeutic environment'. To promote change and healing, they argue, the therapeutic environment must be inviting, non-institutional, homelike, and welcoming with culturally appropriate decorations and pictures' (Covington and Bloom 2007: 23). Their emphasis on the therapeutic environment stresses the role of trauma and how the penal system can trigger painful memories, the role of 'experienced' and gender aware staff, and the importance of accommodating and planning for women's practical needs upon release. Another essential characteristic of a therapeutic environment for women is safety, an issue that for women in prison is without doubt contentious and fraught with complexity.[19] Feminist-inspired approaches seek to incorporate safety into the structure, content and location of the programme (community where possible) and the choice of treatment provider. These issues are all salient to treatment 'successes'. The RNR and gender responsive approaches continue to understate the fact that prisons are not necessarily warm, caring, safe places in which women can be empowered to create meaningful connections. In fact, quite the opposite is typically the case.

This is not to suggest that meaningful intervention cannot, or should not, occur in prison but rather to suggest new lines of inquiry into the importance of the treatment context. For women in particular it may allow for a revisiting of the community as a more appropriate and under used space for treatment. Further, there is a well-established literature on the effects of imprisonment (Liebling and Maruna 2005) that current and emerging models of gender responsivity and RNR do not engage with. The context of imprisonment and its iatrogenic effects can contribute to our theorisation of 'responsivity' and gender responsive models. Such considerations could prompt us to think more broadly about the 'spirit of responsivity'. Perhaps the ideal of responsivity necessitates a greater emphasis on the treatment environment and the issues of power inherent in these therapeutic relationships.

Uneasy connections

The history of women's penal reform confirms that correctional institutions have the ability to absorb, integrate and temporarily silence critical discourses. Moving beyond the disjuncture between the intent of gender responsiveness and its misinterpretations, reflection on how gender responsive punishment is conceptualised and practised in oppressive disempowering contexts is needed. The articulation and interpretation of 'gender' in social policies should be more forcefully evaluated and debated. Serious consideration needs to be given to definitions of gender and/or culturally relevant criteria, particularly given the punitive context in which this 'empowering therapeutic' logic is mobilised.

Notwithstanding the proliferation of research on gender responsivity, well-intentioned policy makers and academics have not fully explored the assumptions and limitations of gender responsive penality, or the possible (inevitable) contradictions that exist between pre-existing penal logics (such as risk-need approaches) and gender responsiveness. The blending of RNR and gender responsive models on the axis of responsivity simply masks the more fundamental problem of how gender should inform assessment, treatment and penality. Moreover, with few exceptions, the research on gender and responsivity fails to carefully theorise or 'study' the importance of race and culture. Each model identifies the importance of culture, though little is said about how race and culture matter to treatment or to the assessment of risk-need.

Unlike Blanchette and Brown (2006), I am less certain about the compatibility of gender responsive logics and RNR. What is even less certain is what gendered responsiveness 'in practice' *means* in terms of how practitioners organise and deliver correctional treatment. Treatment is currently viewed as an integral part of the risk management continuum and, therefore, treatment responsivity is a critical issue for correctional programmes (see Kennedy 2000).

Clearly, the drive towards 'best practices' in women's corrections necessitates some assurances about the purpose and effectiveness of treatment. I do not dispute the need for research and programming that is attentive to gender and meaningful to women and practitioners working toward the goal of reintegration, whether that research takes the form of RNR or an alternate.

Gender responsiveness has not replaced or produced an alternative to hegemonic correctional models like the RNR. Although the RNR model now acknowledges gender, it does so only peripherally. At the core of the RNR model is the premise that risk, need and responsivity are calculable, which plays an important role in strengthening the authority and legitimacy of current penal practices. By challenging this premise and/or re-framing the 'rehabilitation' question as Ward and Maruna (2007) have, new penalities can be imagined. Yet the imagining of a gendered penalty requires a much more sophisticated understanding of gender and penal environments that we can only hope to gain by closing the considerable and lamentable distance between interdisciplinary studies of gender, race and penal policy. This distance continues to weaken our understanding and use of concepts of gender responsiveness, leaving us with more questions than answers.

Notes

1 A criminogenic need is a dynamic risk factor that is statistically correlated to recidivism – that is, substance abuse, employment, marital family relations.

2 There are some preliminary discussions in Canada about aboriginality and the RNR, but this debate is not well developed in the academic literature.

3 Debates about the how and the extent to which 'gender' should be considered when developing assessment instruments and treatment programmes for women continue (Hubbard 2007).

4 Pat Carlen has used the more specific term 'woman-wise' in her discussions of gender-informed penal policy.

5 Professional discretion is often included as a fourth principle. The principle of professional discretion strategically reasserts the importance of retaining professional judgment, provided that it is not used 'irresponsibly' and is systematically monitored. While important, it has received little empirical research attention, rather it appears to be a principle of classification that allows a practitioner within a highly structured system to maintain autonomy and exercise limited discretion.

6 An extended critique of the theoretical underpinnings of the RNR model (see Ward and Maruna 2007) is beyond the scope of this paper; instead I focus on how responsivity is interpreted and applied to women prisoners.

7 There are three recognised forms of structured treatment interventions: operant conditioning, social learning and cognitive behavioral (Blanchette and Brown 2006: 116).

8 There is some international literature addressing the issue of race and rehabilitation, but it is rarely discussed in the context of correctional programming and the RNR. See for instance: Bhui 1999; Dawson 1999.

9 This statement is not meant to imply that the framing of 'gender' in gender responsive models is unproblematic (Goodkind 2005; Hannah-Moffat 2007).

10 This refers to the adoption of the recommendations of the 1990 Task Force on Federally Sentenced Women – *Creating Choices*, not to the actual implementation of women-centred programmes. There is contested history of the operationalisation of the principles embodied in the Task Force. For additional detail, see Hayman 2006 and Hannah-Moffat 2001b.

11 For a complete list of factors, see Bloom *et al.* 2003.

12 Without doubt, advocates of gender responsivity likely faced institutional resistance, discrimination and budgetary limitations in their attempts to address the specific needs of female offenders. This paper is not suggesting that this struggle did not occur nor that changes in programming for women in prison were not desperately needed. (See Goodkind 2005).

13 The reforms were inspired by the renowned report of the Task Force on Federally Sentenced Women, titled *Creating Choices* (1990), and established Canada as an international model of woman-centred penality. The recommendations of the Task Force which were accepted by the federal government enabled a gendered knowledge of punishment and offending to filter from feminist critiques into Canadian penal policy and, over time, into the managerial regimes governing women's prisons.

14 It suggests that while the now muted principles (empowerment, meaningful and responsible choices, respect and dignity, supportive environment and shared responsibility) at the foundation of the original 1994 strategy continue to be of importance, the strategy itself is outdated.

15 The silencing of knowledge often occurs through the framing of critics or alternative explanations as 'knowledge destruction'. See Andrews and Bonta 1998; Bonta in press.

16 A concern about the state of research on gender differences is echoed in the literature on gender specific substance abuse treatment. For instance Pelissier and Jones (2005: 362) note that: 'The limited literature on treatment outcomes is fraught with conflicting findings with respect to

gender. This is not surprising given that these studies address different questions, use different methods of studying gender differences, are conducted in different settings, use different measures, and use a different follow-up time frame. Such differences impede our ability to arrive at clear conclusions about the differential effects of treatment for men and women.'

17 The debate about CBT is well formed in Shaw and Hannah-Moffat 2004; Pollack and Kendall 2005; Pollack 2005. Here the concern is with the dovetailing of responsivity and gender responsivity.

18 Empowerment in this context is characterised as a mechanism of developing competencies and achieving independence (Austin *et al.* 1992; Blanchette and Eldjupovic-Guzina 1998; Blanchette and Brown 2006: 120). See Hannah-Moffat 2001a for a more detailed critique of empowerment and punishment.

19 Women prisoners view safety within the prison from a relativistic perspective. They reportedly 'perceive prison to be generally as safe as or safer than living in the community. However, they did not see prison as a generally safe environment. Rather, they viewed both the community and prison as dangerous, identifying different kinds of risks' (Bradley and Divine 2002, cited in van Wormer and Kaplan 2006: 144).

Chapter 11

Risking desistance: respect and responsibility in custodial and post-release contexts

Mark Halsey[1]

My aim in this chapter is to explore the lived experience of (dis)respect and responsibility as narrated by young men within juvenile and adult custodial contexts. The discussion is prompted by the simple yet fundamentally critical contention that when residents[2] and prisoners are denied opportunities for engaging and practising the performance of respect, and denied opportunities to care for self and others in 'non-trivial'[3] ways, the process of desisting from crime is severely compromised. As Liebling and colleagues have written, '[H]uman beings need fairness and respect: that is, they need to know that actions and decisions taken in relation to them are morally justifiable and to be in environments that treat them with dignity' (Liebling *et al.* 2005: 211–2). Custody, as will become apparent below, provides disproportionately for scenarios of unfairness and disrespect. In order to survive successive custodial sentences prisoners must closely adhere to particular kinds of scripts (Phillips 2001; Rumgay 2004). These scripts stipulate that young male prisoners must a) show unwavering respect to all authority figures (even though respect will often not be given them in return), and b) conceive of themselves and what they have done as solely the product of personal and 'impulsive' decisions rather than as situated within, and influenced by, various structural conditions or, at least, by more complex social relations. It is the sustained exposure to forms of institutional disrespect (Margalit 1998; Sennett 2003) along with the (forced) investment in what I term a 'hyper-responsible' form of subjectivity, which together pose a threat to desistance.

In order to work through the issues involved here I ask and respond to two key questions: (1) What importance do residents/prisoners give to demonstrations of (dis)respect within and beyond custodial environments? and (2) What do residents/prisoners say when questioned about who or what is responsible for their past behaviour and, importantly, for making the best of release? Drawing on four years of interviews (n=92)[4] with young men sentenced to juvenile and adult custodial contexts, I show that respect and responsibility (more particularly, the nurturing of interdependent selves) are indeed critical to the negotiation of custodial and post-release life and, specifically, for maximising the potential for primary desistance to occur (which is, of course, the logical and necessary precondition for transitioning to secondary desistance).[5] But more than this, I show that many young male residents/prisoners experience an institutionalised form of disrespect which teaches them that they are first and foremost offenders, and secondarily, if at all, persons who can and should be trusted with meaningful opportunities to make their way in the world in non-violent ways. And, in contradistinction to strength-based approaches to offender reintegration (which propose a fully social and cultural understanding of respect and responsibility) (see McNeill 2006), the creation of hyper-responsible custodial subjects means that such persons are rarely, if ever, permitted to conceive of life as a *collective* project – as a journey rightfully and necessarily involving connections with and degrees of reliance upon persons and resources beyond the fully volitional "responsibilised" (imagined) self (see Bosworth 2007: 81).

Contextual remarks

Notions of respect and responsibility feature prominently in the lexicon of criminal justice administration. In the absence of individual responsibility there would be no capacity for the state to hold persons accountable for their actions, let alone to impose sanctions (custodial or other). As Duff (2005: 442) puts it, 'Responsibility is answerability; to be responsible is to be liable to be called to answer for something by and to somebody.' Deterrence, denunciation, retribution and even restitution only make sense in a world where responsibility and its recourse to agency (or self-directed wilful conduct) are given concrete form and taken seriously by various bodies. Joel Feinberg (1970) put debates about responsibility within criminal justice settings squarely on the map, and the centrality of responsibility to matters juridical has been recently captured by Nicola Lacey (2001: 350) who comments, 'At the start of the twenty-first century, it is little exaggeration to say that the question of responsibility – indeed the question of individual responsibility – stands as *the* question of normative criminal law theory.' Other commentators have suggested that law is a very narrow instrument for gauging or encouraging responsibility and that the real challenge is to develop what Emmanuel Levinas has termed an 'ethics of intersubjectivity' and for this ethics to be guided by broader debates concerning what he calls the 'spatial scope of care' (Smith quoted in Popke 2003: 310 and 303).

Criminologically, the concept of responsibility has had a direct impact on the way in which various theorists have conceived of offenders, motivations for crime and, importantly, responses to crime (including incarceration) (see Halsey 2006a). Classical, positivist and constitutive schools of criminological thought have written responsibility as residing, respectively, within the cognitive (decision making) processes of individuals, within the biological, psychological or social maladies impacting the individual, or as akin to the discursive and affective relations pertaining between people and their political, cultural and legal contexts (Muncie *et al.* 1996; Einstadter and Henry 1995). In this latter instance, it is the complexity of these relations (the impossibility of locating an originary cause or unified subject) which points toward the need to develop a collective yet suitably nuanced notion of responsibility (something which will be returned to later in this discussion) (Henry and Milovanovic 1996).

Respect, by way of contrast, has had a quite different juridical and criminological genealogy than that of responsibility. Indeed, until very recently, criminal justice had arguably made the performance of *dis*respect into an art form. Treating victims with varying degrees of disdain or suspicion (Kaspiew 1995); envisaging the community as little more than an abstraction whose ideal responsible citizens exist everywhere at law and in public policy but few places in lived experience; reminding court users that deference is a one way street leading directly to the bench; are all examples of what might be called a widespread juridical disregard for those principles it purports to uphold. This is particularly problematic given that, as Middleton (2004: 228) puts it, respect 'forms "the moral infrastructure" on which justice sits'. But there is evidence that respect has emerged, and is continuing to emerge, as a concept – if not always as a practice – of some politico-legal weight. Community justice centres in the US (New York), UK (North Liverpool) and Australia (Melbourne), all envisage the upholding of respect as central to their processes and goals (Karp and Clear 2000; Kurki 2000; Maloney and Holcomb 2001). Restorative justice – whether involving adult or juvenile offenders – conceives respect (for one's story and one's emotional needs) as key to restoring victims' well-being and confidence in the justice system more generally (Johnstone and Van Ness 2006). Therapeutic jurisprudence is also very much based on the idea that respecting and meeting the needs of each and every court user is central to overcoming the often traumatic and humiliating aspects of being the subject of juridical processes (McMahon and Wexler 2003).

There are other signs that respect is being attributed greater symbolic standing. In 2003, the Home Office published its White Paper 'Respect and Responsibility'. In Austin, Texas, the 'Expect Respect Project' aims to stem the tide of bullying and sexual harassment through education in schools (Meraviglia *et al.* 2003). The Department of Families and Communities in South Australia promotes itself as being 'Connected, Ethical, Brave, Respectful'. In 2002, the Victorian Government released its youth policy statement, 'Respect: The Government's Vision for Young People'. The New South Wales Police Service in the context of their 'Ride for Respect Crime Prevention Initiative' has gone as far as to assert that 'Respect is the fundamental law of life'. And very recently, in the context of publicising the New Australian Citizenship Test, the then federal government nominated 'mutual respect' as one of three key elements given to characterise the Australian way of life.[6]

Beyond this, there is a growing academic literature on respect and its relation to crime. This commences most notably with Philippe Bourgois' (2003 [1996]) classic ethnography of crack cocaine dealing in East Harlem, continues with Elijah Anderson's (1999) study of ghetto life in Philadelphia, and culminates more recently with Alison Liebling's (2004) provocative (and I think, well founded) contention that the pain of disrespect should be added to the five 'pains of imprisonment' originally formulated by Gresham Sykes (1958) a half century ago. Of course, there is also a broad literature (for example, Sennett 2003; Margalit 1998; Middleton 2004; Hooks 2000; Currie 2004) dealing directly and indirectly with the concept of respect, and I will return to relevant aspects of this.

Precisely what the politico-popular invocation of respect and responsibility signifies is an open question. One reading would be that these concepts function as (the desired) markers of social cohesion and/or the means for a possible reclaiming of public order and so-called 'common decency' (Bauman 1993; Sevenhuijsen 2000). In simple political and populist terms, respect and responsibility are the things which, according to many state officials, have gone missing or have been trampled on in a world overrun by technologies of violence and a hyper-individualism (Virilio and Lotringer 1997). By such a reckoning, people are now judged by the speed of the transactions they engage in or are subjected to, rather than by the quality, duration and impacts of relationships forged (whether between persons or between people and their (built/natural) surroundings). As lost or displaced articles, respect and responsibility therefore enter the political and cultural imaginary in the form of a yearning: 'If only people respected one another (or respected each other's property, or the environment ...'; 'If only persons took responsibility for their own (and, more pointedly, their children's) behaviour ...', then the world (its homes, workplaces, neighbourhoods) would somehow be transformed into a better, less troublesome (fearful, violent) place. This, at least, is my sense of the performative and political value of the major discourses which seek to summon forth the possible worlds bound up with being respectful and responsible.

Putting the utopian dimensions of such visions aside, there is good reason to think that these terms in fact mean very different things dependent upon contexts and actors. It has even been suggested, rightly, in my estimation, that 'Respect seems to be such a protean notion that it resists a singular meaning; instead it is used in multiple ways as part of various discursive positionings' (Buttny and Williams 2000: 110). The same might also be said of responsibility. By such an account, there is nothing universal about showing respect or acting responsibly. Conversely, there is nothing immutable about the performance of disrespect or acting irresponsibly. Indeed, perhaps one of the primary shortcomings of political manifestos, departmental mission statements and the like, is that they bear little relevance to the rich and varied conditions in which the dimensions of respect and responsibility are negotiated. Accordingly, unless one is prepared to grapple with and theorise the stuff of everyday life (de Certeau 1988), there is, surely, little hope of moving beyond quite abstract, indeed obtuse, renderings of 'the social'[7] and how it acts upon and shapes notions of respect and responsibility.

The correctional system offers an important point of departure for talking about respect and responsibility. On the one hand, correctional departments – whether based in the mass-incarceration culture of the US, or in low incarceration cultures such as the Netherlands – refer repeatedly to respect and responsibility in the key documents informing their operation (mission statements, annual reports, custodial codes of conduct, educational and vocational programmes, therapeutic programmes, release plans, and the like) (see Bosworth 2007). On the other, there is good reason to think that particular custodial settings and post-release environments make it very difficult for 'clients' to demonstrate the kinds of respect and responsibility likely to be of most use in piecing together and sustaining what might be termed conventional life.

Contrary to popular representations of (male) residents prisoners as physically tough and emotionally shallow, and of the process of being released from custodial sentence as a time of unrestrained optimism, both incarceration and release have been shown to be fraught with practical (economic, social, familial) and existential uncertainties. The classic studies of Sykes (1958), Irwin (1970) and Toch (1992) attest to the prison as a complex mix of order and turmoil and of incessant psycho-social challenges of highly intense kinds. Similarly, the works of Farrall (2004) and Maruna and Immarigeon (2004) offer stark evidence of the uncertainties and threats to self-esteem which often characterise attempts to rejoin the community following extended periods in custody. What is implicit in the majority of work on the pains of imprisonment and release is that the capacity to 'make good' is unmistakably connected to the economies of respect and responsibility. However, very few correctional oriented studies explicitly engage with respect or responsibility in a sustained way (but see for notable exceptions: Toch 1992; Liebling *et al.* 2005; Maruna 2004b; Maruna and Mann 2006). It makes sense to think that the giving and receiving of respect, and the witnessing of and opportunity to practise responsibility, are central components for the development and negotiation of the kind of subjectivity[8] demanded of residents/prisoners and those about to re-enter 'society'. In the remainder of this discussion, therefore, I aim to give weight to this claim by drawing on interviews conducted with young men who have attempted to 'go straight' on several occasions, and, who, by default, have experienced multiple detention orders or prison sentences. My contention is that particular custodial and post-release settings conflate routinisation of conduct, imposition of obligations, and deference to authority, with the nurturing of respect and responsibility. What will become clear, therefore, is that to talk of respect and responsibility in the incarceration and post-release context is, ironically, very much to speak of being disrespected by authorities and of being subjected to irresponsible forms of (state) conduct.

Narrating respect and responsibility

The aim below is to bring the lived experience of respect and responsibility to life through the narratives of those who have attempted, and will once again attempt, the transition from custody to the community. I preface each section with a brief statement on the significance of respect and responsibility and then move to relay the relevant narrative excerpts of residents/prisoners.

Talking about respect

In their illuminating piece, Buttny and Williams (2000: 236) remark,

> Respect matters because it structures our social lives in very meaningful ways ... [W]hat seems clear is that without respect we cannot be social citizens. Without respect it is difficult to engage in the business of giving respect, for what worth is the respect of the worthless person?

Respect, in other words, is a social practice. But more than this, respect is the currency which should be afforded to and given by persons regardless of their perceived or actual social status. In order for respect to be sustained, to have the opportunity to flourish, there must exist the unconditional preparedness to initially suspend judgment of the Other (see Hudson 2006b). This unconditional respect – or *prima facie* acceptance or 'hospitality' – can then be said to endure or founder according to the subsequent series of judgments each makes of the Other's behaviour (including their discursive acts) over time. It is probably true to say that respect – which is distinct from understanding or empathy – is the central starting point for non-violent interaction between bodies. This is why, in the words of Buttny and Williams (2000: 230), 'It is not insignificant that we tend to notice respect far less than disrespect.' Simply put, the experience of being disrespected is visceral and interruptive whereas the experience of being respected tends to be anticipated and seamless. But the question, 'What worth is the respect of the worthless person?', none the less stands as central to discussions below. For in many senses those in custody face the almost unassailable task of having to gain the respect of those who have a deep suspicion of their motives and potentials – of those who view residents and prisoners if not as worthless, then as certainly deserving of 'their lot' and of a particular kind of attention (unemotional, distant, regimented, infantilising, masculinised). The respect which emerges or more often fails to emerge between youth workers/custodial officers and the residents/prisoners they are responsible for, is critical to the development of another precondition for 'rehabilitation' and desistance – namely, trust. More specifically, respect is the device for unlocking the trust of those who hold the cards of service delivery (within and beyond custody), job opportunities, educational pathways, housing options and so forth. Sometimes respect and trust are established. But there are many barriers to this becoming the norm rather than the exception.

Respect according to participants
The following excerpts give some insight into the general manner by which respect is conceived by participants.

Interviewer: What is respect?
Participant: It's like … you got to treat them how you want to be treated and that. Treat people how you want to be treated back. (A, 24:24)

P: I've always had my three rules. I've always respected females, respected old people, and young people, like little kids and that … I respect 90 per cent of people in here [in prison] because they haven't done wrong by me, I haven't done wrong by them … So I respect them, you know. (B, 24:25 I2)

P: Like, if I meet somebody, I give them respect straight away.
I: What is respect to you if you had to define it? What does it mean?
P: Just treat other people the way you want to be treated … If they want to be nice to me, I'll be nice to them. If they want to be pricks, well, they're gonna get it back twice as bad. (C, 36:46)

P: Respect to me is like someone that treats you right, and the way they talk, like manners and that, you know? Friendship is respect … That's the way I see it because that's all I've got is a bunch of mates … (D, 44:18)

I: And what is respect? …
P: Someone that you know looks up to you. (E, 25:23)

225

There are subtle differences here. In the first three excerpts respect is narrated as a two way street invoking a 'do unto others as you would have them do unto you' stance (with the third statement playing specifically to the idea that respect involves the *a priori* suspension of judgment mentioned earlier). In the fourth excerpt, respect is reduced to an oral performance – of the words uttered and the tone in which they are spoken. In the last, respect calls upon a sense of authority – of being in a position whereby others aspire to be like those they 'look up to', or of, possibly, being someone whom others are indebted to. The challenge is to discern the conditions under which any or all of these idealised notions become workable or untenable.

Respect in the context of policing
Without doubt, police occupy a key nodal point for the maintenance or compromise of respect with regard to those released from custodial sentences (Loader 1996: 125–9; Reisig *et al.* 2004). Starting again – attempting to make good – requires not only that each would-be desister begins to conceive of themselves and their relationship to the world in new ways. More than this, it requires that other people (police, release workers, family members, peers, teachers) grant the space and time for change to occur, and to believe that it *can* so occur. In other words, desistance from crime requires that the master status of offender be suspended and preferably discarded (over time) by actor and significant others alike. The weight of suspicion – the surveiled space suspicion carves out for those within its purview – needs for a time to be lifted. This, however, very rarely occurs and indeed goes against the very *raison d'être* of certain kinds of bodies. The police constitute one body who have made an art form out of suspicion and distrust, and in so doing, help to nurture these qualities within those they pursue or wish to question.

> The [police] all know me ... As soon as they see me they come straight on my case ... Like, even in town when I'm shopping with my mum – just recently – and I was out, a cop knew me ... Bang, he just come straight up to me [and] says, 'I want to search you' ... And my mum was like shocked that he just come up and said [that]. Like he didn't say, 'What's your name?', cause he knew it ... He goes, 'I know your history' ... and he goes, 'Empty out your pockets.' And he didn't find nothing ... It was just disrespect and embarrassed me in front of my mum ... It made me feel, like, upset. I was like shattered because they

come and done it in front of my mum. It would have been better if they took me to the station … Cause you've done wrong in the past they think you're always going to do wrong … So it's like every time they see you, it's like they're trying to pin you to anything they can. (A, 24:18 I2)

All the cops know us and they all want to get us fuckin' runnin' amok in their faces. They know we're tryin' to straighten up, do the right thing … Fuckin' cops come out and hassle me all the time and shit. You can't do the right thing any more. You get blamed for shit even if it isn't you, you know. Just 'cause it's your kind of style, you know, they just blame you for it. (F, 27:45)

It is difficult to convey in brief excerpted form the kinds of humiliation embedded in such experiences. The first scenario is particularly harrowing in view of the fact that this was one of the few times in many years that this young man had spent any time with his biological mother. In a few seconds, the act of being approached by the police served to transform him from son to suspected criminal. What is often overlooked is that the impact of this seemingly discrete or isolated event exceeds its temporal specificity. One might only guess at the kinds of conversations and explanations which took place subsequent to this (unjust) encounter, not to mention the damage done to one's self concept. The second excerpt speaks to the perceived futility of 'tryin' to straighten up' in the face of police harassment. Here, police adhere doggedly to the tired mantra 'once a crim always a crim'. A more liberal reading would of course suggest that police are only assisting those who would otherwise stray to keep on the straight and narrow – that police do young men a disservice by not 'checking up on them'. This of course obscures the fact that what police most often seek in the wake of a crime is a result. And, most typically, results require that the usual suspects be paid a visit ('All the cops know us …').

But there is a far more serious way of disrespecting the rights of young men in the context of policing. It is one thing to put suspects in humiliating situations through unnecessary or inappropriate questioning (where police pay little or no attention to the emotional, familial and vocational knife edge on which many young (ex)offenders' lives are positioned, and give little or no regard to the capacity for one's good efforts to be instantly undone by the assumption that one has not moved, indeed should not be permitted to move, beyond the status of 'offender'). It is another matter altogether for police to engage in physical violence against young men whilst under their care. The young men I have interviewed to date are evenly divided about their treatment by police. Some acknowledge that police are just doing their job, and that what goes around comes around – that a punch or a scuffle here or there is nothing to get worked up about, and that young men give as good as they get, and therefore 'deserve' the treatment dealt them by police on particular occasions. But there have also been examples related, such as that evinced in the excerpt below, that speak to a violence of a different, more serious kind – a violence designed to unequivocally disempower and humiliate those to whom it is directed.

> ... They [i.e. the police] give you shit in the cells and that ... I've been bashed from them a few times ... They stir you up and they don't like you because say if you get chased ... in a car and you [outrun them] ... They [might eventually get] you but they don't have evidence, they can't do you. So then they get you when you're locked up ... They done it to my dad, they done it – that's how it goes ... They just know I'm going to be like my dad so they do the same as what they done to my dad when he was young ... I've got hit a few times ... But they just put a phone book on there [to my stomach area] and go in like that [participant demonstrates angle and position of fist] so I don't get no bruise on the outside, can't show nothin' ... And when they take you into [participant mentions police cell], they'll just come in and pick you up, handcuff you, and then they'll get you in a padded cell, it's pitch black, nothing's in there so they'll just belt into you and they leave you there ... And if you keep going off then they just – come in and spray you with a [fire] hose ... Then they ... laugh at you and say, 'You look hot. Do you need to cool down?' And they'll just sit there spraying you like a dog in a corner. Just kept on spraying me with the hose ... Like a dog ... You'd think that they're meant to, when you get locked up, they're meant to protect you, that's what they're there for ... And they just treat you like a dog ... [T]his time when I got locked up I got handcuffed with a chair in my throat ...You know. In the cop car. The seats. They handcuffed me with my hands with the chair – the chair in my mouth, like the head thing 'cause they thought I was gonna escape. So I couldn't move. (G, 27:3, age 15, 3 detention orders)

How does a young person – any person – recover their dignity in such situations? What possible reason is there for such persons to be persuaded that violence does not work, that it is an impotent force, and that it is far better to engage in dialogue with those we might otherwise wish to denounce or be distanced from when they themselves have been rendered powerless through violence? Violence does work. It works to strip people (temporarily and sometimes permanently) of their moral worth, and, more crucially, injures their sense of self respect. In such situations, young men also lose what little respect they may have had for authorities, and, more tragically, for the idea that no one is above the law and all can be held accountable before it. In police cells, accountability (sometimes) finds itself missing in action, as absent without leave. When asked if there seems to be any commonalities among those police prepared to engage in behaviour such as that outlined above, the overwhelming majority of young men remarked that the chief perpetrators are, ironically, young male police officers. Women and older, more experienced (male) officers were by and large praised by the participants of this research as fair and reasonable. Clearly, it is not just the masculinity of young offenders which is at stake and in need of refashioning.

Respect in the context of sentencing
For those whose lives are deeply caught up in cycles of arrest, court and incarceration, the sentencing process can appear to outsiders as one of the more mechanical and 'scientific' aspects of this process. But what is frequently glossed over is the relationship between what is said during sentencing and the impact of these enunciations upon those sentenced (see Tombs and Jagger 2006). Most young men interviewed knew of the judge's style and had a good sense of how punitive they were likely to be. The comments that most resonated with participants, however, were not those which may have been encouraging or which may have been more measured and empathetic in tone, but those which cast those convicted of crimes as lost causes, or beyond help.

I: So you went to the Youth Court ... again?
P: Yeah.
I: And I take it the judge knew who you were? ...
P: Yeah, they knew who I was ... He was telling me that I'm a menace to society. It was in the news and in the paper ... Telling me I should be locked away for a long time. That I can't read, I can't write. (H, 14:20 I2, age 18, 5 detention orders)

People certainly notice respect when it is given. But they are more likely to be attuned to those occasions when it is not – particularly when the source of disrespect, the source of kicking one's character when it is already down, so to speak – is someone who occupies a position of state authority. It is commonly held that young offenders could not care less about what the system and those who work for this system think of them. This, to my mind, is generally untrue. Ellemers *et al.* (2004: 157) have eloquently discussed the relationship between 'ingroups' and 'outgroups' arguing that it is not merely imperative that people receive respect, but 'that it is important for people to know that they are respected by the "right" others'. It *is* possible for judges and police to be perceived as the 'right others'. But when figures such as these (including custodial officers) make disparaging remarks to or about young people convicted of criminal offences, they *entrench* the division between outgroups and ingroups. The challenge for judges and other stakeholders in the criminal justice system is to find ways to blur the boundaries between the ingroups associated with offending (and who approve of its occurrence – either as necessary for getting by or as a means of short-lived excitement), and the outgroups responsible for dealing with such behaviour. Ellemers *et al.* (2004: 170) remark upon the way the disconnection between workers (substitute, 'young offenders') and top level managers (substitute, 'juridical and correctional personnel') might be bridged through the performance of respect:

> [R]espect from multiple sources causes interactive effects … Leaders who are successful in building trust may be able to change the perception that they represent an outgroup ('management') into the conviction that the leader is part of the ingroup … which in turn should increase the impact this leader has (and the way this leader evaluates the contribution of individual workers) on the perceptions and behaviours of work team members.

Although being part of an ingroup (which in all cases functions as the Other's outgroup) can have emotional, social and economic benefits, it is necessary to venture beyond the familiar worlds drawn by our ingroups in order to meet the Other on mutually unfamiliar ground – ground which no one party has sovereignty over and which therefore must be continually (re)negotiated by those prepared to venture toward it (see Hudson 2006b).

Respect in the context of custody
Elsewhere, I have spoken of the idea that custody should not be constructed or presumed to be an inherently traumatic or violent experience for those residing in such institutions (Halsey 2006b, 2007b, 2007a). Indeed I have argued that one of the more complex areas of penological research is (or should be) that which examines the impact of custody as a site of emotional respite and physical protection as against custody as a site of existential, cultural, social and familial turmoil (see Irwin and Owen 2005). That said, it is absolutely critical to acknowledge and make plain that custody imposes numerous counter-productive and humiliating circumstances upon those required to serve time. The traditional pains of confinement (Sykes 1958), in other words, are rarely in short supply. In relation to respect, the ways and means by which young men successfully trade in this currency in the eyes of custodial officers often result in a depletion of the reservoirs of respect among fellow residents/prisoners (see Toch 1992: 136–40 and 156–61). This is neatly captured in the following exchange.

P: There's different levels of respect ... 'Cause you got prison level respect, and you got outside level respect, the respect from the community, that comes in a different deal ... You get respect from the community by doing good things. You get respect in prison by being a hard-arsed fucker that won't take shit from anyone. It's weird, the different levels of respect ... you get from the outside and you get from the inside. Yeah, they're totally two different things.

I: Does that mean that you feel as though you have to be a different person when you're inside ... versus the person that you are or want to be when you are in the community?

P: You have to ... Because if you come in here and you try to do good things, like, you help staff out, and all that. You're nothing. You're a staff suck-up ... [But] if you do something, like, you know, you punch on once in a while, then you're all right, you're cool, you're in, it's all good, you're loved. But on the outside it's a different thing. You get on the outside and you punch on with people then people start to get scared of you, they hate you, they don't like you. You get kicked out of parties just for being who you are. (I, 16:1 12, age 18, 4 detention orders)

Respect, to come back to Buttny and Williams' comment, is indeed a 'protean' and fluid phenomenon. It has to be lived in different ways at different times in order that the most critical kind of respect wins out against less tenable versions (however reasonable or desirable these other versions might appear to members of ingroups and outgroups). I am reminded here of Judith Rumgay's (2004) work pointing to the importance of having a range of scripts to draw upon when attempting to desist from crime. Typically, the scripts of young offenders are very 'skeletal' in nature since they are built on the recognisable but poorly experienced 'global identities such as parent, intimate partner, or employee' (Rumgay 2004: 409). An important question here is to ask what it would mean to assist those in custody (and here I count custodial staff among such persons) to populate their skeletal 'scripts for survival' with a more fully social and cultural set of skills for living? For one thing, it would mean developing processes which facilitate not just changes in residents prisoners but changes in staff and managers of custodial facilities as well. Disrespect in custody is very closely aligned with the continued enactment of rules, structures and beliefs which do not permit persons to aspire to something beyond skeletal scripts. Disrespect, again, is the unwillingness to temporarily suspend judgment or to entertain the possibility that persons are not reducible to one kind of subjectivity or essence, but can actively flirt with, develop an affinity for, and reject particular personas (in the non-clinical sense of the term) within the 'one' biography. But whether one kind of subjectivity prevails is not entirely controllable by the person in question. Instead, who one is and who one is perceived to be, or more accurately, who one is perceived to be in the process of *becoming*, is as much a group or social activity as it is the business of the private self.

Totalising institutions have a way of making the smallest gestures or the most trivial of happenings turn into events of great magnitude involving significant stakes. This is particularly so in the context of the period of time immediately following a lock down (where all residents or prisoners are ordered into their cells whilst problematic bodies are taken to isolation rooms where they can 'cool down'). In the following excerpt, the power of perception – the meanings attributed to facial gestures and bodily movements – comes to the fore as a force of humiliation.

They fucking harsh on them fellas having rough times, you know. They're harsh on us, harsh … When people get restrained and taken away they go to this room and all the staff [yell], 'Lock down. Get the fuck in your room.' … You get taken to this room and this room's right near the office … And after restraint, [the staff] go in there [into the office] and they have a cup of tea and laugh … Other units have got it, but our unit's got that fucking room right there and that's not fucking good having that room right there because all [the staff] do is go in there and laugh and give people fucking big dagger looks … This fella's in the thing trying to cool down, have a cool down time before he goes back to his room and all the stares, the laughing … The staff was laughing about how they got the restraint and all that, and having a cup of tea, joking around, and they might even be laughing at something else, but that boy is paranoid that … they're laughing at him ... They're laughing, you know? ... What the fuck are they laughing at? (J, 22:49)

These kinds of events – where respect for young men is perceived to have been comprehensively trampled on – tend not to be easily forgotten. They live on in the minds of those who witness them and impact the steeliness or otherwise of the disposition of residents and prisoners toward staff in subsequent interactions. The effect of this is that the already substantial gulf between staff and prisoners/residents becomes more entrenched. Part of the reason for this is that there are precious few avenues for voicing dissent in ways which guarantee the privacy of those residents prisoners who see fit to make a complaint. What reason is there to work against the subtle and not so subtle recriminations levelled against persons who are, in all kinds of ways, judged to be at the bottom of the social heap, judged to be untrustworthy, and made out to be constantly 'on the make'? To paraphrase Buttny and Williams, why would or should the state and its personnel trust or respect 'the worthless person?' This may seem overly emotive or conspiratorial. But there is good evidence to show that even where custodial staff privately believe residents prisoners to be of moral and social worth, residents and prisoners nonetheless themselves *feel* that they rate very lowly in the eyes of others. This goes to the importance of the distinction drawn by Margalit (1998: 128–9) between *humiliating agents* as against *humiliating situations*. This distinction 'is important because institutional humiliation is independent of the peculiarities of the humiliating agent, depending only on the nature of the humiliation' (Margalit 1998: 129).

I: Has there ever been anyone that you have come in contact with [like] social workers, release workers, [where you've thought]: 'I can relate to them, they can help me, they understand me.' Has that ever happened?

P: I suppose it has always sort of been a mismatch. Because most of the social workers that are in here ... look at us young people that come through the juvenile system and just think that we're not worth it, you know, we're not worth their help or something, I don't know. (K, 2:50 I2)

On many occasions I have asked young men in custody to relay an example of when someone (other than another resident or prisoner) remarked that what they did or who they are has importance or is of value. No one has yet been able to remember such an occasion. The resilience of persons in the face of this moral wasteland – in the face of such entrenched disrespect for the emotional needs of the Other – is quite remarkable.

Respect in the context of release

Feelings of worthlessness, and its close counterpart, hopelessness, also pertain in the post-release environment. Rex (1999) and Farrall (2004) have shown that the path to desistance from crime has both subjective and social dimensions, and that certain persons (such as probation or parole officers, but also employers and family members) can play, if not an instrumental role in this process, then certainly an important one. In all cases, the nurturing and reinforcement of a positive sense of self is critical to the maintenance of the will to desist. Maruna *et al.* (2004a) have convincingly argued that desistance, just like offending, has primary and secondary dimensions meaning that continued desistance, just like continued offending, requires a particular kind of symbolic relationship between (ex)offenders and those with the power to confer the label criminal or, as the case may be, desister. Here, 'desistance may be best facilitated when the desisting person's change in behaviour is recognized by others and reflected back to him [sic] in a "delabeling process" ' (Maruna *et al.* 2004a: 274). In short, 'Not only must a person accept conventional society in order to go straight, but *conventional society must accept that person as well'* (Maruna *et al.* 2004a: 273, emphasis added). However, the willingness to remove the veil of suspicion in relation to those young men with a history of offences against them, is not always forthcoming.

I: [W]hat's been the hardest thing ... in terms of making connections to people and places and things that will help when you're [out]?

P: When you have a life of crime, and that, people don't trust you ... They haven't got faith in you, you know? They think you're just one big fuck up and you always will be, you know. Sorry about the swearing all the time. That you will be a screw up ... and you won't get anywhere in life. You know, you're just a bum ... Go away 'cause you gonna rip me off or something ... (L, 16:13 I2)

P: Now that I look back on it, I wish I never started doing crime ... Because it's hard for me now to go out there and do – try and do the right thing, when there's people who just look at you, you know, like, you're a criminal and you're always going to be a criminal ... You try to do the right thing and then they just look at you, you know, like ... treat you like you're nothing ... You're not – you're not worth giving a chance to. (M, 29:8)

Young men's willingness to 'do the right thing' when released from custody is, in my estimation, a very fragile commodity. It can be broken by the smallest of setbacks. Alternatively, it can be buoyed by things taken for granted or viewed as trivial by outsiders. If broken, the willingness to desist might be repairable, but this reparation process often takes a long time and comes at substantial personal and social cost (in terms of further periods in lock up). Labels, as categorically demonstrated by Lemert (1951), Becker (1963), MacKinnon (1993) and others, are more than words. They literally inform and prescribe for particular bodies the spaces, events, pathways and aspirations they are permitted to desire, engage and hope for. Respect in the context of post-release therefore means understanding something of the simultaneous feelings of anxiety and joy felt by those formally judged to be 'free'. More than this, it means recognising that for many young men, being 'free' is actually tantamount to being in a different kind of prison – not that of conditional release or parole, but that of the confined and intensely nuanced space of public suspicion and opinion (Halsey 2007a).

Talking about responsibility

Monica Barry (2006: 141) has commented,

> There are subtle nuances in the meaning of the word 'responsibility'. It can mean 'having responsibility' which suggests being accountable (to someone) for something; 'acting responsibly' where expectations are placed on the actor by others; or alternatively 'taking on responsibility' which suggests the opportunity of being trusted with something for someone.

These distinctions are critically important. Overwhelmingly, young men in secure care prison get to engage (are forced to connect with) the first two kinds of responsibility, but rarely, if ever, with the third. As will be seen below, *passive* responsibility – a responsibility based on reckoning with past events (or, more accurately, reckoning with the content of particular correctional programmes and what these require young men to think and say about such events) – tends to predominate (Maruna and Mann 2006: 167). There are, in short, very few ways in which residents and prisoners can engage with an *active* form of responsibility (Halsey 2007b). The premise of active responsibility is quite simple. People cannot change the past, but they can forge new relationships in the here and now of a creative and positive kind which in turn can generate, both for the actor and the audience, new perceptions of who someone is or has worked hard to become (see Maruna and Mann 2006: 167; Maruna *et al.* 2004a; Maruna *et al.* 2004b).

Subjectivity – for each and all – is a work in progress. But for those with extensive criminal histories and custodial experiences, one's subjectivity tends to become stuck on or reduced to the series of criminal acts undertaken by each person. The irony is that these persons are precisely those most in need of being trusted by the state, but who are instead made to answer to the state at every turn (to the point, indeed, where each unlearns what it means and how it feels to make non-trivial decisions on their own behalf and in relation to the lives of others). Here, to be responsible is, as Duff (2005) observes, to be *answerable* to a higher (authoritarian) power. It is to be reduced to a virtual automaton. From this point, it is a long way back to the place where someone might be permitted to 'take on' (Barry 2006) responsibility not only for their own lives, but for those they potentially impact on. This is a major hurdle on the path toward primary desistance since it is generally established that persons able to cease offending for varying lengths of time following release, are those who believe they are increasingly viewed as trustworthy and valued citizens (and not just ex-prisoners). Moreover, the best means of demonstrating responsibility is to have opportunities for *doing* (contributing meaningfully and non-trivially to social, cultural, economic and familial life) rather than saying (regurgitating programme rhetoric, or making grandiose promises about the future). There are, though, all manner of obstacles to the emergence of an active responsibility.

Responsibility and biography
Contrary to popular conceptions that offenders will blame anyone but themselves for their actions, the young men interviewed in this research were eager to take responsibility for their crimes. Moreover, they were quite willing to 'cop it sweet' in terms of the penalties they received.

> If you're gonna, like offend, of course you need to get punished, like if you get caught. Don't, like, get heaps mad and crack up and that because you got caught; it's your own fault. If you're gonna steal the car and get caught, you got to do your time. (N, 19:16)

This rhetorical display of responsibility may have as much to do with the lack of alternative subject positions available given the stark realities of confinement. Or it may reflect the kind of truth games (Foucault 1984) that one inevitably enters into when engaging in interviews such that participants – even offenders! – want to be viewed as essentially 'good people'. Or, and I will say more about this below, it may reflect the unspoken rule that qualifying one's involvement in crime with statements which speak to factors 'outside' individual volition, is the penultimate sign of someone in denial and who lacks any sense of self respect. As McKendy (2006: 478) writes, 'Offenders are coaxed, cajoled, threatened and bribed to stop making excuses and to accept responsibility for their own actions. Confession of guilt is a prerequisite for entry into certain programmes, which in turn are required in order for the individual to be considered for early parole.' The strength of the unremarked rule that one shall not mention external factors as playing a part in one's predicament, can be detected in the following excerpts narrated by the same participant in separate interviews.

P: [M]y mother, she has a drug problem, she sold some of my belongings to Cash Converters and stuff like that and I got a bit angry at her for it and she kicked me out of the house and withdrew her guarantor, so I was basically on my own. So I started stealing cars as places to sleep in, and yeah, I used to go out every night, make my money in that car … used that car just to make a living, yeah, … I was selling marijuana for a while … It was getting pretty bad … I had my friend's house I could go back to but his nanna's pretty sick, so I didn't really want to intrude on them … So I was just using cars as bedrooms and after a while it just escalated to going back to making money by doing shop breaks and stuff like that … Just to live, survival money. (O, 3:16, I2)

I: Looking back, would you say that you chose to commit crime or would you say that you were forced into it…?

P: Both … It's always the one, you know, one person's decision but, you know, the lifestyle I grew up in, you know, I'm not surprised I went down that road 'cause you know, my lifestyle wasn't that good when I was younger, in my childhood and stuff. (O, 12:15)

In spite of all, this young man proves reluctant to categorically ascribe much weight to external factors as the reason for his offending ('It's always the … one person's decision'). Indeed, of the 50 unique participants interviewed for this research over the last four years, this is as close as an interviewee has come to countenancing the idea that the paths taken in life *might* reasonably be said to be composed of both subjective *and* social aspects. This is a remarkable situation given the assumed situation of most citizens. As Maruna and Mann (2006: 158) remind, 'When challenged about having done something wrong, all of us reasonably account for our own actions as being influenced by multiple, external and internal factors. Yet, we pathologize prisoners and probationers for doing the same thing.'

I mentioned earlier that the enforcement, juridical and custodial spheres have the effect not of holding persons accountable in nuanced and productive ways, but of making persons into hyper-responsible subjects. This is, to my mind, a very worrying state of affairs. When the state reduces people's lives to the behaviours carried out by a so-called unified, rational subject, it leaves little or no room to consider the collective nature of 'individual' biographies and the implications of this for the policy and practice of offender re-integration.

P: I was put in foster care at the age of seven ... [Since then] I've moved 63 times ... I used to trust no one ... Like, there were times when I just felt life wasn't worth living ... I had to do whatever FAYS told me to do ... I had no say in anything ... One [family] I remember had a bamboo stick and they put duck tape around it and they hit me with that.

I: ... Why would they do that?

P: Well, because one night I was hungry and I woke up while everyone else was asleep. I went and grabbed one of those little small packets of chips. And in the morning [the parents] come in and [the father] smacked me across the fingers, broke my fingers ... It was put in a cast. And the next day when I walked in the door, I got yelled at, and I thought of calling the police on them ... Then they hit me with a stick again ... And I waited till they left and then I burned their house down and I went to FAYS and told them to move me. (P, 1:29, age 16, 5 detention orders)

P: At night time [in lock-up] I just sit there when you got nothing to do. I just think about, like, 'Why did you get yourself into this mess?' (P, 13:27)

The dismissal of the role played by background factors in shaping an individual's life can also be seen in the following excerpt.

P: [In terms of schooling], I've done up to year 10, but I've only   passed about 4 years of it ... My dad looked after me since I was 2 to about 5, and since that time I was in foster care ... I got fostered in 42 different foster places from then till, like, early last year [when I was 14].

I: Why that number [of places]? ...

P: Because I keep ... thinking to myself if I keep playing up on the people they'll run out of places to put me and then I'll just come back to my family ... [But now] I've chosen to disown [my father] ... He was violent because he was an alcoholic ... He used to drink and beat on me and my brothers and sisters ... (Q, 1:41, age 16, 3 detention orders)

I: Looking back, would you say that you chose to commit crime ... or would you say that someone forced you into it, or something forced you into it?

P: I chose it ... I could have chose to be good, stayed at the one foster place and went to school, you know, growing up and staying there and went into independent living and got a job and did everything good but I – I didn't choose to do that. I chose to take the quick and easy path of getting something. (Q, 35:48)

This is passive responsibility in its most dangerous form. The juxtaposition of these clearly conflicting situations is testimony to the way the system has imposed what Foucault (1979) and Rose (1996a) term the 'psy-complex' upon those it seeks to control and rehabilitate. It is a graphic example of a system which has wrested away the capacity for young male offenders to narrate their lives, their backgrounds, their offending, their hopes and fears, with all the necessary complexity, messiness and vagaries that one would expect under almost any other circumstances. This hyper-responsibility is reflected in young men's narratives about who or what is responsible for doing well or making good when next released (oft-repeated refrains include 'I've got to do it by myself', 'I can't rely on anyone else', 'Only I can change my behaviour', and the more forthright, 'It's all down to me').

P: This time I just want to see if I can do it myself, you know.

I: Right. Do you think it'll be different this time around seriously?

P: Yeah ... I'll be a lot hard – it'll be a lot harder for me 'cause I'll be doing it by myself and that ... But that's what I want to do. I just want to do it

- I just want to – I don't want no one telling me
what to do when I open my mouth, you know. I
just want to see if – see if I can stay out myself.
Yeah ... Without anybody's help. 'Cause if I do, I'll
be happy, you know ... I bloody – I'll bloody feel
good about myself, you know.

I: Right. How many detention orders have you had
now?...

P: Six. (R, 30:12 I3)

Here, life is recounted as a project constructed along strictly
isolationist lines. There is, of course, something admirable and
possibly even useful about this. But there is also something deeply
tragic and problematic about the emergence of a generation of young
incarcerated males who feel, or have been taught to believe, that
making one's way in the world is mostly if not solely about the
kind of person one is able to become through constant inner struggle
(with one's psyche, soul, consciousness), rather than knowing that an
absolutely critical dimension of successful citizenship is the capacity
and preparedness to ask and receive assistance from others – that
one's fate is intimately tied to the actions and assumptions of other
people and the institutions governing life. As Currie (2004: 281)
writes,

There is a need ... to look hard at what we might call the
meta-assumptions that, often in subterranean ways, guide ...
approach[es] to the troubles of adolescents – in particular, what
I've called the pejorative assumption, the reflexive tendency
to locate the source of problems within the individual and to
avoid (or reject) exploring the ways in which those problems
are shaped by institutions and actions outside the individual's
control.

Responsibility in the context of custody
Confinement deals in the currency of a very particular kind of
responsibility – namely, the responsibility of each resident or prisoner
to obey written rules, verbal commands, and, to stay true to prison
argot or etiquette (see Phillips 2001; Einat 2005), the unwritten and
unspoken rules of custodial institutions as well. In a sense this is
what the essence of punishment is about – the (further) discursive
stripping away of people's dignity. As McKendy (2006: 496) incisively
observes,

Imprisonment involves not just physical confinement, but also discursive or ideological confinement. What men in prison are prompted to say, the sorts of discursive opportunities they are afforded, the kinds of stories that are officially ratified – all of these are severely restricted ... Even as demands are placed on them to take on the project of making themselves over into rational, self-possessed responsible agents, opportunities to actually do that are sorely lacking.

A key means for constraining responsibility is the effective removal of the capacity for young incarcerated males to make meaningful choices about any and all aspects of their lives.

P: You can't go out, you can't go to bed when you want to, you can't ... go to the toilet or get your room open when you want to. (S, 17:49 I2)

P: These staff [in juvenile] look over you like, like you're at fuckin' kindy, man, you know, like, like you're a child ... That's why everyone in here ... like all the older people, they're just starting to put in requests to go to Yatala [Labour Prison], because they want to be ... by themselves. They want to be able to look after themselves. Not these people, man. They change your diapers. (T, 41:19)

P: It's just ... the same shit day in, day out. No responsibility. Oh, except for wipe the windows every now and again ... On the outside you've got rent to pay, bills to pay, shit to do ... Here you've got nothing to do ...
I: ... [D]o you feel as though you're learning anything from being in here?
P: Oh yeah, I learned the other night how to get through a VY [Holden Commodore] immobiliser ... that's about all I learned. (U, 31:53; 32:1)

On occasion, prison does provide avenues for 'self-improvement' (vocational training, education, health programmes, and so forth). But such opportunities are often closed off as quickly as they arise.

P: There was this Good Beginnings course ... Almost straight away, as soon as I started it, the prison shut it down. They said they wouldn't be able to fund it anymore and yeah, all our programmes went out the window.

I: So what was it that you did day in, day out, in [prison] then? ...

P: Smoke weed and just watch fights. Get into fights. Do PE [physical education], sports, play football. That's about it. Nothing that really benefits me for when I get out. There was no rehabilitation in gaol at all ... I don't think the system's desperate enough to rehabilitate people. They need more government funds to cover these programmes because when ... the programmes were happening, it was benefiting me. I was getting a free call to my partner each week [interstate], so that was keeping my mind at ease. I was doing parenting programmes and I was learning things that I didn't know ... And in a blink of an eye, it was all cut and taken away ... (O, 8:25 I3)

This kind of occurrence serves to exacerbate the powerlessness of those in custody – that whilst each is expected to assume responsibility for their future beyond lock up (to be actively working on their 'rehabilitation') – the reality is more likely to be that these same persons will find themselves structurally unable to do so. This is chiefly because there is very little that residents and prisoners can do to control or influence the kinds of capital (social, cultural, symbolic, economic) (Barry 2006 citing Bourdieu 1997) on offer to them (and therefore technically attainable) whilst in confinement (see Bosworth 2007: 73). Incarceration does things *to* people not *for* them (Halsey 2007b: 362). It requires things of people regardless of their desire or will to actively participate. The effect of this is to produce ill-prepared and distrustful (even resentful) (post)custodial subjects rather than socially skilled and connected citizens.

Responsibility in the context of release
To expect people whose lives have been characterised by the structural inability to assume responsibility for non-trivial relationships and events for extended periods to suddenly turn this situation on its head overnight because they are now formally 'free' to do so, surely rates as one of the most bizarre and unrealistic social experiments in penal practice. Learning to be responsible, just like learning to do

crime, takes time. It takes practice and, just as critically, it requires a willingness on behalf of so-called mainstream networks to place their trust in persons afflicted by severely depleted levels of social and symbolic capital.

P: If you got nothing, you know, what else you meant to do? ... I've got nothing, you know, I might as well do crime ... That's what you think out there, you know, when you got nothing to be out there for. (V, 22:37 I3)

P: I thought [prison] was a complete waste of time. Didn't benefit me at all. Didn't learn nothing.

I: ... How much money did you walk out with last time?

P: About $300 ... All I had was the clothes on my back, so I had to start afresh ... Once you buy some better clothes and your bus ticket ... you've got nothing left ... I was on my own as soon as I left prison, I was on my own. (O, 9:48 I3)

P: They ... don't give you that much support ... They expect you after you've been here for about two years, three years, you know, or a couple of months, you know, they expect you to do it all yourself ... So you've got to have help ... Once you've been here for a long time, you know ... out there's a different world, you know. In here you're used to it. But out there you're not, you know ... Coming back in, in and out, it's just – it's just a routine. In and out, in and out, in and out ... That's what people are used to. In and out, in and out ... And then once they turn 18, they'll get out and go through Yatala. In and out at Yatala. In and out at Yatala. (R, 33:36 I2)

One of the most serious blows to those who manage, against all odds, to get on track – who manage, that is, to turn primary desistance into a reality – is having to deal with the aftermath of past offences which are brought to resolution some years after their perpetration. The majority of young men who have experienced multiple cycles of custody and release know only too well the truth of the phrase that whilst they might be done with the past it may not be done with them. This is graphically illustrated in the following extended excerpt narrated by a young man who had tried many times to do the 'right thing' upon release only to be constrained by previous events.

P: Yeah I was living my own life, making my own choices … [But then I had to go to court because of an old matter]. I'd broken into somewhere and stole some things [when I was younger] … [My lawyer said], "I'll try to get you a suspended sentence" … But the Judge … gave me seven months … I was pretty shocked.

I: Now this is after your lawyer putting forward where you'd been, what you were doing, getting into an independent living scenario – like not even Housing Trust, [that you were in] a private rental unit? That you'd basically stayed out of trouble since you got out [three months earlier]?

P: Yeah.

I: And did the Judge give any consideration to that?

P: Yeah, well, he said that three months doesn't mean anything. He said it's not … long enough to say that … I'm fully rehabilitated and out of trouble. He said maybe if it was six months it would be different. But he said, like, 'It's only three months. That's no proper trial period.' Something along those words, and then he – I think he took into account that I had been doing all right lately and tried to stay out of trouble. At first I think he said he was going to give me nine months, instead of only seven.

I: What was your reaction … when he said seven months? …

P: I felt that that was pretty hard, you know. Something that happened quite a while ago. I had appointments to go to, medical things to do. Like I'm staying out of trouble and I've got myself a unit … I was pissed off about it. I thought that, you know, that every time I get sort of where I want to be, you know – I felt that it wasn't right … I thought, well, if he wasn't too sure that I wasn't doing the right thing, you know, he could have given me a suspended sentence … [Then] if

> I [did] the wrong thing, I would have been locked
> straight back up again ... I guess while I'm here
> I can reflect, can try and set myself up, try to get
> myself back to where I was before I was locked
> up. [One of the staff here said] 'Oh well, you've
> got to take responsibility for what you've done.' I
> guess that's fair enough. That's his point of view. I
> guess at the end of the day I did do it ... It's made
> me probably more hungrier to do the right thing,
> to get myself set up in a unit ... And just stay out
> of the system, you know ... Because once I had a
> unit back when I was 16 and I stuffed it up, and it
> made me really want to get my own property again
> and do the right thing ... And then I got back up
> there and I was thinking, look, well everything will
> be all right. I'm in my unit just taking it day by
> day ... And then I got locked back up again and it
> – yeah, it crushed me a little bit. (X, 10:17 I4, age
> 18, 5 detention orders)

This passage speaks not simply of a system holding people to account, but of the arbitrariness of sentencing (three months being 'no proper trial period' sufficient to demonstrate the categorical sign of rehabilitation, six months being up to the task) and the violence to the primary desistance process which accompanies judgment. It is not a matter of letting people get away with crime. Rather, it is a matter of weighing the damage done to the victim against the damage incurred to the offender by the penalty imposed. This is truly one of the most vexed issues concerning the reformation of self following successive periods of confinement. Presently, the 'reward' for primary desistance – for at least being on the path toward secondary desistance – tends to equate to a reduction in custodial time rather than its suspension or dismissal. The idea here is that forcing someone to serve a reduced amount of time in lock up is less likely to hurt the long-term future of the individual (but will none the less satisfy the demands of retribution and deterrence). But it is more than the individual who suffers in such situations. Instead, conventional social connections are invariably severed by further time in lock up, and the slowly forged familiarity with (even liking for) the routines of keeping house, looking for work and attending classes is undone (sometimes irrevocably). Here, authorities must decide whether to reward the most recent displays of responsibility (of the very kind the system tries to instil in each of its clients) or whether to punish past displays of irresponsibility toward property or persons. In the above case, the imposition of further custodial time appears to have made the recipient of the sentence 'more hungrier to do the right thing'. But this result is surely arrived at by accident rather than by design. There is, in short, an unbelievably thin line dividing the capacity for such persons to reassemble hope (to take something good from something bad) as against their preparedness to adopt a thoroughly nihilistic attitude toward the correctional system and society at large.

Concluding remarks

The young men whose narratives compose this chapter are often accused of many things – of not making the best of help given them, of having little regard for the victims of their crimes, of wasting taxpayers' money, of living fast, chaotic and hedonistic lives with little thought for tomorrow and therefore little sense of deferred gratification. And there is, to call it straight, some truth to these accusations. But on the whole I would argue such criticisms seriously misjudge the nature of the problem at hand – that such finger pointing speaks to the image or stereotype of young custodial subjects rather than to the multiple and competing realities attached to each of their situations. In place of this image – in place of this chimera which guides policy and practice down the redundant paths of control or treatment – are the very real concerns of those subject to various rehabilitative strategies and techniques (see Maruna *et al.* 2004b: 139–40). When one asks young men in custody to discuss the things which prevent them coping well with lock up or doing better upon release, the obstacles mentioned coalesce around such well known issues as housing, peers, money, drugs, as well as the inability to cope with the various tragedies which touch upon their lives (Halsey 2007a).

But this chapter has shown that there are also other less 'tangible' but equally important factors narrated by young men in custody, and these relate fairly and squarely to respect and responsibility. These are not simply abstract or disembodied concepts. Rather, they are practices which have an undeniably *affective* dimension. They make people feel particular things about themselves and about others. This is the sense in which Buttny and Williams (2000: 236) hint that respect gets things done – it is the webbing which gives any 'mass' of persons its sociality over and above its mere geographic commonality. And it is the sense in which responsibility – in the generative sense of the term – helps people to feel good about themselves as trusted and valued persons with the capacity to care about and for the future (the future of loved ones, of their children, perhaps even of the environment, or the world of ideas and public policy). Beyond all this, respect and responsibility to young men in custody are firmly wedded to the notion of balance, or more colloquially, the idea of being given a 'fair go'. Here, young men – indeed most persons – seek the right kind of mix between the way they are treated and the way they treat others, and the things they are permitted to take responsibility *for*, as against the things they are *forced* to do or be involved in. One participant eloquently reflects this desire by commenting,

> I think most people need support, but I think they need a bit of breathing space as well. I mean that they gotta stand on their own two feet. With too much support, you know, when that support breaks they're going to be stuck ... And I think when they decide, if someone decides to do something ... and then they feel that it's hard, support workers shouldn't pressure them. They should just let them change it ... It's their life, you know? Nothing has to be set in concrete ... I don't necessarily think you've got to be busy going to school everyday ... Yeah, it would be good to get a job and that, but you know some people have to do things in their own time ... when they're ready ... Like too much structure, you know, once the wheel falls off, everything crumbles ... Everything just breaks ... That's how I feel anyway. (X, 20:9 I4)

This excerpt closely echoes the statement made by Clear and Karp that, 'Once a function is being performed by one party it becomes unnecessary for another to take it on' (quoted in Maruna *et al.* 2004b: 134). I take this to mean, again, that within custody and following release there is too often a poor balance between opportunities to be responsible for non-trivial things as against the requirement simply to be answerable to a system of rules and programmes. Such an imbalance, I submit, creates overly-dependent rather than *interdependent* selves. This trend toward either hyper-dependent or, at the opposite extreme, *a*social bodies, is inimical to the nurturing of the view that life is and should be a collective endeavour, and that the collective nature of this pursuit is a strength to be reinforced (not a weakness to be shunned or denied). Correctional and post-release systems are premised on highly problematic conceptions of personhood or subjectivity. Indeed, it is clear from the above discussion that the system works with and perpetuates a schizophrenic (more properly, manic) understanding of those to whom it has a duty of care. At one pole, residents and prisoners are perceived (diagnosed) to be suffering from chronic over-dependency on services and support (and that they therefore need (more) exposure to programmes aimed at teaching individual resilience and self-sufficiency). At the other pole, these *same* persons are cast as *a*social or as having some fundamental and long-lived aversion to various kinds of support (and that they therefore need to (again) participate in programmes aimed at teaching them how to be more trusting, more caring, in short, less self-sufficient). In both these scenarios, young male prisoners' subjectivities, histories and experiences are essentialised. The diversity and messiness of their lives is rewritten as 'background noise', or as clinically irrelevant, or as actuarially worthless. This, I submit, is the penultimate form of institutional disrespect. The affective impact of this manic (peristaltic) movement between constructions of over-dependency and under-dependency has been the primary concern of this chapter. The problem, of course, is that within the generally infantilising atmosphere of totalised institutions, respect and responsibility (or suitable states of *inter*dependency) are constantly put asunder and made to re-emerge as deference to and over-dependence on authority. As Bosworth (2007: 80) writes, 'What is clear is that despite their assertions about the importance of individual rights and responsibilities, prisons do not want inmates to express themselves freely.' This statement, while made in relation to sexual activity within custodial settings, applies, I think, to all aspects of incarceration, and, even more problematically, to post-release environments.

If, as demonstrated at the outset of this chapter, respect and responsibility are held to be preconditions of liberal democratic community, then it follows that these practices should be upheld within custodial institutions. For such places are a *part of the community*, however brutish, undesirable, or monstrous they are judged or imagined to be. Society and prison exist as locales on the same plane – what happens in one locale impacts other positions and relations on this plane (as evidenced by the way society produces crime and the way prisons produce a particular kind of social reaction to crime and (ex)prisoners). Indisputably, desistance from crime requires, perhaps above all, the 'choice' to make good. But this choice (or the decision to act 'responsibly' or with appropriate degrees of interdependency) is a socially and culturally mediated event. It is not and cannot be the work of the autonomous subject because there is no such thing as this type of subject. Desistance from crime – at least the likelihood that a break from offending might morph into something more durable at the level of the 'private' self – requires that people value and trust (in short, *respect*) the institutions and processes which purport to assist them or hold them accountable for their actions. Institutional and social disrespect (the disregard for the biographical, situational and generative aspects of people's lives) undermines in subtle but no less real terms the capacity to do well in the days and weeks following release. In such circumstances, desistance remains an image projected by authorities without any tangible means to bring it to reality. Perhaps, therefore, desistance (both primary and secondary varieties) is compromised (put at risk) not by obstinate or foolhardy offenders so much as by the social and institutional relationships on offer to such persons prior to, within, and beyond custody.

Notes

1 I want to express my sincere appreciation to Andrew Goldsmith for suggesting it might be useful to examine the concept of respect and, more especially, disrespect in the context of youth offending. The conversations we have had very much inform this chapter. For this, I am most grateful.

2 'Resident' is the term formally used by authorities to describe those remanded or sentenced to secure care facilities. In the majority of instances, residents are aged 10 to 17 years. 'Prisoner' denotes persons remanded or sentenced to adult custodial facilities.

3 Hays (1994) makes the useful distinction between trivial and non-trivial action in the context of the exercise of agency. She further distinguishes between two kinds of agency – *structurally reproductive agency* where 'people are agents in that alternate courses of action are possible, and in that they make (conscious or unconscious) choices among an available set of structurally provided alternatives' (1994: 63) and *structurally transformative agency* denoting 'those human social choices that have "non-trivial" consequences – that is, those actions that affect the pattern of social structures in some empirically observable way' (1994: 64).

4 Interviews of up to two hours' duration were (and continue to be) conducted at seven custodial institutions in South Australia under the auspices of a Flinders Small Grant (2003–2004) and an Australian Research Council Discovery Grant (2005–2008). To date, 92 interviews involving 50 unique participants aged 15 to 22 have been completed. All initial interviews take place in Cavan Training Centre (CTC) (the 36-bed secure facility for young men aged 15 to 17/18 years located north of Adelaide's

central business district) and explore the three broad themes of pathways into crime, experiences of incarceration, and the transition/challenges of release. Repeat interviews are conducted in CTC or in the relevant adult facility which the participant 'progresses' to since first being interviewed. Interviews are only conducted with those serving or who return to serve a fully custodial sentence. Since September 2003, 22 participants have been interviewed once, 17 have been interviewed twice, five have been interviewed on three occasions, four on four occasions, and one young man has been interviewed five times over the past four years. Half of all young men interviewed have progressed from the juvenile to adult custodial system since the project commenced.

5 Maruna *et al.* (2004a: 274), through an inversion of Lemert's approach to deviance, write that 'Primary desistance would ... refer to any lull or crime-free gap in the course of a criminal career'. By way of contrast (or extension), secondary desistance would connote 'the movement from the behaviour of non-offending to the assumption of the role or identity of a "changed person"'.

6 Australian government advertisement, 20 September 2007. The other two elements mentioned in the advertisement were democracy and equality of opportunity.

7 Clearly, society does not exist in any unified sense except in discourse (Rose 1996b), that is, except in those texts which would (ideally) turn a multitude of complex relationships and forces into *a* people, *a* nation, *a* society. Following Foucault's (more accurately, Nietzsche's) genealogical method, I think it important to remain deeply suspicious of categorical and universalising terminology. Instead, a more productive line of inquiry would perhaps examine how particular bodies (especially those assigned a marginal place in the social order of things), in line with discernible historical convergences, become subjects of power (ascribed, for instance, the capacity to act responsibly) and objects of knowledge (cast as bodies displaying such and such a quantum of respect).

8 Mansfield (2000: 3) defines subjectivity as 'an abstract or general principle that defies our separation into distinct selves and encourages us to imagine that, or simply helps us to understand why, our interior lives inevitably seem to involve other people, either as objects of need, desire and interest or as necessary sharers of common experience. In this way, the subject is always linked to something outside of it – an idea or principle or the society of other subjects. It is this linkage that the word "subject" insists upon.'

Chapter 12

'The best seven years I could'a done': the reconstruction of imprisonment as rehabilitation

Megan Comfort

Introduction

The steep rise in the United States' carceral population over the last three decades has resulted in incarceration becoming a modal event in the lives of low-income men, particularly African-American men. In a political climate that continues to advocate for harsh punishments and disapproves of spending on the 'coddling' of inmates, rehabilitative programmes remain scarce and the majority of prisoners serve their sentences without recourse to job training, education, drug treatment or therapeutic counselling. Yet in interviews conducted with men who had recently been released from prison and their wives or girlfriends, an unexpected theme emerges: rather than portraying the incarceration period as time wasted, couples convert the meaning of the prison sentence from condemnation to redemption, framing it as a period of self improvement and relationship strengthening. A close analysis of these interviews indicates that, as low-income people are increasingly denied social-welfare provisions and instead are relegated with intensified frequency and severity to the penal arm of the state, they engage in the project of *imaginary rehabilitation*, or acting 'as if' (see Carlen, Chapter 1) the penitentiary were an acceptable and indeed effective social institution for preparing people to 're-enter' society. This analysis provides a further lens for examining the extraordinary degradation of life conditions for poor African Americans in the era of mass incarceration.

In May 2005, Governor Arnold Schwarzenegger signed into law bill SB 737, a 'Reorganization Plan' concerning what had previously been known as the California Department of Corrections (CDC). Responsible for the daily operations of the state's 34 adult prisons, eight juvenile facilities, 44 'conservation camps' (detention facilities where adults and juveniles are put to work fighting wildfires, responding to natural disasters and conserving public lands) and the state parole system, in 2005 the CDC housed 165,700 inmates, supervised 126,300 ex-felons, and encompassed 54,000 employees (Office of the Governor 2005). In addition to changes such as organisational restructuring, the introduction of a Global Positioning Satellite to track 'high risk sex offender parolees' and the undertaking of a 'comprehensive risk management programme', SB 737 amended the name of the CDC by adding two key words: as of 1 July 2005, the newly redesigned department was to be known as the California Department of Corrections *and Rehabilitation*. Under the aim of 'reducing criminality', this change was to be reflected in 'expanding and improving existing, evidence-based educational vocation and training programmes to prepare an inmate for their return to the community from which they came'(California Department of Corrections and Rehabilitation 2007b).

Two years later, on 2 May 2007, the CDCR issued a press release: 'Governor Schwarzenegger Signs Historic Prison Reform Agreement' (Unger and Kostyrko 2007). Assembly Bill 900, also known as the Public Safety and Offender Rehabilitation Services Act, was touted as 'a historic measure to help reform California's overburdened correctional system' (in reference to the surplus of bodies that exceeded the state prison system's capacity by nearly 100 per cent) that would 'provide critical relief to prison overcrowding and increase public safety by dramatically changing California's approach to rehabilitating prisoners'. In a state that has been singled out for the fact that its highly punitive parole system results in almost twice the national average (67 per cent compared to 35 per cent) of offenders being reincarcerated for violating the conditions of their parole (Butterfield 2003; Little Hoover Commission 2003), one might expect that a bill aimed at reducing prison overcrowding and transforming rehabilitation would ease parole terms and shore up community-based substance-use treatment options, mental health services and employment programmes, thereby decreasing the number of people being sent or re-sent behind bars. Instead, Governor Schwarzenegger announced that, 'With this bill, we will add 53,000 [prison] beds – the most built in a generation. But we will also put management reforms in place so that these beds are built quickly *and the rehabilitation programmes tied to each and every new bed are strong*' (my emphasis).

With this odd turn of phrase, Governor Schwarzenegger summed up the state of rehabilitation in the state of California and, indeed, largely throughout the United States of America. Rehabilitation has become *de facto* 'tied' to the penitentiary, with whatever forms it is purported to take – mental-health services, job training, education – being dispensed in their carceral versions, behind prison walls and only once those in need of assistance have been squarely tucked into an institutional bed (Bottoms *et al.* 1996; Currie 1998; Kupers 1999; for a discussion of the carceral 'net widening' that encompasses non-custodial treatment, see Cohen 1985). As the newly named department indicates, the mission to rehabilitate has been assigned to custodial authorities (emphasised to the point of redundancy, since the term 'corrections' already connotes the idea of rehabilitation), and as such is designed, evaluated, paid for and delivered through the arm of the government that is otherwise occupied with punishment – a setup described by Coyle (1992: 3), writing while serving as governor of Her Majesty's Prison in Brixton, as 'misunderstood rehabilitation'.

Although this conjoining of punishment and rehabilitation has become commonsensical in the American public imagination, research has cast doubt on the compatibility of such a coupling. In a review of meta-analyses of the effectiveness of correctional rehabilitation, Lipsey and Cullen (2007: 302) note that there is no support for any argument that punishment has a specific deterrent effect (meaning that it has not been found to be effective in reducing individuals' subsequent criminal behaviour), and that 'a significant portion of the evidence points in the opposite direction – such sanctions may increase the likelihood of recidivism.' By contrast, the authors find rehabilitative treatment in the forms of multisystemic therapy, family counselling, cognitive-behavioural therapy, aggression replacement training, drug courts, social casework, and educational, vocational and employment programmes to show mean effect sizes favourable to treatment (Lipsey and Cullen 2007: 303–5). Although some of the rehabilitation programmes evaluated were administered behind bars, Lipsey and Cullen observe that the 'gap between this body of research and current practice and policy [in jails and prisons] … is large and not easily bridged', due in part to the fact that 'the types of programmes used in correctional practice are not the same mix represented in the research literature', with the former sometimes constituting no more than a work assignment or participation in an occasional Alcoholics Anonymous meeting and the latter being theory-based and administered by a research team (Lipsey and Cullen 2007: 314–15).

Even when inmates *are* able to access theory-based prᴄ
administered by research teams and community organisa...
institutional barriers may significantly shape the intervention that
is delivered. Conducting treatment programmes within correctional
facilities involves complying with security measures such as
lockdowns, when all inmates are confined to their living quarters for
days or weeks on end and therefore are not able to attend sessions,
or having prison officers present in the classroom, which may inhibit
participants' willingness to speak openly about temptations to engage
in illegal activities (Grinstead *et al.* 1999). Underlying these logistical
impediments is the reality that, as Carlen and Tombs (2006) remind
us, 'a prison is a prison,' and the first order of correctional facilities
is to confine people against their will, a process that inherently
places inmates in a position of submission, disempowerment and
humiliation as they suffer the 'pains of imprisonment' meticulously
analysed by Sykes (1958). These facilities are also false environments
in which certain needs are met – food, shelter, medical care, all of
which may be problematic for people to access 'on the outside' – and
other needs are categorically denied – intimacy, gainful employment,
parenting opportunities, each of which can present unique stresses that
are difficult to prepare for in the abstract. The carceral environment
in which people may be taught a set of skills therefore is radically
different than the home environments in which people will ultimately
need to exercise them, making it likely that their efforts to do so will
fail.

Schwarzenegger's proclamation announcing a massive increase in
prison beds that will be 'tied' to rehabilitative programmes therefore
can be seen as an exercise in the 'as if' penality described by Carlen
in the Introduction to this volume. His announcement is made *as
if* punishment and rehabilitation were scientifically proven to be
mutually beneficial bedfellows; it is applauded by those who will be
charged with carrying it out *as if* there were really enough funding,
and time, and resources to accomplish such a mission; the bill is
inscribed into law *as if* the rehabilitation component will not trail
behind and ultimately be lost in the construction and management of
the new institutions, cellblocks, kitchens, cafeterias, laundry services,
hospitals, and other structures needed to house those 53,000 bodies
behind bars.

Carlen highlights in her Introduction that one of the dangers of
'the imaginary' in penality and corrections is that it impedes or flat-
out stops the development of alternative ideas of how harm can be
reduced. One can easily imagine how the co-opting of rehabilitation

by state officials into the correctional domain depletes the coffers for non-custodial efforts and simultaneously blocks the conceptualisation of rehabilitative treatment as something that could be separated from punitive control. Discussions of these perils might logically focus on state officials, correctional authorities, policy makers or members of the general public, but typically left out are those who themselves undergo this 'imaginary rehabilitation'. How do former prisoners describe their experiences of rehabilitation – imaginary or otherwise – behind walls? How are their conceptions of their own needs shaped by carceral discourses and forms of rehabilitation? This chapter focuses on these questions to make the following arguments:

- As the social-welfare state dwindles to near extinction and the penal state inflates to gargantuan proportions, poor people in the United States – particularly African-American men – are being routinely diverted into the criminal justice system when they are in need of social assistance.

- A tremendous amount of money is spent incarcerating these individuals, yet virtually none of these funds go toward the provision of rehabilitative programming. When people exit correctional facilities they leave without having received treatment for the conditions or assistance with the circumstances that contributed to their arrest.

- None the less, with other avenues of social-welfare provision closed down by the ideological dominance and rapacious expense of the rehabilitation-tied-to-punishment model, former prisoners themselves learn to participate in the 'closure' described earlier in this volume by Carlen. Seeking to give meaning to the years they spent behind bars, people create narratives that lend credence to the rhetoric of imaginary rehabilitation by crediting the penitentiary with significant life transformations.

- Yet when these stories of redemption are carefully analysed, they are revealed to be grounded primarily in individual efforts and personal reflection, void of substantial or sustained help provided by the institution. Thus their telling points to the deep penetration of the imaginary, as even those at the bull's eye of the punishment apparatus amplify and perpetuate notions of rehabilitation that coalesce with those promoted by correctional authorities despite evidence of considerable disjuncture.

Incarceration in the United States

The tremendous rise of the incarceration rate in the United States over the last 30 years has become legendary among scholars of crime and punishment. After hovering around a stable mean of 150 inmates per 100,000 US residents for half a century, in the mid-1970s the national incarceration rate began a spectacular upward surge.[1] By 2006, 750 of every 100,000 US residents were behind bars (Sabol et al. 2007), a rate six to twelve times higher than that of Western European countries (International Centre for Prison Studies 2006; see also Tonry 2001). The dramatic differences in the prevalence of incarceration among ethnic groups have also become infamous: in 2006 African-American men accounted for 13 per cent of men in the US general population and 41 per cent of men behind bars. Approximately 4.8 per cent of all African-American men were incarcerated in 2006, compared to 0.7 per cent of white men and 1.9 per cent of Hispanic men. Women comprise a much smaller number of inmates, constituting 13 per cent of jail detainees and 7 per cent of prisoners, but African-American women were also greatly over-represented in the carceral system with an incarceration rate 3.8 times that of white women in 2006. That same year, Hispanic women were 1.6 times more likely to be incarcerated than white women (all statistics from Sabol et al. 2007).

'Rehabilitation' is something of a misnomer when speaking about the needs of incarcerated and formerly incarcerated people, because the 're' indicates that people are being returned to a level of habilitation, integration and civic participation that they formerly enjoyed. Yet it is those who have been chronically marginalised who are most likely to spend time in the custody of the state. According to data from the Bureau of Justice Statistics, 33 per cent of US state prisoners were unemployed at the time of their arrest. Nineteen per cent had less than an eighth-grade education (typically achieved at age 14) and only 34 per cent had completed high school (typically achieved at age 18). Fifty per cent had used drugs in the month prior to their arrest, and 61 per cent identified drugs or alcohol as being connected to the reason for their arrest. Sixteen per cent of state prisoners were deemed to be mentally ill, with 50 per cent of these people being prescribed medication for their mental illness during their incarceration (Bureau of Justice Statistics 1990; Ditton 1999). Socioeconomic and ethnic disparities in incarceration result from lack of access to housing, employment, education, mental-health and substance-use treatment, and a host of other factors that profoundly affect people's likelihood of turning to illegal means for survival, psychological relief or acceptance by a peer group – not to mention institutionalised discrimination and the heavy-handed policing of low-income people of colour (Miller 1996; Tonry 1995; Western 2006).

Background to the study

In 2000, I conducted nine months of ethnographic research focusing on women visiting their male partners who were incarcerated in California's San Quentin State Prison (Comfort 2008). In the in-depth interviews I conducted with 50 women whose boyfriend, fiancé, or husband was behind bars, a counterintuitive theme that emerged repeatedly was that the imprisonment period provided an opportunity for couples to renew their romantic bonds since it interrupted men's difficult or dangerous behaviours in the home (such as substance use or conjugal violence) and simultaneously provided them with time and motivation to cultivate their intimate relationships. Indeed, much to my surprise and contrary to the dominant strand in the sociological and criminological literature, many women recast the incarceration in positive terms, providing examples of how imprisoned men became more reflective, family oriented and committed to traditional goals of legal employment and 'settling down' than they had been prior to their arrest. Notably, although women identified these paradoxical benefits that accompanied the confinement of their partners, they also clearly recognised its concomitant harms, leaving them mired in a state of profound ambivalence toward the penitentiary and the powerful role it played in their and their partners' lives. As one woman succinctly expressed, 'It's a lot of good men behind walls! You know, it's just that it took them *to be* behind the walls to wan' to get their self in order. An' that's sad' (Comfort 2008: 174).

From this initial study, the question logically arose as to whether men, too, recast their own incarceration as a time of self-improvement. In 2005 and 2006, with colleagues from the Center for AIDS Prevention Studies at the University of California San Francisco, I conducted a pilot study of ten heterosexual couples in which the male partner had been released from a California state prison within the previous 15 months. Study recruitment focused on the city of Oakland, CA, which has 19 per cent of its population living below the federal poverty line, is 35 per cent African American, and receives 3,000 parolees from California state prisons annually (US Census Bureau 2000; City of Oakland 2003). Participants were recruited from multiple and varied sites: a meeting that parolees were mandated to attend within two weeks of their release from custody; a support group for parolees and their families run by a non-profit organisation in conjunction with a state-funded post-release programme; the centre for visitors at San Quentin State Prison; and the sidewalk in front of a day labour agency. Participating couples came to a scheduled appointment together and were interviewed separately and simultaneously by gender-matched interviewers. Couples were paid for their participation, and no identifying or contact information was retained after the interview.

All participating couples had been romantically involved prior to, during, and after the man's most recent incarceration. Three couples had been in a relationship together for between 11 and 15 years, three had been together for between three and seven years and four had been romantically involved for one to two years. One of the men had been incarcerated most recently for seven years, one for six years, four for between one and three years, and four for between two and six months. Seventeen participants were African American and three were Hispanic, with ages ranging from 19 to 50 years (the average participant age was 34 years).

A close analysis of these interviews indicates that, as low-income people are increasingly denied social-welfare provisions and instead are relegated with intensified frequency and severity to the penal arm of the state, they engage in the project of imaginary rehabilitation, acting 'as if' the penitentiary were an acceptable and indeed effective social institution for preparing them to 're-enter' a society from which they have been consistently excluded. However, what on the surface may sound like an endorsement of the punishment-and-rehabilitation coupling is not intended by former prisoners and their partners to express support for a political move to link rehabilitative treatment to punitive sanctions. Rather, people primarily become involved in strategies of 'preserving identities, structuring reminiscences, and sustaining emotional attachment' (Unruh 1983: 346) as they retroactively make sense of periods of incarceration, and in so doing salvage aspects of that experience that can be recast in a positive light.

The 'as if' of punishment as rehabilitation

Robert is a 50-year-old man who claims he has 'a rap sheet [that] ... would go all the way down the stairs' of the three-storey building in which he was interviewed. Starting with arrests when he was an adolescent and encompassing approximately 15 incarcerations in jails

259

and prisons, he estimates he has spent a total of 23 years of his life behind bars. According to Robert, his numerous run-ins with the law were related to his drug use, repeated burglaries ('I couldn't keep my hands off other people's property. I was like the Zorro guy – I'd take from the rich and give to the poor'), and one assault charge in the early 1980s for which he was sentenced to three years. At the time of his interview, he had been out of the penitentiary for 14 months and was approaching his one-year wedding anniversary with Rose, whom he had begun intermittently courting almost a decade earlier. Diagnosed as HIV-positive during his most recent sojourn in prison (stretching from early 1998 until 31 December 2004), Robert now volunteers his time to speak to groups of troubled juveniles about the health-related perils and legal hazards of injection drug use and criminal activity. Several minutes into his interview, in the course of explaining how he met his wife, he offers his account of the last time he was arrested:

> Well, *I got rescued*. What I did was, I was on drugs so bad that I just walked up to a police officer … he had stopped my friend and I kept walking and [I thought to myself], 'That's it. This is my chance to get clean.' So I turned around and I walked back and I asked him about what he was doin' with my friend and he just looked at me. … I felt like I was asking about my friend but then again I felt like I was telling him help me, [to] take me with him or something. And he said, 'Excuse me sir, would you have anything that I might need to know about?' I said, 'Yes I do, sir.' I went in my pack and I pulled out a syringe with some heroin in it and I gave it to him. And that was – a lot of people would think that that was a disaster point. *That right there was my road to recovery*. Because they took me to jail and it was – a few things happened. I was so glad to be off the streets, because I was homeless at the time; I was so glad to be off the streets that it wasn't even funny. It was such a blessing to have a bed to lay down every night regardless if I was incarcerated or not. … [I spent seven years in prison.] That was the best seven years I could'a done. I pulled myself together, educated myself, learned a lot of things about people, you know being around people, trusting people. I worked in a hospice in prison. I seen a lot of death. And I seen me. That could be me any time. … Because in 2000 I was diagnosed with HIV. … I seen – that was a dose of reality, you know. That was the end of the road as far as what I was doin'. 'If you keep doin' what you're doin'

that's gonna be you, Robert. You get outta here and start again, that could be you right there.' That was so scary for me.

Robert's story of his 'rescue' follows the same lines of Schwarzenegger's announcement: the road to recovery that begins literally with a prison bed. Is this not then the quintessential validation of the incarceration-partnered-with-rehabilitation thesis, straight from the reformed soul's mouth? Narratives like Robert's ostensibly refute those who argue that help for people in need of education, treatment for addiction, housing, employment and other social services is inherently tainted if provided through the correctional apparatus. And in fact, the 'prison saved my life' mantra is not uncommon, being heard in autobiographical accounts of overcoming the odds offered by numerous ex-convicts, including in their published memoirs (McCall 1994; Shakur 1998). How does one reconcile the first-hand interpretation of incarceration-as-salvation and the seemingly more theoretical contradiction between punitive and integrative missions?

The correctional apparatus as gatekeeper for social services

In the tale that Robert tells, there are the clear signs that this homeless, drug-addicted man felt he had nowhere else to turn for a chance at shelter and substance-abuse treatment than a police officer: walking down the street, the sight of the law-enforcement authority triggers the thought, 'This is my chance to get clean.' Exactly as Schwarzenegger described, what used to be considered services to be delivered by the social-welfare state have now become tied – in reality, and therefore also in the minds of the people who need them – to correctional beds. The way that Robert describes his 'rescue' must be analysed in the context of what forms of help are available to him: significantly, he does not recount having the opportunity to pass a social worker whom he could ask for assistance on the street, or to walk by an agency that could accept him immediately into a residential treatment programme. Looked at in the framework of available options, Robert's ostensible choice of correctional intervention in his life is more fundamentally a profound desire for assistance grounded in his knowledge that such assistance is only to be accessed through interfacing with the criminal justice system. Indeed, upon his release from prison Robert continued to turn to the correctional apparatus as the means by which he could have recourse to social services:

When I [was released from prison and I] got to the parole office I said, 'I cannot be on the streets. Will you put me somewhere or just handcuff me right in this office and take me back to prison or another jail or something – I'm not going out in the streets [again]. I'm going to give myself a chance and if you can't do that for me take me to jail.' And that told me right there I was serious about making it. So that's what they did. They put me in a [housing] programme and I had time to put my feet on the ground and get focused – you know, get some tools so when things come up, when life shows up like they say, I have some tools to deal with that.

Although Robert tells his story with unequivocal conviction, through Rose we hear that he sometimes expresses abiding ambivalence about relying on imprisonment as his primary means of service access. When asked about how Robert's incarceration had affected her, Rose responds, 'I missed him, but at the same time it was like I knew because of the situation, of his drug addiction, he needed time out. So I didn't have a problem with it. … He'll tell me, "That's not what I needed." And I said, "Well yeah, you can't do it on your own." … That's what he needed.' Rose was previously married to an alcoholic who did not spend time in prison, and her matter-of-fact acceptance that incarceration provides the 'time out' that is 'needed' by substance users reveals much about her (lack of) history finding treatment and assistance away from correctional institutions for the men in her life. In her comments, she expresses the stark view that Robert's options are to conquer addiction 'on his own' or to go behind bars and let the environment enforce his sobriety, and though she may not take pleasure in the latter, she does not second-guess its utility.[2]

Michael, another interview participant, also describes a connection between the services he needs and the correctional system. An infrequent, low-level lawbreaker, Michael is 49 years old and at the time of his interview had been incarcerated five times since the age of 21 for just over three years in total. When not behind bars, Michael grapples with alcoholism and finding employment, the lack of which creates an uneasy imbalance in his relationship with his common-law wife, Diana, since they are unequal providers for their ten-year-old son. In his interview, Michael repeatedly speaks of his high hopes for an upcoming appointment he was able to obtain through his parole officer with a vocational rehabilitation training programme, and his awareness that it was only because of his prison record that he could participate in the programme: 'I have an appointment with voc rehab and I got that out of CDC [the California Department of Corrections] – and if I wasn't in CDC I couldn't do that.' He also explains the direct channels between his parole officer and his access to mental-health treatment and financial assistance: 'I go to the parole office once a month [on] Tuesday and see a psychiatrist … [who] sends me to General Assistance. And General Assistance gave me a paper for the psychiatrist to sign. So it's all entwined.' Not insignificantly, Michael asserts that he was referred to the psychiatrist for 'severe mental depression' stemming from the trauma he experienced during his most recent incarceration, when he was housed with high-level offenders despite his own low-security status. Although he claims that he did not suffer physical violence, Michael feared for his life as a series of cellmates serving life sentences threatened him, a situation to which he refers repeatedly and with pronounced anxiety during his interview. Hence the services provided to him are even more 'entwined' since his access to mental-health treatment is not only controlled but also necessitated by his contact with the criminal justice system (for discussions of the psychological trauma of incarceration, see Haney 2003; Kupers 1996).

Although Michael speaks excitedly of his appointment with the vocational training programme, he is sceptical overall of the will of the correctional authorities to support rehabilitation efforts: 'Really they [the prison authorities] don't have enough [programmes] though. And it seemed like they're counting on you not to use them, and they're taking them away all the time.' With this statement, he demonstrates a lucid understanding of how the carceral institution operates (what could be called the 'hard reality' view) that is juxtaposed against the 'imaginary work' (in the sense of Hochschild's (1979) 'emotion work') being performed when he articulates his hopes for what might transpire at the vocational training office. Michael expresses similar scepticism about parole officers, recounting the story of how in 2000 he asked his parole officer to help him remove a conviction for driving while under the influence of alcohol from his record. According to Michael, the parole officer replied that he had not known Michael had this conviction but now that he was aware of it he would start testing Michael for alcohol in addition to the other supervisory checks he was already performing. Michael responded angrily, 'This is eight years ago and I'm trying to clean up and rectify, and here you go putting more stress on my back. Come on, man!' These experiences exemplify the inherent contradictions in charging the same authorities with punitive and rehabilitative missions: unable to give equal time, funding and priority to both, prison and parole officers will default to maintaining order and enforcing punishment while maintaining lip service to rehabilitation, leaving those in their charge conflicted, confused and feeling short-changed (Lynch 2001).

The price of doing time

In California, taxpayers spend an average of $35,587 a year to imprison one person and $4,338 to supervise each parolee (California Department of Corrections and Rehabilitation 2007a). The 2007–08 budget for the CDCR was $9.77 billion (or 8.6 per cent of the state's General Fund), and, despite a budget crisis precipitating substantial cuts in state services, at the time of writing it was projected at $10.65 billion for 2008–09 (following closely behind the $12.83 billion proposed for California institutions of higher education) (California Department of Finance 2008). At the average rate, the price tag for Robert's most recent incarceration would have been in the ballpark of $249,109, and the lifetime bill for his estimated 23 years behind bars plus many years of parole would run close to one million dollars. But Robert was no longer an average-cost prisoner as of 2000, when he tested positive for HIV. Inmates of jails and prisons are the only people in the United States who are guaranteed by the Constitution to receive health care (denying them such care is considered cruel and unusual punishment under the Eighth Amendment to the United States Constitution, see McDonald 1999). Although this health care is often substandard, and in California led to a major lawsuit that resulted in the medical system in the CDCR being taken over by a receivership (Reiterman 2004; Sterngold 2005; Bee 2005), it can be more adequate than the nonexistent or sub par services people receive when they are not incarcerated (Freudenberg 2001; Glaser and Greifinger 1993). Due to his diagnosis, Robert began taking antiretroviral medications while incarcerated, which, combined with doctor's visits to follow his progress, would have added several thousand dollars a year to the cost of imprisoning him.

What did Robert receive for the investment of over a quarter-million dollars in him? Although he did not participate in any substance-use treatment programme while incarcerated, he did stop using drugs there and continued his sobriety when he left prison. He also learned of his HIV infection, started taking medication, and understood how to maintain his health through continued medical treatment and lifestyle choices. But beyond these two important changes, Robert left the penitentiary with no additional skills or information to help him enter a society in which he had never been a gainfully employed, non-substance-addicted, civically integrated adult member. Since Rose had been homeless for a period during Robert's incarceration and was also living in transitional housing when he was released, he went directly to a transitional housing programme because he had no other relatives or friends with whom he could stay (homelessness and incarceration often go hand-in-hand, see Gowan 2002). He had no job or training lined up (through his own initiative he pursued training to become a personal fitness trainer, and was employed in this capacity at the time of his interview). Given Robert's strong motivation to 'go straight' and the relatively long period he was imprisoned, one may question the dearth of pre-release planning for housing and employment provided to him. His ability not to re-offend in the 14 months prior to his interview indicated remarkable determination on his part, since returning a formerly drug-addicted, homeless and chronically unemployed man to the streets after seven years behind bars with no housing, job prospects or support structure would seem to be a perfect recipe for recidivism.

Robert is not the only participant who was incarcerated for many costly years, only to be released unprepared for the challenges that lay ahead of him. Calvin is a 23-year-old father of two who has been in correctional custody twice in his lifetime: once for one day in jail, and once for two and a half years in prison. Like Robert, Calvin characterises his time behind bars as positive: 'I think I came out of it good. Because I took some courses and stuff. I took my GED. I took a couple of college courses, like English and writing and stuff, math. A couple parenting [classes], anger management.' During his interview, the young man repeatedly articulates precise goals for his life, saying he wants to work a steady job so he can be a financial provider for his girlfriend, Alana, and their three-year-old son, as well as his four-year-old daughter from a previous relationship. He also wants to go to university and ultimately embark on a career in fabricating prosthetic limbs. Calvin explains that being incarcerated gave him the time to reflect on his life and decide upon these goals but, despite his enthusiasm when talking about them, he has few answers for the interviewer's questions about his specific plans for actually achieving them. The son of substance-addicted parents, Calvin never held a legal job before he was locked up and he left prison without knowing where he would live (he gave a relative's address to his parole officer but knew this would not be a lasting arrangement), where he would find employment, or how exactly he should go about obtaining work outside of the underground economy. His reflections on how he had imagined that 'going legit' would be easy reveal the lack of preparation provided during his 30 months in correctional custody:

> Interviewer: What kind of job were you thinking that you might be able to get with your skills?
>
> Calvin: To be honest I didn't even know. ... I just knew what I wanted. I just knew I wanted stuff to go good when I got out, everything to fall into place. But I didn't know exactly what it was gonna be. I had goals, I had wanted to get in school, wanted to get a job. Wanted to be with my kids, wanted to have a good girlfriend. But I never got in-depth of what exactly what I was gonna be doing. It was like, 'Dang!' Whatever came. So I was like really undecided.

Through attending a job fair for ex-felons, Calvin eventually obtained work installing alarms and intercom systems, which helped him meet his financial obligations but did not advance him toward his goal of completing a university degree. He spent a period living with a variety of friends and relatives, ultimately managing to move into a small apartment with Alana and their son with the help of a non-profit programme providing assistance to young men exiting prison. As with Michael, the forms of assistance that made a difference in Calvin's life were available to him only due to his status as a former prisoner, and were accessible only once he left the institution's walls.

At the time of their interviews, both Robert and Calvin had managed to avoid breaking the law for over a year. One might wonder if the same ends could have been met by applying those hundreds of thousands of taxpayer dollars toward non-custody programmes such as job training, housing assistance and residential drug treatment for the two men (and many others like them, since non-custodial programmes are less expensive to operate than correctional facilities). Also, both were still on parole when they were interviewed, and there is no guarantee that they have been able to sustain their law-abiding behaviour in the time since. Certainly there were hundreds of men who had experienced the exact same 'carceral therapy' as Robert and Calvin who were not recruited as participants for the study because they had been reincarcerated and were no longer available in free society. In Robert's case, his numerous previous incarcerations had not proven effective in helping him conquer his addiction, making it unlikely that the mere application of 'more of the same' catalysed his recovery this time around. The tens of thousands of released prisoners who relapse and re-offend in California each year are blunt testimony to the fact that the CDCR emperor is wearing very few rehabilitative clothes.

Although very different in the details of their life circumstances at the time of their most recent arrests, Robert and Calvin possessed the profile of individuals who would be likely to have responded well to rehabilitative rather than punitive treatment, and these profiles might explain why they were able to leverage their incarceration into a 'turning point' (Sampson and Laub 2005). Robert's narrative indicates a man aging out of crime, worn out by his years of substance use, who was willing to go to extreme lengths just to get a roof over his head. His subsequent HIV diagnosis served to cement his resolve to turn his life around and inspired his choice of a career in physical fitness, while his relationship with Rose, who did not have a history of substance use or incarceration, provided emotional support and motivation to avoid his previous habits. Taken at face value, his account of exposing his heroin use to the police officer as a means of obtaining help with his addiction indicates a high level of 'treatment readiness and problem recognition', both of which have been found to be predictors of retention in substance-abuse programmes (Brocato and Wagner 2008; Joe et al. 1998). For his part, after having had 'nothing but time to reflect' while behind bars, Calvin articulates a strong desire to channel his youthful energy into the conventional outlets of gainful employment, paternal responsibility and romantic partnership. Having avoided the ravages of addiction and side-stepped extensive contact with the criminal justice system until the point of his most recent arrest, the primary barrier to his achievement of his scholastic and professional goals is now the black mark of his prison record (Western 2006) – precisely the supposedly 'rehabilitative' event that provided him with time to evaluate his life trajectory.

Reframing rehabilitation

Despite Governor Schwarzenegger's rhetoric, actual programmes and services in correctional institutions are very limited and often nonexistent. The programmes that do exist typically enrol inmates for a relatively short period (several weeks or months as opposed to years), and participants often do not follow a full course of treatment but rather cobble together a scattering of classes (as described by Calvin earlier, 'I took a couple of college courses … A couple parenting [classes], anger management …'). Given these limitations, it is not surprising that none of the men interviewed identified having benefited from a solid, extensive preparation for (re)entering the legal work force, arranging permanent housing, maintaining sobriety or other activities commonly associated with rehabilitative treatment.

Instead, when former prisoners describe the purportedly rehabilitative or positive aspects of their confinement, they signal a shift in the definition of rehabilitation itself. Rather than talking about social assistance or civic integration – which would be the responsibility of a social-welfare state – they describe the progress they made during their time behind bars in terms of individual efforts at self improvement. Men often refer to incarceration as a 'wake-up call' that motivated them to reflect on past mistakes and future goals. For example, Duane, a 42-year-old man who estimates he has been incarcerated 11 times in his life for a total of just under 11 years, says of his most recent three-month stay in prison for violating his parole, 'I hated it and it was positive. It just woke me back up to reality.' He also notes that his time away brought him closer to his 49-year-old fiancée, Kim: 'It made me feel, which I already knew, our love was solid. … And in some ways it also brung us closer, which made us realise what we have and what we've missed.' For her part, Kim, who describes herself as 'shut down' emotionally due to a previous abusive relationship, finds it to be 'therapy for me to write somebody and communicate' and therefore takes pleasure in sending letters to Duane while he is behind bars. Her increased ease of expression by post adds to the couple's feelings of closeness during periods of separation: 'It's so weird because I can't say what I'm thinking. What I'm thinking just comes out through my hands as opposed to try to express it verbally to where he can understand what I'm trying to – it comes out better on paper' (see also Comfort 2008). When Duane is in prison, then, the couple engages in a joint effort to affirm their commitment to each other, define their goals for their life together, and concentrate on the personal growth they see as necessary to achieving those goals. Rehabilitation in a more classic sense does not play a part in their discussion, and is substituted by an inwardly focused exploration that extends at most to the couple, who are isolated from the surrounding milieu.

Likewise, Michael frames his incarceration in individualistic terms. Asked by the interviewer whether he felt his most recent incarceration was a 'positive, neutral, or negative experience', Michael replies:

Well, when I go in [to prison] I try to use the time for positive things. To work on myself and work on things I need to work on. ... The first couple of times it was a pretty good experience but I went in a negative way. ... I got depressed ... that's what I always do at first, I get a lot of sleep and then I have to face reality. ... It was pretty positive. Because I searched for all the knowledge and the help that I can get from CDC. Everything they had to offer I really applied for it this time and followed up.

In his response, Michael expresses ambivalence over whether he or the prison is responsible for the quality of the time he spends therein, indicating that he primarily believes he is accountable for assuming an upbeat mindset, scouting out opportunities, and taking advantage of whatever the institution might have to offer. Michael's wife, Diana, is less inclined to try to see the bright side of a prison sentence. After a 14-year on-and-off relationship with Michael during which he has struggled with his alcoholism and incarceration while she raised their son and maintained a steady job as a teacher before taking a disability leave due to chronic back pain, Diana has lost patience with the phenomenon of men who announce plans for reformation only after landing behind bars:

And then he'll have revelations when he's in there, 'I know that I shouldn't be here and I really miss you and I know I shouldn't have been at this place at this time. When I get out I'm going to change.' I attribute all that to you being there [in prison]. When you come out let's see what you're going to do. But everybody wants God and wants to do a wonderful thing once they're in there and when you come home is the real deal. I pretty much ix-ne [the 'pig Latin' form of 'nix'] the godliness stuff that happens in his mind in there. I want to see what's happening once you're here. ... And I know a lot of times you have a lot of idle time there so you are able to think a lot clearly, but bring that clarity home when you come physically.

The fact that men have 'idle time' during which they can ruminate about their lives while in prison plays a large role in how people characterise the 'benefits' of incarceration. Greg is a 31-year-old man who had gone to jail a handful of times before he was sent to prison in 1999. At the time of his sentencing, he and his wife Sonia made a clear decision that they would maintain their relationship for the six years he would spend behind bars. Eleven months after his release from custody, he reflected on the changes he observed in himself during that time:

> That was a time to where I got to really understand myself. When I was on the streets I was moving so fast you know. The street life and what not, it just got you moving so much to where from the time you wake up in the morning you're moving until the time you go to sleep. So it's like I've never had no solitude time for me to know who I am, to understand myself, to analyse things that took place within that day or whatever. And most importantly to reflect on my family. Before I went to prison I neglected them a lot.

Sonia shares her husband's perspective. Left on her own to raise her daughter from a previous relationship and hungering for more out of life than hardship and heartache, she embarked upon a similar path of introspection and self improvement:

> We both felt like, okay this is our time to be away from each other. We can grow. I can grow as a woman. I can grow as a mother. He can grow as a man. And when you come out [of prison] we'll know exactly where we want to go. And it was basically college to us. ... It's a bad thing to be separated from your family and everything but I looked at this as a beautiful experience.

Similarly, Calvin gives an account of confinement as a time of personal transformation, particularly regarding his revelation that his previous interactions with women were hurtful and his decision to settle into a monogamous relationship. Responding to the question as to whether his most recent imprisonment was positive, neutral or negative, he asserts:

Calvin: I think it was a positive experience all the way around. Because I look at it as a blessing. Because the stuff I was into, it was like I was hanging around the wrong crowd. All my friends now that I was hanging around with are either dead or in prison for a long time, for like murders and stuff. So I think it was like a blessing from God, or whoever, that I was taken away to learn that lesson. Because I don't think I'd be the person I am right now if it wasn't for that. One, because it gave me time to focus … I was thinking about how could I be a better person. … I really never had an idea of what a man was. So when I was incarcerated I was doing a lot of reading and just reflecting on past relationships, like, 'Dang. That was wrong. You was wrong for doing that girl like that.' So I just went back, all the way just like re-evaluating myself, like, 'Man! What type of man is that? What's the definition of a man?'…

Interviewer: So tell me what a man is to you?

Calvin:　To me a man is honest, hard working, a role model. I think a man is accountable, to hold himself accountable for his actions. Like, I don't know, a good role model. That's what a man is to me. … Someone with integrity.

Calvin's desire to 'be a man' resonates with such expressions in many other interviews, and indeed signals a pivotal conceptualisation of rehabilitation among these former felons. Stark lines are drawn between the way men characterise their pre-incarceration behaviour (womanising, not working, engaging in illegal activities) and the ideas they form while in prison about what it means to 'be a man' – that is, to assume the identity of someone who has learned from past experiences and moved on to a position of moral worthiness that is deserving of respect. Robert describes writing letters from prison in which he explains this transformation to Rose:

I wrote a lot of powerful, things that I thought were powerful, in telling her, 'I'm a changed person. … Because today I'm the man that I felt I shoulda been a long time ago in your life. Somebody who wants to take care of you and do the things that man does. I understand what a man is today.' So I would write things like that to her in the letter and she would tell me her expectations of a man. And that was right up my alley, you know. Because that's what she was saying, that's how I seen me. … You're under somebody else's rule when you're in prison. You gotta do this and do this the way they want you. Get your own place! A *man*'s supposed to have his own. So I told myself, 'I have to find a job. I have to do something.' … And it just feels good today to be able to stand up and feel like I am a man, a real man.

271

Robert's words did not fall on deaf ears. For her part, Rose believed that the troubles in their relationship would benefit from such a change: 'And [in earlier years, when Robert would leave prison] he wanted to see me but I didn't want to see him 'cause he had hurted me. He hurted me too bad, too bad. So I just [said], 'No. You get yourself together, and once you through with this out here, and when you're ready to settle down and be a man, let me know.'

By framing rehabilitation as the process of 'getting oneself together', 'settling down', and 'being a man', couples imbue a prison sentence with possibility. Anyone counting on therapeutic programming, assistance making concrete plans for post-release job and housing aid, or other forms of rehabilitative treatment that require personnel, budgets and infrastructure behind bars would be sorely disappointed while doing time in the vast majority of US correctional institutions. But finding deliverance in merely having time to think quietly about one's life, deciding to adhere to a certain code of masculinity, and articulating that decision to loved ones opens the potential for betterment to virtually all inmates, paradoxically leading them to cast an environment barren of social-welfare services as fertile ground for redemption.

Conclusion: a better seven years

At the beginning of this chapter, Robert states that his most recent incarceration was 'the best seven years' he 'could have done' in terms of overcoming his addiction, getting off the streets and settling into employment and marriage. By analysing his trajectory and that of other men leaving prison, I have demonstrated that the use of the word 'could' in this exclamation can be understood to refer to the extreme paucity of options available to America's poor when it comes to finding housing, health care or other forms of help. To escape his desperate circumstances, Robert could have overdosed, been the victim of a homicide or gradually faded into mental illness. Taken against this backdrop of choices, one agrees with his assertion that turning himself over to the police to be housed, fed and patrolled in an institution of punishment was most likely his 'best' plan of action.

To make the jump to agreeing that a bare minimum of services, a haphazard smattering of classes, and a near-total lack of pre-release preparation constitute the best rehabilitative options is more difficult. And indeed, when speaking about the ways incarceration has affected their lives, the men and women quoted in this chapter do not offer praise for successful, effective programmes or life-changing treatment. Rather, they laud the correctional facility only for interrupting the incessant perils and torments of life on the street, framing rehabilitation in the entirely personal terms of introspection, emotional growth and perseverance.

It is possible, therefore, to conceive of a better seven years than such a period consumed by the imaginary rehabilitation offered within penitentiary walls. While describing his enjoyment at being able to take a break from the streets and ponder what he wanted from life, Calvin provides a telling insight:

[When you're in prison] … you got a perfect chance to really find *you*. [Having that chance] was refreshing. Not the sense of being in jail, like if I could go away like that like and *not* be in jail, like go somewhere on *an island or a mountaintop* or something and just think and really be able to just think and not [have] all these … distractions. It's good [to have time to reflect]. I think people should do that.

Here is something to imagine: a socio-economically disadvantaged young man having an opportunity to contemplate his place in the universe while sitting on an island or a mountaintop – just like his more privileged peers during their family vacations, gap years and post-university holidays. Imagine the flattening of social inequality and economic disparity. Imagine the poor receiving the same mental-health and substance-use treatment as the rich. Imagine …

Notes

1 Discussions of correctional statistics in the United States often confound prison and jail populations. People who are sentenced to more than one year of incarceration typically are sent to prison to serve their time; if they later are reincarcerated for violating the conditions of their parole, they will also serve time for the violation in prison. Jails hold people awaiting trial and people who have been sentenced to under one year of detention. Incarceration statistics refer to both prison and jail populations, but do not include those held in the juvenile system or in police lock-ups.

2 See Comfort (2008) for a detailed account of women's reliance on correctional institutions as their sole source for help with substance-

addicted, mentally ill and abusive men. Richie (1996) provides a penetrating analysis of women who rely on their own incarceration to escape violent men.

Chapter 13

Re-imagining justice: principles of justice for divided societies in a globalised world

Barbara Hudson

Introduction

The underlying premise of this chapter is that theories, models and practices of justice should be based on the idea of encounters with strangers. This is, of course, contrary to actually existing theories, models and practices of justice in contemporary western societies, which are based on the idea of rules to secure fairness and co-operation between members of a community of people with shared history and traditions, a community of people who share common values and who recognise common principles of justice.

Criminologists and socio-legal theorists have provided extensive critique of existing theories and practices of justice, establishing that it is the particular subjectivity of the white male that is the 'subject of law' and that other subjectivities have struggled to achieve recognition, to achieve protection of law, and to receive proportionate and appropriate responses to transgressions of law. While there has been critique and there have been proposals for reform in specific areas of law, understandings of the shortcomings of approaches to justice in modern societies with regard to unrecognised, marginalised or repressed identities have not led to fundamental rethinking of the grounding of justice on the idea of the elucidation and implementation of rules and processes in a community of shared values and understandings. In both the domestic sphere and the international sphere, the idea of common rationalities is the bedrock of 'justice'.

This chapter will outline and advocate a theory of justice which is based on the idea of dealing justly with strangers. *Cosmopolitan justice*, which is not new, is however newly elaborated and it is increasingly influential among political and social theorists, and is coming to the attention of criminologists and socio-legal theorists. Its basic ideas will be outlined, and applications to justice policy and practice will be discussed. Cosmopolitan justice has, until recently, been proposed mainly in international and transnational spheres: war, terrorism, migration, transnational crime, crimes by non-nationals. This chapter will raise issues involved in these fields, but will also argue that because of the radical diversity of contemporary societies, cosmopolitan justice is a more appropriate basis for criminal justice within single states than models premised on common rationalities.

All modern societies face issues of extending rights and protections to groups who have been marginalised and excluded from discourses of justice – indigenous groups in colonised societies; migrant groups in all societies; minority cultural groups; minority ethnic, sexual or religious identities; women and children. Responding to crime means responding to unsought-for encounters, and often involves responding to strangers who, while they may or may not be fellow citizens, are strangers in the sense that their behaviour may be extremely difficult to comprehend.

After explaining the important ideas of cosmopolitan justice, the chapter will continue by discussing its modalities: cosmopolitan justice cannot proceed by impartially applying rules to a 'standard' subject. Its requirement to try to reach understandings of strangers before classifying and before applying rules and selecting remedies means that its processes must be far more openly discursive than formal criminal justice has been hitherto. Cosmopolitanism incorporates an 'ethics of hospitality' and the meaning of hospitality and its implications for justice will be discussed.

Justice, identity and difference

Even the most democratic societies are divided by gender, race, ethnicity, socio-economic status, lifestyle, religion and so on. Diversity and division are unavoidable; they are conditions of modernity, made more complex over the centuries by population movements associated with wars, famines, imperialism, the slave trade and other drivers of migration. The citizens of modernity do not live in the near-homogeneous societies envisaged both by traditional forms of indigenous justice, and by the Enlightenment philosophers and politicians who developed the theories and institutions of justice that were implemented in Europe and exported around the globe. Post-Enlightenment liberal theories were based on the lives and interests of a narrow group of persons: white, property-owning males. The grounding of liberal models of law on the subjectivity of this restricted group has led to modernist justice being, rightly, characterised as 'white man's justice' (Naffine 1990; Hudson 2006a).

Contemporary divided societies, however, must respond to difference and diversity. They must adjudicate competing rights claims, for example the right of women to protection from violence against the right of men to fair trial; they must find ways of including the hitherto excluded and marginalised, such as ethnic and cultural minorities; they must acknowledge and accommodate hitherto unrecognised identities, such as travellers and gay and lesbian persons; they must define rules of membership and decide which rights are membership rights and which are universal human rights; they must establish rights and responsibilities in relation to fields new to governance, such as environmental concerns. Contemporary divided societies must find modes of accommodation and establish procedures of fair co-operation between groups and individuals who may have different and even conflicting interests and ideas of the good life.

While differences of gender and race may be acknowledged in modern western societies, the logic of identity has meant that in the discourses of justice, difference and diversity are either repressed, or denied. The most influential theory of justice in the second half of the twentieth century – John Rawls' justice as fairness – hides difference behind a 'veil of ignorance', where rule-makers do not know their social position and must therefore, it is presumed, make decisions for the general good (Rawls 1971). The criminal justice model based closely on Rawls' theory – the justice or just deserts model – ruled non-legal characteristics such as gender, race, religion and sexuality 'out of court' in order to secure impartiality of judgment. This expulsion of difference means that while the subject of justice remains the dominant white male, the object of justice is the 'generalised other', rather than the flesh-and-blood 'concrete other', the actual other whose harms suffered and inflicted claim attention (Benhabib 1992).

Encounters with strangers

Recognition of difference in contemporary societies is limited to that of 'reciprocity of perspectives', the idea that if she were in my shoes,

277

she would behave as I do, and if I were in her shoes, I would behave like she does. When justice is called upon to respond to someone who does not fit within this range of difference: someone whose perspective is in no way reciprocal; someone who would not be deterred by what would deter me or who would not be appeased by what would appease me, justice is in difficulty, and the outcome is more likely to be repression, ineffectiveness, inappropriateness and exclusion rather than fair remedy or sanction.

Contemporary modern societies are not societies of shared perspectives, they are societies of strangers. As well as divisions of gender, race/ethnicity, socio-economic status, and religion, contemporary societies include both citizens and non-citizens; they receive people who do not have a shared history of living alongside each other; they receive people from different social, religious and cultural traditions; they receive people driven to migrate by war, oppression and deprivation; they receive many who will make significant contributions to the culture and economy; they receive some who may desire to integrate and those who wish to remain separate; they receive some who may wish harm to the host country. If traditional differences of race, gender and sexuality become less salient in some social spheres, new differences arise. Cultural differences may become the core of racial tensions rather than 'biological hierarchy' (Gilroy 2004: 33). Groups are divided into those who integrate, those who don't; moderates and fanatics; democrats and anti-democrats: people like us, and strangers.

The repressive and exclusionary criminal justice outcomes of difference arise because of the strangeness of the Other: men cannot understand women's feelings of powerlessness after experiences of violence and abuse; the secular cannot understand the centrality of religion to the faithful and the imperative of religious observance throughout all the daily routines rather than just on special occasions; the modernist mind cannot understand the desire to maintain traditions; the static and settled cannot understand the imperatives to move of the migrant; the respected cannot understand the resentments of the disreputable and the disregarded; the prosperous and secure cannot understand the desire for escape and for hope felt by the impoverished and insecure.

As societies become more and more individualised and fragmented, the stranger is not only the person who comes from outside. People in different positions within a society lead such disparate, separate lives that they become incomprehensible to each other. To most middle-class, respectable people, for example, carrying a weapon is seen as a reckless act, signifying the carrier's potential aggression and criminality; for young people in our dangerous places, it seems more like a sensible precaution, something that has to be done to demonstrate that they are not easy targets for bullies and gang members. Violence perpetrated for small amounts of money seems a sign of vicious depravity; for the perpetrator it may be the cash needed for escape from grim reality through drink or drugs. Sexual crimes against the very young and the very old are beyond understanding as well as beyond empathy for most of us; we cannot possibly encompass such acts within a 'reciprocity of perspectives' construct.

The stranger we encounter may be the stranger-at-the-gates, the uninvited guest that Bauman invokes, drawing on Simmel's essay *The Stranger*. For Simmel, the stranger is 'the man who comes today and stays tomorrow'. The stranger claims our attention, appears at our border posts; the stranger may be friend or foe; the encounter necessitates responsive action before there can be understanding and classification. By coming into our territory, the stranger has forced the encounter; such forcing

is a notorious mark of the *enemy*. Yet, unlike other, 'straightforward' enemies, he is not kept at a secure distance, nor on the other side of the battle-line. Worse still, he claims a right to be an object of *responsibility* – the well-known attribute of the *friend*. If we press upon him the friend/enemy opposition, he would come out simultaneously under- and over-determined. And thus, by proxy, he would expose the failing of the opposition itself. He is a constant threat to the world's order. (Bauman 1991: 59)

The stranger poses a threat not just to our physical or economic security and stability, but also to the security and stability of our categories, of our ability to interpret events and to classify persons with whom we are thrown into contact (Hudson 2006b).

The stranger already inside the gates poses similar challenges to our attempts to categorise, to interpret and to understand even within our own social world. People carrying out acts which we cannot imagine ourselves doing under any circumstances, but who are our fellow citizens, who share our history and our geography, pose challenges about ourselves and our divided societies. These strangers challenge our self-perceptions of inclusivity and of belonging to a recognisable moral community. They expose the depths of our inequalities and of our fears and hatreds. They reveal the limits to our willingness to care about those whom we do not acknowledge as belonging to our narrow moral community, even if they may belong to our geo-political community. These strangers-in-our-midst are thought undeserving of our concern, our taxes, or our shared spaces as more and more of the prosperous and respectable seek residential, educational and recreational segregation.

For justice based on presumptions of shared traditions, shared fates and shared values, difference and diversity are inevitably threatening. They are, therefore, either largely unacknowledged, or are the basis for repressive response (Melossi 2000; Young 1999). In contemporary societies of strangers, established theories and institutions of justice have not proved effective for the extension of rights, remedies and protections to all citizens. Issues of rights of minority groups to cultural recognition; rights of women; rights of temporary workers; and rights of those who appear to threaten the physical security, economic well-being or preservation of culture of democratic societies make new principles and procedures of justice necessary. New theories and modes of justice, where rights and remedies are not available only to those within the reciprocity of perspectives range of difference are called for. The new justice models should be able to accommodate difference as normal, and should be able to draw on difference as a resource for showing where the subjectivity of justice needs to be made looser and more accommodating to the radical diversity of contemporary societies. (Young 2002).

Cosmopolitan justice

The ideal of cosmopolitanism which is increasingly influential in social and political thinking about justice in a globalised world, has two elements: a moral element and a political element. The moral element is found in Levinas's ethical theory of alterity. His ethical theory claims that we have a responsibility to all who come to our attention, a responsibility that arises merely from the presence of the Other within our gaze, a responsibility that is not dependent on any reciprocity of understanding or obligation (Levinas 1981, 1992; Bauman 1993). The political element stems largely from Kant's political writings, not the *Critiques* of pure and practical reasoning which have underpinned much of post-Enlightment justice theory, but his essay *To Perpetual Peace* (1983/1784–1795). In this essay he addresses the problem of maintaining peace between nations, and also the issue of dealing with strangers who are encountered through trade, war, migration and imperialism. Kant puts forward three propositions in this essay which he claims are essential for the maintenance of peaceful relationships between states and between individuals and strangers. The third proposition, which is the basic principle of cosmopolitan justice, is that there should be a 'cosmopolitan right' of universal hospitality (Kant 1983/1784–1795: 118).

As Paul Gilroy argues, Kant did not acknowledge the inhabitants of the territories entered by colonialists and traders as sharing a 'recognizable subjectivity' that would admit them to the community of justice on the basis of common identity (Gilroy 2004: 90). Kant therefore needed to move beyond premising principles of justice on what people have in common; his premise for responding to the presence of strangers is that of a common situation, rather than a common rationality. For him, cosmopolitanism rests on the shared possession by all persons of the earth's surface. Since the earth is a globe rather than a flat plane, persons cannot disperse over an infinite area and avoid each other's company, but must accommodate to the fact that every move away from someone brings us closer to someone else. Humans must, therefore, necessarily tolerate each other's company, even when this company may be undesired. This necessity of accommodation to the unsought-for presence of others yields a right and a duty of hospitality; '... hospitality means the right of an alien not to be treated as an enemy in someone else's country' (Kant 1983/1784–1795: 118).

Derrida (1999, 2001, 2003) and Bauman (2004a) draw these two strands of cosmopolitanism together, moving from Levinasian moral philosophy to Kantian political philosophy to derive a model of justice premised on encounters with strangers. Other writers (Benhabib 2004, 2006; Habermas 1999) draw more closely on Kant than on Levinas, but they also incorporate elements of the moral philosophy of responsibility to the Other. The moral strand provides a grounding for obligations to strangers that goes beyond obligations to those with whom we share a sense of community, or a sense of common values, while the political strand moves towards the realm of rules, processes and institutions. Kant's cosmopolitanism moves from the face-to-face morality of ethics to the political imperative of persons in contact with people of other societies to deal with them on the basis of acknowledgement of rights and of non-aggressive relationships.

Kant was writing in an era of expanding trade and European imperialism, and he condemned the institution of slavery and the treatment of colonised peoples. He argued that 'a transgression of rights in *one* place in the world is felt *everywhere*' (1983/1784–1795: 119, emphasis in the original), and called for the establishment of international institutions to guarantee the rule of law between nations, and between states and non-citizens. Kant did not propose a single world government, but a federation of the world's nations, with a tier of supra-national institutions to regulate international relations. This idea of 'cosmopolitan federalism' is currently being advocated by Habermas (2003) and by Benhabib (2004, 2006).

Kant's right of hospitality is the essence of cosmopolitanism, and it moves beyond the identity/difference binary because it is predicated on the inevitability of encounters with strangers; it responds to the existential condition of life in modern societies which is that it is not possible to live one's life only among people of one's own kind and of one's own choosing. Kant makes clear that the stranger is not a guest; the stranger is uninvited (Bauman 1991: 59). The uninvited visitor is also a stranger from beyond the moral/cognitive community of shared traditions and values.

Strangers are to be treated with justice; unlike Mill, Kant did not cast persons with whom he could not presume a common rationality as barbarians for whom tyranny is good enough (Brown 2005). The grounding of justice therefore moves from identity of subjectivity to identity of situation, from co-operation within a shared community of values to the management of unsought-for encounters with others, with whom there might not be shared community but with whom there is shared possession of the earth. For contemporary cosmopolitan theorists, the foundation of obligations to others is the situation of common inhabitancy of a fragile earth, where life is always unpredictable and potentially dangerous (Turner 1995).

The discursive modality of cosmopolitan justice

Cosmopolitanism is a universalist perspective in that it holds that every human is of value, and every human has rights. It is a cosmopolitan universalism in that it holds that we have obligations 'that stretch beyond those to whom we are related by the ties of kith or kind, or even the more formal ties of a shared citizenship' while acknowledging that 'People are different, the cosmopolitan knows ... we neither expect nor desire that every person or every society should converge on a single model of life ...' (Appiah 2006: xv). Processes of justice in these circumstances must seek not merely to apply rules and apportion rewards and penalties which it can be assumed will obtain common assent, but must first of all seek to reach understanding, so that even if consensus cannot be achieved, a range of tolerance and acceptability can be arrived at. Cosmopolitan justice is, therefore, discursive justice; its modality is discussion; conversation is its precondition for living together.

Within our diverse societies, discursive justice has obvious resonance for dealing with questions such as the degree to which other traditions of justice should be incorporated within the dominant processes of justice, or should be allowed to exist as parallel systems. In the UK and other western European countries, this issue of other justice traditions arises most controversially in relation to Sharia law and the possibilities of marital conflict, partner violence and other intra-communal conflicts being dealt with by community justice rather than formal UK law. In countries such as Canada, Australia, New Zealand, the USA and other former colonies, the question of recent migrants' rights to draw on their own traditions of justice also arises, but so too does the issue of community justice using the traditions of first peoples.

The need for a more discursive mode of justice can also be seen in the ineffectiveness of judicial response to crimes involving women, as victims or perpetrators. Much concern is evinced by politicians, lawyers and legal theorists over the low conviction rate for rape; sympathy is expressed for women who kill their abusive partners, yet there is resistance to changing rules of evidence to secure more rape convictions, or changing constructions of self-defence and provocation which make these defences and mitigations unavailable to abused women. As Celia Wells has commented in relation to women, looking at issues subject to legal concern may give the impression of feminist arguments being significantly influential, but looking at outcomes demonstrates the continuing influence of traditional stereotypes and prejudices (Wells 2004). The same can, of course, be said in relation to issues concerning race/ethnicity and law.

Discursive justice calls for those who will be affected by rules to be included in discourse, so offender groups, migrant groups, minority religious, cultural, race/ethnic groups, sexual groups as well as both men and women, should have rights of participation. The groups themselves should choose their representatives; the representatives should be accountable to the groups. Inclusion of those who will be affected means that the formerly excluded will be included in justice discourses within single states and between states. It means that internationally and nationally, deliberations on rules for migration and asylum should include representatives of migrants and asylum seekers, representatives of poor as well as rich nations, powerless as well as powerful states.

Advocates of discourse as the fundamental principle of justice, with the aim of reaching intersubjective understanding prior to rule-making and rule-enforcement, have highlighted the need for discourse to have some special characteristics (Young 1990, 2002; Fraser 1997, 2003; Hudson 2006a). Inclusion of those formerly excluded from democratic deliberations, or treated only as objects rather than subjects, demands first of all that discourse be *open*: participants should be able to raise any issue they wish, and should be able to do so in their own terms. Feminist critics of justice, for example, have challenged the public/private divide, arguing that harms suffered in the private domain should be brought to public attention and receive public sanctioning and remedies; women who have suffered violence from abusive partners and those who have suffered racial or religious discrimination or hatred need to be granted recognition, and to be able to put in their own terms the fears, the humiliations, the restriction of their freedom of action that they have experienced.

Discourse should also be *relational*. Iris Marion Young has argued that justice discourse should take account of relationships between social groups, not just relationships between the individual and the state (Young 1990, 2002). Persons are disadvantaged because the groups to which they belong are disadvantaged: black people are disadvantaged compared to white people; in some spheres women are disadvantaged compared to men; immigrants may be disadvantaged compared to citizens, for example. To promote understanding between persons and groups whose situation and outlook is very different, criminal justice should be more open to relational concerns, which can see an offender or a claimant to justice as part of their group as well as in their uniqueness.

Discourse should also be *reflective*. This does not mean merely that judges and magistrates should be thoughtful, but also that consideration of individual incidents should not be restricted to legal categories, to precedents and to prior opinions, but that events should be seen in all their circumstances. The individual responsibility model of western criminal justice emphasises agency (the capacity to act) rather than the circumstances in which the act is performed (Hudson 1999; Norrie 2000). As well as looking relationally at the groups of which offenders and victims are members, looking at the circumstances surrounding an act means looking at concepts of justice and injustice beyond the narrow confines of legal categories of defence, mitigation, aggravation and provocation. Cases should be measured against 'horizons of justice' (Young 1990) such as oppression, violence, inequality and cultural domination. The question should be not that of what is the prescribed sanction or remedy, but 'what would be justice in this case'.

Without reflectiveness, relational concerns could mean that groups are defined by only one element of identity; that identity is either/or rather than both/and: male/female, black/white, rather than black-and-female, for example (Harris 1990; Hudson 2006a). Recognition of between-group differences too often means that within-group differences are unacknowledged and all members of a group are assumed to share the same values, aspirations and priorities. As Iris Young argues, individual identities are conditioned by group membership, but not determined by it; each individual is enmeshed in different constellations of circumstances and relationships:

Social groups do indeed position individuals, but a person's identity is her own, formed in active relation to social positions, among other things, rather than constituted by them. Individual subjects make their own identities, but not under conditions they choose. (Young 2002: 99)

In criminal proceedings, openness of discourse calls for widening categories of expert witnesses, for example calling upon persons with experience of working with abused women to explain to courts the feelings of powerlessness and lack of realistic choices to change their circumstances that are experienced by women who have been abused (Valverde 1998). Irregular immigrants and asylum seekers should be able to recount their sufferings and privations, and should be represented by people who know the circumstances prevailing in their countries of origin. Courts should take account of relational disadvantages, for example a defence or mitigation of hardship should be considered for those whose criminality is linked to patterns of disadvantage or discrimination suffered by groups of which they are members. Reflectiveness should be included by asking about the circumstances of oppression or other dimensions of injustice that may be relevant to the particular case; legal categories should be changed or precedents disregarded if they do not allow for substantive justice in a particular case.

Restorative justice and other forms of community justice, including truth and reconciliation commissions, are generally more discursive than formal criminal justice. Victims, offenders and their representatives are able to give their own accounts of what happened, for what reasons, and with what consequences, and one of the primary aims of restorative justice is for the parties to appreciate each other's viewpoint. Understanding may not always be achieved, but the search for understanding is much more to the fore than in formal criminal justice. Even in these forms of justice, however, there is usually some discursive closure. In restorative justice processes there are often, for instance, restrictions on who may appear on behalf of offenders, and victims may have the right of veto on some aspects of proceedings (Hudson 2006a). Relational concerns may be neglected and reflective horizons absent if the process is focused entirely on the relationships between the particular victim, perpetrator and their narrowly drawn communities.

In formal criminal justice processes within modern western societies, discourse is strictly confined, and it may be difficult to envisage how the discursive openness that is proposed here could be approached. Glimpses can, however, be found. Since the introduction of the Charter of Rights and Freedoms for example, the Canadian Supreme Court has become more discursively open, and has incorporated elements of relationalism and reflectiveness.

Relational concerns have been incorporated into discussions by the Canadian Supreme Court and by the Canadian Parliament in relation to rape, where debates about admissible defences and the conditions for establishing consent have moved away from women's sexual history and towards the behaviour of men. The premises of these debates have been the vulnerability of women and children as a group to assault by men as a group, and the promises contained in the *Charter of Rights and Freedoms* to equal protection by the law.

Relational issues have been included in appeal judgments in cases concerning Aboriginal-Canadians and African-Caribbean Canadians, whose criminality has been seen in a context of systemic disadvantage and discrimination in comparison to white Canadians (*R. v Gladue* 1999; *R.v Borde* 2003; *R. v Hamilton* 2004). Lower courts have been instructed to determine in individual cases whether disadvantages associated with the groups of which defendants are members are implicated in the offending of the particular individuals in cases being dealt with.

The Supreme Court's judgment in the Ruzic case demonstrated reflectiveness in judicial discourse (*R. v Ruzic* 2001). Mariana Ruzic, a Serbian, was convicted of importing two kilograms of heroin into Canada. She claimed that a man in Belgrade, where she lived with her mother, had threatened to harm her mother if she did not import the drug, and explained that she did not seek police help because she believed the Serbian police to be corrupt. Section 17 of the Canadian Criminal Code, which defines the requirements for a defence of duress, requires immediacy of the threat and presence of the threatener, and an implicit requirement is that the threat is to the person who commits the offence. Ruzic did not meet these conditions. The judgment on appeal was that the section did not meet the Charter's ideals to avoid punishment of the morally innocent, and so the conditions of the defence would have to be widened (Shaffer 1998). What this judgment demonstrates is that the Supreme Court did not confine itself to the Code's formulations; it did not stay within legal definitions and rules about admissible circumstances, but looked towards wider horizons and principles of 'fundamental justice'.

Another case which demonstrates elements of reflective discourse is that of Lavallee, a woman who killed her abusive partner (*R. v Lavallee* 1990). The circumstances of the killing did not fit the criteria for self-defence because although Lavallee shot her partner after he had been physically and verbally abusive, she did so with a rifle shot to the back of the head as he was leaving their bedroom. Self-defence, according to section 34 of the Criminal Code, requires that the individual has a reasonable apprehension of death or grievous bodily harm from an immediate assault by the victim and a reasonable belief that there is no other way to preserve their own life. Lavallee did not meet these criteria, but the evidence of the expert witness on the effects of abuse led to expansion of the criteria of 'reasonable apprehension' and 'reasonable belief' (Manfredi 2001: 89). The judgment acknowledged that women who had suffered abuse might not believe themselves to have the same range of choices that men or non-abused women might perceive.

Unfortunately, in the UK, USA and many other countries, discursive closure has been more marked than discursive opening in recent years. Decreased attention to personal and social circumstances in probation reports; increased use of mandatory penalties, and the general tendency to 'understand less and punish more' have narrowed the justice discourse and increased marginalisation and exclusion.

The claims of hospitality

Justice discourse needs not only to attempt to understand the other, but also to determine the limits of hospitality. The ethical-political dualism of cosmopolitanism is to be central to the meaning, and to the operation, of hospitality. As Derrida explains, the ethical moment of hospitality aspires to unconditionality, whereas the political moment is the conditionality of deciding what hospitality can be extended, what must be denied, to a particular stranger (Derrida

2001, 2003). The demand of the ethical strand that the stranger needs to be received without hostility must be reconciled with the realities of the political moment that a society must protect itself against the stranger who might actually be dangerous:

> Pure and unconditional hospitality, hospitality *itself*, opens or is in advance open to someone who is neither expected nor invited, to whomever arrives as an absolutely foreign *visitor*, as a new arrival, non-identifiable and unforeseeable, in short, wholly other. I would call this a hospitality of *visitation* rather than *invitation*. The visit might actually be very dangerous, and we must not ignore this fact, but would a hospitality without risk, a hospitality based by certain assurances, a hospitality protected by an immune system against the wholly other, be true hospitality? (Derrida 2003: 128–9, emphasis in the original)

Questions are obviously raised by the concept of hospitality about exactly what is meant by terms such as violence and hostility; what curtailments and impositions are acceptable and what are not; for limits and curtailments that might be acceptable, what kinds of dangers, and what sort of proof, can justify imposition?

Conditionality, for cosmopolitans, is limited by the requirement of demonstrable actual danger, and it is limited by the requirement to receive the stranger with hospitality prior to categorisation as dangerous or safe, and prior to setting limits or restrictions on hospitality. Derrida's call for the unconditional trace is that the hospitality to be afforded should be 'undecided' at the moment of the stranger's reception.

Measures to control migration adopted by many western nations violate norms of hospitality. Hostility is expressed at all levels: policies adopted by inter-governmental institutions such as the European Union; national and local government policies; violence and verbal abuse by individual citizens. Sea patrols in the southern Mediterranean and the oceans around Australia as well as the establishment of enclaves in north Africa to prevent movement to southern European countries such as Spain, restrict the rights of people to leave countries where they are being persecuted or where they cannot obtain the basic needs of human flourishing. The refusal of migrants from countries such as Sudan and Iraq means that the right to life is not being fully protected; narrow interpretation of the Geneva Conventions which leaves women vulnerable to violence such as genital mutilation means that the right to integrity of the person is not being protected. Potential immigrants are being detained in prison-like institutions, a practice which symbolically identifies them as threats to national well-being (Bosworth 2007a). Denial of rights to education, medical care, financial assistance and other welfare necessities is the very opposite of 'hospitality'.

Cosmopolitans such as Benhabib (2004) and Moellendorf (2002) have discussed the issue of what rights are due to non-citizens, and for what reasons they may be suspended (Hudson 2007). The cosmopolitan vision is that human rights are universal, and so non-citizens as well as citizens are entitled not only to the fundamental rights of life, freedom from torture, and freedom from detention without due process of law, but also to more positive rights including the right to move to where they can flourish. Cosmopolitans challenge nation-states' rights to impose restrictions on immigration, arguing that a right to emigrate is of no value without a corresponding right to immigrate. With other cosmopolitans, Benhabib and Moellendorf state that immigration and co-relative rights of non-citizens can only be denied if the person concerned demonstrably threatens the physical security of the host state: threats to culture or 'way of life' are not sufficient to restrict hospitality.

Benhabib and Moellendorf support the establishment of cosmopolitan federalism not only, as Kant envisaged, to prevent violence between nation-states, but also to secure the equitable distribution of life chances in the global sphere. Moellendorf appeals to the doctrine of equality of opportunity, arguing that economic opportunities as well as opportunities to freedom of religion, sexuality, participation in political processes and rule of law, should be equally available to the inhabitants of all nations. As well as making rights enjoyed by the affluent available more generally, some arguments for open borders rest largely on the belief that it is only if the rich nations could not refuse admittance (and hospitality) to migrants from poorer nations that there would be serious commitment to trade and aid policies which would lessen global inequalities significantly (Carens 2000; Unger 2005).

The idea of 'respect' for the identity of the other has close parallels to the ideal of hospitality in the reception of strangers from both within and without the borders of a state (Carson 2007). Respect is a principle of discourse theory, made explicit in many models of restorative justice; respectful listening is often stated as a condition of participation in restorative meetings and conferences. Pavlich (2002), for example, explains that hospitality does not demand that the stranger must surrender her identity. Treating the other with respect for her identity is imperative if understanding is to be achieved in discourse; it is implied by the principle of openness of discourse, allowing anyone to raise any topic, and to state their claims in their own terms. Respect is also a prerequisite for responding to the stranger as someone to whom one has an obligation of hospitality; equal respect is also said to be the concept which overlaps most modern theories of justice, the one moral imperative of all conceptions of justice (Reiman 1990: 123–4).

This requirement for respect acknowledged as the right to maintain one's identity is clearly not met by immigration and citizenship policies which restrict citizenship to those who can demonstrate 'Britishness' (or Frenchness, Germanness or any other identity with the host culture). Refraining from crime or any other actual harm to the state or to its residents, is the only limit on hospitality that is compatible with cosmopolitan justice.

Respect, too, is conditional; respect may require recognition for the identity of the other, but it does not mean endorsement of all possible forms of life (Fraser 1997). While many identities, such as those associated with culture, sexuality, religion or gender, should be supported, other identities, such as racist or violent criminal, should be restricted and their manifestations reduced as far as possible. In the global sphere and within a single nation-state, justice discourses seek to negotiate respect for identity and the form of life associated with it. The goal of discourse might not be consensus on all values and goals, the outcome of discourse might not be unconditional respect for all identities; the goal should, however, be to achieve such understanding and accommodation as to achieve the mutual respect necessary to extend hospitality without provoking harm.

Concluding comments

The ideas put forward by cosmopolitan theorists pose challenges not just for social theory, but for social justice. Justice is performed in a world of great inequalities, globally and within single states. The claimant for justice, whether a would-be immigrant or asylum seeker, a member of a marginalised or disadvantaged social group, a victim of crime, or a perpetrator whose criminality is linked to inequality or oppression, will often be powerless in relation to those who dominate discourse, those who have the power to give or withhold hospitality.

'Inclusion of the marginal and excluded in discourse', 'conditionality' of hospitality, and 'negotiation' of respect raise issues of the asymmetry of the host and the stranger, the dominant and the powerless. Relationalism and reflectiveness must be considered in the context of discourse itself, not only in the context of the behaviour or claim that occasioned the discourse. Sennett (2003) asks how can there be *Respect in a World of Inequality*, and while discourse should be structured so as to facilitate respect, inequality should not be unrestrained; inequality should not be allowed to reach a degree likely to inhibit parity of discourse and to discourage respect. Similarly, cosmopolitans ask whether the tolerance of the other which is necessary in a world where encounters with strangers are unavoidable, is a tolerance where the powerful host sets the limits according to what she finds acceptable or repugnant (Benhabib 1995). Inequality on such a scale that one party can dominate the other means that any tolerance extended is a tolerance of condescension rather than of necessity; it will be a tolerance which can be given or withheld by the powerful, not a just accommodation which is acknowledged as a right of the powerless.

Cosmopolitan belief in the universalism of rights, and in the obligation of hospitality even to those whose behaviour poses danger or is otherwise demonstrably unacceptable, dictates that all sanctions, all conditions and limitations, should respect the rights of the other. Hospitality, in such cases, may be constrained in order to achieve protection from danger, but hospitality should be conditional rather than absent. This means, for example, that even if there are reasonable grounds for suspicion that someone may be dangerous, they should not be detained beyond a legally limited term, conditions of detention should be humane, they should have access to lawyers, and they should not be tortured or in any way mistreated. Offenders should be sanctioned in the least restrictive way consistent with avoidance of real and demonstrable danger to others, and if they need to be incarcerated this should be in humane conditions, with all possible measures in place to secure their safety and well-being. Whether in custody or in the community, offenders should receive any necessary treatment and rehabilitative measures to help them lead a life less threatening to public safety and more fulfilling for themselves. Since for cosmopolitan justice, hospitality is an obligation, the model of 'state-obligated rehabilitation' (Carlen 1989) should be revived to place obligations on the party setting the limits on hospitality, as well as on the party to whom hospitality is owed.

If justice is to be premised on encounters with strangers, it is fundamental that strangers should be treated with justice. In contemporary societies the stranger – whether the stranger from beyond the borders or the stranger from within our midst – is too easily constructed as a monster (Hudson 2006b). The essence of the ethical strand of cosmopolitanism is that we accept obligations to the other before we demand she makes herself understandable; the impulse in our fearful, divided societies in our unpredictable world seems to be to do the opposite: we categorise before we understand, and we repress and exclude before we accept the obligations of justice. Ameliorating inequalities is a pre-requisite for promoting understanding, and for reducing our defensive corralling of ourselves behind the walls of migration controls, segregated cities, and of our others in enclaves, detention centres and fortress prisons.

Cosmopolitanism is challenging, bringing division and diversity to the forefront in the search for justice. Cosmopolitanism entails acceptance that the context of justice is a society of inequalities, differences of values, traditions and beliefs, and that we cannot expect that we will be dealing with persons who are within our moral community or, at least, within a range of reciprocal perspectives. Repressing or excluding otherness is the easy option and it is not difficult to appreciate its attractions. In the contemporary condition of modernity which is that we inhabit divided societies in a globalised world, however, repression or exclusion of otherness is a denial of justice. Encounters with strangers are unavoidable, and therefore need to be the premise of justice in responding to conflicts both internationally and within single states.

Cosmopolitans are well aware of the difficulties of countering interpretations of strangers not only as different and other, but as people to be isolated and repelled, at the borders of the nation-state and at the internal borders of our tightly-drawn communities of affinity. They are optimistic that although concepts of right and wrong, good and bad, may take on different interpretations because of the contexts in which they operate, differences in the range of application do not override the commonalities we derive from our situation of being together on this fragile earth. Cosmopolitans suppose that all cultures have enough overlap in their vocabulary of values to begin a conversation, and they suppose that when

> the stranger is no longer imaginary, but real and present, sharing a human social life, you may like or dislike him, you may agree or disagree; but if it is what you both want, you can make sense of each other in the end. (Appiah 2006: 99)

Cases cited

R. *v Borde* [2003] 172 C.C.C. (3rd) 225, 63 Ontario Reports (3rd) 417

R. *v Gladue* [1999] 1 S.C.R. 688

R. *v Hamilton* [2004] 72 Ontario Reports (3d) 417

R. *v Lavallee* [1990] 1 S.C.R. 577

R. *v Ruzic* [2001] 1 S.C.R. 687

References

Aas, K.F. (2005) *Sentencing in the Age of Information: From Faust to Macintosh.* London: GlassHouse Press.

Agomoh, U. and Ogun, B. (2000a) *Manual for the Training of Prison Officer-trainers on the United Nations Standard Minimum Rules for the Treatment of Prisoners.* Lagos: Prisoners Rehabilitation and Welfare Action (PRAWA).

Agomoh, U. (2000b) *Prison Link Training Guide.* Lagos: Prisoners Rehabilitation and Welfare Action (PRAWA).

Allen, R. (1999) 'Is what works what counts? The role of evidence-based crime reduction in policy and practice', *Safer Society*, 2 (February): 21–3.

Allison, E. (2007) 'Beyond Justice?', *Guardian*, 7 February 2007: 10–13.

Althusser, L. (1971) *Lenin and Philosophy and Other Essays.* London: New Left Books.

AMS (2003) *Förmedlingsarbete med ökat sökandeansvar. Åtgärdsprogram för förbättrad sökaktivitet.* Stockholm: Arbetsmarknadsstyrelsen.

Anderson, B. (1983) *Imagined Communities.* London: Verso.

Anderson, E. (1999) *Code of the Street.* New York: W.W. Norton.

Andrews, D. and Bonta, J. (1998) *Psychology of Criminal Conduct* (2nd edn). Cincinnati, Ohio: Anderson Publishing Company.

Andrews, D., Bonta, J. and Hoge, R. (1990) 'Classification for effective rehabilitation: Rediscovering psychology', *Criminal Justice Behaviour*, 17 (1): 19–52.

Andrews, D., Bonta, J. and Wormith, S. (2006) 'The recent past and near future of risk and/or need assessment', *Crime and Delinquency*, 52 (1): 7–27.

Andrews, D.A. and Dowden, C. (2006) 'Risk principle of case classification in correctional treatment: A meta-analytic investigation', *International Journal of Offender Therapy and Comparative Criminology*, 50 (1): 88–100.

Anttila, I. (1971) 'Conservative and Radical Criminal Policy in the Nordic Countries', *Scandinavian Studies in Criminology*, 3: 9–21.

Appiah, K.A. (2006) *Cosmopolitanism: Ethics in a World of Strangers*. London: Penguin/Allen Lane.

Arsovska, J. and Verduyn, P. (2008) 'Globalisation, Conduct Norms and "Culture Conflict": Perceptions of Violence and Crime in an Ethnic Albanian Context', *British Journal of Criminology*, 48(2): 226–46).

Asad, T. (2000) 'What Do Human Rights Do? An Anthropological Enquiry', *Theory and Event*, 4 (4).

Ashworth, A. (2001) 'The Decline of English Sentencing' in M. Tonry and R. Frase (eds) *Sentencing and Sanctions in Western Countries*. New York: Oxford University Press.

Ashworth, A. (2005) *Sentencing and Criminal Justice* (4th edition). Cambridge: Cambridge University Press.

Auge, M. (1995) *Non-places*. London: Verso.

Austin, J.L. (1976) *How To Do Things with Words* (2nd edn). Oxford: Oxford University Press.

Bailey, R., Knight, C. and Williams, B. (2007) 'The Probation Service as part of NOMS in England and Wales: fit for purpose?' in L. Gelsthorpe and R. Morgan (eds) *Handbook of Probation*. Cullompton: Willan Publishing.

Barry, M. (2006) *Youth Offending in Transition*. London: Routledge.

Bauman, Z. (1991) *Modernity and Ambivalence*. Cambridge: Polity Press.

Bauman, Z. (1993) *Postmodern Ethics*. Oxford: Blackwell.

Bauman, Z. (2002) *Society Under Siege*. Cambridge: Polity.

Bauman, Z. (2004) *Wasted Lives*. Cambridge: Polity.

Bauman, Z. (2004a) *Europe: An Unfinished Adventure*. Cambridge: Polity Press.

Beck, U. (1992) *Risk Society: Towards a New Modernity*. London: Sage.

Beck, U. (1998) 'The Politics of the Risk Society' in J. Franklin (ed.) *The Politics of the Risk Society*. London: Polity Press.

Beck, U. (2000) *World Risk Society*. London: Polity Press.

Beck, U. (2002) 'The terrorist threat: world risk society revisited', *Theory, Culture and Society*, 19 (4): 39–55.

Becker, H. (1963) *Outsiders*. New York: Viking.

Bee, C.C. (2005) 'Prison health care seized citing some "outright depravity"', US judge will pick overseer', *Sacramento Bee*, San Francisco.

Belknap, J. and Holsinger, K. (1998) 'An Overview of Delinquent Girls: How Theory and Practice Have Failed and the Need for Innovative Changes' in R. Zapich (ed.) *Female Offenders: Critical Perspectives and Effective Interventions*. Gaithersburg MD: Aspen Publishers.

Belknap, J. and Holsinger, K. (2006) 'The Gendered Nature of Risk Factors for Delinquency', *Feminist Criminology*, 1 (1): 48–71.

Benhabib, S. (1992) *Situating the Self: Gender, Community and Postmodernism in Contemporary Ethics*. Cambridge: Polity Press.

Benhabib, S. (1995) 'Subjectivity, historiography and politics' in S. Benhabib, D. Cornell and N. Fraser (eds), *Feminist Contentions*. London: Routledge.

Benhabib, S. (2004) *The Rights of Others: Aliens, Residents and Citizens*. Cambridge: Cambridge University Press.

Benhabib, S. (2006) *Another Cosmopolitanism*. R. Post (ed.) Oxford: Oxford University Press.

Bennett L.W. and Feldman, M.S. (1981) *Reconstructing Reality in the Courtroom*. London: Tavistock.

Bentham, J. (1962) *The Works of Jeremy Bentham*, Vol. 1. J. Bowring (ed.) New York: Russell and Russell.

Bentham, J. (1995) *The Panopticon Writings*. London: Verso.

Bhui, H.S. (1999) 'Race, Racism, and Risk Assessment: Linking Theory to Practice with Black Mentally Disordered Offenders', *Probation Journal*, 46 (3): 171–81.

Birgden, A. (2002) 'Therapeutic jurisprudence and "good lives": A rehabilitation framework for corrections', *Australian Psychologist*, 37 (3): 180–6.

Birgden, A. (2004) 'Therapeutic jurisprudence and responsivity: Finding the will and the way in offender rehabilitation', *Psychology, Crime and Law*, 10 (3): 283–95.

Blair, T. (2006) 'Prime minister's speech on criminal justice reform'. Tony Blair's speech in Bristol, 23 June 2006. (http://society.guardian.co.uk/ crime and punishment/story/0,,1804484,00html). (Downloaded 26 June 2006).

Blanchette, K. and Brown, S.L. (2006) *The Assessment and Treatment of Women Offenders: An Integrative Perspective*. West Sussex: John Wiley and Sons.

Bloom, B. (ed.) (2003a) *Gendered Justice: Addressing Female Offenders*. Durham, NC: Carolina Academic Press.

Bloom, B. (2003b) 'A New Vision: Gender Responsive Principles, Policy and Practice' in B. Bloom (ed.) *Gendered Justice: Addressing Female Offenders*. Durham, NC: Carolina Academic Press.

Bloom, B. (1999) 'Gender-Responsive Programming for Women Offenders: Guiding Principles and Practices', *Forum on Corrections Research*, 11 (3): 22.

Bloom, B. and Covington, S. (1997) 'Gender Specific Programming For Female Offenders: What Is It and Why Is It Important?', paper presented at the 50th Annual Meeting of the American Society of Criminology, 11–14 November, Washington, DC.

Bloom, B., Owen, B. and Covington, S. (2003) *Gender Responsive: Research, Practice and Guiding Principles for Women Offenders*. Washington DC: National Institute of Corrections, US Department of Justice.

Bloom, B. and Covington, S. (2006) 'Gender Responsive Treatment Services in Correctional Settings', *Inside and Out: Women, Prison and Therapy*, 29 (3): 9–33.

Bloom, B., Owen, B. and Covington, S. (2004) 'Women Offenders and the Gendered Effects of Public Policy', *Review of Policy Research*, 21 (1): 31–48.
Bloom, B., Owen, B. and Covington, S. (2005) 'Gender Responsive Strategies for Women Offenders: A Summary of Research, Practice and Guiding Principles for Women Offenders'. Washington DC: National Institute of Corrections, US Department of Justice.
Bloom, B., Covington, S. and Raeder, M. (2002) *Gender-responsive Strategies: Research, Practice, and Guiding Principles for Women Offenders. Final Draft.* US Department of Justice, Washington, DC: National Institute of Corrections.
Boardman, M. (2004) *Known Unknowns: The Delusion of Terrorism Insurance.* http://law.bepress/expresso/eps/244.
Bondeson, U. (1974) *Fången i fångsamhället.* Stockholm: Norstedt.
Bonomy, Lord (2002) *Improving Practice: 2002 Review of the Practices and Procedures of the High Court of Justiciary.* Edinburgh: The Stationery Office.
Bonta, J. (2002) 'Offender Risk Assessment: Guidelines for Selection and Use', *Criminal Justice and Behavior*, 29 (4): 355–80.
Bonta, J. and Andrews, D. (2007) 'Risk-Need-Responsivity model for offender assessment and rehabilitation'. Ottawa: Public Safety. http://www.publicsafety.gc.ca/res/cor/rep/_fl/Risk_Need_2007-06_e.pdf
Bonta, J., Pang, B. and Wallace-Capretta, S. (1995) 'Predictors of recidivism among incarcerated female offenders', *Prison Journal*, 75 (3): 277–94.
Bosworth, M. (2007) 'Creating the Responsible Prisoner: Federal Admission and orientation packs', *Punishment and Society*, 9 (1): 67–85.
Bosworth, M. (2007a) 'Immigration detention in Britain', in M. Lee (ed.) *Human Trafficking.* Cullompton: Willan Publishing.
Bottoms, A. (2001) 'Compliance and Community Penalties' in A. Bottoms, L. Gelsthorpe and S. Rex (eds) *Community Penalties: Change and Challenges.* Cullompton: Willan.
Bottoms, A., Sparks, R. and Hay, W. (1996) *Prisons and the Problem of Order.* Oxford: Clarendon Press.
Bourdieu, P. (1997) 'The Forms of Capital' in A. Halsey, H. Lauder, P. Brown and H. Stuart Wells (eds) *Education: Culture, Economy, Society.* Oxford: Oxford University Press.
Bourgois, P. (2003) *In Search of Respect* (2nd edn). Cambridge: Cambridge University Press.
Bowers, K.J. and Johnson, S.D. (2003) *The Role of Publicity in Crime Prevention: findings from the Reducing Burglary Initiative.* Home Office Research Study 272. London: Home Office Research, Development and Statistics Directorate.
Bowles, R. and Pradiptyo, R. (2004) *Reducing Burglary Initiative: and Analysis of Costs, Benefits and Cost Effectiveness.* Home Office Online Report 43/04. London: Home Office.

BRÅ (2002) *Att lära ut ett nytt sätt att tänka: utvärdering av Cognitive Skills-programmet i kriminalvården 1995–2001.* BRÅ 2002:11 Stockholm: Brottsförebyggande rådet.

Bradshaw, D. (1993) 'Introduction' in A. Huxley (1994) *Brave New World.* London: Flamingo.

Braithwaite, J. (2000) 'The New Regulatory State and the Transformation of Criminology in D. Garland and R. Sparks (eds) *Criminology and Social Theory.* Oxford: Oxford University Press.

Brake, M. and Hale, C. (1992) *Public Order and Private Lives.* London: Routledge.

Brocato, J. and Wagner, E.F. (2008) 'Predictors of Retention in an Alternative-to-Prison Substance Abuse Treatment Program', *Criminal Justice and Behavior*, 35 (1): 99–119.

Brown, G.D. (2007) *Serious Violent and Sexual Offenders: The Influence of the New Penology and Actuarial Justice on Contemporary Sentencing Practice.* Unpublished MSc dissertation, Glasgow Graduate School of Law.

Brown, M. (2000) 'Calculations of Risk in Contemporary Penal Practice' in M. Brown and J. Pratt (eds) *Dangerous Offenders: Punishment and Social Order.* London: Routledge.

Brown, M. (2005) 'Liberal exclusion and the new punitiveness' in J. Pratt, D. Brown, M. Brown, S. Hallsworth and W. Morrison (eds) *The New Punitiveness: Trends, Theories, Perspectives.* Cullompton: Willan.

Brown, M. and Pratt, J. (eds) (2000) *Dangerous Offenders: Punishment and Social Order.* London: Routledge.

Brown, P., Hesketh, A. and Williams, S. (2003) 'Employability in a Knowledge-driven Economy', *Journal of Education and Work*, 16 (2): 107–26.

Bullock, K. and Tilley, N. (2003) (eds) *Crime Reduction and Problem-oriented Policing.* Cullompton: Willan.

Bureau of Justice Statistics (1990) *Survey of Inmate Characteristics.* Washington DC: National Institute of Justice.

Burnett, R. (2004) 'To reoffend or not to reoffend? The ambivalence of convicted property offenders' in S. Maruna and R. Immarigeon (eds) *After Crime and Punishment: Pathways to Offender Reintegration.* Cullompton: Willan.

Burton, F. and Carlen, P. (1979) *Official Discourse.* London: Routledge and Kegan Paul.

Butler, J. (1990) *Gender Trouble: Feminism and the Subversion of Identity.* London: Routledge.

Butterfield, F. (2003) 'Study Calls California Parole System a $1 Billion Failure', *New York Times*, New York: A24.

Buttny, R. and Williams, P. (2000) 'Demanding Respect: The Uses of Reported Speech in Discursive Constructions of Interracial Contact', *Discourse and Society*, 11 (1): 109–33.

Byrne, M. and Howells, K. (2002) 'The Psychological Needs of Women Prisoners: Implications for Rehabilitation Management', *Psychiatry, Psychology and the Law*, 9 (1): 34–43.

California Department of Corrections and Rehabilitation (2007a) 'Facts and Figures'. www.cdcr.ca.gov/Divisions_Boards/Adult_Operations/Facts_and_Figures.html

California Department of Corrections and Rehabilitation (2007b) 'History of the Re-Organization'. http://www.cdcr.ca.gov/About_CDCR/History. html

California Department of Finance (2008) 'Governor's Budget 2008–09'. http://www.ebudget.ca.gov/agencies.html

Callon, M. (ed.) (1998) *The Laws of Markets*. Oxford: Blackwell.

Campbell, D.T. (1969) 'Reforms as Experiments', *American Psychologist*, 24: 409–29.

Campbell, D.T. (1978) 'Reforms as experiments' in J. Bynner and K.M. Stribley (eds), *Social Research: Principles and Procedures*. Oxford: Oxford University Press.

Carens, J. (2000) *Culture, Citizenship and Community: A Contextual Exploration of Justice as Even-handedness*. Oxford: Oxford University Press.

Carlen, P. (1976) *Magistrates' Justice*. Oxford: Martin Robertson.

Carlen, P. (1989) 'Crime, Inequality and Sentencing' in P. Carlen and D. Cook (eds) *Paying for Crime*. Milton Keynes: Open University Press.

Carlen, P. (2002a) 'Controlling Measures: The Repackaging of Common-sense Opposition to Women's Imprisonment in England and Canada', *Criminal Justice*, 2: 155–72.

Carlen, P. (2002b) 'Carceral Clawback,' *Punishment and Society* 4 (1): 115–21.

Carlen, P. (2002c) *Women and Punishment: The Struggle for Justice*. Cullompton: Willan.

Carlen, P. (2007) 'Imaginary Penalties and Risk-Crazed Governance.' Paper presented to the British Society of Criminology, North West Branch, University of Liverpool, 27 March, and to The Scandinavian Studies of Confinement Research Network Working Group Meeting 'Multidisciplinary perspectives on prison research', Copenhagen, 14–15 May.

Carlen, P. and Tombs, J. (2006) 'Reconfigurations of Penality: The Ongoing Case of Women's Imprisonment', *Theoretical Criminology*, 10 (3): 337–61.

Carson, W.G. (2007) 'Calamity or Catalyst: Futures for Community in Twenty-First-Century Crime Prevention', *British Journal of Criminology*, 47 (5): 711–27.

Carter, P. (2003) *Managing Offenders, Reducing Crime – Correctional Services Review*. London: Home Office.

Carter, P. (2007) *Securing the Future*, Lord Carter's Review of Prisons. London: House of Lords.

Chesney-Lind, M. and Pasko, L. (2004) *The Female Offender: Girls, Women, and Crime*. Thousand Oaks, CA: Sage.

Chomsky, N. (1971) 'Topics in the Theory of Generative Grammar' in J. Searle *The Philosophy of Language*. Cambridge: University of Cambridge Press.

Chouard, G. (2003) 'Patchwork, or the "pile-up of possibles" in "How to make an American Quilt"', *Mosaic*, Winnipeg, June.

Christie, N. (1993) *Crime Control as Industry. Towards GULAGS, Western Style?* New York: Routledge.

Chylicki, P. (2000) *Cognitive Skills i svensk kriminalvård 1999. Rapport 4.* Norrköping: Kriminalvårdsstyrelsen.

City of Oakland (2003) 'Oakland Mayor Jerry Brown Comments on Visit to San Quentin Prison'. Press Release. Oakland: City of Oakland. http://www.oaklandnet.com/government/mayor/press-releases/SanQuentin.html

Clarke, R.V. and Eck, J. (2003) *Become a Problem-Solving Crime Analyst in 55 Small Steps.* London: Jill Dando Institute, University College London.

Clarkson, C. and Morgan, R. (1995) 'The Politics of Sentencing Reform', in C. Clarkson and R. Morgan (eds), *The Politics of Sentencing Reform.* Oxford: Clarendon Press.

Clear, T.R. and Cadora, E. (2001) 'Risk and Correctional Practice' in K. Stenson and R.R. Sullivan (eds), *Crime, Risk and Justice: The Politics of Crime Control in Liberal Democracies.* Cullompton: Willan.

Clegg, S. (1993) 'Narrative, Power and Social Theory' in D.K. Mumby (ed.), *Narrative and Social Control: Critical Perspectives.* London: Sage.

CNN online law center (2004) 'Early Database Project Yielded 120,000 Suspects.' (http://www.cnn.com/2004/LAW/05/20/terror.database.ap/)

Cohen, S. (1985) *Visions of Social Control.* Oxford: Polity Press.

Coleman, R. (2004) *Reclaiming the Streets: Surveillance, Social Control and the City.* Cullompton: Willan.

Coleman, R. (2005) 'Surveillance in the City: Primary Definition and Urban Spatial order', *Crime, Media and Culture,* 1 (2): 131–48.

Coleman, R. and Sim, J. (2005) 'Contemporary Statecraft and The Punitive Obsession' in J. Pratt, D. Brown, M. Brown, S. Hallsworth and W. Morrison (eds) *The New Punitiveness: Trends, Theories, Perspectives.* Cullompton: Willan.

Coleman, R. Sim, J. and Whyte, D. (2002) 'Power, politics and partnerships: The State of Crime Prevention on Merseyside' in G. Hughes, and A. Edwards (eds) *Crime Control and Community: The New Politics of Public Safety.* Cullompton: Willan.

Comfort, M. (2008) *Doing Time Together: Love and Family in the Shadow of the Prison.* Chicago: University of Chicago Press.

Congressional Record (2001) 29 November (wais.access.gpo.gov)

Congressional Record (2002) 13 June (wais.access.gpo.gov)

Congressional Record (2003) 13 February (wais.access.gpo.gov)

Congressional Record (2006) 1 February (wais.access.gpo.gov)

Cook, T.D. and Campbell, D.T. (1979) *Quasi-Experimentation.* Boston, MA: Houghton Mifflin.

Correctional Service of Canada (CSC) (2003) *Standards for Correctional Programs* 726-1. Issued under the authority of the Assistant Commissioner, Correctional Operations and Programs 2003-11-19. http://www.csc-scc.gc.ca/text/prgrm/correctional/documents/standards_726-1_e.pdf (Accessed 1 December 2007).

Corrigan, P. and Sayer, D. (1985) *The Great Arch*. Oxford: Blackwell.

Cosgrove, Lady (2001) *Reducing the Risk*. Edinburgh: Scottish Executive.

Cover, R. (1986) 'Violence and the Word', *The Yale Law Journal*, 95: 1601–29.

Covington, S.S. and Bloom, B.E. (2006) 'Gender Responsive Treatment and Services in Correctional Settings', *Women & Therapy*, 29 (3–4): 9–33.

Covington, S.S. and Bloom, B.E. (2007) 'Gender Responsive Treatment and Services in Correctional Settings', *Women & Therapy*, 29 (3–4): 9–33.

Coyle, A. (1992) 'The Responsible Prisoner: Rehabilitation Revisited', *Howard Journal of Criminal Justice*, 31 (1): 1–7.

Coyle, A. (2002) *A Human Rights Approach to Prison Management Handbook for Prison Staff*. London: International Centre for Prison Studies.

Crawford, A. (1997) *The Local Governance of Crime: Appeals to Community and Partnerships*. Oxford, Clarendon Press.

Crawford, A. (1998) *Crime Prevention and Community Safety: Politics, Policies and Practices*. London: Longman.

Crawford, A. (2001) 'Joined-up but fragmented: Contradiction, ambiguity and ambivalence at the heart of New Labour's "Third Way" ', in R. Matthews and J. Pitts (eds), *Crime, Disorder and Community Safety: A new agenda?* London: Routledge.

Critchley, S. (2007) *Infinitely Demanding: Ethics of Commitment, Politics of Resistance*. London: Verso

Croall, H. (2004) 'Community Safety and Economic Crime', paper delivered to the 4th Annual Conference of the European Society of Criminology, Amsterdam.

Cruikshank, B. (1999) *The Will to Empower: Democratic Citizens and other Subjects*. Ithaca: Cornell University Press.

Currie, E. (1998) *Crime and Punishment in America*. New York: Henry Holt.

Currie, E. (2004) *The Road to Whatever*. New York: Metropolitan Books.

Dawson, D. (1999) *Risk of Violence Assessment: Aboriginal Offenders and the Assumption of Homogeneity*. Paper presented at the Best Practice Interventions in Corrections for Indigenous People Conference. Australian Institute of Criminology and Department for Correctional Services SA, Adelaide, October.

Davis, A. (2003) *Are Prisons Obsolete?* New York: Seven Stories Press.

Davies, N. (2003) 'Using New Tools to Attack the Roots of Crime', *Guardian*, 12 July 2003.

Dean, M. (1999) *Governmentality: Power and Rule in Modern Society*. London: Sage.

de Certeau, M. (1988) *The Practice of Everyday Life* (trans. S. Rendall). Berkeley: University of California Press.

Defense Advanced Research Program Agency (DARPA) (2003) *Report to Congress regarding the Terrorism Information Awareness Program*. http://epic.org/privacy/profiling/tia/may03_report.pdf

De Giorgi, A. (2006) *Re-thinking the Political Economy of Punishment: Perspectives on Post-Fordism and Penal Politics*. Aldershot: Ashgate.

Degnan, J.J. (2004) *Statement before the Senate Committee on Banking, Housing and Urban Affairs*. May 18.

Dembour M.-B. (2006) *Who Believes in Human Rights: Reflections on the European Convention*. Cambridge: Cambridge University Press.

Deleuze, G. and Guattari, F. (2004/1987) *A Thousand Plateaus: Capitalism and Schizophrenia*. London: Continuum.

Derrida, J. (1999) *Adieu to Emmanuel Levinas* (trans. P.A. Brault and M. Hughes), Stanford, CA: Stanford University Press.

Derrida, J. (2001) *Cosmopolitanism and Forgiveness* (trans. M. Dooley and M. Hughes). London: Routledge.

Derrida, J. (2003) 'Autoimmunity: Real and Symbolic Suicide' in G. Borradori (ed.) *Philosophy in a Time of Terror: Dialogues with Jurgen Habermas and Jacques Derrida*. Chicago: University of Chicago Press.

Dhiri, S., Brand, S. Harries, R. and Price, R. (1999) *Modelling and Predicting Property Crime Trends in England and Wales*. Home Office Research Study 199. London: Home Office.

Ditton, P.M. (1999) *Mental Health and Treatment of Inmates and Probationers*. Washington, DC: Bureau of Justice Statistics.

Donzelot, J. (1979) *The Policing of Families*. New York: Pantheon.

Doob, T. and Webster, C. (2006) 'Countering Punitiveness: Understanding Stability in Canada's Imprisonment Rate', *Law and Society Review*, 40 (2): 325–67.

Dowden, C. and Andrews, D.A. (1999) 'What Works for Female Offenders: A Meta-analytic Review', *Crime and Delinquency*, 45 (4): 438–52.

Downes, D. (1998) 'Toughing it Out: From Labour Opposition to Labour Government', *Policy Studies*, 19 (3–4): 191–8.

Downes, D. and Morgan, R. (2002) 'The Skeletons in the Cupboard: The Politics of Law and Order at the Turn of the Millennium', in M. Maguire, R. Morgan and R. Reiner (eds) *The Oxford Handbook of Criminology* (3rd edn). Oxford: Clarendon Press.

Downes, D. and Morgan, R. (2002a) 'Hostages to Fortune?: The politics of Law and Order in Post-War Britain', in M. Maguire, R. Morgan and R. Reiner (eds) *The Oxford Handbook of Criminology* (3rd edn). Oxford: Clarendon Press.

Downes, D. and Hansen, K. (2006b) *Welfare and Punishment: The Relationship between Welfare Spending and Imprisonment*. London: Crime and Society Foundation.

Drakeford, M. (2005) 'Wales and the third term of New Labour: Devolution and the Development of Difference', *Critical Social Policy*, 25 (4): 497–506.

Dreier, O. (2001) 'Virksomhed – læring – deltagelse', *Nordiske Udkast*, 2.

Dreier, O. (2003) *Subjectivity and Social Practice*. Aarhus: Center for Health, Humanity, and Culture, Department of Philosophy, University of Aarhus.

Duff, R.A. (2005) 'Who is Responsible, For What, To Whom?', *Ohio State Journal of Criminal Law*, 2: 441–61.

Dunbar, I. and Langdon, A. (1998) *Tough Justice: Sentencing and Penal Policies in the 1990s*. London: Blackstone.

Durkheim, E. (1995/1896) *The Rules of Sociological Method*. New York: Free Press.

Edwards, A. and Hughes, G. (2005) 'Comparing the Governance of Safety in Europe: A Geo-historical Approach', *Theoretical Criminology*, 9 (3): 345–63.

Edwards, A. and Hughes, G. (2008a) 'Resilient Fabians? Anti-social Behaviour and Community Safety Work in Wales', in P. Squires (ed.) *ASBO Nation*. Bristol: Policy Press.

Edwards, A. and Hughes, G. (2008b) *The Role of the Community Safety Officer within Wales: Challenges and Opportunities*, A Report for the Wales Association of Community Safety Officers, Cardiff.

Edwards, H. (2007) 'Implementation of the Offender Management Act 2007', Letter from the Chief Executive, NOMS, Ministry of Justice (www.justice.gov.uk)

Esmée Fairbairn Foundation (EFF) (2004) *Crime, Courts and Confidence: Report of an Independent Inquiry into Alternatives to Prison* (The Coulsfield Inquiry). London: The Stationery Office.

Einat, T. (2005) '"Soldiers", "Sausages" and "Deep Sea Diving": Language, Culture and Coping in Israeli prisons' in A. Liebling and S. Maruna (eds) *Effects of Imprisonment*. Cullompton: Willan.

Einstadter, W. and Henry, S. (1995) *Criminological Theory*. New York: Harcourt Brace.

Ellemers, N., Doosje, B. and Spears, R. (2004) 'Sources of Respect: The Effects of Being Liked by Ingroups and Outgroups', *European Journal of Social Psychology*, 34: 155–72.

Elliott, L. and Atkinson, D. (2007) *Fantasy Island*. London: Constable.

Ericson, R. and Haggerty, K. (1997) *Policing the Risk Society*. Oxford: Clarendon Press.

Ericson, R.V. and Doyle, A. (2004) *Uncertain Business*. Toronto: University of Toronto Press.

Ewald, F. (1999) 'Insurance and Risk' in G. Burchell, C. Gordon and P. Miller (eds) *The Foucault Effect. Studies in Governmentality*. London: Harvester/Wheatsheaf.

Ewald, F. (2002) 'The Return of Descartes's Malicious Demon: An Outline of a Philosophy of Precaution', in T. Baker and J. Simon (eds) *Embracing Risk*. Chicago: University of Chicago Press.

Falshaw, L., Friendship, C., Travers, R. and Nugent, F. (2003) *Searching for 'What Works': An Evaluation of Cognitive Skills Programmes*. Home Office Research Findings No. 206. London: Home Office.

Farmer, D.J. (1995) *The Language of Public Administration*. Tuscaloo: University of Alabama Press.

Farrall, S. (2002) *Rethinking What Works With Offenders*. Cullompton: Willan.

Farrall, S. (2004) *Rethinking What Works With Offenders*. Cullompton: Willan.

Farrall, S., Mawby, R.C. and Worrall, A. (2007) 'Prolific/Persistent Offenders and Desistance' in L. Gelsthorpe and R. Morgan (eds) *Handbook of Probation*. Cullompton: Willan.

Farrell, G., Bowers, K., Johnson, S. and Townsley, M. (eds) (2007) *Imagination for Crime Prevention: Essays in Honour of Ken Pease. Crime Prevention Studies*, 21. Cullompton: Willan Publishing and New York: Criminal Justice Press.

Farrington, D.P. and Painter K. (2004) *Gender Differences in Offending: Implications for Risk-Focused Prevention*. London: Home Office, Research, Development, and Statistics Directorate.

Feeley, M. (2004) 'Actuarial Justice and the Modern State' in G. Bruinsma, H. Ellfers and J. de Keijser (eds) *Punishment, Places and Perpetrators – Developments in Criminology and Criminal Justice Research*. Cullompton: Willan.

Feeley, M. and Simon, J. (1992) 'The New Penology; Notes on the Emerging Strategy of Corrections and its implications', *Criminology*, 30 (4): 449–75.

Feeley, M. and Simon, J. (1994) 'Actuarial Justice: The Emerging New Criminal Law' in D. Nelken (ed.) *The Futures of Criminology*. London: Sage.

Feinberg, J. (1970) *Doing and Deserving*. Princeton: Princeton University Press.

Field, S. (1990) *Trends in Crime and Their Interpretation: A Study of Recorded Crime in Post-war England and Wales*. Home Office Research Study 119. London: HMSO.

Field, S. (1999) *Trends in Crime Revisited*. Home Office Research Study 195. London: Home Office.

Fitzgibbon, D. (2007) 'Risk Analysis and the New Practitioner: Myth or Reality?', *Punishment and Society*, 9 (1): 87–98.

Fortin, D. (2004) *Program Strategy for Women Offenders*. Ottawa: Correctional Service of Canada. http://www.csc-scc.gc.ca/text/prgrm/fsw/fsw18/fsw18_e.pdf.

Foster, J. (2002) '"People Pieces": The Neglected but Essential Elements of Community Crime Prevention' in G. Hughes and A. Edwards (eds) *Crime Control and Community: the new politics of public safety*. Cullompton: Willan.

Foucault, M. (1979) *Discipline and Punish*. London: Penguin.

Foucault, M. (1984) 'Truth and Power' in P. Rabinow (ed.) *The Foucault Reader*. London: Penguin.

Foucault, M. (1988) *Madness and Civilization*. New York. Vintage Books Edition.

Foucault, M. (1991) 'On Governmentality' in G. Burchell, C. Gordon and P. Miller (eds), *The Foucault Effect: Studies in Governmentality*. England: Harvester Wheatsheaf.

Foucault, M. (2004) *Society Must Be Defended*. (trans. D. Macey) London: Penguin.

Frankel, M.E. (1972) *Criminal Sentences: Law Without Order*. New York: Hill and Wang.

Fraser, N. (1997) *Justice Interruptus: Critical Reflections on the Post-socialist Condition*. New York: Routledge.

Fraser, N. (2003) 'Social Justice in the Age of Identity Politics: Redistribution, Recognition, and Participation', in N. Fraser and A. Honneth *Redistribution or Recognition: A Political-Philosophical Exchange*. London: Verso.

Freudenberg, N. (2001) 'Jails, Prisons, and the Health of Urban Populations: A Review of the Impact of the Correctional System on Community Health', *Journal of Urban Health*, 78 (2): 214–35.

Friedman, S. (2006) *It's Party Time for TRIA Backers*. http://www.property-casuality.com/2006/12/its_party_time_for_tria_backer.html

Garland, D. (1996) 'The Limits of the Sovereign State', *British Journal of Criminology*, 36 (4): 445–71.

Garland, D. (1997) '"Governmentality" and the Problem of Crime', *Theoretical Criminology*, 1 (2): 173–214.

Garland, D. (1999) 'Penal modernism and postmodernism' in R. Mathews (ed.), *Imprisonment*. Dartmouth: Ashgate.

Garland, D. (2001) *The Culture of Control: Crime and Social Order in Contemporary Society*. Oxford: Oxford University Press.

Garsten, C. (2004) ' "Be a Gumby": The Political Technologies of Employability in the Temporary Staffing Business' in C. Garsten and K. Jacobsson (eds) *Learning to be Employable: New Agendas on Work, Responsibility, and Learning in a Globalizing World*. Basingstoke: Palgrave Macmillan.

Gendreau, P., Little, T. and Goggin, C. (1996) 'A Meta-Analysis of the Predictors of Adult Offender Recidivism: What Works!', *Criminology*, 34 (4): 575–607.

Gendreau, P., French, S. and Gionet, A. (2004) 'What Works (What Doesn't Work): The Principles of Effective Correctional Treatment', *Journal of Community Corrections*, XXII (Spring): 4–30.

Giddens, A. (2000) *The Third Way and its Critics*. Cambridge: Polity Press.

Gilling, D. (1997) *Crime Prevention: Theory, Policy and Politics*. London: UCL Press.

Gilling, D. (2007) *Crime Reduction and Community Safety: Labour and the Politics of Local Crime Control*. Cullompton: Willan Publishing.

Gilroy, P. (1987) *There Ain't No Black in the Union Jack*. London: Hutchinson.

Gilroy, P. (2004) *Between Camps: Nations, Cultures and The Allure of Race*. London: Routledge.

Glaser, J.B. and Greifinger, R.B. (1993) 'Correctional Health Care: A Public Health Opportunity', *Annals of Internal Medicine*, 118 (2): 139–45.

Goldblatt, P. and Lewis, C. (eds) (1998) *Reducing Offending: An Assessment of Research Evidence on Ways of Dealing with Offending Behaviour*. Home Office Research Study 187. London: Home Office.

Goldstein, A. (1973) *Structured Learning Therapy: Toward a Psychotherapy for the Poor*. New York: Academic Press.

Goldstein, A. (1976) *Skill Training for Community Living: Applying Structured Learning Therapy*. New York: Pergamon Press.

Goodkind, S. (2005) 'Gender-Specific Services in the Juvenile Justice System: A Critical Examination', *Affilia*, 20 (1): 52–70.

Gough, D. (2005) 'Tough on Probation: Probation Practice under the National Offender Management Service' in J. Winstone and F. Pakes (eds), *Community Justice: Issues for Probation and Criminal Justice*. Cullompton: Willan.

Government Accountability Office (2004a) *Data Mining: Federal Efforts Cover a Wide Range of Uses*. http://www.gao.gov/cgi-bin/getrpt?GAO-04-548

Government Accountability Office (2004b) *Effects of the Terrorism Risk Insurance Act of 2002*. http://www.gao.gov/cgi-bin/getrpt?GAO-04-806T

Government Accountability Office (2007a) *Data Mining: Early Attention to Privacy in Developing a Key DHS Program could Reduce Risks*. GAO-07-293.

Government Accountability Office (2007b) *Homeland Security: Continuous Attention to Privacy Concerns is Needed as Programs are Developed*. GAO-07-293.

Gowan, T. (2002) 'The Nexus: Homelessness and Incarceration in Two American Cities', *Ethnography* 3 (4): 500–34.

Grinstead, O.A., Zack, B. and Faigeles, B. (1999) 'Collaborative Research to Prevent HIV Among Male Prison Inmates and their Female Partners', *Health Education and Behavior*, 26 (2): 225–38.

Habermas, J. (1999) *The Inclusion of the Other: Studies in Political Theory* (C. Cronin and P. De Grieff, eds). Cambridge: Polity Press.

Habermas, J. (2003) 'Fundamentalism and Terror – A Dialogue with Jurgen Habermas' in G. Borradori (ed.), *Philosophy in a Time of Terror: Dialogues with Jurgen Habermas and Jacques Derrida*. Chicago: University of Chicago Press.

Haggerty, K. and Ericson, R. (2000) 'The Surveillant Assemblage', *British Journal of Sociology*, 51 (4): 605–22.

Hague, G. and Wilson, C. (1996) *The Silent Pain: Domestic Violence 1945–1970*. Bristol: The Policy Press.

Hall, S. (1988) *The Hard Road to Renewal*. London: Verso.

Hall, S., Clarke, J., Critcher, C., Jefferson, T. and Roberts, B. (1978) *Policing the Crisis: Mugging, the State and Law and Order*. London, Macmillan.

Hallsworth, S. (2002) 'Representations and Realities in Local Crime Prevention: Some Lessons from London and Lessons for Criminology' in G. Hughes and A. Edwards (eds) *Crime Control and Community: the new politics of public safety*. Cullompton: Willan.

Hallsworth, S. (2008) *Interpreting Violent Street Worlds*. An inaugural lecture by Professor Simon Hallsworth, Department of Applied Social Sciences, London Metropolitan University, 27 February 2008.

Halsey, M. (2006a) 'Social Explanations for Crime' in A. Goldsmith, M. Israel and K. Daly (eds) *Crime and Justice: A Guide to Criminology* (3rd edn). Sydney: Lawbook Company.

Halsey, M. (2006b) 'Negotiating Conditional Release: Juvenile Narratives of Repeat Incarceration', *Punishment and Society*, 8 (2): 147–82.

Halsey, M. (2007a) 'Assembling Recidivism: The Promise and Contingencies of Post-release Life', *Journal of Criminal Law and Criminology*, 97 (4): 1209–60.

Halsey, M. (2007b) 'On Confinement: Client Perspectives of Secure Care and Imprisonment', *Probation Journal*, 54 (4): 339–68.

Hamilton-Smith, N. (ed.) (2004) *The Reducing Burglary Initiative: Design, Development and Delivery*. Home Office Research Study 287. London: Home Office.

Hampton, T. and Thompson, D. (2004) '*Where Big Brother Snoops on America 24/7*'. http://www.capitolhillblue.com.artman/publish/article_4648.shtml

Haney, C. (2003) 'The Psychological Impact of Incarceration: Implications for Postprison Adjustment' in J. Travis and M. Waul (eds) *Prisoners Once Removed: The Impact of Incarceration and Reentry on Children, Families, and Communities*. Washington, DC: Urban Institute.

Hannah-Moffat, K. (2001a) 'Prisons that Empower: Neoliberal Governance in Canadian Women's Prisons', *British Journal of Criminology*, 40 (3): 510–31.

Hannah-Moffat, K. (2001b) *Punishment in Disguise: Penal Governance and Federal Imprisonment of Women in Canada*. Toronto: University of Toronto Press.

Hannah-Moffat, K. (2007) 'Gendering Dynamic Risk: Assessing and Managing the Maternal Identities of Women Prisoners' in K. Hannah-Moffat and P. O'Malley (eds) *Gendered Risks*. London: Routledge Cavendish Publishing.

Hannah-Moffat, K. and O'Malley, P. (2007) *Gendered Risks*. London: Routledge Cavendish Publishing.

Hannah-Moffat, K. and Shaw, M. (2001) *Taking Risks: Incorporating Gender and Culture into the Classification and Assessment of Federally Sentenced Women in Canada*. Canada: Status of Women Canada's Policy Research Fund.

Hanson, R. (n/d) '*The Policy Analysis Market (and FutureMAP) Archive*'. http://hanson.gmu.edu/PAM/govt/FutureMAP-call-for-proposals-12-19-02.htm

Hardyman, P.L. and Van Voorhis, P. (2004) *Developing Gender-specific Classification Systems for Women Offenders*. Washington, DC: United States Department of Corrections.

Harris, A.P. (1990) 'Race and Essentialism in Feminist Legal Theory', *Stanford Law Review*, 42: 581–616.

Hay, C. (1996) *Re-Stating Social and Political Change*. Buckingham, Open University Press.

Hay, D. (1977) 'Property, Authority and the Criminal Law' in D. Hay, P. Linebaugh, J. Rule, E.P. Thompson and C. Winslow (eds) *Albion's Fatal Tree*. Harmondsworth: Penguin.

Hayman, S. (2006) *Imprisoning Our Sisters: The New Federal Women's Prisons in Canada*. Montréal: McGill-Queens University Press.

Hays, S. (1994) 'Structure and Agency and the Sticky Problem of Culture', *Sociological Theory*, 12 (1): 57–72.

Hedderman, C. and Gelsthorpe, L. (eds) (1997) *Understanding the Sentencing of Women*. Home Office Research Study 170. London: Home Office.

Hedderman, C. and Hough, M. (2004) 'Getting Tough or Being Effective: What Matters?' in G. Mair (ed.) *What Matters in Probation*. Cullompton: Willan.

Hedderman, C. (2006) 'Keeping a Lid on the Prison Population – Will it Work?' in M. Hough, R. Allen and U. Padel (eds) *Reshaping Probation and Prisons: The New Offender Management Framework*. Bristol: The Policy Press.

Henry, S. and Milovanovic, D. (1996) *Constitutive Criminology*. London: Sage.

Hillyard, P., Pantasis, C., Tombs, S. and Gordon, D. (eds) (2004) *Beyond Criminology: Taking Harm Seriously*. London: Pluto.

Hillyard, P. and Tombs, S. (2005) 'Beyond Criminology?' *Criminal Obsessions: Why Harm matters More Than Crime*. London: Crime and Society Foundation.

Hirschfield, A. (2005) 'Analysis for Intervention', in N. Tilley (ed.) *Handbook of Crime Prevention and Community Safety*. Cullompton: Willan.

Hirst, P. (1976a) *Problems and Advances in the Theory of Ideology*. Cambridge University Communist Party.

Hirst, P. (1976b) 'Althusser and the Theory of Ideology', *Economy and Society*, 5 (4).

Hollin, C.R. and Palmer, E.J. (2006) 'Criminogenic Need and Women Offenders: A Critique of the Literature', *Legal and Criminological Psychology*, 11, 179–95.

HM Inspectorates of Prisons and Probation (2001) *Through the Prison Gate: A Joint Thematic Review*. London: HMI Prisons and Probation.

HM Inspectorate of Prisons (2005) *Recalled Prisoners: a Short Review of Recalled Adult Male Determinate-sentenced Prisoners*. London: HMI Prisons.

HM Inspectorate of Probation (2006a) *An Independent Review of a Serious Further Offence Case: Damien Hanson and Elliot White*. London: HM Inspectorate of Probation.

HM Inspectorate of Probation (2006b) *Anthony Rice: An Independent Review of a Serious Further Offence Case*. London: HM Inspectorate of Probation.

HM Treasury (n/d) *Green Book, Appraisal and Evaluation in Central Government* http://greenbook.treasury.gov.uk/ (accessed 14/12/07).

Hobsbawm, E. (2002) *Interesting Times*. London: Abacus.

Hochschild, A.R. (1979) 'Emotion Work, Feeling Rules, and Social Structure', *American Journal of Sociology*, 85(3): 551–75.

Holtfreter, K. and Cupp, R. (2007) 'Gender and Risk Assessment: The Empirical Status of the LSI-R for Women', *Journal of Contemporary Criminal Justice*, 23 (4): 363–82.

Holtfreter, K. and Morash, M. (2003) 'The Needs of Women Offenders: Implications for Correctional Programming', *Women and Criminal Justice*, 14 (2/3): 137–60.

Hollin, C.R. and Palmer, E.J. (2006) 'Criminogenic Need and Women Offenders: A Critique of the Literature, *Legal and Criminological Psychology*, 11: 179–95.

Home Office (1991) *Safer Communities: The Local Delivery of Crime Prevention Through the Partnership Approach* (Morgan Report). London: Home Office.
Home Office (1998) *Joining Forces to Protect the Public*. London: Home Office.
Home Office (1999) *The Government's Crime Reduction Strategy*. London: Home Office.
Home Office (2001) *Making Punishment Work: Report of a Review of the Sentencing Framework for England and Wales*. London: Home Office.
Home Office (2002) *Justice for All*. Criminal Justice White Paper. London: Home Office.
Home Office (2003) *Home Office Self-Assessment Framework for Crime and Disorder Reduction Partnerships and Drug Action Teams*. London: Home Office.
Home Office (2004) *Reducing Crime – Changing Lives*. London: Home Office.
Home Office (2006) *Rebalancing the Criminal Justice System in Favour of the Law-Abiding Majority. Cutting Crime, Reducing Reoffending and Protecting the Public*. London: Home Office.
Homel, P., Nutley, S., Webb, B. and Tilley, N. (2004) *Investing to Deliver: reviewing the implementation of the UK Crime Reduction Programme*. Home Office Research Study 281. London: Home Office.
Hood, R. (1992) *Race and Sentencing*. Oxford: Oxford University Press.
Hooks, B. (2000) *Where We Stand*. New York: Routledge.
Hope, T. (2004). 'Pretend it Works: Evidence and Governance in the Evaluation of the Reducing Burglary Initiative', *Criminology and Criminal Justice*, 4 (3): 287–308.
Hope, T. (2005) 'The New Local Governance of Community Safety in England and Wales', *Canadian Journal of Criminology and Criminal Justice*, 47 (2): 367–87.
Hope, T. (2006) 'Things Can Only Get Better', *Criminal Justice Matters*, 62 (Winter 2005/06) http://www.kcl.ac.uk/depsta/rel/ccjs/cjm62.html
Hope, T. (2007) 'The Distribution of Household Property Crime Victimization: Insights from the British Crime Survey' in M. Hough and M. Maxfield (eds) *Surveying Crime in the 21st Century. Crime Prevention Studies*, 22. Monsey NY: Criminal Justice Press and Cullompton: Willan.
Hope, T. (2008) 'A Firing Squad to Shoot the Messenger', London: CCJS.
Hope, T., Bryan, J., Crawley, E., Crawley, P., Russell, N. and Trickett, A. (2004) *Strategic Development Projects in the Yorkshire and the Humber, East Midlands and Eastern Regions*. Home Office Online Report 41/04. London: Home Office. http://www.homeoffice.gov.uk/rds/onlinepubs1.html
Hörnqvist, M. (2007) *The Organised Nature of Power. On Productive and Repressive Interventions Based on Considerations of Risk and Need*. Stockholm: Kriminologiska institutionen
Hough, M., Jacobson, J. and Millie, A. (2003) *The Decision to Imprison: Sentencing and the Prison Population*. London: Prison Reform Trust.
Hough, M. (2006) 'Introduction' in M. Hough, R. Allen and U. Padel (eds) *Reshaping Probation and Prisons: The New Offender Management Framework*. Bristol: The Policy Press.

House of Commons Science and Technology Committee (2004) *Scientific Publications: Free for All?* Tenth Report of Session 2003-04. Volume 1. London: House of Commons: HC 399-1.

Hubbard, D. (2007) 'Getting the Most Out of the Correctional Treatment: Testing the Responsivity Principle on Male and Female Offenders', *Federal Probation*, Reform Trust (1): 2–8.

Hudson. A. (2007) *Homeland Security Revives Supersnoop, The Washington Times*, 8 March.

Hudson, B. (1987) *Justice Through Punishment: A Critique of the 'Justice' Model of Corrections*. Basingstoke: Macmillan.

Hudson, B. (1998) 'Doing Justice to Difference' in A. Ashworth and M. Wasik (eds) *Fundamentals of Sentencing Theory*. Oxford: Oxford University Press.

Hudson, B. (1999) 'Punishment, Poverty and Responsibility: The Case for a Hardship Defence', *Social and Legal Studies*, 8 (4): 583–91.

Hudson, B. (2002) 'Gender Issues in Penal Policy and Penal Theory' in P. Carlen (ed.) *Women and Punishment: The Struggle for Justice*. Cullompton: Willan.

Hudson, B. (2006a) 'Beyond White Man's Justice: Race, Gender and Justice in Late Modernity', *Theoretical Criminology*, 10 (1): 29–47.

Hudson, B. (2006b) 'Punishing Monsters, Judging Aliens: Justice at the Borders of Community', *Australian and New Zealand Journal of Criminology*, 39 (2): 232–47.

Hudson, B. (2007) 'The Rights of Strangers: Policies, Theories, Philosophies' in M. Lee (ed.), *Human Trafficking*. Cullompton: Willan.

Hudson, K., Maguire, M. and Raynor, P. (2007) 'Through the Prison Gate: Resettlement, Offender Management and the "Seamless Sentence"' in Y. Jewkes (ed.) *Handbook on Prisons*. Cullompton: Willan.

Hughes, G. (1998) *Understanding Crime Prevention*. Buckingham: Open University Press.

Hughes, G. (2006) 'Community Safety' in E. McLaughlin and J. Muncie (eds) *The Sage Dictionary of Criminology*, 2nd edn. London: Sage.

Hughes, G. (2007) *The Politics of Crime and Community*. London: Palgrave.

Hughes, G. and Edwards, A. (2002) *Crime Control and Community: The New Politics of Public Safety*. Cullompton: Willan Publishing.

Hughes, G. and Gilling, D. (2004) 'Mission Impossible: The habitus of the community safety manager,' *Criminal Justice*, 4 (2): 129–49.

Hughes, G., McLaughlin, E. and Muncie, J. (eds) (2002) *Crime Prevention and Community Safety: New Directions*. London: Sage.

Hunter, J.R. (2004) *Testimony on behalf of the Consumer Federation of America*, before the Senate Committee on Banking, Housing and Urban Affairs. May 18.

Hutton, W. (2007) *The Writing on the Wall: China and the West in the 21st Century*. London: Little, Brown.

INQUEST (2007) 'Jury Condemns Prison Service Management Following Death of Mentally Ill Woman in HMP Durham–Government Response to Corston Review Inadequate to Prevent Further Deaths', London: INQUEST.

International Centre for Prison Studies (2006) *World Prison Brief*. London: Kings College, University of London.

Irwin, J. (1970) *The Felon*. Englewood Cliffs: Prentice-Hall.

Irwin, J. and Owen, B. (2005) 'Harm and the Contemporary Prison', in A. Liebling and S. Maruna (eds), *Effects of Imprisonment*. Cullompton: Willan.

Jacobson, J. and Hough, M. (2007) *Mitigation: The Role of Personal Factors on Sentencing*. London: Prison Reform Trust.

Jasanoff, S.S. (1987). 'Contested boundaries in policy-relevant science'. *Social Studies in Science*, 17: 195–230.

Jacoby, R. (2005) *Picture Imperfect*. New York: Columbia University Press.

Jefferson, A. (2005) 'Reforming Nigerian Prisons: Rebuilding a "Deviant" State', *British Journal of Criminology*, 45: 487–503.

Jefferson, A. (2007a) 'The Political Economy of Rights: Exporting Penal Norms to Africa', *Criminal Justice Matters*, 70 (1): 33–4.

Jefferson, A. (2007b) 'Prison Officer Training and Practice in Nigeria. Contention, Contradiction and Reform Strategies', *Punishment and Society*, 9 (3): 253–69.

Johnstone, G. and Van Ness, D. (eds) (2006) *Handbook of Restorative Justice*. Cullompton: Willan.

Joe, G., Simpson, D. and Broome, K. (1998) 'Effects of Readiness for Drug Abuse Treatment on Client Retention and Assessment of Process', *Addiction*, 98: 1177–90.

Judd, C.M. and Kenny, D.A. (1981) *Estimating the Effects of Social Interventions*. New York: Cambridge University Press.

Jutte, R. (1994) *Poverty and Deviance in Early Modern Europe*. Cambridge: Cambridge University Press.

Kant, I. (1983/1784–95) 'To Perpetual Peace' in *Perpetual Peace and Other Essays*. Cambridge: Hackett Publishing.

Karp, D. and Clear, T. (2000) 'Community Justice: A Conceptual Framework' in C.M. Freil (ed.), *Boundary Changes in Criminal Justice Organizations, Criminal Justice 2000*, 2 (special issue): 323–68. National Institute of Justice, US Department of Justice.

Karstedt, S. and Farrall, S. (2006) 'The Moral Economy of Everyday Crime', *British Journal of Criminology*, 44 (6): 1011–36.

Kaspiew, R. (1995) 'Rape Lore: Legal Narrative and Sexual Violence', *Melbourne University Law Review*, 20: 350–82.

Kendall, K. (2002) 'Time to Think Again About Cognitive Behavioural Programmes' in P. Carlen (ed.) *Women and Punishment: The Struggle for Justice*. Cullompton: Willan.

Kendall, K. (2004) 'Dangerous Thinking: A Critical History of Correctional Cognitive Behaviouralism' in G. Mair (ed.) *What Matters in Probation?* Cullompton: Willan.

Kendall, K. and Pollack, S. (2003) 'Cognitive Behaviouralism in Women's Prisons: A Critical Analysis of Therapeutic Assumptions and Practices' in B. Bloom (ed.) *Gendered Justice: Addressing Female Offenders*. Durham, NC: Carolina Academic Press.

Kennedy, S. (2000) *Responsivity: Reducing Recidivism by Enhancing Treatment Effectiveness* Ottawa: Correctional Service of Canada.http://www.csc-scc. gc.ca/text/rsrch/compendium/2000/chap_5_e.shtml

Klein, M. W. (1995) *The American Street Gang: Its Nature, Prevalence and Control*. Oxford: Oxford University Press.

Kodz, J. and Pease, K. (2003) 'Reducing Burglary Initiative: Early Findings on Burglary Reduction', *Findings 204*. Research, Development and Statistics Directorate. London: Home Office.

Kupers, T. (1996) 'Trauma and Its Sequelae in Male Prisoners: Effects of Confinement, Overcrowding, and Diminished Services', *American Journal of Orthopsychiatry*, 66 (2): 189–96.

Kupers, T. (1999) *Prison Madness: The Mental Health Crisis Behind Bars and What We Must Do About It*. San Francisco: Jossey-Bass Publishers.

Kurki, L. (2000) 'Restorative and Community Justice in the United States', in M. Tonry (ed.) *Crime and Justice: A Review of Research*. Chicago: University of Chicago Press, 235–303.

KV (2006a) *Kriminalvård och statistik 2005*. Norrköping: Kriminalvården.

KV (2006b) *Kriminalvård i Sverige*. Norrköping: Kriminalvården.

KV (2007) 'Antal timmar arbetsdriften 2005', *Agresso*, Norrköping: Kriminalvården.

KVS (1966) *Kriminalvården 1965*. Stockholm: Kriminalvårdsstyrelsen.

KVS (1967) *Kriminalvården 1966*. Stockholm: Kriminalvårdsstyrelsen.

KVS (2004) *Ackreditering av Brotts-och Missbruksrelaterade program i svensk kriminalvård*. Norrköping: Kriminalvårdsstyrelsen.

KVV (2000) *Reasoning and Rehabilitation (reviderad upplaga). Utdrag ur Handbok för undervisning i Cognitive Skills*. Norrköping: Kriminalvårdsverket/T3 Associates Training & Consulting Inc.

KVV (2002) *Cognitive Skills Teorimanual*. Norrköping: Kriminalvårdsverket.

KVV (2005) 'Vår vision', <www.kvv.se> (Accessed 14 June 2005).

KVVFS (2004) *Kriminalvårdsstyrelsens föreskrifter och allmänna råd om planering av kriminalvårdspåföljd m.m.* KVVFS 2004: 19 Norrköping: Kriminalvårdsstyrelsen.

Lacan, J. (1977) *Ecrits*. London: Tavistock.

Lacey, N. (2001) 'In Search of the Responsible Subject: History, Philosophy and Social Sciences in Criminal Law Theory', *Modern Law Review*, 64 (3): 350–71.

Lave, J. (1993) 'The practice of learning' in S. Chaiklin and J. Lave (eds) *Understanding Practice: Perspectives on Activity and Context*. Cambridge, New York, NY: Cambridge University Press.

Lave, J. and Wenger, E. (1991) *Situated Learning: Legitimate Peripheral Participation*. Cambridge: Cambridge University Press.

Law, J. (2004) *After Method: Mess in Social Science Research*. London: Routledge.

Lemert, E. (1951) *Social Pathology*. New York: McGraw Hill.

Levinas, E. (1981) *Otherwise Than Being, or Beyond Essence* (trans A. Lingis). Pittsburgh: Duquesne University Press.

Levinas, E. (1992) *Ethics and Infinity*. Pittsburgh: Duquesne University Press.

Lewis, C. (ed.) (2003) *Modelling Crime and Offending: recent developments in England and Wales*. Occasional Paper No. 80. Research, Development and Statistics Directorate, Home Office. London: Home Office.

Levi, M., Burrows, J., Fleming, M. and Hopkins, M. with Matthews, K. (2007) *The Nature, Extent and Economic Impact of Fraud in the UK*. London: ACPO.

Liebling, A. (2004) 'The Moral Climate of the Prison', paper presented at International Symposium on the Effects of Imprisonment, Cropwood Conference, University of Cambridge, 14–15 April.

Liebling, A., Durie, L., Stiles, A. and Tait, S. (2005) 'Revisiting Prison Suicide: The Role of Fairness and Distress' in A. Liebling and S. Maruna (eds) *Effects of Imprisonment*. Cullompton: Willan.

Liebling, A. and Maruna, S. (eds) (2005) *The Effects of Imprisonment*. Cullompton: Willan.

Lipsey, M.W. and Cullen, F.T. (2007) 'The Effectiveness of Correctional Rehabilitation: A Review of Systematic Reviews', *Annual Review of Law and Social Science*, 3: 297–320.

Little Hoover Commission (2003) 'Back to the Community: Safe and Sound Parole Policies', Sacramento.

Loader, I. (1996) *Youth, Policing and Democracy*. London: Macmillan.

Loader, I. (2006) 'Fall of the Platonic Guardians: Liberalism, Criminology and Political Responses to Crime in England and Wales', *British Journal of Criminology*, 46 (3): 561–86.

Loader, I. and Walker, N. (2007) *Civilising Security*. Cambridge: Cambridge University Press.

Loader, I. (2007/8) 'A "new politics" of crime?' in P. Carlen (ed.) *Politics, Economy and Crime. Criminal Justice Matters*, 70: 41–2.

Lothian, A. (2006) 'Guiding Hand', *The Journal Magazine: The Journal of the Law Society for Scotland*, November: 18–22.

Lukacs, G. (1971/1923) *History and Class Consciousness* (trans. R. Livingstone). London: Merlin.

Lynch, M. (2001) 'Rehabilitation as Rhetoric: The Ideal of Reformation in Contemporary Parole Discourse and Practices', *Punishment and Society*, 2 (1): 40–65.

MacKinnon, C. (1993) *Only Words*. Cambridge: Harvard University Press.

MacLean, Lord (2000) *Report of the Committee on Serious Violent and Sexual Offenders*. Edinburgh: Scottish Executive.

Maguire, M. (2007) 'The Resettlement of Ex-prisoners' in L. Gelsthorpe and R. Morgan (eds) *Handbook of Probation*. Cullompton: Willan.

Maidment, D. (2006) 'We're Not All that Criminal: Getting Beyond the Pathologizing and Individualizing of Women's Crime', *Women and Therapy* 3–4 (29): 35–56.

Mair, G. (2004) *What Matters in Probation*. Cullompton: Willan.

Maloney, D. and Holcomb, D. (2001) 'In Pursuit of Community Justice: Deschutes County, Oregon', *Youth and Society*, 33 (2): 296–313.

Management Model (London: NOMS) www.noms.justice.gov.uk

Manfredi, C.P. (2001) *Judicial Power and the Charter: Canada and the Paradox of Liberal Constitutionalism* (2nd edn). Ontario: Oxford University Press.

Mannheim, K. (1960/1936) *Ideology and Utopia*. London: Routledge.

Mansfield, N. (2000) *Subjectivity*. St Leonards: Allen and Unwin.

Margalit, A. (1998) *The Decent Society*. Cambridge: Harvard University Press.

Marshall, T.H. and Bottomore, T. (1992) *Citizenship and Social Class*. London: Pluto Press.

Maruna, S. (2004a) '"California Dreamin": Are We Heading Towards a National Offender "Waste Management" Service?', *Criminal Justice Matters*, 56: 6–7.

Maruna, S. (2004b) 'Is Rationalization Good for the Soul?: Resisting "Responsibilization" in Corrections and the Courts', in B. Arrigo (ed.) *Psychological Jurisprudence*. Albany, NY: SUNY Press.

Maruna, S. and Immarigeon, R. (eds) (2004) *After Crime and Punishment*. Cullompton: Willan.

Maruna, S. and Mann, R. (2006) 'A Fundamental Attribution Error? Rethinking Cognitive Distortions', *Legal and Criminological Psychology*, 11: 155–77.

Maruna, S., LeBel, T., Mitchell, N. and Naples, M. (2004a) 'Pygmalion in the Reintegration Process: Desistance from Crime through the Looking Glass', *Psychology, Crime and Law*, 10 (3): 271–81.

Maruna, S., LeBel, T. and Lanier, C. (2004b). 'Generativity Behind Bars: Some "Redemptive Truth" about Prison Society', in E. de St. Aubin, D. McAdams and T. Kim (eds) *The Generative Society*. Washington, DC: American Psychological Association.

Mascini. P. and Houtman, D. (2006) 'Rehabilitation and Repression: Reassessing their Ideological Embeddedness', *British Journal of Criminology*, 46 (5): 837–58.

Mathiesen, T. (1974) *The Politics of Abolition*. London: Martin Robertson.

Mathiesen, T. (1990) *Prison on Trial*. London: Sage.

Mathiesen, T. (1997) 'The Viewer Society: Michel Foucault's Panopticon Revisited' in *Theoretical Criminology*, 1 (2): 215–34.

Mathiesen, T. (2000) *Prison On Trial* (2nd edn). Winchester: Waterside Press.

Mathiesen, T. (2004) *Silently Silenced: Essays on the Creation of Acquiescence in Modern Society*. Winchester: Waterside Press.

Matthews, R. and Pitts, J. (eds) (2001) *Crime, Disorder and Community Safety*. London: Sage.

Matthews, R. and Young, J. (eds) (2003) *The New Politics of Crime and Punishment*. Cullompton: Willan.

Maurutto, P. and Hannah-Moffat, K. (2005) 'Assembling Risk and the Restructuring of Penal Control', *British Journal of Criminology*, 45 (1): 1–17.

Mawby, R.C., Crawley, P. and Wright, A. (2007) 'Beyond "Polibation" and Towards "Prisi-polibation"? Joint Agency Offender Management in the Context of the Street Crime Initiative', *International Journal of Police Science and Management*, 9 (2): 122–34.

McCain, L.J. and McCleary, R. (1979) 'The Statistical Analysis of the Simple Interrupted Time-series Quasi-experiment', in T.D. Cook and D.T. Campbell *Quasi-Experimentation*. Boston, MA: Houghton Mifflin.

McCall, N. (1994) *Makes Me Wanna Holler: A Young Black Man in America*. New York: Vintage Books.

McDonald, D.C. (1999) 'Medical Care in Prisons' in M. Tonry and J. Petersilia *Prisons*. Chicago: University of Chicago Press.

McKendy, J. (2006) '"I'm Very Careful About That": Narrative and Agency of Men in Prison', *Discourse and Society*, 17 (4): 473–502.

McInnes, Sheriff J. (2004) *The Summary Justice Review Committee: Report to Ministers*. Edinburgh: Scottish Executive.

McMahon, M. and Wexler, D. (eds) (2003) *Therapeutic Jurisprudence*. Cullompton: Willan.

McNeill, F. (2006) 'A Desistance Paradigm for Offender Management', *Criminology and Criminal Justice*, 6 (1): 39–62.

McQuaid, R. and Lindsay, C. (2005) 'The Concept of Employability', *Urban Studies*, 42 (2): 197–219.

Meidner, R. (1992) 'Comment – The Rise and Fall of the Swedish Model', *Studies in Political Economy*, 39: 159–71.

Melossi, D. (1981) 'The Penal Question in *Capital*', in T. Platt and P. Tagaki (eds) *Crime and Social Justice*. London: Macmillan.

Melossi, D. (2000) 'Social Theory and Changing Representations of the Criminal', *British Journal of Criminology*, 40 (2): 296–320.

Melossi, D. and Pavarini, M. (1981) *The Prison and the Factory*. London: Macmillan.

Meraviglia, M., Becker, H., Rosenbluth, B., Sanchez, E. and Robertson, T. (2003) 'The Expect Respect Project: Creating a Positive Elementary School Climate', *Journal of Interpersonal Violence*, 18 (11): 1347–60.

Merrington, S. and Stanley, S. (2004) " 'What Works"?: Revisiting the Evidence in England and Wales', *Probation Journal*, 51 (1): 7–20.

Merton, R. (1968/1949) *Social Theory and Social Structure*. New York: Free Press.

Middleton, D. (2004) 'Why We Should Care About Respect', *Contemporary Politics*, 10 (3/4): 227–41.

Messina, N., Burdon, W. and Hagopian, G. (2006) 'Predictors of Prison-based Treatment Outcomes: A Comparison of Men and Women Participants', *American Journal of Drug and Alcohol Abuse*, 32 (1): 7–28.

Millie, A., Tombs, J. and Hough, M. (2007) 'Borderline Sentencing: A Comparison of Sentencers' Decision-making in England and Wales, and Scotland', *Criminology and Criminal Justice*, 7 (3): 243–67.

Miller, J.G. (1996) *Search and Destroy: African-American Males in the Criminal Justice System.* New York: Cambridge University Press.

Moellendorf, D. (2002) *Cosmopolitan Justice.* Boulder, Colorado: Westview Press.

Monahan, J. (2004) 'The Future of Violence Risk Management' in M. Tonry (ed.) *The Future of Imprisonment.* New York: Oxford University Press.

Moretti, M.M., Odgers, C.L. and Jackson, M.A. (eds) (2004) *Girls and Aggression: Contributing Factors and Intervention Principles. Perspectives in Law and Psychology,* 19. New York: Kluwer Academic Plenum.

Morgan, R. (2006) 'With Respect to Order the Rules of the Game have Changed: New Labour's Dominance of the "Law and Order Agenda" ' in T. Newburn and P. Rock (eds) *The Politics of Crime Control.* Oxford: Oxford University Press.

Morris, N. (1974) *The Future of Imprisonment.* Chicago: University of Chicago Press.

Muncie, J., McLaughlin, E. and Langan, M. (eds) (1996) *Criminological Perspectives.* London: Sage.

Murray, C. (1990) *The Emerging British Underclass.* London: Institute of Economic Affairs.

Myrick, A. (2004) 'Escape from the Carceral: Writing by American Prisoners 1895–1916', *Surveillance and Society,* 2 (1): 93–109 (http://www.surveillance-and-society.org)

Naffine, N. (1990) *Law and the Sexes.* Sydney: Allen and Unwin.

Nassetta, C. (2004) *Testimony on behalf of the Coalition to Insure against Terrorism, before the Senate Committee on Banking, Housing and Urban Affairs.* May 18.

National Association of Professional Insurance Agents. *President Bush Signs TRIA Extension into Law.* http://www.pianet.com/IssuesOfFocus/HotIssues/tria/12-28-05 6.htm

National Commission on Terrorist Attacks Upon the United States (2004) *The 9/11 Commission Report.* http:// govinfo.library.unt.edu/911/report/911Report.pdf

National Offender Management Service (NOMS) (2006) *The NOMS Offender.* London: NOMS. www.noms.justice.gov.uk

National Probation Service and Home Office (2001) *A New Choreography, Strategic Framework 2001–2004.* London: National Probation Service.

Nellis, M. (2003) 'Review of "Understanding Community Penalties"', *Punishment and Society,* 5 (4): 478–91.

Neocleous, M. (2000) *The Fabrication of Social Order.* London: Pluto Press.

Neocleous, M. (2003) *Imagining the State.* Maidenhead, Buckingham: Open University Press.

Nichol, D. (2007) 'Chairman Calls for Debate on Impact of IPP Sentences', *The Board Sheet Issue 5.* London: Parole Board.

Nielsen, K. and Kvale, S. (1999) *Mesterlære: Læring som Social Praksis.* København: Hans Reitzels Forlag.

Nilsson, A. (2002) *Fånge i marginalen* Stockholm: Kriminologiska institutionen.

Nilsson, A. (2005) 'Vad är nytt med "det nya klientelet"?', *Nordisk Tidskrift for Kriminalvidenskab*, 92 (2): 147–61.

9/11 Commission Final Report. http://www.gpoaccess.gov/911/index.html

Normand, A. (2003) *Proposals for the Integration of Aims, Objectives and Targets in the Scottish Criminal Justice System.* Edinburgh: The Stationery Office.

Norrie, A. (2000) *Punishment and Responsibility: A Relational Critique.* Oxford: Oxford University Press.

O'Brien, P. and Young, D.S. (2006) 'Challenges for Formerly Incarcerated Women: A Holistic Approach to Assessment'. *Families in Society*, 87 (3): 359–66.

Office of the Governor (2005) 'Governor Schwarzenegger Signs Legislation to Transform California's Prison System', http://gov.ca.gov/index.php?/press-release/1935/

Ogloff, J.R.P. and Davis, M.R. (2004) 'Advances in Offender Assessment and Rehabilitation: Contributions of the Risk, Need, Responsivity Approach', *Psychology, Crime and Law*, 10 (3): 229–42.

O'Malley, P. (1992) 'Risk, Power and Crime Prevention', *Economy and Society*, 21 (3): 252–75.

O'Malley, P. (1996) 'Post-Keynesian Policing', *Economy and Society*, 25 (2): 137–55.

O'Malley, P. (2004) *Risk, Uncertainty and Government.* London: GlassHouse Press.

O'Malley, P. (2006) 'Governmentality', in E. McLaughlin and J. Muncie (eds) *The Sage Dictionary of Criminology* (2nd edn). London: Sage.

O'Malley, P. and Hutchinson, S. (2007) 'Reinventing Prevention: Why Did "Crime Prevention" Develop So Late?' *British Journal of Criminology*, 47(3): 373–389.

O'Malley, P., Weir, L. and Shearing, C. (1997) 'Governmentality, Criticism, Politics', *Economy and Society*, 26: 501–17.

Padfield, N. and Maruna, S. (2006) 'The Revolving Door at the Prison Gate: Exploring the Dramatic Increase in Recalls to Prison', *Criminology and Criminal Justice*, 6 (3): 329–52.

Panitch, L. and Leys, C (2005) 'Preface' in L. Panitch and C. Leys (eds) *The Socialist Register 2006*. London: The Merlin Press.

Parole Board (2007a) *40 Years: Parole Board for England Wales Annual Report and Accounts 2006–07*. HC1022 London: The Stationery Office.

Parole Board (2007b) *The Board Sheet Issue 11*. London: Parole Board.

Partridge, S. (2004) *Examining Case Management Models for Community Sentences.* Home Office Online Report 17/04. London: Home Office.

Pavlich, G. (2002) 'Deconstructing Restoration: The Promise of Restorative Justice' in E. Wietekamp and H. Korner (eds) *Restorative Justice: Theoretical Foundations*. Cullompton: Willan.

Pease, K. (1994) 'Crime Prevention', in M. Maguire, R. Morgan and R. Reiner (eds) *The Oxford Handbook of Criminology*. Oxford: Oxford University Press.

Pease, K. and Wiles, P. (2000) 'Crime Prevention and Community Safety: Tweedledum and Tweedledee?', in K. Pease, S. Ballintyne and V. McLaren (eds) *Key Issues in Crime Prevention, Crime Reduction and Community Safety*. London, IPPR.

Peck, J. and Theodore, N. (2000) 'Beyond "Employability"', *Cambridge Journal of Economics*, 24: 729–49.

Pelissier, B. and Jones, N. (2005) 'A Review of Gender Differences among Substance Abusers', *Crime & Delinquency*, 51 (3): 343–72.

Phillips, J. (2001) 'Cultural Construction of Manhood in Prison', *Psychology of Men and Masculinity*, 2 (1): 13–23.

Piacentini, L. (2006) 'Prisons During Transition: Promoting a Common Penal Identity through International Norms' in S. Armstrong and L. McAra (eds), *Perspectives on Punishment: The Contours of Control*. Oxford: Oxford University Press.

Poindexter, J.M. (2003) *Official Letter of his Resignation from DARPA*. http://www.washingtonpost.com/wp.srv/nation/transcripts/poindexterletter.pdf

Policy Hub (n/d) *Magenta Book: Guidance Notes on Policy Evaluation*. http://www.policyhub.gov.uk/magenta_book/ (accessed 14/12/07)

Pollack, S. (2006) 'Therapeutic Programming as Regulatory Practice in Women's Prisons' in E. Comack and G. Balfour (eds) *Criminalising Women*. Halifax: Fernwood.

Pollack, S. and Kendall, K. (2005) 'Taming the Shrew: Regulating Prisoners through Women-centered Mental Health Programming', *Critical Criminology*, 13 (1): 71–87.

Popke, E.J. (2003) 'Poststructuralist Ethics: Subjectivity, Responsibility and the Space of Community', *Progress in Human Geography*, 27 (3): 298–316.

Poulantzas, N. (1978) *State Power Socialism*. London: Verso.

Power, M. (1997) *The Audit Society*. Oxford: Oxford University Press.

Pratt, J. (1995) 'Dangerousness, Risk and Technologies of Power', *The Australian and New Zealand Journal of Criminology*, 28: 3–31.

Pratt, J. (2000) 'Dangerousness in Modern Society', in M. Brown and J. Pratt (eds) *Dangerous Offenders – Punishment and Social Order*. London: Routledge.

Pratt, J. (2007) *Penal Populism*. London: Routledge.

Pratt, J., Brown, D., Brown, M., Hallsworth, S. and Morrison, W. (2005) *The New Punitiveness: Trends, Theories, Perspectives*. Cullompton: Willan.

Pridemore, W.A. (2004) 'Review of the Literature on Risk and Protective Factors of Offending among Native Americans', *Journal of Ethnicity in Criminal Justice*, 2 (4): 45–63.

Prison Officers' Association (2007) Press Release, 4 September, PR44/07.27 (3): 298–316.

Procacci, G. (1998) 'Against Exclusion: The Poor and the Social Sciences' in M. Rhodes and Y. Mény (eds) *The Future of European Welfare*. Houndmills: MacMillan Press.

Prop. (2002/03) *Arbetsmarknadspolitiken förstärks*, Proposition 44. Stockholm: Regeringskansliet.

Quadrennial Defense Review Report (2001) US: Department of Defense.

Raine, J. (2006) 'NOMS and its Relationship to Crime Reduction, Public Confidence and the New Sentencing Context' in M. Hough, R. Allen and U. Padel (eds) *Reshaping Probation and Prisons: The New Offender Management Framework*. Bristol: The Policy Press.

Ramsbotham, D. (2003) *Prisongate: The Shocking State of Britain's Prisons and the Need for Visionary Change*. London: The Free Press.

Rawls, J. (1971) *A Theory of Justice*. Oxford: Oxford University Press.

Raynor, P. and Vanstone, M. (2002) *Understanding Community Penalties*. Buckingham: Open University Press.

Raynor, P. and Maguire, M. (2006) 'End-to-end Management or End-in-tears? Prospects for the Effectiveness of the National Offender Management Model' in M. Hough, R. Allen and U. Padel (eds) *Reshaping Probation and Prisons: The New Offender Management Framework*. Bristol: The Policy Press.

Read, T. and Tilley, N. (2000) *Not Rocket Science? Problem-solving and Crime Reduction*, Home Office Crime Reduction Research Series Paper 6. London: Home Office.

Reiman, J. (1990) *Justice and Modern Moral Philosophy*. New Haven, Conn: Yale University Press.

Reiner, R. (2007) *Law and Order: An Honest Citizen's Guide to Crime and Control*. Cambridge: Polity.

Reisig, M., McCluskey, J., Mastrofski, S. and Terrill, W. (2004) 'Suspect Disrespect Toward the Police', *Justice Quarterly*, 21 (2): 241–68.

Reisig, M.D., Holtfreter, K. and Morash, M. (2006) 'Assessing Recidivism Risk across Female Pathways to Crime', *Justice Quarterly*, 23 (3): 384–405.

Reiterman, T. (2004) 'Scathing Report on Prison Doctors: A Panel of Experts Ordered by Court to Review State System Calls Physician Quality "Seriously Deficient", *Los Angeles Times*.

Report to Congress regarding the Terrorism Information Awareness Program (2003). In response to Consolidated Appropriations Resolution, 2003, Pub.L. No. 108–7, Division M, 111(b)

Report of the President's Working Group on Financial Markets (2006). *Terrorism Risk Insurance*. http://www.ustreas.gov/offices/domestic-finance/financial-institutions/terrorism-insurance/pdf/report.pdf

Rex, S. (1999) 'Desistance from Offending: Experiences of Probation', *The Howard Journal*, 38 (4): 366–83.

Rex, S. and Tonry, M. (eds) (2002) *Reform and Punishment: The Future of Sentencing.* Cullompton: Willan.

Rhodes, R.A.W. (1997) *Understanding Governance.* Buckingham: Open University Press.

Richie, B. E. (1996) *Compelled to Crime: The Gender Entrapment of Battered Black Women.* New York, Routledge.

Riksrevisionen (2004) *Återfall i brott eller anpassning i samhället, RiR.* Stockholm: Riksrevisionen.

Robinson, D. (1995) *The Impact of Cognitive Skills Training on Post-Release Recidivism among Canadian Federal Offenders,* Research Report No R-41. Ottawa: Correctional Service Canada.

Robinson, G. (2005) 'What Works in Offender Management?', *The Howard Journal of Criminal Justice,* 44 (3): 307–18.

Rock, P. (1990). *Helping Victims of Crime: The Home Office and the Rise of Victim Support in England and Wales.* Oxford: Clarendon.

Rodaway, P. (1995) 'Exploring the Subject in Hyper-reality' in S. Pile and N. Thrift (eds) *Mapping the Subject.* London and New York: Routledge.

Romilly, S. (1810) *Observations on the Criminal Law of England as it Relates to Capital Punishments and on the Mode in which it is Administered.* London: Cadell and Davies.

Rose, N. (1996a) *Inventing Ourselves.* Cambridge: Cambridge University Press.

Rose, N. (1996b) 'The Death of the Social? Refiguring the Territory of Government', *Economy and Society,* 25 (3): 327–56.

Rose, N. (1999) *Powers of Freedom: Reframing Political Thought.* Cambridge: Cambridge University Press.

Rose, N. (2000) 'Government and Control', *British Journal of Criminology,* 40: 321–39.

Rose, N. and Miller, P. (1992) 'Political power beyond the state: problematics of government', *British Journal of Sociology,* 43 (2): 173–205.

Rothman, D.J. (2003) 'The Crime of Punishment' in T.G. Blomberg and S. Cohen (eds) *Punishment and Social Control* 2nd edn. New York: Aldine de Gruyter.

Ryan, T. (1978) *The Acceptable Pressure Group.* Farnborough: Saxon House.

Ryan, T. (2005) 'Engaging with Punitive Attitudes towards Crime and Punishment: Some Strategic Lessons from England and Wales' in J. Pratt, D. Brown, M. Brown, S. Hallsworth and W. Morrison *The New Punitiveness: Trends, Theories, Perspectives.* Cullompton: Willan.

Rumgay, J. (2004) 'Scripts for Safer Survival: Pathways out of Female Crime', *The Howard Journal,* 43 (4): 405–19.

Rusche, G. (1978/1933) 'Labor Market and Penal Sanction: Thoughts on the Sociology of Justice', *Crime and Social Justice,* 10: 2–8.

Rusche, G. and Kirschheimer, O. (2003/1939) *Punishment and Social Structure.* New Brunswick: Transaction Publishers.

Sabol, W.J., Minton, T.D., Harrison, P.M. (2007) *Prison and Jail Inmates at Midyear 2006*. Washington, DC: Bureau of Justice Statistics.

Sampson, R.J. and Laub, J.H. (2005) *Crime in the Making: Pathways and Turning Points through Life*. Cambridge, MA: Harvard University Press.

Sayer, A. (1992) *Method in Social Science: A Realist Approach*. London: Routledge.

Sayer, A. (2000) *Realism and Social Science*. London: Sage.

Scott, R. (2005) 'Reflections on Over Quarter of a Century as a Sheriff', *The Scottish Journal of Criminal Justice Studies*, 11: 22–9.

Scottish Executive (2000) *Managing the Risk*. Edinburgh: Scottish Executive.

Scottish Executive (2004) *Supporting Safer Stronger Communities: Scotland's Criminal Justice Plan*. Edinburgh: Scottish Executive.

Scottish Executive (2006) *Reducing Reoffending: National Strategy for the Management of Offenders*. Edinburgh: Scottish Executive.

Scottish Government (2007) *Reforming and Revitalising: Report of the Review of Community Penalties*. Edinburgh: The Scottish Government.

Scraton, P. (1987) *Law, Order and the Authoritarian State*. Buckingham: Open University Press.

Scruton, R. (1974) *Art and Imagination*. London: Methuen.

Sennett, R. (2003) *Respect in a World of Inequality*. New York: W.W. Norton.

Sentencing Commission for Scotland (SCS) (2006) *The Scope to Improve Consistency in Sentencing*. Edinburgh: The Sentencing Commission for Scotland.

Sentencing Guidelines Council (2004) *Overarching Principles: Seriousness – Guideline*. London: Sentencing Guidelines Council.

Sevenhuijsen, S. (2000) 'Caring in the Third Way: The Relation between Obligation, Responsibility and Care in *Third Way* discourse', *Critical Social Policy*, 20 (1): 5–37.

Shaffer, M. (1998) 'Scrutinizing Duress: The Constitutional Validity of Section 17 of the Criminal Code', *Criminal Law Quarterly*, 40: 444.

Shakur, S. (1998) *Monster: The Autobiography of an LA Gang Member*. Boston: Addison-Wesley.

Shaw, M. and Hannah-Moffat, K. (2004) 'How Cognitive Skill Forgot about Gender and Diversity' in G. Mair (ed.) *What Matters in Probation Work*. Cullompton: Willan.

Shaw, S. (2007) 'Deaths Following Release from Custody' in *On the Case* 23, November.

Sherman, L.W., Gottfredson, D. Mackenzie, D. and Eck, J. (1997) *Preventing Crime: What Works, What Doesn't and What's Promising: A Report to the United States Congress*. Washington DC: US Department of Justice, Office of Justice Programs.

Shute, S. (2007) 'Parole and Risk Assessment' in N. Padfield (ed.) *Who to Release? Parole, Fairness and Criminal Justice*. Cullompton: Willan.

Sim, J. (2000) 'Against the Punitive Wind: Stuart Hall, the State and the Lessons of the Great Moving Right Show' in P. Gilroy, L. Grossberg and

A. McRobbie (eds) *Without Guarantees: In Honour of Stuart Hall*. London: Verso.

Sim, J. (2004a) 'Thinking About Imprisonment' in J. Muncie and D. Wilson (eds) *Student Handbook of Criminal Justice and Criminology*. London: Cavendish.

Sim, J. (2004b) 'The Victimised State and the Mystification of Social Harm' in P. Hillyard, C. Pantazis, S. Tombs and D. Gordon (eds) *Beyond Criminology*. London: Pluto.

Sim, J. (2005) 'At the Centre of the New Professional Gaze: Women, Medicine and Confinement' in W. Chan, D.E. Chunn and R. Menzies (eds) *Women, Madness and the Law*. London: GlassHouse Press.

Sim, J. (2007) '"An Inconvenient Criminological Truth": Pain, Punishment and Prison Officers' in J. Bennett, B. Crewe and A. Wahidin (eds) *Understanding Prison Staff*. Cullompton: Willan.

Sim, J. (in press) *The Carceral State*. London: Sage.

Simon, J. (1998) 'Managing the Monstrous: Sex Offenders and the New Penology', *Psychology, Public Policy and Law*, 4 (1/2): 452–67.

Simon, J. (2007) *Governing through Crime*. Oxford/New York: Oxford University Press.

Smandych, R. (ed.) (1999) *Governable Places: Readings on Governmentality and Crime Control*. Dartmouth: Ashgate.

Smith, M.J., Clarke, R.V. and Pease, K. (2002) 'Anticipatory Benefits in Crime Prevention' in N. Tilley (ed.) *Analysis for Crime Prevention. Crime Prevention Studies*, 13. Monsey, NY: Criminal Justice Press.

Snow, C.P. (1961) *Science and Government*. The Godkin Lectures at Harvard University, 1960. London: Oxford University Press.

Sorbello, L., Eccleston, L., Ward, T. and Jones, R. (2002) 'Treatment Needs of Female Offenders: A review', *Australian Psychologist*, 37: 196–205.

Social Exclusion Unit (2002) *Reducing Reoffending by Ex-Prisoners*. London: Cabinet Office.

Solomon, E., Eades, C., Garside, R. and Rutherford, M. (2007) *Ten Years of Criminal Justice under Labour. An Independent Audit*. London: Centre for Crime and Justice Studies.

SOU (1971) *Kriminalvård i anstalt*, SOU 1971: 74. Stockholm: Justitie-departementet.

Statskontoret (2003) *Effektivitetsgranskning av kriminalvården*. Stockholm: Statskontoret.

STC (2006) House of Commons Science and Technology Committee. *Scientific Advice, Risk and Evidence Based Policy Making*. Seventh Report of Session 2005–06, Volume I Report HC 900-I; Volume II Oral and Written Evidence HC 900-I. The House of Commons, 26 October 2006.

STC (House of Commons Science and Technology Committee) (2007) *Scientific Advice, Risk and Evidence Based Policy Making: Government Response to the Committee's Seventh Report of Session 2005–06*. First Special Report of Session 2006-07, HC 307. The House of Commons, 21 February 2007.

Steffensmeier, D. and Allan, E. (1998) 'The Nature of Female Offending: Patterns and Explanations in R.T. Zaplin (ed.) Female Offenders: Critical Perspectives and Effective Interventions. Gaithersburg, MD: Aspen Publishers.

Stenson, K. (1993) 'Community Policing as a Governmental Technology', Economy and Society, 22 (3): 373–99.

Stenson, K. (2002) 'Community Safety in Middle England – The Local Politics of Crime Control' in G. Hughes and A. Edwards (eds) Crime Control and Community: The New Politics of Public Safety. Cullompton: Willan.

Stenson, K. and Edwards, A. (2004) 'Policy Transfer in Local Crime Control: Beyond Naïve Emulation' in T. Newburn and R. Sparks (eds) Criminal Justice and Political Cultures: National and International Dimensions of Crime Control. Cullompton: Willan.

Stenson, K. and Sullivan, R. (2001) (eds) Crime, Risk and Justice: The Politics of Crime Control in Liberal Democracies. Cullompton: Willan.

Sterngold, J. (2005) 'Grim Reality of Prison Health Care: Doctors, Nurses and Inmates Suffer Inside Broken System. San Francisco Chronicle. San Francisco: A15.

Stone, N. (2007) 'Criminal Justice Act 2003' in R. Canton and D. Hancock (eds) Dictionary of Probation and Offender Management. Cullompton: Willan.

Sundin, B. (1970) Individ, institution, ideologi – anstaltens socialpsykologi. Stockholm: Bonniers.

Svensson, T. (2001) Marknadsanpassningens politik. Den svenska modellens förändring 1980–2000. Uppsala: Acta Universitatis Upsaliensis.

Sykes, G. (1958) Society of Captives. Princeton: Princeton University Press.

Task Force on Federally Sentenced Women (TFFSW) (1990) Creating Choices: The Report of the Task Force on Federally Sentenced Women. Ottawa: Correctional Service of Canada. http://www.csc-scc.gc.ca/text/prgrm/fsw/choices/toce-eng.shtml

Tata, C. (2007) 'Sentencing as Craftwork and the Binary Epistemologies of the Discretionary Decision Process', Social and Legal Studies 16 (3): 425–47.

Tata, C. and Hutton N. (eds) (2002) Sentencing and Society: International Perspectives. Aldershot: Ashgate.

Taylor, C. (2004) Modern Social Imaginaries. Durham and London: Duke University Press.

Thigpen, M., Solomon L., Hunter, S. and Buell, M. (2004) Developing Gender Specific Classification Systems for Women Offenders. Washington: National Institute of Corrections.

Thomas, D. (1979) Constraints on Judgment: The Search for Structured Discretion in Sentencing, 1860–1910. Cambridge: Institute of Criminology Occasional Series, no. 4.

Thomas, D. (2003) 'Judicial Discretion in Sentencing' in L. Gelsthorpe and N. Padfield (eds) Exercising Discretion: Decision-making in the Criminal Justice System and Beyond. Cullompton: Willan.

Thomas, J.E. (1978) 'A Good Man for Gaoler? Crisis, Discontent and Prison Staff' in J.C. Freeman (ed.) *Prisons Past and Future*. London: Heinemann Educational Books.

Thomas, M. (2007) 'Black and Minority Ethnic Prison Officers' Experience within HM Prison Service', in *Prison Service Journal*, 174: 27–31.

Thompson, J. (2007) 'The Recall and Re-release of Determinate Sentence Prisoners' in N. Padfield (ed.) *Who to Release? Parole, Fairness and Criminal Justice*. Cullompton: Willan.

Thornton, A. (2007) 'Current Practice and Future Changes: A Judicial Member's Perspective' in N. Padfield (ed.) *Who to Release? Parole, Fairness and Criminal Justice*. Cullompton: Willan.

Tilley, N. and Laycock, G. (2000) 'Joining up Research, Policy and Practice about Crime', *Policy Studies*, 21: 213–27.

Tilley, N., Pease, K., Hough, M. and Brown, R. (1999) *Burglary Prevention: Early Lessons from the Crime Reduction Programme* Crime Reduction Research Series Paper 1. London: Home Office.

Toch, H. (1992) *Living in Prison*. Washington, DC: American Psychological Association.

Tombs, J. (2004) *A Unique Punishment: Sentencing and the Prison Population in Scotland*. Edinburgh: Scottish Consortium on Crime and Criminal Justice.

Tombs, J. (2005) *Reducing the Prison Population: Penal Policy and Social Choices*. Edinburgh: Scottish Consortium on Crime and Criminal Justice.

Tombs, J. and Jagger, E. (2006) 'Denying Responsibility: Sentencers' Accounts of their Decisions to Imprison', *British Journal of Criminology*, 46: 803–21.

Tombs, S. (2006) 'Violence, Safety Crimes and Criminology', *British Journal of Criminology*, 47 (4): 531–50.

Tombs, S., Croall, H. and Whyte, D. (2007) *Safety Crimes*. Cullompton: Willan Publishing.

Tonry, M. (1992) 'Judges and Sentencing Policy – The American Experience' in C. Munro and M. Wasik (eds) *Sentencing, Judicial Discretion and Training*. London: Sweet and Maxwell.

Tonry, M. (1995) *Malign Neglect: Race, Crime, and Punishment in America*. New York: Oxford University Press.

Tonry, M. (1996) *Sentencing Matters*. New York: Oxford University Press.

Tonry, M. (2001) 'Punishment Policies and Patterns in Western Countries' in M. Tonry and R.S. Frase (eds) *Sentencing and Sanctions in Western Countries*. Oxford: Oxford University Press.

Tonry, M. (2002) 'Setting Sentencing Policy through Guidelines' in S. Rex and M. Tonry (eds) *Reform and Punishment: The Future of Sentencing*. Cullompton: Willan.

Tonry, M. (2004) *Punishment and Politics: Evidence and Emulation in the Making of English Crime Control Policy*. Cullompton: Willan.

Trotter, C. (1999) *Working with Involuntary Clients*. London: Sage.

Turner, B.S. (1995) *Globalism, Orientalism and Postmodernism*. London: Routledge.

Unger, R. (2005) *What Should the Left Propose?* London: Verso.

Unger, S. and Kostyrko, G. (2007) 'Gov. Schwarzenegger Signs Historic Bipartisan Agreement, Takes Important Step Toward Solving California's Prison Overcrowding Crisis'. http://www.cdcr.ca.gov/News/2007_Press_Releases/Press20070503.html

Unruh, D.R. (1983) 'Death and Personal History: Strategies of Identity Preservation', *Social Problems*, 30 (3): 340–51.

US Census Bureau (2000) *Population by Race and Population by Hispanic or Latino and Race.* Washington DC: City of Oakland.

US Department of the Treasury (2005) *Assessment: The Terrorism Risk Insurance Act of 2002.* http://www.treas.gov/press/releases/reports/063005%20tria%20study.pdf

US House of Representatives (2001) *Subcommittee on Capital Markets, Insurance and Government Sponsored Enterprises.* Serial 107–48.

US House of Representatives (2004) *Subcommittee on Capital Markets, Insurance and Government Sponsored Enterprises.* Serial 108–81.

Vaihinger, H. (1965/1924) *The Philosophy of As If: A System of the Theoretical, Practical, and Religious Fictions of Mankind* (trans. C.K. Ogden). New York: Harcourt Brace and Co.

Valverde, M. (1998) 'Social Facticity and the Law: A Social Expert's Eyewitness Account of Law', *Social and Legal Studies*, 5 (2): 201–8.

van Berkel, R., Hornemann Møller, I. and Williams, C. (2002) 'The Concept of Inclusion/Exclusion and the Concept of Work' in R. van Berkel and I. Hornemann Møller (eds) *Active Social Policies in the EU. Inclusion through Participation?* Bristol: Policy Press.

van Wormer, K. and Kaplan, L.E. (2006) 'Results of a National Survey of Wardens in Women's Prisons: The Case for Gender-specific Treatment', *Women & Therapy*, 29 (1/2): 133–51.

Vanstone, M. (2000) 'Cognitive-Behavioural Work with Offenders in the UK: A History of Influential Endeavour', *The Howard Journal*, 39 (2): 171–183.

Virilio, P. and Lotringer, S. (1997) *Pure War* (trans. M. Polizzotti) New York: Semiotext(e).

von Hirsch, A. (1976) *The Choice of Punishments.* New York: Hill and Wang.

von Hirsch, A. (1986) *Past or Future Crimes.* Manchester: Manchester University Press.

von Hirsch, A. (1993) *Censure and Sanctions.* Oxford: Oxford University Press.

von Hirsch, A. and Ashworth, A. (2005) *Proportionate Sentencing: Exploring the Principles.* Oxford: Oxford University Press.

Wacquant, L. (2004) *Fattigdomens fängelser.* Eslöv: Symposion.

Wacquant, L. (2008) *Punishing the Poor: The New Government of Social Insecurity.* Durham and London: Duke University Press.

Walker, A., Kershaw, C. and Nicholas, S. (eds) (2006) *Crime in England and Wales, 2005/06*. Home Office Statistical Bulletin, 12/06. London: Home Office.

Wall Street Journal (2006) *'Terrorizing Congress'*, 27 October.

Walmsley, R. (2006) *World Prison Population List* (7th edn). London: International Centre for Prison Studies.

Ward, T. and Maruna S. (2007) *Rehabilitation*. London: Routledge.

Weber, M. (1947) *Theory of Social and Economic Organization*. New York: Oxford.

Wells, C. (2004) 'The Impact of Feminist Thinking on Criminal Law and Justice: Contradiction, Complexity, Conviction and Connection', *Criminal Law Review*, 4: 503–15.

Western, B. (2006) *Punishment and Inequality in America*. New York: Russell Sage Foundation.

Western, B. and Beckett, K. (1999) 'How Unregulated is the US Labor Market? The Penal System as a Labor Market Institution', *The American Journal of Sociology*, 104 (4): 1030–60.

White, J. (1986) *The Worst Street in North London*. London: Routledge.

Whitty, N. (2007) 'Risk, Human Rights and the Management of a Serious Sex Offender', *The German Journal of Law and Society*, Special Issue on International and Comparative Perspectives, 265–76.

Whyte, D. (2007) 'The Crimes of Neo-Liberal Rule in Occupied Iraq', *British Journal of Criminology*, 47 (2): 177–95.

Wilson, D., Bouffard, L. and MacKenzie, D. (2005) 'A Quantitative Review of Structured, Group-Oriented, Cognitive-Behavioral Programs for Offenders', *Criminal Justice and Behaviour*, 32 (2): 172–204.

Wilson Gilmore, R. (2007) *Golden Gulag. Prisons, Surplus, Crisis, and Opposition in Globalizing California*. Berkeley: University of California Press.

Windlesham, D.J. and Baron, G.H. (1993) *Responses to Crime Vol. 2, Penal Policy in the Making*. Oxford: Clarendon Press.

Wood, J. and Shearing, C. (2007) *Imagining Security*. Cullompton: Willan.

Woodward, J.D., Webb, K.W. and Newton E.M. (2001) *Biometrics: A Technical Primer, Army Biometrics Applications: Identifying and Addressing Sociocultural Concerns*. Appendix A, RAND/MR-1237-A. Santa Monica, CA: RAND.

Worrall, A. and Hoy, C. (2005) *Punishment in the Community: Managing Offenders, Making Choices* (2nd edn). Cullompton: Willan.

Worrall, A. and Mawby, R.C. (2004) 'Intensive Projects for Prolific/Persistent Offenders' in A. Bottoms, S. Rex and G. Robinson (eds) *Alternatives to Prison: Options for an Insecure Society*. Cullompton: Willan.

Wyden, R. and Dorgan, B. (2003) *Wyden, Dorgan Call for Immediate Halt to Tax-Funded 'Terror Market' Scheme*. http://wyden.senate.gov/media/2003/07282003_terrormarket.h

Young, I. M. (1990) *Justice and The Politics of Difference*. Princeton, NJ: Princeton University Press.

Young, I.M. (2002) *Inclusion and Democracy*. Oxford: Oxford University Press.

Young, J. (1999) *The Exclusive Society*. London: Sage.

Young, J. (2004) 'Voodoo Criminology and the Numbers Game' in J. Ferrell, K. Hayward, W. Morrison and M. Presdee (eds) *Cultural Criminology Unleashed*. London: Glasshouse Press.

Young, J. (2007) *The Vertigo of Late Modernity*. London: Sage.

Zaplin, R.T. (1998) *Female Offenders: Critical Perspectives and Effective Interventions*. Gaithersburg, MD: Aspen Publishers.

Zizek, S. (1994) 'The Spectre of Ideology' in S. Zizek (ed.) *Mapping Ideology*. London: Verso.

Index

9/11, xiii, 28, 30, 32–33, 40, 43–44

Aas, K., 87
accreditation, 4
actuarialism, xviii, 9, 11, 16–17, 40,
   92, 249
African Commission of Human and
   People's Rights., 159
Althusser, L., xvii, 7, 71, 73
Andersen, Hans Christian, xiii
Anderson, E., 221
Andrews, D., 179, 196
Anti-Social Behaviour Order
   (ASBO), 16, 69–70, 75, 89
Aristotle, xiv
Asad, T., 169, 171
'as if', xv, 1, 4, 5, 6, 8, 10–11, 18, 97,
   146–147, 190, 252, 255
audit, xv, 2, 6, 8–10, 17, 87–88, 100
Austin, J.L., 82

Barry, M., 236
Bauman, Z., 279, 281
Beck, U., 27, 39, 43, 60
Becker, H., 235
Benhabib, S., 282, 289
Bentham, J., 28

Birgden, A., 213
Blair, T., 135–137, 153
Blanchette, K., 210–211, 214
Bloom, B., 200–201, 208, 211, 213
Bonta, J., 196
Bosworth, M., 190, 249
Bottoms, A., 131
Bourgois, P., 221
broken windows, 71
Brown, S.L., 210–211, 214
bureaucracy, xviii, xxiv, 32, 86
bureaucratisation (routinisation) of
   imagination, 31–33, 36–37, 39, 42
Burton, F., xvii
Buttney, R., 224, 232–233

Campbell, D.T., 59–60
capital accumulation, 71–72
carceral clawback, 212
Chomsky, N., xi
Chouard, G., 115–116
citizens/citizenship, 191, 221, 280,
   289–290
Clancy, C., 31–32
Clear, T., 248
cognitive behaviouralism/skills/
   theory, xxii, 179, 182–183, 187–191

Cohen, S., 132
Coleman, R., 24, 73, 156
competing knowledges, 23
Conservative Governments, UK., 14,
    49–51, 119, 152, 154
Correctional Service of Canada, 207
cosmopolitanism, xxii
cosmopolitan justice, xvii, 275–292
Cover, R., 144
Covington, S., 213
Coyle, A., 254
Cullen, F.T., 254
Currie, E., 241

Davies, N., 56–57
De Giorgi, A., 11, 17
Deleuze, G., 75–76, 79–80
Dembour, M., 169, 171
Derrida, J., 281, 287
discretion in criminal justice, 23, 85,
    88, 91–92, 97, 119
Doyle, A., 38
Dreier, O., 167
Duff, R., 219
Durkheim, E., 22, 132

Edwards, A., 120
Ellemers, N., 230
Ericson, R. 38, 76–77, 80
Eriksson, T., 173
evidence-based policy, 21
Ewald, F., 27–30, 33–34, 36, 40, 43

Farrall, S., 223, 234
Feeley, M.,16
Feinberg, J., 219
fictions, 10
Final Report of the National
    Commission on Terrorist Attacks
    on the United States (National
    Commission) 31–32
Fordism/Fordist, 172–173, 177–178
Foucault, M., 26, 29–31, 36, 43, 73,
    77, 138, 142, 150, 190, 251

Garland, D., 74–75
Gendreau, P., 179
Ghanaian Prison Officers, 163
Giddens, A., 39
Gilroy, P., 281
Goldstein, A., 183
Gramsci, A., 71, 73, 136, 148
Guattati, F., 75–76

Habermas, J. 282
Haggerty, K., 76–77, 80
Hall, S., 136
Hallsworth, S. 76–80
harm, 21, 22, 23, 284
Hillyard, P., 21
Hirst, P., xviii
Hobsbawm, E., xiii
Hope, T., 20
hospitality, 224, 276, 282, 288,
    290–291
Hudson, B., 169
human rights, 157, 160, 169–171
Hutchinson, S., 16

ideology, 9
Immarigeon, R., 223
International Centre for Prison
    Studies, 158
Irwin, J., 223

Jacoby, R. 154
Jarma, A.I., 159

Kant, I., 280, 281–282, 289
Karp, D., 248
Karstedt, S., 22
Kavle, S., 167
Kenall, K., 180
Kirschheimer, G., 175

Labour Party, 68–69
Lacan, J., xvii
Lacey, N., 220
Lave, J., 167

left realism, 71
Lemert, E., 235, 251
Levi, M., 21
Levinas, E., 220, 280
Leys, C., 150
Liebling, A., 218, 221
Lipsey, M.W., 254
Lindsay, C., 181–182
Loader, I., 24

Mackinnon, C., 235
Maguire, M., 115
Mann, R., 238
Mansfield, N., 251
Margalit, A., 233
Marshall, T.H., 191
Maruna, S., 215, 223, 234, 238, 251
Marx/Marxism, 71, 191–192
Mathiesen, T., 59, 78, 140–141, 155
  'silently silencing', iv, 8, 17, 59
  'the unfinished', 155
McKendy, J., 237, 241
McQuaid, R., 181–182
Merrington, S., 188
Merton, R., 74
Middleton, D., 220
Mill, J., 282
Moellendorf, D., 289
Morgan, R., 15
Murray, C., 11
Murray, K., 156
Myrick, A., 149–150

National Offender Mangement
  Service (NOMS), 114, 116, 120,
  127–129
New Labour, 14–15, 45, 48–49, 60,
  117, 137–139, 141–142, 152, 154
Nielsen, K., 167
Nigerian Prison Service, 158,
  160–161, 165–166

O'Malley, P., 16, 75
Orwell, G., 76–77
Other, xxi, xxiii, xxv, 6, 7, 8, 10, 118,
  169, 230, 278, 280, 281, 289

Panitch, L., 150
partnerships, 21, 83
Patten, J., 118
Pavlitch, G., 289
Pease, K., 71, 82
Peck, J., 180
populism, xiv, 21, 23, 89, 148
Porporino, F., 179
Poulantzas, N., 144
Prisoners' Rehabilitation and
  Welfare Action (Nigeria)
  (PRAWA) 159, 162–163
Prison Staff College in Kaduna, 160
privatisation, 17–18
professionals in criminal justice
  system, 5, 11–12, 15–18
programming, vi, xxii, 3–4, 6, 8, 10,
  157–158, 182, 187, 193–217, 236,
  243, 249, 255, 272
punitive populism, 23

Ramsbotham, D., 19–20
Rawls, J., 277
Raynor, P., 115
Reasoning and Rehabilitation
  Training Programme, 182
rehabilitation deficit, 7
Rex, S., 234
Richie, B., 274
risk assessment (of offenders), 5,
  92–96, 99, 102, 122–125
Risk, Need and Responsivity (RNR),
  193–205, 210–216
role-playing, 163–164, 184–186
Romilly, S., 86
Ross, R., 179
rule usage, xiv, 9, 86, 91
Rusche, O., 175

San Quentin State Prison, 258–259
Sennett, R., 291
Sim, J., 24
Simmel, G., 279
Simon, J., 16
Snow, C., 61–62

Standard Minimum Rules (SMR), 158– 159, 163–165, 169–170
Stanley, S., 188
State-obligated rehabilitation, 291
Stone, N., 121
strangers, 276–279, 288, 291–292
substantive penalities, 11, 24, 45
surplus knowledge, 11, 18, 21
Swarzenegger, A., 252–255, 261, 267
Sykes, G., 221, 223, 255
symbolic penalities, 11, 24, 45, 177

Task Force for Federally Sentenced Women [Canada], 203, 216
Taylor, C., xvi, xvii
Thatcher, 14
The Emperor's New Clothes, xiii
Theodore, N., 180
therapunitive prison, 5
Thomas, A., 149
Thomas, J.E., 168
Thompson, J., 130–131
Toch, H., 223
trapped administrator, 60

United Nations, 160
US National Institute of Corrections, 199
United States Incarceration Rate, 257, 273

Vaihinger, H., 7, 10

Ward, T., 215
Waskow, A., 155
Weber, M., xiv, 30, 37, 42
Wells, C., 283
what works, 65, 178–179, 190
Whyte, D., 21
Williams, P., 224, 232–233
woman-wise, 215
women-centred programmes, 194, 203
World Trade Centre, xiii

Young, I.M., 284

Zizek, S., 184